The MICHELIN Guide

San Francisco
Bay Area & Wine Country

RESTAURANTS
2013

Michelin Travel Parner

Société par actions simplifiées au capital de 11 629 590 EUR
27 Cours de L'Île Seguin - 92100 Boulogne Billancourt (France)
R.C.S. Nanterre 433 677 721

Dépot légal Octobre 2012
Made in Canada
Published in 2012

The MICHELIN Guide
One Parkway South
Greenville, SC 29615 USA
www.michelinguide.com
michelin.guides@us.michelin.com

Dear Reader

We are thrilled to present the seventh edition of our MICHELIN Guide to San Francisco.

Our dynamic team has spent this year updating our selection to wholly reflect the rich diversity of San Francisco's restaurants and hotels. As part of our meticulous and highly confidential evaluation process, our inspectors have anonymously and methodically eaten through all the city's neighborhoods including the bay area and wine country to compile the finest in each category for your enjoyment. While these inspectors are expertly trained food industry professionals, we remain consumer driven: our goal is to provide comprehensive choices to accommodate your comfort, tastes, and budget. Our inspectors dine, drink, and lodge as 'regular' customers in order to experience and evaluate the same level of service and cuisine you would as a guest.

Furthermore, we have delved deeper into the dining scenes south of San Francisco in order to provide a more thorough selection of notable and unique restaurants in both the Peninsula and South Bay. Don't miss the scrumptious "Small Plates" category, highlighting those establishments with a distinct style of service, setting, and menu; and the further expanded "Under $25" listing which also includes a diverse and impressive choice at a very good value.

Additionally, you may follow our Michelin Inspectors on Twitter @MichelinGuideSF as they chow their way around town. Our anonymous inspectors tweet daily about their unique and entertaining food experiences.

Our company's two founders, Édouard and André Michelin, published the first MICHELIN Guide in 1900, to provide motorists with practical information about where they could service and repair their cars, find quality accommodations, and a good meal. Later in 1926, the star-rating system for outstanding restaurants was introduced, and over the decades we have developed many new improvements to our guides. The local team here in San Francisco enthusiastically carries on these traditions.

We sincerely hope that the MICHELIN Guide will remain your preferred reference to San Francisco restaurants and hotels.

Contents

© SF Travel Association/Phil Coblentz

The MICHELIN Guide

"This volume was created at the turn of the century and will last at least as long".

This foreword to the very first edition of the MICHELIN Guide, written in 1900, has become famous over the years and the Guide has lived up to the prediction. It is read across the world and the key to its popularity is the consistency in its commitment to its readers, which is based on the following promises.

→ Anonymous Inspections

Our inspectors make anonymous visits to hotels and restaurants to gauge the quality offered to the ordinary customer. They pay their own bill and make no indication of their presence. These visits are supplemented by comprehensive monitoring of information—our readers' comments are one valuable source, and are always taken into consideration.

→ Independence

Our choice of establishments is a completely independent one, made for the benefit of our readers alone. Decisions are discussed by the inspectors and the editor, with the most important decided at the global level. Inclusion in the guide is always free of charge.

→ The Selection

The Guide offers a selection of the best hotels and restaurants in each category of comfort and price. Inclusion in the guides is a commendable award in itself, and defines the establishment among the "best of the best."

How the MICHELIN Guide Works

→ Annual Updates

All practical information, the classifications, and awards, are revised and updated every year to ensure the most reliable information possible.

→ Consistency & Classifications

The criteria for the classifications are the same in all countries covered by the Michelin Guides. Our system is used worldwide and is easy to apply when choosing a restaurant or hotel.

→ The Classifications

We classify our establishments using XXXXX-X and 🏨🏨🏨-🏨 to indicate the level of comfort. The ✿✿✿-✿ specifically designates an award for cuisine, unique from the classification. For hotels and restaurants, a symbol in red suggests a particularly charming spot with unique décor or ambiance.

→ Our Aim

As part of Michelin's ongoing commitment to improving travel and mobility, we do everything possible to make vacations and eating out a pleasure.

How to Use This Guide

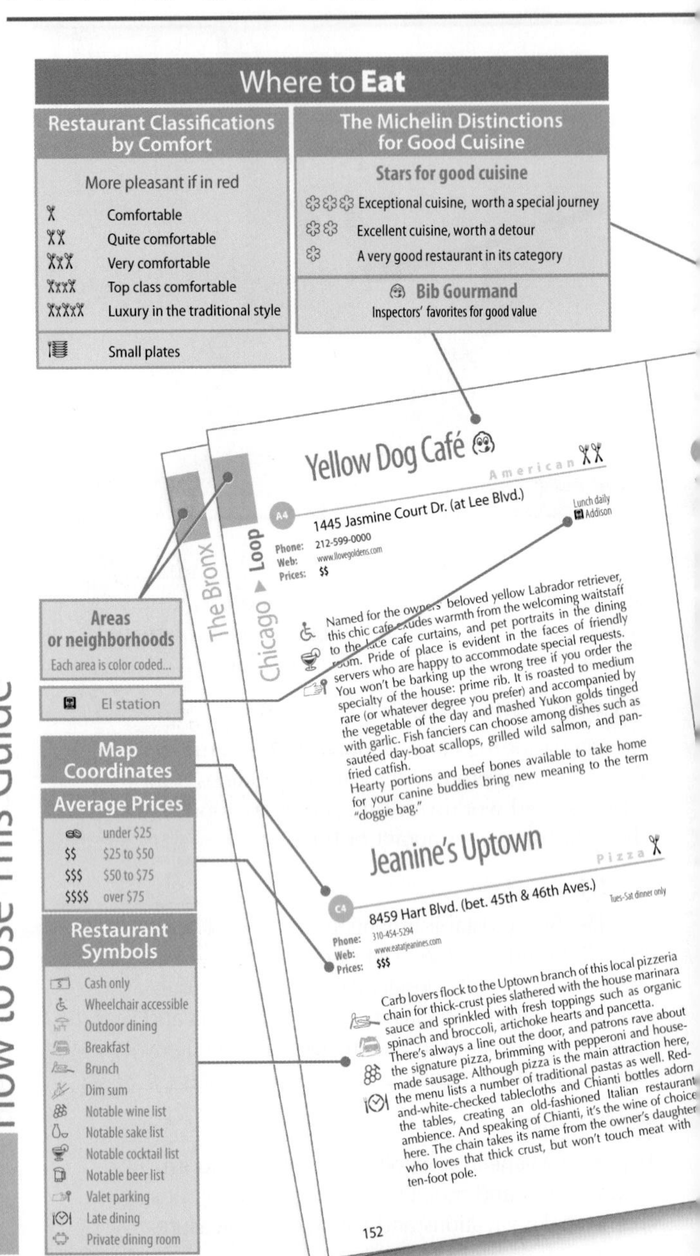

Where to **Stay**

Average Prices	Hotel Symbols	Hotel Classifications by Comfort
Prices do not include applicable taxes	149 rooms – Number of rooms & suites	More pleasant if in red
$ under $200	Wheelchair accessible	Comfortable
$$ $200 to $300	Exercise room	Quite comfortable
$$$ $300 to $400	Spa	Very comfortable
$$$$ over $400	Swimming pool	Top class comfortable
	Conference room	Luxury in the traditional style
	Pet friendly	
	Wireless	

Map Coordinates

Palace

Italian

Pl. (at 30th Street)

Dinner daily

ulouspalace.com

Manhattan ▶ Chelsea

David Buffington/Getty Images

me cooked Italian never tasted so good than at this pretentious little place. The simple décor claims no big-me designers, and while the Murano glass light fixtures e chic and the velveteen-covered chairs are comfortable, is isn't a restaurant where millions of dollars were spent n the interior.

nstead, food is the focus here. The restaurant's name may not be Italian, but it nonetheless serves some of the best pasta in the city, made fresh in-house. Dishes follow the seasons, thus ravioli may be stuffed with fresh ricotta and herbs in summer, and pumpkin in fall. Most everything is liberally dusted with Parmigiano Reggiano, a favorite ingredient of the chef.

For dessert, you'll have to deliberate between the likes of creamy tiramisu, ricotta cheesecake, and homemade gelato. One thing's for sure: you'll never miss your nonna's cooking when you eat at Sonya's.

153

The Fan Inn

D1

135 Shanghai Street, Oakland

Phone: 650-345-1440 or 888-222-2424
Web: www.superfaninnoakland.com
Prices: $$

45 Rooms
5 Suites

John A. Rizzo/Getty Images

San Francisco ▶ Civic Center

oused in an Art Deco-era building, the venerable Fan Inn ently underwent a complete facelift. The hotel now fits with the new generation of sleekly understated hotels ring a Zen-inspired aesthetic, despite its 1930s origins.

othing neutral palette runs throughout the property, uated with exotic woods, bamboo, and fine fabrics. e lobby, the sultry lounge makes a relaxing place for mixed cocktail or a glass of wine.

ens and down pillows cater to your comfort, while n TVs, DVD players with iPod docking stations, less Internet access satisfy the need for modern For business travelers, nightstands convert to les and credenzas morph into flip-out desks. nter, fax or scanner? It's just a phone call away. st, the hotel will even provide office supplies.

alf of the accommodations here are suites, xury factor ratchets up with marble baths, ng areas, and fully equipped kitchens. nn doesn't have a restaurant, the nearby rly everything you could want in terms of dumplings to haute cuisine.

315

Where to Eat

San Francisco Travel Association photo by Phil Coblentz

San Francisco

Castro

Cole Valley · Haight-Ashbury · Noe Valley

It's raining men in the Castro, the world famous "gayborhood" that launched the career of civil rights icon, Harvey Milk, and remains devoted to celebrating the gay and lesbian community (yes, ladies are allowed here too). The hub for all things LGBT–including Gay Pride in June and the Castro Street Fair each October–the Castro is a constant party with a mélange of bars from shabby to chic and dance clubs that honor the ruling class of multi-platinum wonder women—think Madonna, Beyoncé, Babs, Cher, and Lady Gaga.

The Castro teems with casual cafeterias to feed its buzzing population of gym bunnies, leather daddies, and drag queens, as well as a flood of vibrant out-of-towners on pilgrimage to this mecca. **Café Flore**'s quaint patio is more evocative of its Parisian namesake than the plain-Jane continental fare. But, if you go to eat, you're missing the point: This is prime cruising territory with cheap drinks and DJs. There are white napkin restaurants dishing worthwhile cuisine–**La Méditerranée** for instance–but the best flavors of the Castro are served on the run.

Thai House and **Noe Valley Bakery & Bread Company** are mainstays for a quick and heavenly bite; and **Marcello's Pizza** is a satisfying post-cocktail hangout. Speaking of booze, SF's first openly gay bar, **Twin Peaks Tavern**, and **Castro Village Wine Company** continues to lure. The younger hotties, however, sweat it out at **Badlands**' colorful (and sceney) dance floor. **Café du Nord** draws hipsters for live music in a former speakeasy built in 1907. This neighborhood is also chock-full of darling specialty shops: The **Castro Cheesery** pours fresh-roasted gourmet coffees and offers a small selection of cheeses; **Drewes Brothers** struts its meats; **Samovar Tea Lounge** brews artisan loose-leaf; and **Swirl**, a sleek space brimming with stemware and accessories, offers tastings of boutique wine varietals. Take home a snack from Italian foods purveyor **A.G. Ferrari**, or indulge your sweet tooth at the kitschy kiosk, **Hot Cookie**.

Nearby Cole Valley is home to **Say Cheese**, full of quality international cheeses and a small stock of sandwiches; and **Val de Cole**, with value table wines galore. On Monday nights, dog-lovers treat the whole family to dinner on the garden patio at **Zazie**. Counterculturalists, of course, have long sought haven in the hippiefied Haight-Ashbury where, despite recent Gap-ification, head shops and record stores continue to dominate the landscape.

Eschew any notions of fine dining here and join the locals at more laid-back hot spots. **Cha! Cha! Cha!** is a groovy tapas bar flowing with fresh-fruit sangria; and for the morning after, **Pork Store Café** draws a cliquey following for greasy hash browns and fluffy hotcakes.

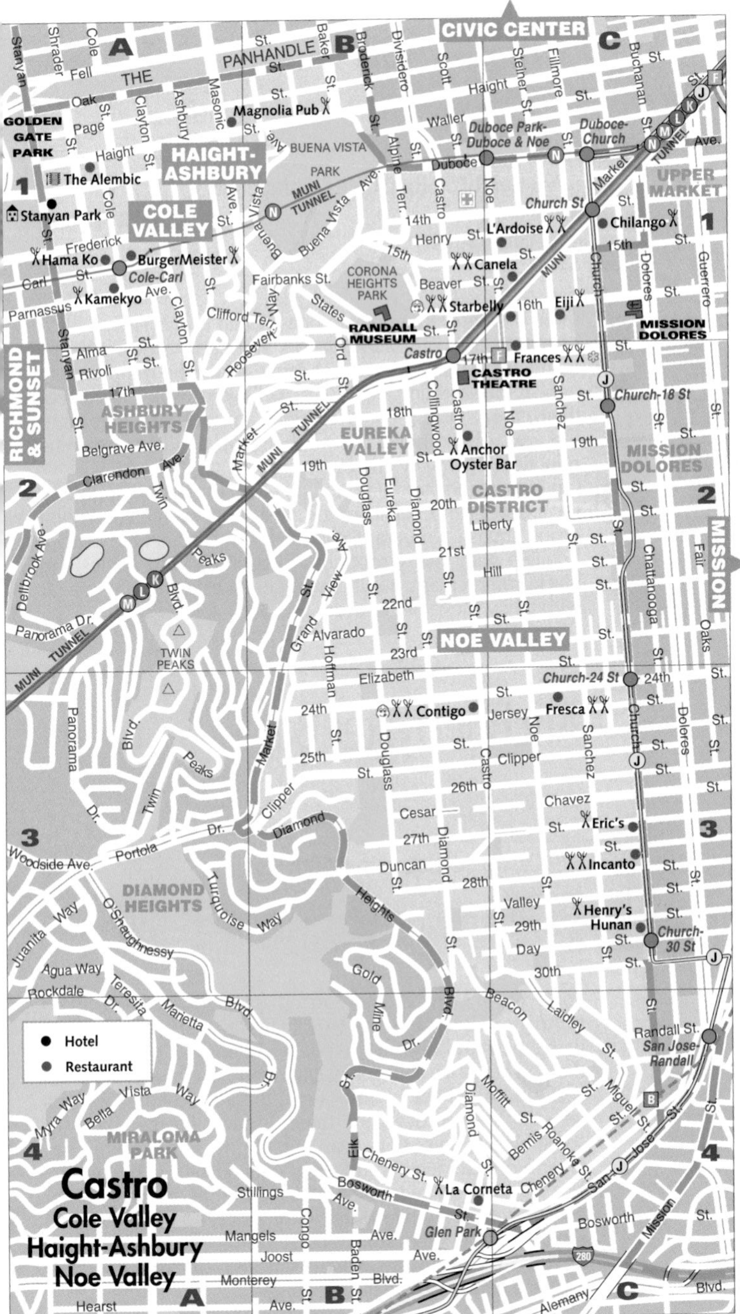
CIVIC CENTER
GOLDEN GATE PARK
HAIGHT-ASHBURY
COLE VALLEY
BUENA VISTA PARK
CORONA HEIGHTS PARK
RANDALL MUSEUM
UPPER MARKET
MISSION DOLORES
RICHMOND & SUNSET
ASHBURY HEIGHTS
EUREKA VALLEY
CASTRO THEATRE
CASTRO DISTRICT
MISSION
TWIN PEAKS
NOE VALLEY
DIAMOND HEIGHTS
MIRALOMA PARK
Magnolia Pub
The Alembic
Stanyan Park
Hama Ko
BurgerMeister
Kamekyo
L'Ardoise
Chilango
Canela
Starbelly
Eiji
Frances
Anchor Oyster Bar
Contigo
Fresca
Eric's
Incanto
Henry's Hunan
La Corneta
Hotel
Restaurant
Castro
Cole Valley
Haight-Ashbury
Noe Valley

The Alembic

Gastropub 

1725 Haight St. (bet. Cole & Shrader Sts.)

Phone: 415-666-0822 Lunch & dinner daily
Web: www.alembicbar.com
Prices: $$

Tired of bars with mediocre bites? Head to this gritty stretch of Haight St., with tattoo parlors and liquor stores aplenty. Its minimalist façade may not impress and the trappings are typical (pressed-tin ceilings and well-worn wood floors), but their crowds know that the drinks and eats are a boon to the area. The bartenders strut their stuff amidst a crowning selection of whiskey and Bourbon.

On busy nights, try for a table in back, but expect to jockey for a seat at the bar to order those pork belly sliders with crispy squash tempura. Other dishes might include porcini bouillon with celery root custard adorned with apples and black truffle cream; and a dense cheesecake layered in a jar with tangy Meyer lemon curd and huckleberry jam.

Anchor Oyster Bar

Seafood 

B2

579 Castro St. (bet. 18th & 19th Sts.)

Phone: 415-431-3990 Lunch Mon – Sat
Web: www.anchoroysterbar.com Dinner nightly
Prices: $$

For a warm bowl of chowder on a foggy day, head home to Anchor Oyster Bar, the 1977 mainstay that's always ready with a beer and a bivalve. While the homey bar may not have the soigné of its younger neighbors, it does have the solid seafood and cheeky humor (note the adult-themed T-shirts for sale) to keep everyone sated. In fact, the place itself is something of an oyster: clean, a bit briny, some claim it has an aphrodisiac quality, and occasional pearls can be found.

Cozy up at a stainless steel table or the marble-topped bar and check the whiteboard for classics such as steamed shellfish, seafood cocktails, and variations on chowder. Their fresh oysters are always expertly shucked—the only thing that changes here are the daily specials.

BurgerMeister

American

86 Carl St. (at Cole St.)

Phone: 415-566-1274 Lunch & dinner daily
Web: www.burgermeistersf.com
Prices: 

This daddy of burger joints with up-market eats and a low-key vibe stacks up to Bay Area standards with all-natural Niman Ranch beef and eco-friendly packaging. Moreover, these juicy quarter- and half-pounders, cooked to order and tossed on a freshly baked bun, are greatly delicious and make a near mockery of the trendy little slider.
Though not cheap, the "Meister Favorites" (starting at nine dollars) offer quality and creativity, as in the "San Diego" topped with roasted jalapeños and melted pepper jack. Fries come in curly, sweet potato, chili, and roasted garlic varieties; beer-battered onion rings arrive without a trace of grease. Salads and wines by the glass are offered, though milk shakes are more popular here, and are best eaten with a spoon.

Canela

Spanish

2272 Market St. (bet. Noe & Sanchez Sts.)

Phone: 415-552-3000 Lunch Fri – Sun
Web: www.canelasf.com Dinner nightly
Prices: $$

Canela is a pretty Spanish respite set on Market Street. Its space emanates warmth via terra-cotta-colored wainscoting, gold-accented walls, and interesting art installations crafted from tree branches. A few tables scattered on the sidewalk are ideal for pet-friendly factions.
The menu spotlights flatbreads and a wide variety of tapas. Try a traditional tortilla, light and flavorful, layered with sliced potato and onion in a fluffy egg omelet, served over drizzles of red pepper coulis. Golden brown *croquetas* filled with *jamon* and creamy béchamel are crunchy on the outside and gooey on the inside; while a bowl of succulent *gambas* drenched in garlicky- buttery- and spicy sauce are served with rustic bread for sopping up every last *yum*.

Chilango

Mexican

C1

235 Church St. (bet. 15th & Market Sts.)

Phone: 415-552-5700 Lunch & dinner daily
Web: www.chilangorestaurantsf.com
Prices: ⊜

Never mind the massive burritos found in most Mexican spots around the Bay Area. It's an ode to Mexico City-style street food here at Chilango—a rockin' little joint spinning out some seriously good stuff. The space is styled in neutral colors with tile-covered tables and floors, and a gallery of black-and-white photos decking the walls.

Capturing the spirit of its homeland are traditional *sopes,* griddled masa cakes piled with chorizo, shredded cabbage, red chile salsa, and drizzled with *crema;* or *tacos de pollo,* grilled chicken tossed in spicy chipotle salsa and stuffed into tortillas with white onion and cilantro. Don't expect to see cheese or sour cream in these renditions—they stay true to their Mexico City roots. End with a soft, caramel-laden flan.

Contigo

Spanish

B3

1320 Castro St. (at 24th St.)

Phone: 415-285-0250 Dinner Tue – Sun
Web: www.contigosf.com
Prices: **$$**

This Noe Valley darling's name (Spanish for "with you") is the first clue that Contigo is best when shared with friends. Single diners sit cozily at the wine bar or front counter, for truly, this contemporary neighborhood eatery was designed in the spirit of conviviality.

Reclaimed wood and ceramic tiles lend an earthy balance to a modish setting, where small groups nosh on authentic Catalan fare–think bite-sized tapas such as salt cod *croquetas* with *piment d'Espelette allioli*–over glasses of sparkling cava. *Raciones* are slightly larger plates ideal for sharing: look for oxtail-stuffed piquillo peppers and fried caper-studded Brussels sprouts. Do not miss the prized *jamòn Iberico,* sliced tissue thin, or the heated garden patio out back.

Eiji

C1 — Japanese

317 Sanchez St. (bet. 16th & 17th Sts.)

Phone: 415-558-8149 — Lunch & Dinner Tue – Sun
Web: N/A
Prices: $$

Differentiating one sushi house from another is a personal matter, but Eiji's wooden shingle siding and tree-flanked façade, marked by an oblong flag reading "sushi" and "tofu" on either side is sure to lure. Eiji Onoda's eponymous eatery brings to life a vegan's dream—think of inordinately luscious custard-soft, fresh homemade tofu and you will start to get the drift.

Go for a bowl of silky, made-to-order *oboro*—delicate curds of tofu just separated from the soymilk; or try the melt-in-your-mouth *ankake* tofu topped with a *konbu*-soy sauce. Aptly representing the "sushi" side is pristine seafood like *ankimo* or monkish liver. Also proffered are *sunomono*, seafood casseroles, *yosenabe*, and *misonabe*—bring your own bowl if you want either *nabe* to-go.

Eric's

C3 — Chinese

1500 Church St. (at 27th St.)

Phone: 415-282-0919 — Lunch & dinner daily
Web: www.ericrestaurant.com
Prices: $$

A neighborhood favorite and Noe Valley fixture with a line out the door since 1991, Eric's is just the sort of godsend that everyone comes to appreciate. This little house packs its bright yellow, mirrored interior with regulars who feast on Hunan and Mandarin lunches for under $10 (including soup and tea) and dinner for just a few bills more.

Prices belie the portions, so expect ample specialties such as rainbow fish with pine nuts in garlic sauce, or tender Shanghai chicken breast with crispy seaweed and al dente brown rice. While some discerning palates may claim the cuisine is somewhat Americanized, no one denies that it is nonetheless delicious.

Reservations are not accepted (hence the line), but service is as very fast as it is friendly.

Frances ✿

C2 — Californian XX

3870 17th St. (at Pond St.)

Phone: 415-621-3870 — Dinner Tue – Sun
Web: www.frances-sf.com
Prices: $$$

Jennifer Yin

In this quiet, residential Castro locale, everything feels as welcoming as those still-warm, roasted almonds with sea salt and rosemary that magically appear while perusing the menu at Frances. Unsurprisingly, this is a true neighborhood gathering place, where everyone seems to know the servers by name and is content to bask in the spirited vibe while waiting for a table or jockeying for a seat at the snug bar.

An urban-rustic aesthetic is fashioned with votive-topped wood tables along a pillow-strewn banquette, and a staff that is relaxed but always attentive.

Frances remains impressively true to its farm-to-table philosophy and seasonal menu no matter the time of year. Wintery meals might feature leaves of baby kale dressed in tangy-sweet fennel *agrodolce*, tossed with shredded duck confit, fried shallots, and sticky slices of Medjool dates. Delicious combinations abound in the likes of roasted Brussels sprouts with bacon lardons and buttery chestnuts; or perfectly fresh red snapper with sunchokes, vibrant tatsoi, and Meyer lemon gremolata. Desserts like chocolate-almond clafoutis do not disappoint, especially when topped with brûléed banana slices and creamy salted caramel ice cream.

Fresca

3945 24th St. (bet. Noe & Sanchez Sts.)

Phone: 415-695-0549 Lunch & dinner daily
Web: www.frescasf.com
Prices: $$

Inside their cheery space, Fresca offers a unique rendition of Peruvian flavors and inventive cocktails to be sampled and sipped in rhythm with the Latin tempo. The front seating area with its bright yellow walls, arched ceilings, lofty skylights, and outdoor views wears a fresh, open feel as does their open kitchen where you are likely to find someone shucking oysters.

Purity is the name of their game and this is deliciously patent in several creative ceviches from the traditional to the black variation tinged with squid ink. The ahi mignon featuring a rose pepper-crusted tuna with purple potatoes; and *trucha enecebollada*, skillet-roasted rainbow trout crowned with tiger prawns, successfully illustrate the concept of culinary invention.

Hama Ko

108 Carl St. (bet. Cole & Stanyan Sts.)

Phone: 415-753-6808 Dinner Tue – Sun
Web: N/A
Prices: $$

It may be easy to miss this simple sushi shop (only a few sake bottles line its sidewalk window and there is no sign), but that would be blasphemous as you won't find a more authentic, mom-and-pop affair than Hama Ko. He mans the sushi bar, deftly assembling nigiri samplers; and she serves the serene space with a cheerful smile. This feels like the home of your (imaginary) Japanese grandparents.

The open kitchen is a touch worn, but the food is super fresh and lovingly prepared. Forget those trendier sushi spots, and be sure to inquire about the chef's hot and cold creations including deliciously succulent tuna, buttery scallops, and simple maki. While the chef is serious and focused, when you share your enjoyment, witness big beams around the room.

Henry's Hunan

Chinese

C3

1708 Church St. (bet. Day & 29th Sts.)

Phone: 415-826-9189 Lunch & dinner daily
Web: www.henryshunan.com
Prices: ⊜

Believe this: Henry's Hunan has some of the best hot and sour soup in San Francisco City, and they *give* it away at lunch. This fourth outpost in Noe Valley is perhaps the most stylish, featuring delicious and fantastically spicy classics for heat-addicts.

Begin, of course, with the aforementioned soup, floating thin slices of carrot and green onion, chopped tofu, scrambled egg, and red chilies in a silky, spicy-hot broth. Howard's special *kung pao* pork and Liling chicken wings provide a unique and tasty turn; while the hot and sour beef has a memorable kick, with tender strips of beef stir-fried with sweet carrots and onions in a pungent vinegar-chili sauce. And with such low prices and large portions, this place is truly a bijou.

Incanto

Italian

C3

1550 Church St. (at Duncan St.)

Phone: 415-641-4500 Dinner Wed – Mon
Web: www.incanto.biz
Prices: **$$**

Incanto is a much beloved ristorante in Noe Valley. The dining room has stone tile archways and walls covered in prints of familiar farm scenes. Servers are friendly and clearly enthusiastic about the menu—a Dante-themed room is available for private dining should you wish to order a whole pig.

Chef Chris Cosentino's passion for offal and nose-to-tail cooking is reflected in the menu, but there are plenty of other less-daring though equally gratifying items. Adventurous diners might want to try a luscious lamb terrine wrapped in fatty bacon and enhanced with mint gelée; or thick, chewy *spaghettoni* tossed with a green garlic purée, slivers of Serrano, and soft shell crab. Tamer palates will love each bite of the pork shoulder with roasted ramps and favas.

Kamekyo

Japanese

943 Cole St. (bet. Carl St. & Parnassus Ave.)

Phone: 415-759-5693 — Lunch & dinner daily
Web: N/A
Prices: $$

Cole Valley's go-to for sushi lovers since 1996, Kamekyo is an intimate dining room anchored by a polished blonde wood bar and minimalist décor. A lavender ceiling and gold-hued walls warm the space, though the stoic chefs can be chilly. Still, a seat at the counter while the seafood is cleaned could yield a taste that should not be refused.

Deftly cut nigiri, sashimi, and maki make big waves here, but wholesome Japanese favorites including piping hot soba and udon noodles, light and crispy shrimp tempura, teriyaki, perfectly steamed white rice, and budget-friendly lunchtime bento boxes should not be overlooked. For visitors looking to keep with the theme, the Japanese Tea Garden in neighboring Golden Gate Park is just a Prius hop away.

La Corneta

2834 Diamond St. (bet. Bosworth & Chenery Sts.)

Phone: 415-469-8757 — Lunch & dinner daily
Web: www.lacorneta.com
Prices: ⓢ

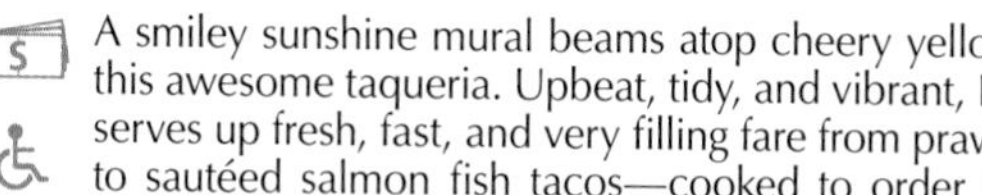

A smiley sunshine mural beams atop cheery yellow walls at this awesome taqueria. Upbeat, tidy, and vibrant, La Corneta serves up fresh, fast, and very filling fare from prawn burritos to sautéed salmon fish tacos—cooked to order from fresh fillets. Queue up and mosey down the food line where servers pile your favorite ingredients into a mouthwatering heap of Mexican deliciousness.

Try to tackle the carne asada super burrito—expertly wrapped to contain the gargantuan mix of grilled beef, beans, rice, cheese, guacamole, sour cream, lettuce, tomato, and *pico de gallo*. If the nachos, tacos, burritos, and quesadillas haven't defeated you, end with a warm, sugary *churro*. A word to the wise: any item with the word "super" means it, so grab a knife and fork.

L'Ardoise

C1 French XX

151 Noe St. (at Henry St.)

Phone: 415-437-2600 Dinner Tue – Sat
Web: www.ardoisesf.com
Prices: $$

Laying low on a tree-lined residential street with tight-knit wood tables, a few seats at the kitchen-facing counter, and a house full of French-speaking ex-pats, L'Ardoise is the traditional Gallic bistro every neighborhood wishes it had. If this were our neighborhood, we would likely become regulars. Still, we might not be guaranteed a seat in their petite and charming interior.

Newcomers may trust the Francophile clientele and know that L'Ardoise is authentic. Here traditional recipes such as coq au vin, falling off the bone and into the *pommes purée* are exquisitely simple and tasty every time. Pair your wine-soaked chicken with a glass of smooth Châteauneuf-du-Pape and finish with an oh-so-buttery and flaky apple-laden tarte Tatin.

Magnolia Pub

A1 Gastropub X

1398 Haight St. (at Masonic Ave.)

Phone: 415-864-7468 Lunch & dinner daily
Web: www.magnoliapub.com
Prices: $$

Hippies and hipsters alike flock to this Haight-Ashbury mainstay where a hoppy aroma fills the wood-clad interior. Tufted leather booths are a cozy spot for noshing despite the steam clinging to the windows—thanks to the beloved work of the micro-brewery.

Obviously, beer is the nip of choice. Locals (and characters who give this place its personality) crowd the bar, made of salvaged wood, for home-brewed draughts whose names are scribbled on the blackboard next to their BUs, or bitterness units, according to Brit tradition. In SF style, Slow Food rules at this gastropub, serving creative updates on classic pub grub like homemade sausages. Pair an artisanal pint with Scotch quail eggs or a seafood boudin; Anglophiles rejoice in the fish and chips.

Starbelly 

C1 Californian XX

3583 16th St. (at Market St.)

Phone: 415-252-7500 Lunch & dinner daily
Web: www.starbellysf.com
Prices: $$

Oh, Starbelly, you devilish creature. Must you tempt us with your salted caramel *pot de crème*, your rosemary oatmeal cookies (limiting us to one at brunch), your orange blossom doughnuts, and your roasted butternut squash pizza with black garlic and chèvre?

It's no wonder this local darling is forever packed–the dynamite menu, welcoming staff, and cheery, kick-back vibe make for a winning combo–and we can't get enough. It's a tough table to score, so expect a line and know it's worth the wait. Freshly fried and golden-crisp spuds; broccoli *de ceccio* scramble; or a grilled steak sandwich are among the delicious options. Hiding on 16th Street, it's easy to miss; just look for the tables out front sporting bright yellow Colman's English mustard tins.

Look for our symbol, spotlighting restaurants with a notable wine list.

San Francisco ▸ Castro

Civic Center

Hayes Valley · Lower Haight · Tenderloin

The gilded Beaux-Arts dome of City Hall marks the main artery of the Civic Center, where graceful architecture houses the city's finest cultural institutions, including the War Memorial & Performing Arts Center and the Asian Art Museum. On Wednesdays and Sundays, the vast promenade outside City Hall hosts **Heart of the City**, San Francisco's oldest farmer's market. Priced to attract low-income neighborhood families, the market brims with such rare Asian produce as young ginger, Buddha's hand, and bergamot lemons. Ground zero for California's marriage equality movement and protests of every stripe, City Hall is also prime territory for festivals, including Love Fest; the SF Symphony's biennial Black & White Ball; and the Lao New Year Festival in April. This same mall also witnessed the harvest of Alice Waters' Slow Food Nation Victory Garden in 2008. With an enormous Asian, and particularly Vietnamese, population in the neighboring Tenderloin, there is an incredible array of authentic dining options, especially on Larkin Street. Mom-and-pop shop **Saigon Sandwiches** leads the way with spicy *báhn mì* made with fresh, crusty baguettes. These tasty subs are only three bucks a pop. Nearby, the *pho ga* at **Turtle Tower** is said to be a favorite of Slanted Door's chef, Charles Phan, while **Bodega Bistro** is a romantic purple nook with a profusion of aromas, French flavors and *pho*. Best known for a seedy mess of strip clubs, liquor stores, and drug deals, the Tenderloin is a go-to for both a dingy and decadent nightlife. On the site of a former speakeasy, **Bourbon & Branch** is a sultry hideaway with a tome full of classic and creative cocktails.

Other sleek hot spots in this region include **Opaque**, a literal dining-in-the-dark establishment where guests rely on their other senses besides sight to appreciate a meal. The place is quite

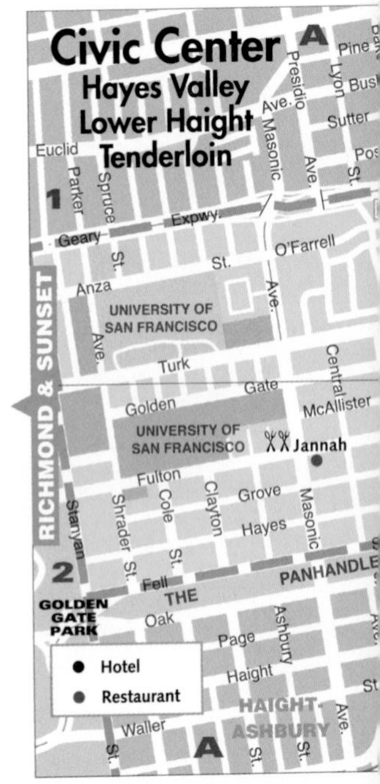

popular and offers a unique experience with interesting eats and delicious concoctions. West of the Civic Center, Hayes Valley is positively polished, with a coterie of chic design shops and boutiques; as well as an interesting medley of stylish restaurants.

The excellent menu at **Chantal Guillon Macarons** includes tantalizingly-flavored macarons (violet cassis and Madagascar vanilla?) in a French-style setting. **Destino** is a mainstay for *"nuevo Latino"* cuisine, and **Miette Confiserie** is an impossibly charming yet old-fashioned candy store that is jam-packed with hard-to-find European chocolates, salted licorice, taffy, and gelées. Apostles of **Blue Bottle Coffee** get their daily dose at the kiosk on Linden Alley. To the west, the Lower Haight draws hipsters for foosball and 21 tap beers at **The Page**; sake cocktails at **Noc Noc**; and live shows at the Independent. However, it's the Fillmore Jazz District that seduces true music lovers. Settled by African-American GI's at the end of World War II, the neighborhood hummed with jazz greats like Billie Holiday and Miles Davis. Today, with the attempted resurgence of the jazz district, large restaurants present live music and contemporary stars grace the stage. The Fillmore still echoes with the voices of American rock stars including Pink Floyd, Jimi Hendrix, and The Dead; and the annual Fillmore Jazz Festival is also a must-see.

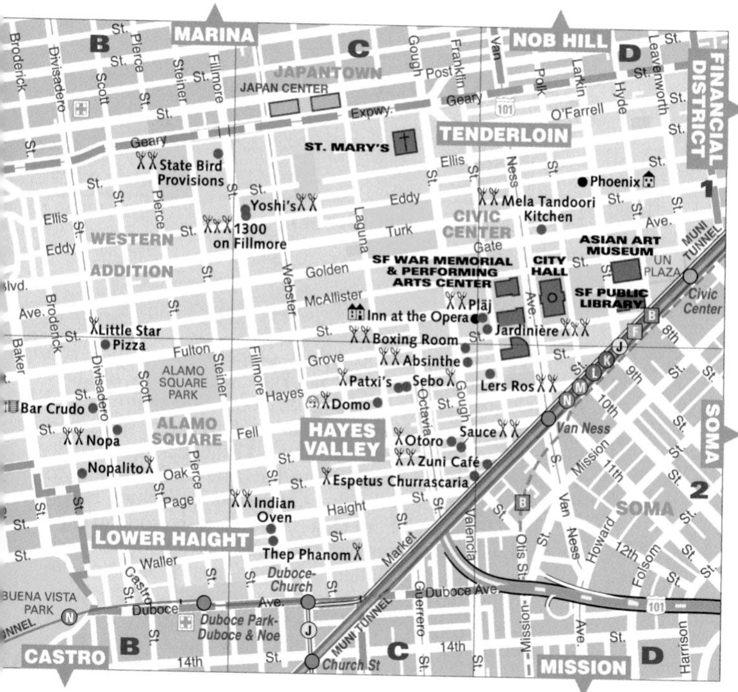

Absinthe

Mediterranean 

C2

398 Hayes St. (at Gough St.)

Phone: 415-551-1590
Web: www.absinthe.com
Prices: $$$

Lunch & dinner Tue – Sun

A longtime favorite among cosmopolites looking for a bite near the performing arts district, Absinthe offers a performance of its own. The set: a bustling Parisian brasserie with pressed-tin ceilings and mischievous green fairies spying on red velvet banquettes from mural-coated walls. The actors: well-heeled ladies and business types at lunch; adoring couples and artisanal cocktail enthusiasts by night.

Choreography in the kitchen focuses on Mediterranean-French delicacies composed of Californian ingredients. Dishes may include country pâté with kumquat marmalade; potato-crusted Arctic char with Niçoise olive tapenade; and Valrhona chocolate *pot de crème*.

Take home a bit of Absinthe in the restaurant's beloved beverage tome, *The Art of the Bar*.

Bar Crudo

Seafood 

B2

655 Divisadero St. (at Grove St.)

Phone: 415-409-0679
Web: www.barcrudo.com
Prices: $$

Dinner Mon – Sat

With super-fresh seafood artfully prepared, Bar Crudo is a bright idea. But be warned: San Francisco is a city of savvy foodies and, on any given night, you'll find them packed like sardines into this modern, narrow Divisadero space and ordering their fill of raw, cold, and hot small plates.

Regulars line the kitchen-facing bar and small balcony to slurp seafood chowder with caramelized applewood bacon and an enticing kick from chilies. A butterfish crudo may be flavored with asparagus-pistachio pesto and garnished with beet *brunoise*, while butterflied Idaho trout is roasted with toasty potatoes. Dessert is not served here, but chalk it up to the chef's expertise—he knows you'll be stuffed anyway. Schooled diners park in the nearby DMV lot.

Boxing Room

Southern

399 Grove St. (at Gough St.)

Phone: 415-430-6590
Web: www.boxingroom.com
Prices: $$

Lunch & dinner daily

Laissez les bon temps rouler at Boxing Room, the Civic Center newcomer serving a raucous taste of the Bayou. A far cry from the neighborhood's more posh post-theater environs, this corner space with floor-to-ceiling windows has a contemporary urban vibe with exposed steel beams, reclaimed wood tables, and a long zinc counter popular among cocktailing bartenders after work. In all, it's a party.

The kitchen too turns out jazzy cuisine with flavorful Cajun and Creole notes. Get your groove on with cornmeal-battered fried alligator (tastes like chicken); spicy andouille sausage and chicken gumbo; or a delicious fried shrimp Po'boy with creamy tartar sauce. For dessert, try fluffy beignets with espresso cream and pretend you're at Café du Monde.

Domo

Japanese 

511 Laguna St. (bet. Fell & Linden Sts.)

Phone: 415-861-8887
Web: www.domosf.com
Prices: $$

Lunch Mon – Fri
Dinner nightly

The secret's out about this tiny, unembellished foodie paradise. And it's no surprise: über fresh sushi at affordable prices plus long waits to boot make for a killer combo. It's a get in-get out affair here at Domo-there's no trying to linger over sake-where a small interior with wood counters and a sprinkling of sidewalk tables keep things simple.

A tidy list of specialty rolls are spelled out on a mirror—try the Apollo Roll, avocado, cucumber and shiso topped with caramelized scallops, crab, and tobiko; or the Alpha, a roll filled with smoky unagi, mango, and avocado, crowned with spicy tuna and pickled jalapeño. Delectable slices of nigiri are another spot-on option like silky, oily, and fresh aji and Spanish mackerel brushed with fresh wasabi.

Espetus Churrascaria

Brazilian

1686 Market St. (at Gough St.)

Phone: 415-552-8792 — Lunch & dinner daily
Web: www.espetus.com
Prices: $$

This is nirvana for carnivores with a penchant bordering on gluttony. "All you can eat" takes on new meaning at this Brazilian *rodizio*-style haven, where gallant *gauchos* deliver (via swords) an endless parade of roasted and grilled proteins. Turn the wheel to green if you want "more please," and show red (or scream "uncle") when you're "taking a meat break." So after several servings of Parmesan pork, homemade sausage, chicken thighs, and beef sirloin, it's code red!

During lunch, you may see a lot of repeat visits from the sirloin guy, but as accoutrements, a generous buffet overflows with salads, fresh veggies, and other side dishes. Dinner ups the meat ante as well as the prices, but one glass of the malbec and you'll be set for a lusty feast.

Indian Oven

Indian

233 Fillmore St. (bet. Haight & Waller Sts.)

Phone: 415-626-1628 — Lunch & dinner daily
Web: www.indianovensf.com
Prices: $$

Fillmore residents who take out from Indian Oven on weeknights can now enjoy the restaurant's two walls of windows flooding the space with sunlight—this colorful little eatery with Indian folk art murals and a second dining room upstairs is stellar for private parties.

Surrounded by upscale boutiques, bustling bars, and restaurants along this popular stretch of Fillmore, Indian Oven is a great respite for an inexpensive bite after dropping your dough at the neighboring shops. The open kitchen turns out milder versions of authentic North Indian signatures such as tandoori chicken; fragrant *murgh masala* with turmeric and cumin; and tender lamb *vindaloo*. Also try homemade cheese dumplings, *gulab jamun*, and the specialty rice dish, *Kashmiri biryani*.

Jannah

A2 Middle Eastern XX

1775 Fulton St. (bet. Central & Masonic Aves.)

Phone: 415-567-4400 Lunch & dinner Tue – Sun
Web: www.yayacuisine.com
Prices: $$

From its walls and ceilings painted with bright blue skies and puffy clouds, to the Arabic music streaming through the dining room, Jannah is like a trip to the Medina without the jet lag. Bright, upbeat, and full of energy, Jannah's boundaries extend to a pleasing outdoor patio—just right for enjoying the hookah pipes that sit at the ready.

It is California-meets-Middle East on the menu, which features interesting, authentic, and unique dishes. A trained team of cooks punctuate their cooking with bold flavors and sweet/savory spices to create their own mark on everything from tabbouleh to *kuzi*—phyllo dough stuffed with lamb, fruit, vegetables, and an enticing blend of spices. Don't dismiss the chef's specials like smoked spice-crusted trout (*maskoof*).

Jardinière

D1 Californian XXX

300 Grove St. (at Franklin St.)

Phone: 415-861-5555 Dinner nightly
Web: www.jardiniere.com
Prices: $$$

For a memorable night in town, don your best dress, find a hand to hold, and head to this dreamy longtime favorite, tinged with a sense of bygone romance. Stop off at the circular bar and join the well-heeled couples sipping cocktails pre-or post-opera. Snag a seat upstairs where tables dot a candle-lit balcony overlooking the lower levels, and stunning arched windows showoff views of the bustling street.

Delectable dishes like wild fennel pappardelle with oxtail ragout, cherry tomatoes, and Niçoise olives; or ravioli bursting with autumnal squash, roasted bell peppers, provolone, and crispy sage keep locals happy. The Monday night three-course prix-fixe (with wine pairings) for $45 is a steal, while the chef's nightly tasting menu makes a fine feast.

Lers Ros

Thai XX

D2

307 Hayes St. (bet. Franklin & Gough Sts.)

Phone: 415-874-9661 — Lunch & dinner daily
Web: www.lersros.com
Prices: $$

It's a straight-up, unapologetic spice explosion here at Lers Ros. Authentic Thai is the name of the game at this trendy outpost—the original sister location still stands strong in the edgy and offbeat Tenderloin.

Contemporary tile accents, stacked stone walls, vibrant paintings by native artists, and black tabletops set the stage for inexpensive offerings (two items for around ten bucks at lunchtime), and dangerously delicious dishes. Crowds keep rolling in to chow on a menu that might feature spicy flash-fried tofu with fresh chili, garlic, bell peppers, and garlic; or scrumptious shrimp in a coconut milk red curry with eggplant, bamboo shoots, and red peppers. A tender half chicken marinated in a sweet smoky glaze is grilled to juicy gratification.

Little Star Pizza

Pizza X

B2

846 Divisadero St. (bet. Fulton & McAllister Sts.)

Phone: 415-441-1118 — Dinner Tue – Sun
Web: www.littlestarpizza.com
Prices: $$

This is a hip, chic, and minimalist spot for local twenty-somethings to pop in, put some of-the-moment music on the jukebox, grab an ice cold P.B.R., and wait for their eponymous Little Star deep dish pies to arrive, topped in creamy spinach, feta, and mushrooms. The Classic deep-dish (sausage, mushrooms, green peppers, and onions) is likewise a favorite, but lovers of thin-crust find nirvana in roasted chicken and basil pesto atop a crispy, flaky cornmeal crust.

The dimly lit dining room is always packed, loud, and not a kid-friendly spot, so the Chuck E. Cheese set should stay home with a sitter. Expect waits during prime time, so consider calling for a pie to-go. Alternatively, give their Valencia Street or Albany location in the East Bay a shot.

Mela Tandoori Kitchen

D1 — Indian XX

536 Golden Gate Ave. (bet. Polk St. & Van Ness Ave.)

Phone: 415-447-4041
Web: www.melatandoori.com
Prices: $$

Lunch Mon – Fri
Dinner nightly

Mela Tandoori Kitchen recently moved to this fresh location and it is quickly becoming a favored spot for the ubiquitous lunch buffet. Dinnertime is quieter, (the non-residential streets empty out, except for that odd homeless person), but those who come will enjoy the wonderful selection of Indian and Pakistani dishes found here, amid a flashy décor of multi-hued striped walls with bright accents and colorful tablecloths.

The kitchen employs halal as well as *zabihah* meats that are prepared and massaged with bold spices. In fact, dishes like an intensely tangy and spicy prawn vindaloo; or delicious spice-coated *pasanda* beef paired with a charred chili-cheese naan might just be some of the spiciest South Asian dishes available around town.

Nopa

Californian

560 Divisadero St. (at Hayes St.)

Phone: 415-864-8643
Web: www.nopasf.com
Prices: $$

Dinner nightly

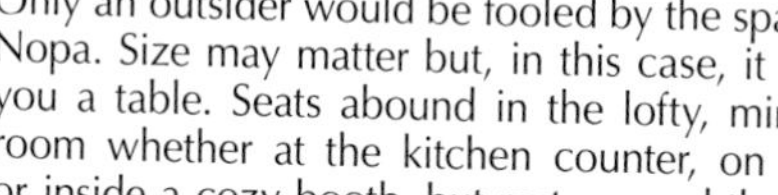

Only an outsider would be fooled by the spacious interior of Nopa. Size may matter but, in this case, it won't guarantee you a table. Seats abound in the lofty, minimalistic dining room whether at the kitchen counter, on the mezzanine, or inside a cozy booth, but rest assured they are filled with savvy locals who made a reservation.

Here the Bay Area's signature organic fare gets the wood-fired treatment, where such dishes as Italian sausage flatbread with seasonal fava beans are soul-warming and delicious. Even a flaky halibut is hearty when wood-roasted, topped with sugar snap peas and earthy wild mushrooms. Nopa is at once urban and rustic—just taste the molten-rich and heavenly chocolate soufflé that flaunts a blooming garnish of lavender.

Nopalito

Mexican

B2

306 Broderick St. (bet. Fell & Oak Sts.)

Lunch & dinner daily

Phone: 415-437-0303
Web: www.nopalitosf.com
Prices:

Painted in zesty shades of green evocative of its namesake, Nopalito is both a piquant bit of edible cactus used in Mexican cooking and the cheeky little sibling of Nopa, the neighborhood's destination restaurant. Here, budget-conscious hipsters come for satisfying Mexican fare of the local, organic variety.

Housed in Falletti Plaza, Nopalito is minimally adorned with just a few canvas coffee bags and a crowded, heated patio—adults convene at the bar rife with tequila and mescal. But flavors are big in dishes like complimentary fried chickpeas tossed in *guajillo* salsa; quesadilla *roja* with braised pork shoulder and crispy *chicharrón*; and a seasonal fish taco spiced with adobo and smoky ancho chile.

Check out the new Nopalito location in the Inner Sunset.

Otoro

Japanese 

C2

205 Oak St. (at Gough St.)

Lunch Mon – Fri
Dinner Mon – Sat

Phone: 415-553-3986
Web: www.otorosushi.com
Prices: $$

Sushi savants know that otoro is the supremely rich tuna belly, but in Hayes Valley it is a petite sushi spot drawing crowds of loving locals. Slate blue tones and wood accents show a contemporary aesthetic, while white porcelain dishes, windowed walls, and perky spotlights lend a splash of cheer. The sushi counter overflows with fresh, flavorful options, but steaming udon bowls are best for those who like to get their slurp on.

Daily specials merit serious attention and reveal such silky nigiri as buttery walu and melt-in-your-mouth otoro. *Takashi* rolls wrapped with albacore slices and filled with crispy pumpkin pieces, or the perfect little otoro maki packed with spicy tuna and crowned with mango slices are other favorites from the ample menu.

Patxi's

C2 — Pizza

511 Hayes St. (bet. Laguna & Octavia Sts.)

Phone: 415-558-9991
Web: www.patxispizza.com
Prices: $$

Lunch & dinner daily

An exuberant din of neighborhood pizza lovers rocks the rafters at Patxi's, the Hayes Valley outpost of the Palo Alto original. Exposed brick walls, concrete floors, and bright paintings from a nearby gallery give this location a distinctly San Francisco feel, though many of the pies actually nod to Chicago.

While Patxi's does offer cracker-crisp cornmeal pies for thin-crust devotees, deep dish is the main draw here. Expect to wait half an hour or more for that flaky-buttery, two-inch-deep sensation stuffed with gooey cheese; the "Favorite" is heavily heaped with pepperoni, mushrooms, and black olives. Salads and pizzas by the slice play well to the loyal lunch crowd, while half-baked take-home pies are a smart reward at the end of a long day.

Pläj

D1 — Scandinavian

333 Fulton St. (bet. Franklin & Gough Sts.)

Phone: 415-863-8400
Web: www.plajrestaurant.com
Prices: $$

Dinner nightly

This fresh spot located in the Inn at the Opera is the love child of Swedish-born Chef/owner Roberth Sundell. Strutting a small bar and two dining areas, inflections like white linen-topped tables and orange accents give the space a stylish yet low-key atmosphere.

The menu is Scandinavian featuring classic ingredients and flavor combinations mingled with Californian influence. Meals may start with toasted rye bread and proceed to pillow-soft potato dumplings arranged atop onion confit, sweet lingonberry sauce, brown butter, and smoky lardons. Try a herring tasting paired with marinades like saffron-tomato and an Asian-inspired ginger and smoked soy, ideally complemented by a Scandinavian wine, beer, or soda—lingonberry-elderflower anyone?

Sauce

American XX

C2

131 Gough St. (bet. Oak & Page Sts.)

Dinner nightly

Phone: 415-252-1369
Web: www.saucesf.com
Prices: $$

Laying off the Sauce isn't an option for Hayes Valley locals who can't help but kick back at their neighborhood mainstay, anticipating comfort food classics like baked mac and cheese with ham hock or fried chicken with whipped potatoes and gravy.

The Gough Street locale is as cozy as the food: upholstered booths are warmed by light from the semi-open kitchen; dark coffered ceilings and white tablecloths add just enough glam to make this a hot night out. An international bent is evident in lettuce steak wraps with chili-garlic sauce or butterfish wrapped with *Prosciutto di Parma*. Desserts are a crowd pleaser as in the cinnamon-sugar donuts with vanilla-Bourbon dipping sauce. Don't forget the other sauce, in a glass of crisp, local rosé.

Sebo

Japanese X

C2

517 Hayes St. (bet. Laguna & Octavia Sts.)

Dinner Tue – Sun

Phone: 415-864-2122
Web: www.sebosf.com
Prices: $$$

Sebo is small, so reservations are suggested at this well-tread spot decked with a sushi counter, sprinkling of trapezoidal wood tables, Japanese ceramic dishes, and back-lit wall panels. For all the hard wood surfaces, this gem is relatively quiet—perhaps it's the Zen-like appreciation of meals?

Sebo is also revered for its variety of superbly fresh seafood. The menu highlights sashimi, maki, and a selection of nigiri which might include an interesting and uncommon assortment such as Arctic char, *hirame*, gizzard shad, bonito, mackerel, scallops, uni, saltwater eel, and monkfish liver. Sebo isn't merely a sushi place: for those looking to splurge, there is a selection of cooked dishes, while the omakase is ideal for those in the mood to linger.

State Bird Provisions

B1 Contemporary 

1529 Fillmore St. (bet. Geary Blvd. & O'Farrell St.)

Phone: 415-795-1272
Web: www.statebirdsf.com
Prices: $$

Dinner Mon – Sat

Who says dim sum-style dining is just for Chinese food? Not the folks behind State Bird Provisions. At this popular haunt, most of the dishes are not on the menu—just flag down the staff parading around with trays and carts amid the industrially styled space.

This Civic Center foodie gem is fun and casual; there's even a high counter for standing diners who just can't wait to sit. Contemporary small plates could include a mound of fresh and creamy *burrata* with green garlic served atop a warm bun; tender slices of smoked duck breast matched with roasted fingerling potatoes; or the signature quail dish from which the restaurant got its name (state bird with provisions) composed of deliciously addictive breaded and fried quail pieces posed upon a confit.

Thep Phanom

C2 Thai

400 Waller St. (at Fillmore St.)

Phone: 415-431-2526
Web: www.thepphanom.com
Prices: $$

Dinner nightly

Fillmore residents tired of the bar scene step up to a different type of bar—the to-go counter at 20-year mainstay Thep Phanom, where a creamy Thai iced tea is as good as any cocktail. Family types not in the mood to sully their kitchens with takeout, however, are content to eat in the friendly dining room, dressed in simple wood furnishings and exotic art with two windowed walls for a view of neighborhood bustle.

Authentic dishes such as grilled beef salad and crispy prawns are boldly flavored with the cuisine's ubiquitous fresh basil, cilantro, garlic, and chili; heat-seekers will relish the sinfully spiced "Thaitanic" chicken with string beans and yellow curry. Don't miss the Birds of Paradise, otherwise known as the chef's famous fried quails.

1300 on Fillmore

American

1300 Fillmore St. (at Eddy St.)

Phone: 415-771-7100
Web: www.1300Fillmore.com
Prices: $$$

Lunch Sun
Dinner nightly

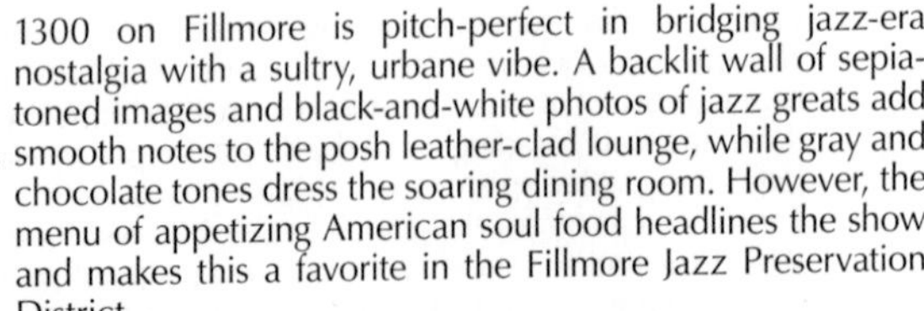

1300 on Fillmore is pitch-perfect in bridging jazz-era nostalgia with a sultry, urbane vibe. A backlit wall of sepia-toned images and black-and-white photos of jazz greats add smooth notes to the posh leather-clad lounge, while gray and chocolate tones dress the soaring dining room. However, the menu of appetizing American soul food headlines the show and makes this a favorite in the Fillmore Jazz Preservation District.

Come hungry and prepared to devour an array of comfort food. A culinary performance might warm up with cornbread smothered in honey butter and pepper jelly; crescendo at supremely tender maple-braised beef short ribs with buttermilk mashed potatoes; and wind down with a hot apple cobbler. Classic cocktails sing spirited backup.

Yoshi's

Japanese

C1

1330 Fillmore St. (at Eddy St.)

Phone: 415-655-5600
Web: www.yoshis.com
Prices: $$$

Dinner Tue – Sun

Inside the Fillmore Heritage Center, Yoshi's exhibition kitchen sets the stage for creative sushi in a jazzy interior that's suited to a grand performance hall. The restaurant has a contemporary-industrial aura with polished wood tables, concrete columns, and a sweeping staircase leading to an upstairs club. Moreover, the vast dining room can accommodate a sold out crowd of concert-goers with two lounge areas and a sleek sushi counter.

Service may be slow but the wait is worth it for such expertly prepared dishes as the "High Note," a sushi-sashimi combo including *maguro*, hamachi, and *unagi*; grilled *robata* plates; and rolls like the spicy dragon with shrimp tempura and creamy avocado. A glass from the well-curated sake list perfectly washes it all down.

Zuni Café

D2 — Mediterranean XX

1658 Market St. (bet. Franklin & Gough Sts.)

Phone: 415-552-2522
Web: www.zunicafe.com
Prices: $$

Lunch & dinner Tue – Sun

Over thirty years young and still thriving, locals and tourists alike remain drawn to this renowned favorite, famous for its laid-back Cali vibe and great, locally sourced eats. The iconic space is styled with exposed brick, contemporary paintings, and a wood-burning fireplace at the center of the action.

Located near the Civic Center, Financial District, and SoMa, Zuni Café makes for a perfect lunch destination. Indeed, many a local business folk can be found noshing on wood-fired pizzas (try the pecorino, pancetta, and arugula); or the grass-fed hamburger on grilled rosemary focaccia, smothered with garlic aioli. Swing by at dinner for the likes of or pork tenderloin and fennel sausage with sautéed rapini, cannellini beans, and breadcrumb salsa.

Your opinions are important to us. Please write to us directly at: michelin.guides@us.michelin.com

Financial District

Embarcadero · Union Square

Though San Francisco may be famed for its laid-back image, its bustling business district is ranked among the top financial centers in the nation. On weekdays, streetcars, pedestrians, and wildly tattooed bicycle messengers clog the routes of the triangle bounded by Kearny, Jackson, and Market streets. Lines snake out the doors of the better grab-and-go sandwich shops and salad bars at lunch; and both day and night, a host of fine dining restaurants in this quarter cater to clients with expense accounts. Along Market Street, casual cafés and chain restaurants focus on floods of tourists and shoppers. Despite all that the area has to offer, its greatest culinary treasures may be within the Ferry Building. This 1898 steel-reinforced sandstone structure was among the few survivors of the 1906 earthquake and fire

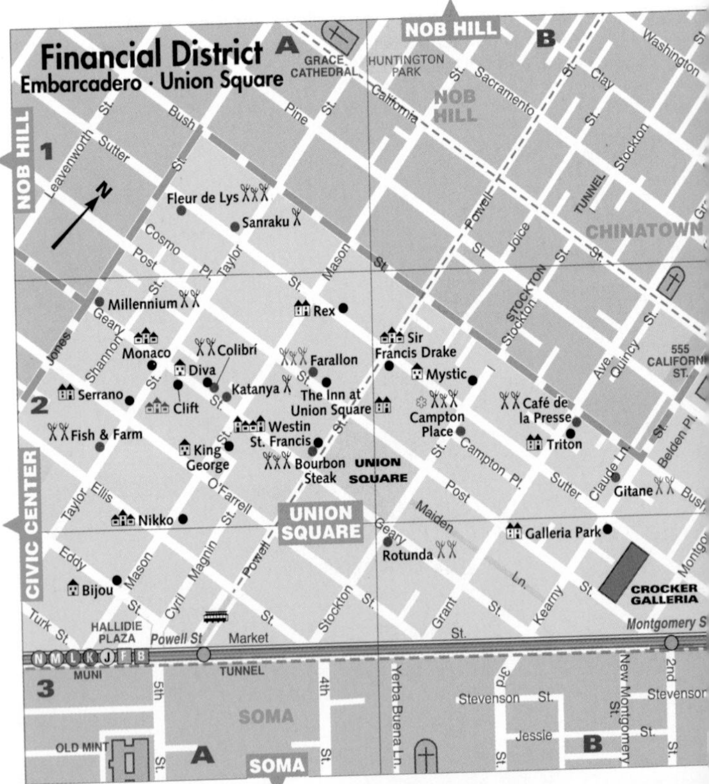

that destroyed most of the area. It remains a clear neighborhood standout, easily recognized by its 244-foot clock tower rising from Market Street above the waterfront promenade known as The Embarcadero ("boarding place" in Spanish). Renovated in 2004, its soaring interior arcade now makes an architecturally stunning culinary showcase for local and artisanal foods, fine Chinese teas, and everything in between. Known as the **Ferry Building Marketplace**, this is a true foodie pilgrimage and includes Lauren Kiino's **Il Cane Rosso**—a quick serve rotisserie and casual sandwich shop that pleases patrons with a weekday brunch starring an olive oil-fried egg sandwich; lunch menus replete with salads, soups, and sandwiches; and family-style three-course dinners prettily priced at $25. The marketplace strives to support the local and artisanal food community by highlighting small regional producers. Among these, two of the most popular are the acclaimed **Cowgirl Creamery** farmstead cheeses, and the organic breads of Berkeley's **Acme Bread Company**. Discover numerous exotic, organic mushrooms, medicinals, and themed products at **Far West Fungi**. Patient enthusiasts can even purchase logs on which

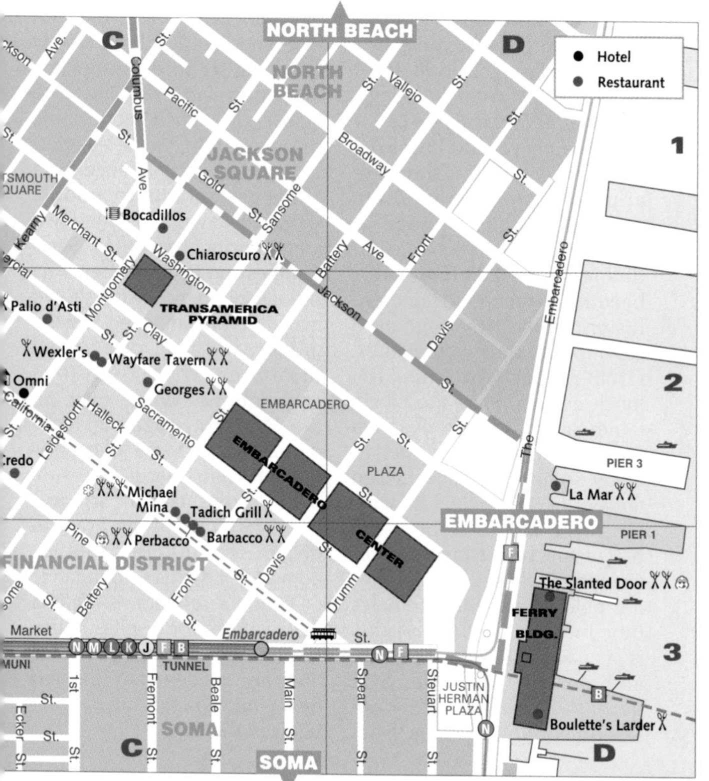

to grow their own harvest. The legendary **Frog Hollow Farms** also has an outpost here, offering luscious seasonal fruit as well as a myriad of organic chutneys and marmalades. **Recchiuti Confections** elevates the art of crafting Parisian-style chocolates and caramels to a level that can only be described as heavenly! The owners (Michael and Jacky Recchiuti) successfully take on the charge of introducing Americans to "real chocolate" via their best sellers.

Even the retail offerings are food-themed here, and include a number of cookware shops and home-design boutiques with a northern Californian flair. **4505 Meats** is hugely popular for Chef Ryan Farr's butchery classes, as well as for his smoked artisan hot dogs, sausages, and *chicarrónes*.

While such world-class food shopping may whet the appetite, more immediate satisfaction can be found in the building's more casual dining spots. **DELICA** offers beautifully-prepared Japanese fusion foods, from signature sushi rolls to savory croquettes. Grab a seat with the FiDi lunch crowds filling the picnic tables at **Mijita** (run by Traci Des Jardins of Jardinière) to enjoy some Oaxacan chicken tamales or Baja-style fish tacos. Or, perch atop a stool at the bar of the **Hog Island Oyster Company**, whose fresh bivalves are plucked from the Tomales Bay in Marin County—this is a great spot to sit, slurp, and take in the view. Still perhaps the most decadent takeout option may be from **Boccalone Salumeria**, where one can find a comprehensive selection of charcuterie that are available for purchase by the platter, pound, or layered in a single-serving "cone" for an unapologetically carnivorous treat. On Tuesday and Saturday mornings, join the chefs and crowds at the **Ferry Plaza Farmers Market** for organic produce, mouthwatering baked goods, fresh pasta, and more.

On market days, stands and tents soak the sidewalk in front of the building and rear plaza that overlooks the bay. Clusters of FiDi office workers head to the Embarcadero Center (spanning five blocks in the heart of the commercial district with reduced parking rates on weekends) to get their midday shopping fix in the sprawling three-story indoor mall and to grab a quick lunch in one of the complex's thirty-some eateries. These food havens range from chain restaurants to noodle shops. Here you'll also find two longtime local favorites, **See's Candies** and **Peet's Coffee**. Any serious shopper or visitor should make the pilgrimage to **Slide,** a unique and chic playground brimming with delicious concoctions. While over on the Western edge, upscale department stores like Saks and Neiman Marcus preside over famed Union Square. Here, as fashionistas flock to designer boutiques, foodies come for the area's abundance of gourmet restaurants. Drama lovers also favor respites in this neighborhood, especially since they are conveniently located near some of the city's most beloved theaters.

Barbacco

220 California St. (bet. Battery & Front Sts.)

Phone: 415-955-1919
Web: www.barbaccosf.com
Prices:

Lunch Mon – Fri
Dinner Mon – Sat

This younger sister of Perbacco (next door) stretches its lanky, lean interior with original brick walls, a long marble bar, shiny stainless steel, and contemporary photos evoking a dizzying sense of motion. Barbacco's style is matched only by its efficiency, and FiDi regulars appreciate that the staff is equipped with hand-held POS systems to keep them on the go.

Busy at all times, Barbacco serves impeccable trattoria fare as well as takeout bites. Braised chicken thighs with Castelvetrano olives, garlic confit, and escarole; or squid stuffed with spicy *pan grattato* and *rucola* make for heart-warming meals. And, as at Perbacco, the rustic, homemade pastas are perfection—imagine *canneroni* coated in a slow-roasted lamb sugo with peas, mint, and chili.

Bocadillos

710 Montgomery St. (at Washington St.)

Phone: 415-982-2622
Web: www.bocasf.com
Prices:

Lunch Mon – Fri
Dinner Mon – Sat

This is a tiny tapas bar that pays homage to a *pequeño* Spanish sandwich loaded with big, blazing flavors. In the same vein, a fiery shade of *piment d'espelette* heats the walls of beloved Bocadillos. At lunch, FiDi suits file in for the $10 duo and choose from hot and cold varieties like fried chicken with spicy coleslaw; tuna salad with Tillamook cheddar; or turkey, Brie, and cranberry sauce.

Assorted tapas like Brussels sprouts with Asian pear and Serrano ham, and crisp salads round out the dinner offerings; while high stools around the polished wood bar are a laid-back perch to enjoy a glass of Spanish wine. Come nightfall, votives illuminate a snug, uncluttered space where the tables are loaded with baskets of utensils and small plates for sharing.

Boulette's Larder

Californian

D3

1 Ferry Building (at The Embarcadero)

Lunch Sun – Fri

Phone: 415-399-1155
Web: www.bouletteslarder.com
Prices: **$$**

A larder is a large pantry, and Boulette is the owner's big black Hungarian sheepdog. And, if every doghouse has a pantry like this, we've been missing out. Buried in the bustling Ferry Building, this is a foodie's version of an apothecary displaying everything from *agar agar* and specialty salts, to Sicilian anchovies in oil and pine needle syrup.

The menu spins to the season, but by day (breakfast and lunch included), Boulette doles out sophisticated creations as well as salads, soups, and heartier items (braised beef short ribs perhaps?). By night, Chef Amaryll Schwertner and partner Lori Regis transform the room into an intimate chef's table with elegant place settings and candlelit floral arrangements that sit pretty beside a lemon meringue tart.

Bourbon Steak

Steakhouse

A2

335 Powell St. (bet. Geary & Post Sts.)

Dinner nightly

Phone: 415-397-3003
Web: www.michaelmina.net
Prices: **$$$$**

Nothing is ordinary about Bourbon Steak, Michael Mina's fine dining destination set off the lobby of the grande dame Westin St. Francis hotel. A flight of steps leads you to this deliciously impressive respite, which brags soaring ceilings, dramatic columns, enormous arched windows, oversized mirrors, and caramel leather chairs.

This mighty space baits an army of suits and tourists in need of replenishing with the likes of golden brown Maine lobster corn dogs enlivened with a whole grain tarragon-mustard sauce; the signature ahi tuna tartare crowned with a quail egg and mint; and an impeccable 8 oz. filet mignon brushed with béarnaise sauce. Every meal starts with a trio of fantastic spice-dusted duck-fat fries guaranteed to induce broad smiles.

Café de la Presse

B2 French XX

352 Grant Ave. (at Bush St.)

Phone: 415-398-2680
Web: www.cafedelapresse.com
Prices: $$

Lunch & dinner daily

After a fashionable stroll through nearby Union Square, Café de la Presse is a lovely spot to brush up on your French with an après-shopping glass of viognier. The sunny streetfront café is dotted with bistro tables and stocked to the rafters with international newspapers and magazines; if you desire to actually speak French, the multi-lingual staff is happy to oblige.

Framed reproductions of vintage posters dress the slightly more formal wood-paneled dining room where Francophiles from near and far nosh on authentic dishes like *cocktail de crevettes*, meaty tiger prawns and avocado cocktail dressed with sweet grapefruit; or *Coquilles St. Jacques* with pan-seared day boat scallops, fennel confit, onion reduction, and potato *gaufrettes. Bon appétit*!

Chiaroscuro

C1 Italian XX

550 Washington St. (bet. Montgomery & Sansome Sts.)

Phone: 415-362-6012
Web: www.chiaroscurosf.com
Prices: $$

Lunch Mon – Fri
Dinner Mon – Sat

Chiaroscuro flies a bit under the radar in the financial district, but those in the know frequent the place for its fantastic homemade pastas. The chef is from Rome and his menu reflects the types of dishes that he grew up eating. Lunch sees a bigger business clientele, but dinner is a mix of young and old. The charming "cement barn" vibe of the décor with its cushioned concrete banquettes reflects the food as grounded, solid, and contemporary, yet well-rooted in its history.

A tasting of signature pastas should be mandatory and may include wonderful vermicelli mingled with pecorino-coated prawns, mussels, sundried tomato, and arugula; or a unique and sublime monkfish dressed with potato foam and perfectly paired with a black disk of squid ink terrine.

Campton Place 

Contemporary XxX

B2

340 Stockton St. (bet. Post & Sutter Sts.)

Lunch & dinner daily

Phone: 415-955-5555
Web: www.camptonplacesf.com
Prices: $$$$

Taj Campton Place San Francisco

From the chilled champagne cart that greets each table, to the modern and gold-toned interior that remains modest and understated, there is a sense of focused ambition and refinement throughout Campton Place. And yet, there is that eye-catching and gorgeous blown-glass arrangement of reddish orchids suspended from the ceiling—a colorful harbinger of the food that will soon arrive, often as beautiful to behold as it is to eat.

The predominantly French contemporary menu highlights pure, seasonal flavors and ingredients that emphasize the haute side of cuisine, but the *très* inventive chef adds wonderful notes of his own traditions. Expect meals to begin with the likes of chopped ahi tuna tartare set upon a narrow strip of watermelon with *papadam* crumbles and a swath of avocado purée. Entrées have featured plump medallions of bronzed chicken roulade with a farce of chicken mousse, neatly positioned around crisp lardons, grilled nebrodini mushrooms, and a trio of broccoli that has been blanched and smoked, tempura-fried, and puréed.

Desserts deliver subtle pleasures through delicate rounds of passion fruit custard with pearls of spherified coffee and a small scoop of icy coconut "snow."

Colibrí

A2 — Mexican XX

438 Geary St (bet. Mason & Taylor Sts.)

Phone: 415-440-2737
Web: www.colibrimexicanbistro.com
Prices: $$

Lunch & dinner daily

A stone's throw from bustling Union Square, this popular crowd pleaser attracts a mainly tourist cluster with its darling digs and fresh plates of modern Mexican. Wrought-iron chandeliers and lanterns illuminate persimmon and gold walls, in a room fitted with bare mahogany tables and chairs, stone tile floors, and bright floral arrangements.

Piping-hot tortillas served with a trio of house salsas are a terrific taste bud teaser. Next, jump to *sopas surtidos*, three griddled masa rounds heaped with refried beans, *queso fresco*, and onions, topped with shredded chicken, pork, or sautéed veggies. Other tantalizers may uncover cheese-laden chicken enchiladas bathed in a tomatillo-jalapeño sauce (or tomato-chipotle), and finished with sour cream and cilantro.

Credo

C2 — Italian XX

360 Pine St. (bet. Montgomery & Sansome Sts.)

Phone: 415-693-0360
Web: www.credosf.com
Prices: $$

Lunch Mon – Fri
Dinner Mon – Sat

Credo has found its groove in the FiDi. The restaurant is minimal in its design, which lets the eye focus on their stunning reclaimed wood tabletops carved by famed Dutch designer Piet Hein Eek and credo-covered walls courtesy of mega-personalities like Andy Warhol, Albert Einstein, and Gisele Bundchen.

The well-tread bar is popular for after-work drinks, while Credo's carte covers rustic Italian cooking. For a more sequestered experience, book the private room or chef's table, and get an up-close view of the kitchen drizzling cracker-thin funghi pizza with truffle oil; finishing a slow-braised *osso buco di maiale* atop buttery cannellini beans and rosemary potatoes; or topping a simple yet superb apple galette with vanilla bean gelato.

Farallon

Seafood

A2

450 Post St. (bet. Mason & Powell Sts.)

Phone: 415-956-6969 Dinner nightly
Web: www.farallonrestaurant.com
Prices: $$$

Some build castles in the air, while others create underwater fantasies. This vastly lauded seafood respite brings ocean to land only feet from Union Square in a spectacular space where every detail captures the life aquatic with octopus stools, jelly fish light fixtures, and shell motifs. Snake through elaborate dining nooks to the stunning pool room, bathed in intricate mosaic and beloved by an operatic set dressed to the nines.

Beneath sea urchin chandeliers, glimpse the flawless symphony between kitchen and staff. Then dive into a menu featuring seared ahi slices fanned over a salad of lentils, frisée, and tapenade; grilled Alaskan salmon made pungent with Chinese black bean sauce; and bittersweet chocolate mousse crested with tequila cream.

Fish & Farm

American

A2

339 Taylor St. (bet. Ellis & O'Farrell Sts.)

Phone: 415-474-3474 Dinner nightly
Web: www.fishandfarmsf.com
Prices: $$

Don't be put off by Fish & Farm's address inside FiDi's Mark Twain hotel; rather, let the evocation of Americana lure you in. Two large canvases depicting aquatic and pastoral scenes dominate the dark wood dining room, and tufted leather banquettes are a comfortable place to settle in. Fish & Farm brings a simply delightful surf and turf experience.

Locally sourced, organic ingredients star in many of the dishes, from oysters on the half shell with malt vinegar mignonette to Southern-style fried Petaluma chicken served with mashed potatoes, wilted collard greens, and cornbread madeleines. Steak lovers will relish the ribeye with corn and chanterelles, while the all-American sweet tooth can sate itself on velvety ricotta cheesecake in a jar.

Fleur de Lys

A1 — French XXX

777 Sutter St. (bet. Jones & Taylor Sts.)

Phone: 415-673-7779
Web: www.fleurdelyssf.com
Prices: $$$$

Dinner Tue – Sat

Immediately identifiable by its canopied entrance and gold lettering, plush Fleur de Lys is proud of its traditional and established first impression. An attentive hostess, enthused yet poised waiters, and elegantly set tables are reminders that this is one of San Francisco's last remaining grandes dames. Still, there is nothing musty about this classic and celebratory spot, with stunning florals and gleaming mirrors that reflect romancing couples and older socialites in their best dress.

The comfort found within is unashamedly glitzy and luxurious. This culminates in the likes of a chilled Dungeness salad with lobster fondant and caviar; Alaskan halibut with a tomato-coriander coulis; or a Mirabelle soufflé splashed with plum sauce.

Georges

C2 — Seafood XX

415 Sansome St. (bet. Commercial & Sacramento Sts.)

Phone: 415-956-6900
Web: www.georgessf.com
Prices: $$

Lunch Mon – Fri
Dinner Mon – Sat

When it was said that Luca Brasi "swims with the fishes" it was bad news. However, this Italian kitchen thrives on such fortune. Set in a former gold rush-era bank, Georges' rush is from financial types for lunch and happy hour. Handsome aesthetics await in the form of a wasabi green bar, sleek paneling, and tables of reclaimed wood.

A John Dory sculpture underlines the menu's focus on sustainable seafood. From the ice cold raw bar, try premium Kusshi oysters served on the half shell with a rosé mignonette; or super fresh ono ceviche neatly topped with hearts of palm and crispy shallot rings. Savor bold fenugreek-dusted albacore tuna placed atop a crunchy chickpea pancake flecked with carrot-harissa. Leave the gun; take the citrus-and-semolina *zeppole*.

Gitane

Mediterranean XX

B2

6 Claude Ln. (bet. Bush & Sutter Sts.)

Phone: 415-788-6686 Dinner Tue – Sat
Web: www.gitanerestaurant.com
Prices: $$

There are a million words to describe this Claude Lane jewel but, honestly, just one will suffice: sexy! Tucked in a clandestine little alley with just a few sidewalk tables to give her away, Gitane–French for "gypsy woman" and also a brand of cigarettes–may have a Gallic name but the reference stops there. This is an exotic hideaway.

Wrought-iron chandeliers and red lamps cast a dim light on mirrored walls, which reflect rich textiles and cushioned banquettes. Sound sultry? The cuisine is equally seductive. You'll salivate for Catalan-style flatbread with cilantro, caramelized onions, and merguez sausage; flaky pan-seared opah with herbed yogurt and seasoned chickpea stew; and a chicken tagine with green olives, almonds, and saffron-tomato broth.

Katanya

Japanese X

A2

430 Geary St. (bet. Mason & Taylor Sts.)

Phone: 415-771-1280 Lunch & dinner daily
Web: N/A
Prices: 

In the heart of what locals fondly call the "Splenderloin," this Tenderloin neighborhood noodle house has all the trappings of a favorite haunt in a gritty locale: questionable décor and a line of mixed patrons loitering outside the door.

That's right, those in the know aren't put off by Katanya's gaudy gilded artwork or well-worn furnishings. Rather, they are in a hurry and here for lunch, which promises rewarding bowls of piping hot ramen. Start with tempura, plump *gyoza*, or offerings from the sushi bar before getting to the good stuff: belly-warming bowls of the house specialty noodles come laden with fried chicken and potatoes as well as corn, egg, and barbecued pork. Even the most tired taste buds will perk up for the kimchi-flavored broth.

La Mar

D2 — Peruvian XX

Pier 1 1/2 (at The Embarcadero)

Phone: 415-397-8880 — Lunch & dinner daily
Web: www.lamarsf.com
Prices: $$

Though La Mar may lack the intensity of its fellow Peruvian eateries, this restaurant makes up for it in location. By virtue of being housed in a grand pier building, the ambience is stately to say the least, with soaring ceilings, oversized windows, and a diligent semi-open kitchen. However, the best seats might be on the patio overlooking the boats and bay.

Lunch sees a blend of loyal corporate types and tourists who adore their lovely selection of small plates. Variety is their forte, so order a cluster of dishes like *causa camarón*, chopped shrimp dressed in a spiced *leche de tigre* aïoli; *empanadas de aji de gallina*, stewed chicken empanadas served with *aji amarillo*; and *rollo norteño*, shrimp and avocado roll crested with finely sliced scallops.

Millennium

A2 — Vegan XX

580 Geary St. (at Jones St.)

Phone: 415-345-3900 — Dinner nightly
Web: www.millenniumrestaurant.com
Prices: $$

Millennium was lauded for its exceptional vegan food long before it was cool to be vegan. Even fervid carnivores trade their steaks for tofu here, where the friendly staff is eager to advise on the area's best organic markets.

Influenced by countless cultures, Millennium's gourmet vegan made at the hands of Chef Eric Tucker personifies flavor and creativity. Sustainable products star in dishes like black bean torte with caramelized plantains, pumpkin-habanero *papazul*, and cashew "sour cream"; maple- and black pepper-glazed smoked tempeh; or Bourbon-and-black salt molten chocolate cake trickled with a smoked pecan ice cream.

Dishes are so tasty that this place is packed nightly, so reserve ahead or pray for a seat at the first-come, first-served bar.

Michael Mina ✿

Contemporary XXX

252 California St. (bet. Battery & Front Sts.)

Phone: 415-397-9222 — Lunch Mon – Fri
Web: www.michaelmina.net — Dinner nightly
Prices: **$$$$**

MICHAEL MINA San Francisco

There is a warmth and excitement here that almost outshines the importance of its namesake chef. It may be grand in scale yet this dining room retains a casual Californian style through oversized mirrors reflecting massive floral arrangements and mixologists pouring their wares into Spiegelau stemware at the polished concrete bar. Proximity to luxury hotels means that this clientele strikes the right balance between relaxed and refined.

Of course, this all originates in the kitchen, where Chef Michael Mina is worthy of all the accolades and Google alerts surrounding him. The signature tuna starter brings new and interesting flavors to each bit of sweet pear, roasted nuts, and spiced oil mixed tableside with freshly chopped fish. Handmade pastas might twirl mushrooms and rabbit with an intense green herb and fiery garlic sauce, and be a prelude to olive oil-poached John Dory with oranges, artichokes, and consommé mixed with silky-smooth tapenade. (Ask for a spoon and don't miss a drop.) Desserts are clever but mostly delicious, as in a deconstructed brown butter cake with rummy bananas and flan ice cream.

Lunches are served with precision—a gift to anyone needing to be out in an hour.

Palio d'Asti

C2 — Italian XX

640 Sacramento St. (bet. Kearny & Montgomery Sts.)

Phone: 415-395-9800
Web: www.paliodasti.com
Prices: $$

Lunch Mon – Fri
Dinner Mon -Sat

Named for Il Palio, a bareback horserace in the Italian town of Asti that harks back to the Middle Ages, this FiDi favorite does not stray from its theme. Equestrian art gallops around concrete columns and across walls, while courtly banners and vibrant coats of arms trumpet contemporary Italian meals of enormous proportions.

The fare hails from various Italian regions and is available in two-, three-, and four-course prix-fixe menus that largely appeal to neighborhood businessmen. Aromatic, authentic, and generous dishes might include hand-rolled penne pasta with herb-rich tomato sauce and Berkshire pork *guanciale*; fennel sausage pizza with smoked mozzarella; or a steaming fisherman's stew with spicy saffron-lobster broth and grilled sourdough.

Perbacco

C3 — Italian XX

230 California St. (bet. Battery & Front Sts.)

Phone: 415-955-0663
Web: www.perbaccosf.com
Prices: $$

Lunch Mon – Fri
Dinner Mon – Sat

Perbacco loosely translates to "good times" in Italian and that's exactly what you'll have when you come here. From the cool marble bar to the sleek furnishings, Perbacco has city-chic written all over it. It is urban and up to the minute, and its smartly dressed and sophisticated crowd knows it.

The highly professional and knowledgeable staff makes this a tightly run ship, while the country Italian cooking is sure to please. The food focuses on Piemonte, with a little bit of Liguria, and even Provence thrown in for good measure. It is comfort food for city slickers and may include *piastra*-seared octopus with olive oil-crushed potatoes; beef short rib *stracotto*; and chocolate custard with whipped cream and amaretti—all at palatable prices.

Rotunda

B3 — Californian XX

150 Stockton St. (at Geary St.)

Phone: 415-362-4777 — Lunch daily
Web: www.neimanmarcus.com
Prices: $$$

Sheltered in Neiman Marcus and with a view of Union Square, drama and glamour attract ladies-who-lunch and tourists to the stained-glass Rotunda. They're here to nibble on salads and raise a tea pinkie while observing models parade the latest fashions along the circular balcony.

Rotunda is known for its fab afternoon tea, but there is also a full lunch menu that begins with a demitasse of hot chicken broth, followed by crispy popovers and strawberry butter. A first course of fresh ahi tuna poke served on butter lettuce leaves may be trailed by sautéed salmon spread over tender farro, Brussels sprouts, and roasted red pepper vinaigrette. Go ahead and indulge in the creamy strawberry cheesecake *sans* guilt—you can always buy some Spanx on the way out.

Sanraku

A1 — Japanese X

704 Sutter St. (at Taylor St.)

Phone: 415-771-0803 — Lunch Mon – Sat
Web: www.sanraku.com — Dinner nightly
Prices: ◎◎

When it comes to consuming raw fish, it's easy to judge a sushi bar by its cover: sleek can be a misleading synonym for fresh. But San Francisco sushi connoisseurs know that the most outstanding seafood hides out in unassuming corners. Welcome to Sanraku, a no-frills favorite with quick, inexpensive, and quality Japanese bites.

Dressed in bare light walls and blonde wood tables, Sanraku isn't much to look at. But natural light and spunky service keep things upbeat, and ample portions do not disappoint the Western palate. Santa Barbara uni is fresh and creamy, and the sashimi platter is loaded with flavorful fluke, Spanish mackerel, and salmon. With small salads and bowls of miso soup, lunch specials appeal to the local working set.

The Slanted Door

Vietnamese

1 Ferry Building (at The Embarcadero)

Phone: 415-861-8032 Lunch & dinner daily
Web: www.slanteddoor.com
Prices: $$

Faraway from the heat of Vietnam, Charles Phan's ever sacred Slanted Door embodies a fortuitous marriage of local bounty kissed with Californian flair and faithful Vietnamese flavors. A virtual emperor of a Bay Area empire, his branches ooze verve and vivacity. Superbly set in the cuisine-centric Ferry Building, the hype still delights at this swank, scenic place.

Cypress tables cradle earthenware parading a litany of delights. Tinged with clean flavors are street foods like spring rolls with pork, shrimp, and peanut sauce at the side of a crispy snapper head with grilled pineapple and ginger jus. Reservations are hard to come by, but the bar is first-come, first-served luring boisterous beauties with a bevy of beers, cocktails, and teas.

Tadich Grill

Seafood

240 California St. (bet. Battery & Front Sts.)

Phone: 415-391-1849 Lunch & dinner Mon – Sat
Web: www.tadichgrill.com
Prices: $$

Tadich Grill is as much a spot for history buffs as it is for local foodies: opened in 1849, San Francisco's oldest restaurant retains its antique charm. While there are a few tables, regulars prefer a niche at the long wood bar where they can catch up with fellow barflies and watch the white-coated staff up close.

Try not to fill up on sliced sourdough—the simple dishes are hearty. Mainstays include a creamy Boston clam chowder; large Dungeness crab cakes with steamed baby bok choy; and fresh seafood entrées that may be broiled, pan-fried, sautéed, poached, deep-fried, or baked *en casserole*. Don't forget about the delightful daily specials, which may include seafood cioppino with garlic bread; broiled lobster tail; and corned beef hash.

Wayfare Tavern

C2 — Gastropub XX

558 Sacramento St. (bet. Montgomery & Sansome Sts.)

Phone: 415-772-9060 — Lunch Mon – Sat
Web: www.wayfaretavern.com — Dinner nightly
Prices: $$

These days, Wayfare Tavern dressed in celebrity chef Tyler Florence's signature style is perennially packed, so make your reservations in advance. Breezy, masculine, and just a bit raucous, this bi-level arena wears an old-world gastropub vibe with classic wood floors and furnishings, subway-tiled walls, wallpaper, and even a private room decked out with a pool table and flatscreen.

The man himself can often be spotted in the seriously animated exhibition kitchen. Grab a seat at the antique bar for the best view as servers whir past with plates of organic fried chicken (in a buttermilk brine with roasted garlic); smoked Sonoma pork ribs sweetened with plums and corn; and tri-tip adorned with truffle butter, watercress, and French fried potatoes.

Wexler's

C2 — American X

568 Sacramento St. (bet. Leidesdorff & Montgomery Sts.)

Phone: 415-983-0102 — Lunch Mon – Fri
Web: www.wexlerssf.com — Dinner Tue – Sat
Prices: $$

Wexler's has a discreet façade, but those who've discovered this friendly, casual spot, simply love it. Local business folks come here to rest their weary legs—under a dark, undulating art installation nicely contrasted with vibrant red chandeliers. Their barbecue-inspired bill of fare is not for the purists, but tender, smoked chicken wings bathed in signature hot sauce and paired with Greek yogurt and tangy Pt. Reyes blue cheese, deserves to be a meal on its own. BBQ brisket *bánh mi* may be a westernized version of the classic filled with pickled cabbage and Fresno chiles, but when coupled with a creamy macaroni salad studded with bacon, the experience is magical. Complete this meaty feast with a slice of cheddar cheese-crusted apple-huckleberry pie.

Marina

Japantown · Pacific Heights · Presidio

If San Francisco were a university campus, the Marina would be Greek Row, for what it lacks in diversity and substance, it makes up with a nod to those with "new money." The Marina's more sophisticated sister, Pacific Heights, thrives on some serious family money and couldn't care less about being edgy. When the tanned denizens of this beautiful bubble aren't jogging with their golden retrievers at Crissy Field, or sipping aromatic chocolate from the **Warming Hut**, they can be seen pushing designer baby strollers in boutiques or vying for parking in Mercedes SUVs.

Cafe Culture

Perhaps surprisingly, fine dining is not a hallmark of the Marina. Rather, this socialite's calling card is the quick-bite café **La Boulange** or **The Grove**; the gastropub, à la **Liverpool Lil's** or the **Balboa Café**; and the pickup joint **Perry's**, said to have been among the world's first. In truth, quality cuisine has little to do with a Marina restaurant's success: The locals are delightfully content to follow the buzz to the latest hot spot, whose popularity seems mandated by the number of pretty people sitting at its tables. However, in the Presidio, where Lucasfilm H.Q. rules, creative and tech geeks opt for convenience at nearby **Presidio Social Club** that serves up a locally sourced bill of fare amid a classic northern Californian setting. "Off the Grid-Fort Mason" features a collection of food trucks, which gather every Friday evening proffering fantastic street eats. For the Marina's physically fit and diet-conscious residents, food is mere sustenance to the afternoon shopper and a sponge for the champagne and chardonnay flowing at plentiful watering holes. In other words, it's really all about the bar scene, baby, and there's a playground for everyone. Oenophiles save the date for the annual ZAP Zinfandel Festival in January. Preppy post-collegiates swap remembrances of European semesters abroad at wine bars like **Ottimista Enoteca-Café** and **Nectar**. Guys relive

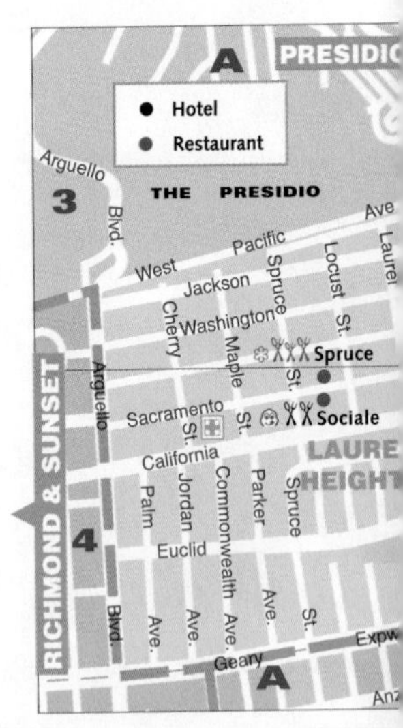

their frat house glory days at **Harry's Bar**, while singles on the hunt for marriageable meat opt for a cozy fireplace at the posh **MatrixFillmore**. With a burgeoning Asian culture, Japantown is the exception to the rule. **Umami Burger** on Union Street is the first Northern Californian location to serve this popular L.A.-based treat; **O Izakaya Lounge** riffs on the Japanese novelty for baseball; and the fab **Sundance Kabuki Cinema** offers a range of treats in their two full bars. Also in abundance here are Japanese cultural events, local shopping, and scores of schools.

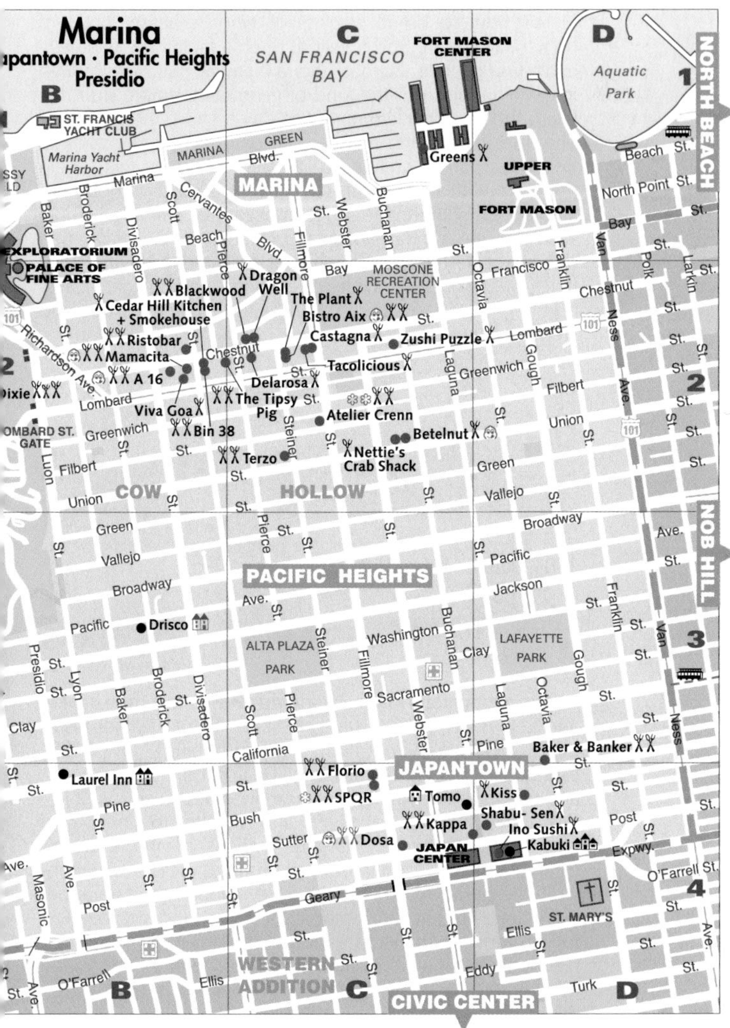

A 16

Italian XX

B2

2355 Chestnut St. (bet. Divisadero & Scott Sts.)

Phone: 415-771-2216 — Lunch Wed – Fri
Web: www.a16sf.com — Dinner nightly
Prices: $$

Here's how to do it: a glass of *vino*, a hearty bowl of homemade pasta, and a seat at a table facing the energetic exhibition kitchen. Named after a highway that runs through Italy, A 16 spins out the kind of exquisitely simple stuff that keeps the place packed night and day.

The appealing menu features seasonal ingredients sourced from local farms, creating a lovely homegrown feel. Begin the feast with Neapolitan-style *salsiccia* pizza (wood-fired and topped with tomato sauce, mozzarella, crumbled fennel seed sausage, rapini, garlic, and chilies); or *scialatiella*, thin ribbons of pasta tossed in chili oil and studded with bits of rich pork. Conclude with a decadent medjool date cake, a buttery sensation served with heady amaretto sauce and crème fraîche.

Baker & Banker

Californian XX

D3

1701 Octavia St. (at Bush St.)

Phone: 415-351-2500 — Lunch Sun
Web: www.bakerandbanker.com — Dinner Tue – Sun
Prices: $$

A true labor of love for husband-and-wife team Jeffrey Banker and Lori Baker, this casual-chic space has a distinct bistro bend. Envisage wood floors and furnishings, low lights, espresso leather banquettes, chalkboards listing beers, wines, and other specials, and the picture becomes clear.

Baker & Banker's love for and loyalty to local and sustainable produce is amply evident in the kitchen's shining dishes. Moving beyond bistro basics is a bacon-wrapped pork loin ladled with tangy cabbage and a juniper reduction. Braised lamb atop a mélange of crispy veggies, mushrooms, and parsnip gnocchi; and a lush Meyer lemon pie topped with whipped cream, candied thyme, surrounded by wonderfully sticky-sweet black olives crown this market-driven deal.

Atelier Crenn ✿✿

Contemporary XX

C2

3127 Fillmore St. (bet. Filbert & Pixley Sts.)

Phone: 415-440-0460 Dinner Tue – Sat
Web: www.ateliercrenn.com
Prices: $$$$

Atelier Crenn

The subtitle of this restaurant, Poetic Culinaria, speaks volumes of its aesthetic and philosophy—the fact that Chef Dominque Crenn is the child of an artist is not lost on this space. Moss, wood, and stones fashion an organic décor. Beneath the reed-lined ceiling is a room filled with lines of poetry and objets d'art, yet the glassed-in kitchen is the rightful focus.

This sense of artistry extends to the plate, or rather the pieces of slate, ribbed glass bowls, and earthen ceramics presented by the staff, who are always on-point. Modernist techniques and local ingredients are the hallmarks of such dishes as allium and ovum, featuring pickled pearl onions, ramps, grilled green onions, chive blossoms, and braised shallots with a quail egg poached sous-vide. Many dishes include miniature renderings of 4D landscapes, as if Thumbelina were about to walk across your plate.

Picture this in a dessert that replicates a beet—the root tip is chocolate covered in beet powder, the round itself is magenta sorbet in a thin layer of gelatin to convey perfectly roasted skin. This is surrounded by "dirt" made of flash-frozen mousse, puffed amaranth, and toasted oats blooming with edible flower petals.

Betelnut 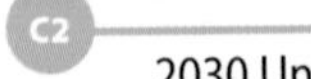

Asian

C2

2030 Union St. (bet. Buchanan & Webster Sts.)

Phone: 415-929-8855 — Lunch & dinner daily
Web: www.betelnutrestaurant.com
Prices: $$

This lively open kitchen cranks out great Far Eastern street food delicacies, with a focus on small plates designed for sharing and pairing with maybe a Tsing Tao or Elephant beer. Sample tasty portions of minced chicken and *lup cheong* sausage with lettuce cups; *shui jiao* pork dumplings in a Sichuan peppercorn broth; braised founder with cucumbers and spicy bean sauce, and myriad other options for those with an asbestos palate.

Its mysterious vibe, sultry lighting, and lazy rotating fans over the street-front Dragonfly Lounge, earn this Marina favorite major points for ambience. Speaking of which, a red lacquered bar is a sleek spot for creative cocktails, and the upstairs dining room is always humming with revelers—reservations are recommended.

Bin 38

American

B2

3232 Scott St. (bet. Chestnut & Lombard Sts.)

Phone: 415-567-3838 — Lunch Fri – Sun
Web: www.bin38.com — Dinner nightly
Prices: $$

It's tragic that most people come to Bin 38 only for a glass of wine. These folks are missing out on some serious talent behind the stoves. While the aura exuded is all wine bar, the small plates in the dining room scream delicious restaurant. Under a clear sky, join the swank Marina set on the back patio by the fire pit for a comforting bowl of ricotta-packed agnolotti combined with caramelized pancetta, a quivering egg, and spring onion slivers.

With such a creative selection of food and wine, sipping and snacking here is oh-so-enjoyable. And, between the lamb trio (mini chops, grilled merguez, and crispy lamb bacon) drizzled with a green garlic purée; and a pristine olive oil cake licked with lavender ice cream, you are bound to leave beaming.

Bistro Aix

Mediterranean XX

C2

3340 Steiner St. (bet. Chestnut & Lombard Sts)

Phone: 415-202-0100 Dinner nightly
Web: www.bistroaix.com
Prices: $$

Bistro Aix, with its glorious glass ceiling and well-tread bar (carved from discarded marble) that routinely pours delicious libations, lures loyalists from far and wide with the scent of an oak-burning grill. A reclaimed and warming redwood banquette lines the back dining room where solid tables are topped with cotton dishcloth napkins; the back atrium is sunny, framing a decade-old olive tree, giving Aix the au naturel aroma of Provence.

Southern French fare has a Californian accent; and from the expert kitchen, expect such luscious dishes as a white bean crostini with tender squid and flavorful *persillade*; fresh salmon *a la plancha* perfectly prepared; and a high-quality dark chocolate cloud cake with whipped crème fraîche and toasted almonds.

Blackwood

Thai XX

C2

2150 Chestnut St. (bet. Steiner & Pierce Sts.)

Phone: 415-931-9663 Lunch & dinner daily
Web: www.blackwoodsf.com
Prices: $$

Thai brunch in the Marina? Newcomer Blackwood serves it all day, so rest easy and arrive when you wish. With sparkling wall panels and tufted banquettes, this sophisticated space mirrors its artistically-presented dishes.

A unique menu of contemporary Thai food has a heavy American influence especially at breakfast and brunch. This is amply evident in a signature dish of caramelized bacon topped with grilled asparagus and a lick of spice-infused homemade maple syrup. Bold flavors work beautifully in pan-seared snapper crested with fiery cashew-basil-garlic pesto and coupled with a refreshing green mango salad; while red coconut curry teeming with beef, bell peppers, bamboo shoots, and fresh basil sided with fluffy rice is a classic.

Castagna

French

2015 Chestnut St. (bet. Fillmore & Steiner Sts.)

Phone: 415-440-4290 — Lunch & dinner Tue – Sun
Web: www.castagnasf.com
Prices: $$

One glimpse at Castagna's (*chestnut* in Niçois) bright red awning and tables arranged out front where patrons dine with their little dogs, and you know she's French. In keeping with the bistro aesthetic, this gem's décor is delicately adorned with wood banquettes, tile floors, and red-painted walls.

The welcoming co-owners are brothers from Nice; expectedly, their menu reflects both French and Italian influences. Dishes like a *salade* Niçoise are simple, fresh, and classic; while the *croque monsieur*, slathered with béchamel, grated Gruyère, and served with skinny frites and garlic aïoli is probably *the* most divine version in town. End this French feast on Chestnut Street with a light, lacy *crème de marron* crêpe, fittingly filled with chestnut paste.

Cedar Hill Kitchen + Smokehouse

Barbecue 

3242 Scott St. (bet. Chestnut & Lombard Sts.)

Phone: 415-834-5403 — Lunch & dinner Tue – Sun
Web: www.cedarhillsf.com
Prices: $$

Cedar Hill Kitchen + Smokehouse is an unlikely (read: refreshing) arrival to the Marina, setting Texas-style barbecue amidst stylish boutiques and hip cafés. Featuring a décor of nostalgic memorabilia blended with ranch details like branding irons, this is an ideal haven for a warm day—glass doors open up for an inside-outside feel where you can nibble on a silky buttermilk pie and sip on sweetened black tea.

The flavors may be Southern but the portion sizes are Californian, so skip the shopping and go straight for moist baby back ribs in a sweet-smoky barbecue sauce; or a mound of tender Texas-style pulled pork infused with a rich, smoky flavor. Brussels sprouts roasted with pork drippings and tangy pit beans with burnt tips are sides to die for.

Delarosa

Italian

2175 Chestnut St. (bet. Pierce & Steiner Sts.)

Phone: 415-673-7100 Lunch & dinner daily
Web: www.delarosasf.com
Prices: $$

It's hard to miss the sleek grey and orange façade or the sexy signage, summoning pizza and beer lovers from afar. Inside, the color scheme continues: steel stools sit under long wooden tables dotted with orange votive holders; a twelve-seat wood-topped bar is backed by neat, cubicle shelving and a rectangular steel slab studded with beer taps. Above, fiery, flame-like light fixtures dangle from high ceilings.

Packed with well-heeled locals and families, Delarosa spins out terrific wood-fired and generously sized pizzas, with fourteen types of beer to complement. Not in the mood for pie? Try the chicken sausage, red grapes, and mustard antipasti; Dungeness crab *arancini*; or the *garganelli* with juicy porcini mushrooms, pancetta, and sage.

Dixie

Southern

1 Letterman Dr. (off Lombard St.)

Phone: 415-829-3363 Lunch & dinner daily
Web: www.sfdixie.com
Prices: $$$

On the edge of the Presido, Dixie has a Southern social club feel with warm wood paneling, barrel ceilings, and unique art in the form of a wall-mounted cello and rope hoop sculpture. This favored newbie attracts the city's cream of crop (wealthy tech types and old-money socialites) that must overlook their inconsistent service for first-rate fare.

Due to the chef's impressive pedigree, Dixie has improved over time. Notice such refined details in a highbrow chicken-fried quail with garlic waffle and spicy cabbage salad; or pan-seared halibut with sassafras and fennel, topped with creamy uni remoulade. Rabbit roulade wrapped in bacon and served over a bed of sweet onions, date paste, and little gem lettuces will ensure that you are never hungry again.

Dosa

Indian

1700 Fillmore St. (at Post St.)

Phone: 415-441-3672 — Lunch Wed – Sun
Web: www.dosasf.com — Dinner nightly
Prices: $$

Regulars to Dosa's Mission home will hardly recognize this second location, across from the Kabuki Theater, where owners Emily and Anjan Mitra are bringing their South Indian flavors to a vast, contemporary interior decked in eco-friendly materials, mismatched chandeliers, and a palette inspired by the spices in the kitchen.

In fact, spice lovers will find much to love. Begin with the complimentary fennel-studded *pappadum*, then try a crispy fish *pakora* marinated in cumin, ginger, and chili, and paired with cilantro chutney. Of course, this is also a worthy start for an introduction to *dosas*—thin pancakes with plentiful fillings including habanero-mango or the more classic masala with spiced potatoes. Exotic cocktails flow at the bustling bar.

Dragon Well

2142 Chestnut St. (bet. Pierce & Steiner Sts.)

Phone: 415-474-6888 — Lunch & dinner daily
Web: www.dragonwell.com
Prices: ⊜

Sandwiched between the posh boutiques and trendy eateries of Chestnut Street, Dragon Well is a modest favorite for fresh Chinese served continuously from 11:30 A.M. until 10:00 P.M. The cozy space sports well-worn wood floors, close tables, and skylights that shed light onto butter-yellow walls. Scenes from China overlook the fully Western clientele who pack the house at lunch to feast on somewhat Americanized fare.

Made with the freshest ingredients, dishes include flavorful tea-smoked duck with plump steamed buns and hoisin sauce; stir-fried chicken and black beans with red bell pepper and chili sauce; and a crisp "bird's nest" of scallops, calamari, and prawns with sugar snap peas, carrots, and ginger. Dragon Well is also terrific for takeout.

Florio

C4 — Italian XX

1915 Fillmore St. (bet. Bush & Pine Sts.)

Phone: 415-775-4300 — Dinner nightly
Web: www.floriosf.com
Prices: $$

Florio is a sparkling Italian jewel set amid the chic boutiques on Fillmore Street. The atmosphere is inviting, service is friendly, and the crowd is mostly local. The softly lit dining room is elegant but easygoing, and there is a front bar where you can snag a seat on jam-packed nights.

Flavorful, hearty comfort food is well-prepared and not the slightest bit fussy. Nightly additions to the menu might reveal well-seasoned meatballs cooked until golden brown and tossed in a deliciously spicy herb-infused tomato sauce; or fat ribbons of pappardelle spiraling around caramelized pancetta, fresh rosemary, and earthy cranberry beans. A wedge of zucchini bread topped with a tangy-sweet Meyer lemon glaze will have you calling this place home in no time.

Greens

C1 — Vegetarian X

Building A, Fort Mason Center

Phone: 415-771-6222 — Lunch Tue – Sun
Web: www.greensrestaurant.com — Dinner Mon – Sat
Prices: $$

This jewel in the crown of vegetarian restaurants procures her ingredients solely from small, local farms including her own Green Gulch farm in Marin. This can only mean inventive, organic food featuring the freshest seasonal vegetables, herbs, and fruits. Greens' Zen philosophy is also amplified in its dining room complete with dazzling views of the marina and Golden Gate Bridge.

The chefs at the helm are in charge of crafting these fine ingredients into flavorful dishes like ricotta-corn griddle cakes with jalapeños, scallions, and cheddar; *gratin Provençal* with roasted eggplant, eight-ball squash, Pt. Reyes Toma and *fromage blanc* custard; and Knoll Farm fig and caramelized onion pizza spread with goat cheese, Asiago, walnuts, and crisp sage leaves.

Ino Sushi

Japanese X

D4

22 Peace Plz., Ste. 510 (bet. Buchanan & Laguna Sts.)

Phone: 415-922-3121 Dinner Tue – Sat
Web: N/A
Prices: **$$**

Japantown locals and film buffs headed to the Kabuki Theater rub elbows (literally) in this teeny authentic sushi joint on the second floor of the neighborhood's Miyako mall. A true mom-and-pop place, Ino serves all combinations of fresh nigiri, maki, and sashimi prepared by a stern, seasoned chef and served by his exceedingly polite wife.

A minimum order applies ($20 for a table, $30 at the counter), but it shouldn't be a problem—sushi aficionados know that even little bits of seafood add up. Start with an assorted nigiri platter piled with Spanish mackerel, tai snapper, *unagi*, toro, and more, spiked appropriately with wasabi. Still hungry? The neat salmon and avocado roll ought to hit the spot. Can't decide? Let the chef do so for you.

Kappa

Japanese XX

C4

1700 Post St. (at Buchanan St.)

Phone: 415-673-6004 Dinner Mon – Sat
Web: www.kapparestaurant.com
Prices: **$$$$**

Located in Japan town on the second level of a small shopping complex, Kappa has a discreet sign that is easy to miss. However, once inside, the kimono-clad hostess offers a warm greeting. Reservations are an absolute must here as there is a loyal patronage (read: regulars) of Japanese business people and local foodies.

The small space has an arching counter that faces the chef's workspace. His wife is the sole server and explains each course of the nightly Koryori menu that has included super fresh sashimi, nigiri, and a hot dish combo of a crispy corn fritter, breaded and fried pork, *tsukune*, a piece of roasted duck, *tamago* egg cake, firefly squid, and green beans dressed in miso paste. A bowl of red bean gelée completes this delicious ensemble.

Kiss

Japanese

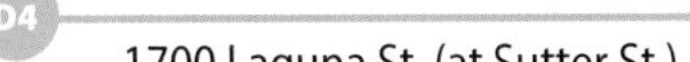

D4

1700 Laguna St. (at Sutter St.)

Phone: 415-474-2866 Dinner Tue – Sat
Web: N/A
Prices: **$$$**

Shaded by the 100-foot-tall Peace Pagoda, Japantown seems the obvious go-to for authentic Japanese cuisine. But, amid the quirky magazine shops, hardware and garden stores, where to eat isn't immediately obvious. Walk a few blocks, and tucked in the corner of a building, find Kiss.

Like its noodle shop neighbors, Kiss doesn't make much of a first impression: the mom-and-pop shop has little décor and even less seating. A keen foodie though will notice that there's not a vacant seat in the house. Book in advance and make like the regulars who order the daily omakase, a multi-course feast of traditional dishes like smoky sardine salad; fresh nigiri; and *chawan mushi s*tudded with halibut and gingko nuts. You will never again wonder where to eat in Japantown.

Mamacita

Mexican

B2

2317 Chestnut St. (bet. Divisadero & Scott Sts.)

Phone: 415-346-8494 Dinner nightly
Web: www.mamacitasf.com
Prices: **$$**

Marina hipsters flock to Mamacita for its flavor-packed Cal-Mex fare that is not 100% authentic, but is 200% delicious. The vibe is casual and the dark wood furnishings, large tequila-lined bar, oversized mirrors, and starburst pendant lights hint of Mexico.

The Mexican-inspired dishes utilize fresh, local ingredients but still somehow taste like delicious south-of-the-border fare. The menu might feature classic *chile rellenos* filled with fava beans and goat cheese; achiote-spiced prawn tacos with grilled pineapple and watercress; and an enchilada casserole of pork meatballs, spicy tomato salsa, refried black beans, and melted *queso*. For a bit of sweet, try the cheesecake "flan" with a tequila-strawberry purée—likely from its vast selection of tequilas.

Nettie's Crab Shack

C2 — Seafood

2032 Union St. (bet. Buchanan & Webster Sts.)

Phone: 415-409-0300 — Lunch Wed – Mon
Web: www.nettiescrabshack.com — Dinner Wed – Sun
Prices: $$

A far cry from the aquatic kitsch that's drowning Fisherman's Wharf, Nettie's Crab Shack is an homage to east coast sensibilities, with a towering palm, solarium-like front, and surfer-chic interior filled with weathered cottage chairs and New England expats pining for home.

More to the point, this crab house is all about the crab (often Dungeness), whether grilled, steamed, half or whole, in a deviled egg, cake, or roll. On Sundays, don't wear your best but do grab a bib for an old-school, seasonal crab feed with salads, boiled potatoes, and artichokes. Those who feel like branching out can try the clam chowder or Anchor Steam-battered cod and chips. Home-style desserts like ginger cake are a sweet indulgence before moving on to the area's chic shops.

The Plant

C2 — Vegetarian

3352 Steiner St. (bet. Chestnut & Lombard Sts.)

Phone: 415-931-2777 — Lunch & dinner daily
Web: www.theplantcafe.com
Prices: 

The tenet behind this eco-friendly eatery has remained the same—to keep body-conscious patrons and the planet healthy. Organic vegetarian and vegan options abound, beginning with a breakfast of sprouted bagels with cream cheese or almond butter. Lunch and dinner bring sandwiches and entrées like a quinoa bowl filled with sautéed vegetables and greens with a ginger-miso sauce. The menu also remembers those coveting meatier choices with the likes of grilled chicken, salmon, and shrimp.

The Plant is popular with business people, families, and single diners, who can opt to sit in the simple dining room, at the counter, or sidewalk tables. If rushed, grab a pre-packed meal from the to-go cooler. Also try waterfront dining at their Pier 3 location.

Ristobar

Italian

2300 Chestnut St. (at Scott St.)

Phone: 415-923-6464
Web: www.ristobarsf.com
Prices: $$

Lunch Sat – Sun
Dinner nightly

With beautiful frescoes dressing its walls and ceilings, a dramatic Venetian glass chandelier hanging overhead, and a long bar on one side, Ristobar is all about Italian-sleek. Whether you're feasting in the pretty, light-filled dining room or out on the lovely patio, take confidence in the fact that the staff is always welcoming and the food consistently good. Pastas divulge homemade *gnocchetti* tossed in an herb-infused tomato sauce studded with *burrata* and basil; or *paccheri* with ahi tuna, favas, and asparagus. If that doesn't fit your mood, opt for a light and sumptuous thin-crust pizza slathered with cherry tomatoes, juicy prawns, and prosciutto. Take your time to linger over a creamy panna cotta sweetened with honey and ripe organic strawberries.

Shabu-Sen

Japanese

1726 Buchanan St. (bet. Post & Sutter Sts.)

Phone: 415-440-0466
Web: N/A
Prices: 

Lunch & dinner daily

Don't be deterred by the simply appointed space. No one comes for the décor; the interactive, fun, and very social experience of dining shabu-shabu style is what draws them in. Choose from beef, pork, chicken, scallops, or prawns–or better yet, a combination–and await a plate of the uncooked meal, ready to be dipped in boiling, flavored broth set on the table-top burner.

The pork and beef shabu-shabu shows up with peanut and soy dips, noodles, mushrooms, shallots, carrots, tofu, and rice—all excellent, fresh, and tasty. Diversify each bite by playing with different dipping combinations, but be sure to skim the broth to keep those flavors crisp. Before the communal cooking begins, grab a starter of fantastic shrimp dumplings to whet the appetite.

Sociale 

Italian

A4

3665 Sacramento St. (bet. Locust & Spruce Sts.)

Phone: 415-921-3200 — Lunch Tue – Sat
Web: www.caffesociale.com — Dinner Mon – Sat
Prices: $$

Sociale is perfect for an intimate rendezvous. A discreet awning marks the spot and a brick path transports you to this sunny, bucolic sanctuary. Inside, find a comfortable room decked with framed photos on buttery yellow walls. The cozy bar is lovely for a sip of sparkling prosecco. Seating in the heated courtyard patio is coveted, so make sure to book ahead

Chef Tia Harrison looks to Northern Italy for inspiration in starters like duck meatballs with dried cherry sugo, that are perfect to share. But if you dine like an Italian, pastas like homemade pappardelle tossed with braised duck and laced with porcini mushrooms may serve as a primer before pan-seared Petrale sole stuffed with shrimp and served atop fingerling potatoes in a chive-beurre blanc sauce.

Tacolicious

Mexican 

2031 Chestnut St. (bet. Fillmore and Steiner Sts.)

Phone: 415-346-1966 — Lunch & dinner daily
Web: www.tacolicioussf.com
Prices: 

If you're pining for Mexican street food, head to Tacolicious and gratify a juicy temptation. Evocative prints and wrestling figurines add local flavor to the "bar" vibe. It's not every taco stand that has area chefs making guest appearances to spread the taco love.

Free your forks and with your fingers tackle tasty tacos packed with seasonal ingredients like summer squash with grilled corn and peppers; fried local cod with cabbage and *crema*; or tender *pollo en mole* Colorado. Other items like Azteca chicken soup with a *chile passila*-tomato broth, or Mexican shrimp cocktail will set you straight. The homemade salsas (chipotle, tomatillo, habanero) and slew of tequilas keep adults jaunty.

Check out Tacolicious II (with Mosto tequila bar) in the Mission.

SPQR 

C4 | Italian XX

1911 Fillmore St. (bet. Bush & Pine Sts.)

Phone: 415-771-7779 | Lunch Sat – Sun
Web: www.spqrsf.com | Dinner nightly
Prices: $$$

Ed Anderson

May SPQR (meaning Senate and the Roman people) be an example of the fine Italian-themed *ristoranti* that are to come. Bringing good value, rusticity, refinement, and an affinity for pork, this is the kind of sophisticated and soulful cuisine that we all wish we ate a little more often. The space is winsome and dim, with its smattering of tables and a very popular marble dining counter. From start to finish, everything feels hip and casual yet without pretense; service is friendly, deeply knowledgeable, and contagiously passionate.

Meals here may begin with the aptly named "textures of Nantes carrot" starring an intense carrot purée, convincing carrot hummus, purple quinoa cake (think "tots"), as well as fried, roasted, and carrot "dust" renditions—a feast worthy of Bugs Bunny in a monocle.

Pastas are a highlight and the squid ink linguine is hauntingly good, tangled and topped with a fat lobe of sea urchin, lumps of crab, a dab of *yuzu kosho*, and flecks of crunchy salt. The suckling pork breast and loin epitomize perfect cooking, served with autumnal garnishes like braised red cabbage, beets, and cranberries as well as apple cider reduction and an invigorating smear of black garlic.

Spruce 

Mediterranean XXX

A4

3640 Sacramento St. (bet. Locust & Spruce Sts.)

Phone: 415-931-5100 — Lunch Mon – Fri
Web: www.sprucesf.com — Dinner nightly
Prices: $$$

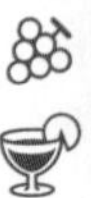

Frankie Frankeny

The temperature-controlled charcuterie room visible through glass windows beyond the courtyard is an apt invitation to enter this local favorite for fine dining with Mediterranean flair. Inside, find affluent regulars who seem always dressed for dinner—the polished staff already knows their drink orders.

The dining room's butterscotch-colored leather chairs, velvety banquettes, and spacious tables ensure comfort; the centrally located cellar cabinet and decanting table extend the focus to wine. A marble bar is well situated for starting with a bit of pre-dinner bubbly or a casual dish of velvety rich country pâté with tangy cornichons and frisée salad.

The dining room serves to showcase the chef's formidable skills through dishes that are a delightful display of technique, quality, and artistry. Meals have included delicate house-made pastas, such as *caramelle* filled with buttery white bean purée, served with salty shavings of speck, tender haricot vert, tarragon, and drizzles of a wonderfully mild mustard emulsion. Hints of familiar classics remain unexpected, as in the warm Pink Lady apple pie with a cube of creamy white cheddar ice cream and drizzle of earthy stout caramel sauce.

Terzo

Mediterranean

C2

3011 Steiner St. (bet. Filbert & Union Sts.)

Phone: 415-441-3200 — Dinner nightly
Web: www.terzosf.com
Prices: $$

The third time's a charm as the saying goes and Terzo, the third restaurant from the group that owns Rose Pistola and Rose's Café, gets it right. Filament bulbs cast a cool light over the dark contemporary interior where chocolate leather covers the banquettes and a central communal table bustles with noshing regulars. Wall-mounted racks display a good selection of global wines, with many available by the glass—de rigueur for washing down these Mediterranean-inspired small plates.

Start with grilled Monterey Bay calamari with lentils, fennel, and a dusting of pimentón; or try the vegetarian hummus and beet salad. Hearty appetites should look for larger entrées like roasted mahi mahi with garbanzo beans and almonds. Terzo is romantic, so do bring a date.

The Tipsy Pig

Gastropub

C2

2231 Chestnut St. (bet. Pierce & Scott Sts.)

Phone: 415-292-2300 — Lunch Wed – Sun
Web: www.thetipsypigsf.com — Dinner nightly
Prices: $$

The Tipsy Pig sports just the right mix of handsome furnishings, pressed-tin ceilings, and exposed brick walls to exude a saloon-like style that combines perfectly with flavorful Californian food. A constant crowd of Marina hipsters can be found lingering at their front bar pouring a delectable selection of spirits and beers sized from the 10 oz. "Piglet" to the 20 oz. "Tipsy Pig."

Settle into the elevated wood-furnished dining room for the main event, perhaps beginning with a bowl of creamy sweet corn clam chowder drizzled with chili oil. The roster of tasty and fresh gastropub fare may reveal a spicy tuna burger served on a bun smeared with *sambal* and smashed avocado; or bite-size pieces of roasted summer squash tossed in melted butter and herbs.

Viva Goa

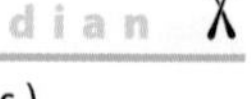

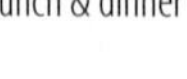

B2 — Indian

2420 Lombard St. (bet. Divisadero & Scott Sts.)

Phone: 415-440-2600 — Lunch & dinner daily
Web: www.vivagoaindiancuisine.com
Prices: $$

Cardamom, curry, and the strums of an Indian sitar hang in the air at Viva Goa, the Lombard Street eatery that offers a rich culinary experience thanks to Goa's coastal life where Portuguese influences mingles with the local cuisine. Once you find parking–this neighborhood can be tricky–slide into a burgundy booth and order a Goan specialty—both the seafood curry and stuffed-and-fried whole pomfret are unexpected standouts.

Indian food lovers will also find tasty executions of the classics: fried chicken lollipops drenched in a peppery red sauce; spicy *vindaloo*; aromatic *biryani*; *tikka masala*; savory *samosas*, and blistered garlic naan. Spice junkies can ask for extra hot, while budget diners will appreciate the $8.99 buffet at lunch.

Zushi Puzzle

C2 — Japanese

1910 Lombard St. (at Buchanan St.)

Phone: 415-931-9319 — Dinner Mon – Sat
Web: www.zushipuzzle.com
Prices: $$

This packed Lombard Street *sushi-ya* may have the oddest name on the block, but its success is no puzzle: a fish is flown in fresh from Japan each day and dozens of specialty maki–including the soft shell and snow crab Dynasty roll–are both beautifully plated and among the tastiest around. The Best Hand Roll isn't just the flourish of a confident chef, but earns its superlative name.

In fact, Chef Roger Chong is a friendly, funny guy from his post at the back counter. Make a reservation (you'll need one) for a view of the master at work. Adventurous types can relinquish the menus and let the chef steer your course, while safer palates find comfort in bowls of soba and udon noodles. Seafood addicts should check the dry erase board for the day's catch.

Peter L. Wrenn / MICHELIN

Mission

Bernal Heights · Potrero Hill

The sun always shines in the Mission, a bohemian paradise dotted with palm trees and home to artists, activists, and a vibrant Latino community. Graffiti murals line the walls of funky galleries, thrift shops, and bookstores; and sidewalk stands burst with Mexican plantains, nopales, and the juiciest limes this side of the border.

The markets here are among the best in town: **La Palma Mexicatessan** brims with homemade *papusa*, chips, and fresh Mexican cheeses. **Lucca Ravioli** stocks imported Italian goods, while **Bi-Rite** is a petite grocer popular for fresh flowers and prepared foods. Across the street find **Bi-Rite Creamery**, a cult favorite for ice cream. From cheese and ice cream, turn the page to hipster coffee hangout, **Ritual Coffee Roasters**. What's so stellar about their coffee? Join the line outside the door, order one of their special roasts from the Barista, and you will start to get the picture.

Countless bargain *mercados* and dollar stores might suggest otherwise, but the Mission is home to many an avant-garde hangout. **Dynamo Donuts** on 24th Street is *the* place for delectable flavors like apricot-cardamom, chocolate-star anise, and maple-glazed bacon-apple. **Walzwerk** charms with East German kitsch and is also the go-to for Deutsch delights. Mission pizza reigns supreme–thin-crust lovers wait in line at **Pizzeria Delfina**–as they serve a wicked pie with crispy edges blistered just so. Carb addicts cannot (and should not) miss the exceptional breads, pastries, and pressed sandwiches at **Tartine Bakery**. To best experience the flavors of the Mission, forgo the table and chairs and pull up at a curb on Linda Street, where a vigilant street food scene has incited a revolution of sorts. The **Magic Curry Kart** plates $5 steaming rice dishes, while the **Crème Brûlée Cart** torches fresh custards, some spiked with Bailey's Irish Cream, *à la minute*. The alley buzzes with locals noshing on homemade pastries, empanadas, and Vietnamese spring rolls until the grub runs out.

The city's hottest 'hood also offers a cool selection of sweets. A banana split is downright retrolicious when served at the Formica counter of 90-year-old **St. Francis Fountain**. The sundaes are made with **Mitchell's Ice Cream**, famous in SF since 1953. Modish flavors–think pink grapefruit-tarragon and salted licorice–are in regular rotation at the newer **Humphrey Slocombe**. **Mission Pie** is a local jewel that lures people far and wide for their sumptuous selection of savory and sweet pies. While their menu spins to the season, it also pays homage to the environment by using only local, sustainable produce sourced from nearby farms, and unveils light savory treats, baked goods, and a mélange of pies.

Dance off your indulgences on Salsa Sunday at **El Rio**, the dive bar with a bustling back patio, or join the hip kids for DJs and live bands at the culturally diverse **Elbo Room**. The lesbian set shoots pool at the **Lexington Club**. On the late night, growling stomachs brave harsh lighting at numerous taquerias, many of which are open till 4:00 A.M. Go see for yourself: Try the veggie burrito at **Taqueria Cancun**; tacos at **La Alteña**; and mind-blowing meats (*lengua* or *cabeza*?) at **El Farolito**. During the day, **La Taqueria**'s *carne asada* burrito is arguably the best. And the **El Tonayense** taco truck, to quote one blogger, is of course "da bomb!"

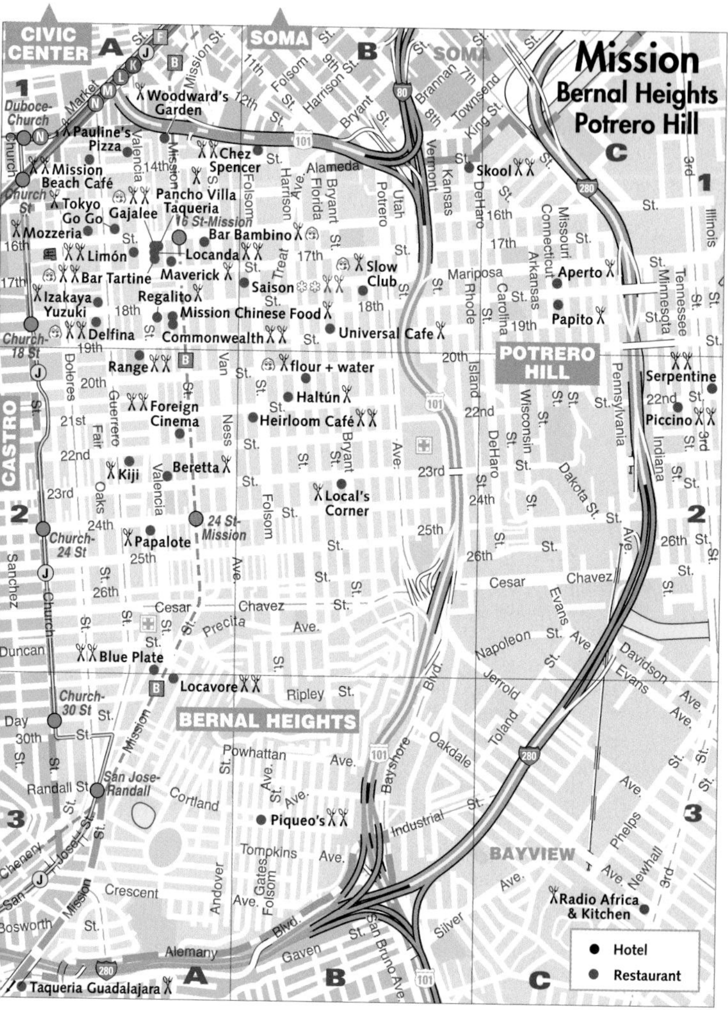

Aperto

Italian

C1

1434 18th St. (at Connecticut St.)

Phone: 415-252-1625 Lunch & dinner daily
Web: www.apertosf.com
Prices: $$

If only everybody could live next to this cheery Italian café. It has all the trappings of an ideal local haunt from yellow walls and towering windows to a large corner nook, perfect for families to gather round. Servers are hospitable and intent; even line cooks might send smiles your way.

The name of their game is rustic Italian food which consists of a great selection of pastas and daily specials. A meal might start with delicious bruschetta brushed with olive oil, a thick fava bean paste, and artichoke hearts. Carb fiends will savor perfectly al dente orecchiette mingled with asparagus stalks in garlic-infused white wine; while meatheads hanker for super tender red wine-braised beef short ribs served over a bed of fresh corn and shelling beans.

Bar Bambino

Italian

A1

2931 16th St. (bet. Mission St. & Van Ness Ave.)

Phone: 415-701-8466 Dinner Mon – Sat
Web: www.barbambino.com
Prices: $$

This polished little refuge in a rather dank Mission alcove holds some of the area's hottest tables. Inside the pleasant wine bar, hooks await your coat and more than 35 European wines by the glass are ready to erase the day. Try for a seat at the white marble bar or heated back patio, as you remember that this bite-sized spot is a SF favorite, so reservations would have been a good idea.

The menu offers shareable plates of artisanal cheese, house-made *salumi,* daily *antipasti* such as fried olives stuffed with prosciutto and pecorino; or a chicken panino with roasted butternut squash. Stylish couples and small groups of friends pack the zinc tables, while singles find conversation at the long communal table, lit by a recycled wine bottle chandelier.

Bar Tartine

Eastern European

A1

561 Valencia St. (bet. 16th & 17th Sts.)

Phone: 415-487-1600
Web: www.bartartine.com
Prices: $$

Lunch Sat – Sun
Dinner Tue – Sun

Bar Tartine's minor revamp resulted in a delightful though diminutive annex. Here, a daytime menu of open-faced rye bread sandwiches topped with smoked trout, chicken liver pâté, or cheeses meets a small menu of snacks and baked goods.

In the evening, the annex closes and the entire wood-ridden restaurant is open for dinner. Friendly servers buzz around the welcoming room with such ambitious creations as a chilled white beet soup with whey, white curry, and coriander, nicely paired with smoky potatoes laid beside a ramp aïoli. Balancing earthy textures with hearty flavors are lentil croquettes served on sesame-*kamut* bread, layered with yogurt, cucumbers, and lentil sprouts. Get your bird on with a chicken stuffed with sausage and crunchy sauerkraut.

Beretta

Italian

A2

1199 Valencia St. (at 23rd St.)

Phone: 415-695-1199
Web: www.berettasf.com
Prices: $$

Lunch Sat – Sun
Dinner nightly

Beretta delivers a bang-up performance with its thin-crust pizzas and shared Italian plates. This well-loved spot is perpetually jamming with Mission hipsters who adore the place for its relaxed vibe, fantastic food, and reasonable prices. From meatballs like *mamma* used to make to tender Dungeness crab *arancini* with Calabrese aïoli, and daily entrée specials, there's plenty on the menu. But, pizzas always emerge as the champion.

The quarters are tight at the bar and tables, but that's just part of the fun. Besides, the menu is designed for sharing. Just make sure you call dibs on the last slice of hot salami-, *coppa*-, tomato-and *diavolicchio*-topped pizza.

Call ahead for a coveted spot on the waiting list, since reservations are for large groups only.

Blue Plate

American XX

A2

3218 Mission St. (bet. 29th & Valencia Sts.)

Phone: 415-282-6777 Dinner nightly
Web: www.blueplatesf.com
Prices: **$$**

Despite San Francisco's outdoorsy image, there is nary a restaurant patio in sight on the dawn of a rare warm day. That's why Missionites have been heading to Blue Plate for more than a decade, where potted plants and blossoming fruit trees overhang café tables in the garden and the kitchen serves mostly organic Cal-Med cuisine inspired by the season. Inside, the narrow space is cool, casual, and ambient with local art lining the walls and skinny-jeaned regulars chowing tasty comfort fare. Chef/owner Cory Obenour's Mediterranean flavor combinations shine in dishes such as grilled Monterey Bay squid with lemon juice and sorrel chiffonade; and slip-from-the-bone pork osso buco cooked in red wine with wilted chard, porcini, and seasoned walnuts.

Chez Spencer

French XX

B1

82 14th St. (bet. Folsom & Harrison Sts.)

Phone: 415-864-2191 Dinner Tue – Sun
Web: www.chezspencer.net
Prices: **$$$**

Chez Spencer is camoflauged amid warehouses, and yet it is considered a darling of the Mission. Upon entering, guests walk through a large wooden gate, followed by a gorgeous garden terrace and covered patio, until reaching the lofty dining room. Under the skylights and soaring arched wooden beams, two kitchens and a wood-burning oven are as integral to the space as the patrons.

Named for his son, Spencer, and owned by Chef Laurent Katgely, Chez Spencer offers both a lengthy tasting menu and à la carte choices like bouillabaisse with saffron aïoli; smoked duck breast *à la Lyonnaise* with poached egg and lardons; or a wood-grilled filet mignon with *morels à la crème* and truffle butter.

For French food fast, look for the Spencer on the Go "mobile bistro."

Commonwealth

A1 — Californian XX

2224 Mission St. (bet. 18th & 19th Sts.)

Phone: 415-355-1500
Web: www.commonwealthsf.com
Prices: $$

Dinner nightly

Commonwealth is a restaurant that takes chances, starting with its edgy Mission locale. Yet the interior is minimal and serene, with a bar offering views of the open kitchen and tables spotlit by filaments. There is a sense of purpose here, both among the progressive owners who donate part of every tasting menu to charity, and the buzz of young foodies.

This kitchen thrills in reformulating ingredients to deliver flavor and textural surprise, as in herring fillets with chicken skin breadcrumbs and beet-miso purée; egg custard with uni, seaweed brioche cubes, and wild greens; and lamb's tongue terrine with gem lettuce, Meyer lemon, artichoke heart, and pistachio cream. At dessert, chocolate and peanut butter semifreddo tops cloud-like frozen popcorn.

Delfina

A1 — Italian XX

3621 18th St. (bet. Dolores & Guerrero Sts.)

Phone: 415-552-4055
Web: www.delfinasf.com
Prices: $$

Dinner nightly

Delfina is one of those spots that is perennially popular with the Mission locals. The pizzeria next door does a booming business, but this spacious dining room is almost always packed, and highlights a neat arrangement of bare wood tabletops, a narrow counter (perfect for solo diners), and a semi-open kitchen. Mirrors on the side walls and a line of windows in the front give this space a larger and airy feel. There is no need to dress up for this casual, welcoming spot. Expect menu items such as hearty, chewy pappardelle tossed with flavorful pork sugo; tender-roasted and crisp-skinned quail served over creamy polenta; and chicken liver *spiedini* with *guanciale* and aged *balsamico*. Close with a lovely chocolate *budino* with salted caramel ice cream.

flour + water

Italian

2401 Harrison St. (at 20th St.)

Phone: 415-826-7000
Web: www.flourandwater.com
Prices: $$

Dinner nightly

In Italian cooking, it all just amounts to flour and water, the two basic ingredients in homemade pasta and pizza dough. And, these are cooked to perfection at this beatnik haunt where artsy twenty-something's are cool with waiting an hour for a blistered pie.

Join the crowd in the standing room bar for a glass of *nebbiolo* as you look around. Concrete floors and a redwood bar lend an industrial vibe, but seafoam walls and aquatic art keeps things oddly warm. The narrow space gets loud with patrons chirping over a squash salad with *lardo*, Brussels sprouts, and pistachios; nightly tastings of seasonal, artisan pastas; and pizzas topped with tasty combos like sunchokes, chanterelles, Taleggio, and horseradish gremolata.

Check out new sib Central Kitchen.

Foreign Cinema

International

2534 Mission St. (bet. 21st & 22nd Sts.)

Phone: 415-648-7600
Web: www.foreigncinema.com
Prices: $$

Lunch Sat – Sun
Dinner nightly

Date night is a wrap at Foreign Cinema, the Mission's art house eatery that projects international films and cult classics onto a white brick wall on the heated courtyard patio. After dinner, get your contemporary art fix in the adjoining gallery and finish with a nightcap at László, the Soviet-themed annex bar.

Subtle, modish accents keep the films in focus, but Foreign Cinema's global translation of Mediterranean fare is worthy of center stage. At dinner, couples share tuna tartare tossed in ginger-lime vinaigrette or moist swordfish with wilted greens and herb-rich *gremolata*. At brunch, locals give fried eggs deglazed with balsamic or the champagne omelet two thumbs up.

Speaking of which, check out baby sis Show Dogs on Market St. for a fab breakfast.

Gajalee 

A1 — Indian XX

525 Valencia St. (bet. 16th & 17th Sts.)

Phone: 415-552-9000
Web: www.gajaleesf.com
Prices: $$

Lunch Fri – Sun
Dinner nightly

Gajalee is an exotic arrival to the Mission. Evoking the Indian coastline, the setting is decked in ceilings painted with waves, golden sand-colored walls, and plenty of natural light—the Bay Area expat community has been showing up routinely and not just for the décor.

This Indo idol specializes in seafood dishes hailing from South India and its coast. The flavors are boldly spiced and nothing is toned-down for American palates—including a fiery fish curry made from deliciously thick yogurt, chilies, and cashew paste. *Kolambi hariyali* unveils fresh shrimp cooked in a zesty sauce of cilantro and mint; while an utterly delish chicken *pulav*, tender pieces of chicken tossed with caramelized onions and saffron rice is a beautiful complement to any meal.

Haltún

B2 — Mexican 

2948 21st St. (at Treat Ave.)

Phone: 415-643-6411
Web: www.haltunsf.com
Prices: 

Lunch & dinner daily

This Mission spot might be Mexican, but don't expect the typical quesadilla and burrito affair here. Instead, Haltún specializes in flavorful Mayan dishes not often seen on other menus. Need to get out of a snit? Their cheery dining room with bright orange walls and tiled floors as well as the warm and friendly service will definitely banish bad moods.

The authentic, home-style food is flavorful, fresh, and filling, so even though chips and salsa arrive right away, don't stuff yourself just yet. Save your appetite for dishes like *pol-can*, fried corn dumplings stuffed with lima beans and crushed pumpkin seeds, or *diabla* shrimp in chile chipotle sauce. *Pollo pibil*, chicken marinated and glazed with annatto seed sauce, is finger-licking good.

Heirloom Café

Californian XX

B2

2500 Folsom St. (at 21st St.)

Phone: 415-821-2500 Dinner Mon – Sat
Web: www.heirloom-sf.com
Prices: $$$

San Francisco foodies may have a new mecca in Heirloom Café, a recent favorite melding the Mission's indie spirit with a vintage interior aesthetic: think wallpaper, worn wood floors, and natural light. The open kitchen lends to a feeling of warmth and bustle, and the limited menu feels a bit like dinner at home—that is, if you happen to be a highly skilled chef.

Seasonal dishes are perfectly prepared and might include marinated calamari coupled with creamy chili flake-studded gigante beans, crunchy endive, and breadcrumbs; duck breast with Bing cherries, mizuna, and roasted fennel; or sautéed wild salmon with corn succotash and currant pesto. At dessert, juicy peaches and zesty ginger cream jazzes up a moist black thread tea cake.

Izakaya Yuzuki

Japanese X

A1

598 Guerrero St. (at 18th St.)

Phone: 415-556-9898 Dinner Mon – Sat
Web: www.yuzukisf.com
Prices: $$$

Izakaya Yuzuki fits right in to this foodie heaven stretch of 18th Street with its authentic dishes and amicable staff. The modest interior showcases simple white walls hand-painted with vegetable outlines.

Almost everything here is made from scratch, from the homemade tofu to the red bean paste. Expect such tantalizers as a salad of Dungeness crab, kelp ribbons, wakame, and house-made pickles dressed in a tangy rice wine vinaigrette. Heart-warming beef *tataki* is slightly seared and served over a sweet onion salad with miso sauce; while skewered chicken meatballs are perfectly seasoned with a sweet-and-smoky glaze. Attention to detail is what sets this *izakaya* apart, so be sure to make reservations because the word is out and space is limited.

Kiji

A2 Japanese

1009 Guerrero St. (bet. 22nd & 23rd Sts.)

Phone: 415-282-0400 Dinner Tue – Sun
Web: www.kijirestaurant.com
Prices: $$

Less is more at Kiji, a super-simple neighborhood sushi joint on a busy stretch of Guerrero Street, in the heart of the Mission. With just a handful of tables and a tiny sushi counter, Kiji is perennially packed: have patience–a table will turn over soon–or make like the locals and call in your order to-go.

While an array of maki are available for Americanized tastes, the menu is best represented by traditional Japanese fare such as hamachi *kama*, a broiled yellowtail collar served with ponzu sauce; and a nightly list of nigiri that may include melt-in-your-mouth *aji*, *tai*, escolar, and ocean trout. Everything here is fresh and good, rather than fancy. Try the Kiji roll, stuffed with snow crab and asparagus and topped with tuna, *tobiko*, and spicy sauce.

Limón

Peruvian 

524 Valencia St. (bet. 16th & 17th Sts.)

Phone: 415-252-0918 Lunch & dinner daily
Web: www.limon-sf.com
Prices: $$

Reinvented as Limón Rotisserie, this location of Limón resides on Valencia Street in the heart of the bustling Mission district. In keeping with its handle, the décor features orange and lime accents along taupe walls hung with colorful paintings. The setting is *mucho* casual and walk-ins are welcome.

Limón features the *pollo a la brasa*, an absolutely worthy focus: this Peruvian slow-roasted bird is perfectly juicy and moist, marinated with garlic and herbs, and paired with a side of *aji*. Other solid hits may include *ensalada ruca*, fresh root vegetables mixed with *choclo*, green peas, and tossed in a creamy mustard dressing; crispy and addictive golden brown yucca fries; or *tacu-tacu*, a fragrant and delicious mixture of rice, beans and *aji amarillo* sauce.

Local's Corner

Californian

2500 Bryant St. (at 23rd St.)

Phone: 415-800-7945 — Lunch & dinner Tue – Sun
Web: www.localscornersf.com
Prices: $$

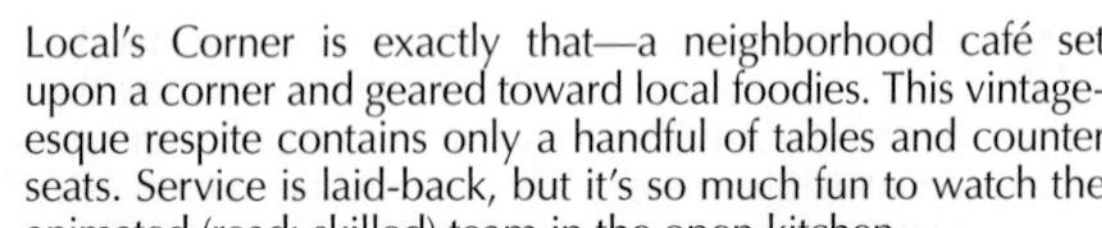

Local's Corner is exactly that—a neighborhood café set upon a corner and geared toward local foodies. This vintage-esque respite contains only a handful of tables and counter seats. Service is laid-back, but it's so much fun to watch the animated (read: skilled) team in the open kitchen.

The menu of light, well-crafted Californian fare spins to the season, so check out the framed mirror listing daily oysters and cheeses. Then embark on dishes that might feature a refreshing chicken salad mingled with yogurt, toasted almonds, raisins, and fresh cilantro; or beef tartare crowned with a quail egg and pickled cauliflower. That smoked salmon salad sandwich with a side of peppery arugula is just begging to be paired with a homemade Meyer lemonade.

Locanda

Italian

557 Valencia St. (bet. 16th & 17th Sts.)

Phone: 415-863-6800 — Dinner nightly
Web: www.locandasf.com
Prices: $$

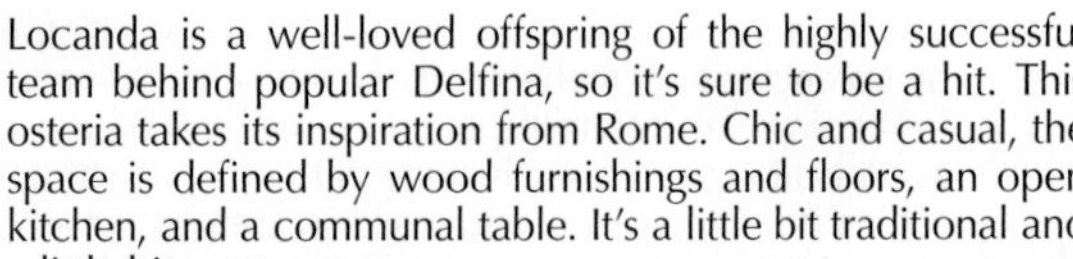

Locanda is a well-loved offspring of the highly successful team behind popular Delfina, so it's sure to be a hit. This osteria takes its inspiration from Rome. Chic and casual, the space is defined by wood furnishings and floors, an open kitchen, and a communal table. It's a little bit traditional and a little bit contemporary.

Antipasti like shaved raw artichokes with grilled ricotta and a refreshing salad with endive, crème fraîche, and cured salmon, are a great way to begin before moving on to heartier pastas and charcoal-grilled dishes. Don't be fooled by the simple-sounding menu, since there's also a selection of offal plates like chilled tongue with salsa verde, tripe with tomato, mint, and pecorino, or fried sweetbreads and artichokes.

Locavore

A m e r i c a n

3215 Mission St. (bet. Fair & Virginia Aves.)

Phone: 415-821-1918
Web: www.locavoreca.com
Prices: **$$**

Lunch Sat – Sun
Dinner Tue – Sat

Locavore's name says it all. They specialize in preparing dishes crafted with local ingredients for the surrounding residents. Mission denizens flock to this brown-shaded haven for such exquisitely simple fare as tender and charred stalks of roasted asparagus topped with smoked almond tapenade, creamy hollandaise, and a soft-poached egg; balanced by a hearty helping of beef brisket with nettle croquette, chard, and pickled turnips. Weekend brunch may include garlicky house-made chorizo served beside scrambled eggs and crispy potato *rosti*.

Locavore is a hipster hangout, but the hype has calmed down. In fact on certain nights, you may even get in without a reservation and find a seat at the small bar back in the back or at the long wooden communal table.

Maverick

A m e r i c a n

3316 17th St. (at Mission St.)

Phone: 415-863-3061
Web: www.sfmaverick.com
Prices: **$$**

Lunch Sat – Sun
Dinner nightly

Posters of the 1950s TV series *Maverick* grace the brown-and-orange walls of this Mission eatery named for the 1800s Texas cattle rancher, Samuel Maverick. The diminutive space has a single high table overlooking a semi-open kitchen up front and close-knit wood tables scattered throughout the rest of the dining room.

The culinary vibe is hipster American and the patrons are mostly from the neighborhood. Familiar comfort food may include a crispy corn tostada with shrimp, black beans, and slaw; and a grilled Berkshire pork chop glazed in honey and Bourbon served with cornbread stuffing and candied pecans. And is there a better way to cap a night than with warm cookies dipped in cool milk?

Love all things ham and oysters? Check out sibling Hogs & Rocks.

Mission Beach Café

American XX

198 Guerrero St. (at 14th St.)

Phone: 415-861-0198
Web: www.missionbeachcafesf.com
Prices: $$$

Lunch daily
Dinner Mon – Sat

Heard the buzz about their amazing homemade pies? We bet you did. But lucky for locals (and us) there's even more to this delightful neighborhood fave than fantastic pastries. Dive right into their delectable goodness with crispy lemon-saffron risotto cakes topped with tea-smoked albacore, fried quail eggs, and caviar, drizzled with chili-crème fraîche and basil oil.

Catch the pot pie menu every Tuesday night with offerings that may include a comforting rabbit pot pie with turnips and baby parsnips; or beef short rib pot pie with earthy trumpet mushrooms. The seafood pot pie boasts fresh shellfish and fennel. Can't decide on sweet? Get spoiled with a trio of desserts—lavender-honey cheesecake; strawberry rhubarb pie; and pear-plum pie.

Mission Chinese Food

Chinese X

A1

2234 Mission St. (bet. 18th & 19th Sts.)

Phone: 415-863-2800
Web: www.missionchinesefood.com
Prices: ⊕

Lunch & dinner Thu – Tue

Some people say it's the most over-hyped spot around, yet Mission Chinese Food is as popular as ever. And the craze has even spread to the East Coast, but this original well-worn dining gem remains the same: strangely set within the defunct Lung Shan Restaurant, and decked with a red dragon that looms overhead.

Servers move around with brusque efficiency as they present flavor-packed, contemporary interpretations of Chinese dishes like smoky and fatty *kung pao* pastrami strewn with shaved potato and peanuts; sizzling cumin lamb chili joined with pickled long beans; or a unique dish of wild pepper leaves swirled with tofu ribbons and pumpkin slices dressed in a chili broth. Reservations not accepted, so be prepared to stand around in your skinny jeans.

Mozzeria

3228 16th St. (bet. Dolores & Guerrero Sts.)

Phone: 415-489-0963 — Lunch Sat – Sun
Web: www.mozzeria.com — Dinner Tue – Sun
Prices:

Oh, the pies at Mozzeria! Whether it's the traditional Margarita, oozing with mozzarella and fresh basil; the California-style slathered with decadent blue cheese, caramelized onions, and thyme; or the Asian-style crowned with roast duck, hoisin sauce, and spring onions, there's a pleaser for every palate.

Specializing in those Neapolitan-style, thin-crust pizzas (fired at a thousand degrees), this brilliant newbie's deaf owners attract a largely non-hearing patronage. But don't fret if you're not proficient in sign language as the wonderful and accommodating staff will steer your way. Though pizza is their main affair, other tasty options abound including flaky and delicate salmon salsa verde served with tangy fried capers and rosemary potatoes.

Pancho Villa Taqueria

3071 16th St. (bet. Mission & Valencia Sts.)

Phone: 415-864-8840 — Lunch & dinner daily
Web: www.sfpanchovilla.com
Prices:

Choice is chief at Pancho Villa, so scope the menu and come ready to make brisk decisions. This masterful Mexican taqueria presents a parade of burritos, tacos, quesadillas, nachos et al. With wrapper and protein in hand, select a refreshing beverage. Then, an immaculate and colorful salsa bar with myriad condiments will spin you right round like a record.

There is no table service here, so grab the first seat in sight. As the mariachis gently lilt, dive into a fit-for-a-family super burrito, jammed with rice, beans, *chile verde* chicken, *pico de gallo*, cheese, guacamole, and sour cream; classic chips made divine with a mélange from the salsa bar; and a side order of fried *flautas* filled with chicken and bathed in a tomato-chile sauce.

Papalote

Mexican

3409 24th St. (bet. Poplar & Valencia Sts.)

Phone: 415-970-8815 Lunch & dinner daily
Web: www.papalote-sf.com
Prices: $$

With a cheerful dining room awash in primary hues and playful kites (*papalotes*) flying overhead, this is the kind of taqueria your mom has always wished for—one that garnishes its menu with fresh ingredients and truly healthy choices. The art-filled Mexican grill may find critics among Mission locals who prefer gritty authenticity, but sometimes breaking tradition just tastes good.

Here, taqueria mainstays have a northern Californian soul: vegetarian burritos share table space with spicy-sweet *mole* chicken, fresh fish, and carne asada tacos, all topped with crisp romaine lettuce, guacamole, ripe Roma tomatoes, and even refreshing jicama. Vegans are also welcome; Papalote offers soy chorizo and grilled tofu as lightweight alternatives to meat.

Papito

Mexican

317 Connecticut St. (at 18th St.)

Phone: 415-695-0147 Lunch & dinner daily
Web: www.papitosf.com
Prices: $$

Potrero Hill foodies may have long praised Chef Jocelyn Bulow for bringing hearty brasserie fare and charming ambience to the neighborhood, but this owner of favorite Chez Papa headed south of the border to Oaxaca for this venture (Papito). With just six copper-topped tables, a casually hip vibe, and organic, sustainably-sourced ingredients, this Connecticut Street eatery is a far cry from the city's taquerias.

Yet tacos are the order of day, piled high with fresh toppings including crispy *pollo*, purple cabbage slaw, and chipotle rémoulade. Also find fat and flavorful quesadillas; chunky (and pricey) guacamole; and *camaron costeño*, sautéed shrimp with fixings atop an organic corn tortilla. Space is limited so locals often place orders to-go.

Pauline's Pizza

A1 — Pizza

260 Valencia St. (bet. Duboce Ave. & 14th St.)

Phone: 415-552-2050
Web: www.paulinespizza.com
Prices: $$

Dinner Tue – Sat

Housed in a sunny yellow building on vibrant Valencia St., Pauline's maintains its reputation as a Mission pet for California-style pizzas topped with organic veggies. Like its food, their mien is comfortable, simply decked with a semi-open kitchen and large windows. Adored by families and locals, private parties can be hosted in the upstairs dining room.

Pizza is their game, and they offer several varieties (like butternut squash with Gruyère) along with a nightly selection of specials. With pre-baked shells available to-go, you may try to recreate their pies at home, but their signature pizza slathered with pesto and pine nuts is best enjoyed in-house. By rule, the spicy Louisiana andouille pizza must be chased by a cool, creamy ice cream sundae.

Piccino

C2 — Pizza

1001 Minnesota St. (at 22nd St.)

Phone: 415-824-4224
Web: www.piccinocafe.com
Prices: $$

Lunch & dinner Tue – Sun

First impressions do matter and with Piccino, you'll be charmed at first sight. Housed on the first floor of a Victorian building painted bright yellow with green trim, Piccino isn't as cutesy inside as it is on the outside. Instead, this chic restaurant employs raw wood planked floors, sleek chocolate brown chairs, and Eames stools at the counter to rather cool effect.

Headed by a skilled cadre of cooks, the kitchen turns out Italian food with California punch. Thin-crust crispy pizza is the shining star, though panini and pastas are a close second. Refreshing salads whet your appetite for the deliciously chewy and crispy pizzas, served on wooden, parchment paper-lined boards. For dessert try the *affogato* made with Pink Squirrel ice cream.

Piqueo's

Peruvian

B3

830 Cortland Ave. (at Gates St.)

Phone: 415-282-8812 Dinner nightly
Web: www.piqueos.com
Prices: $$

This petite candlelit eatery in a Bernal Heights bungalow with walls the shade of ripe avocado, proffers big flavor in small portions. A relative of Mochica and La Costanera, Piqueo's has locals crowding its counter for a view of the open kitchen where Chef/owner Carlos Altamirano deploys unusual Peruvian produce in mouthwatering dishes.

Adventurous diners will enjoy the learning experience. For the full effect, sample an array of small plates like *antichucho de corazón* (marinated beef heart brochettes with potatoes and *sarsa panchita*); *humita dulche* (sweet corn *tamal* with *queso fresco* and *mole Peruano*); and *seco de Cordero* (lamb braised in a cilantro-Peruvian ark beer sauce). Wash it down with a *chicha morada*, made from Peruvian purple maize.

Radio Africa & Kitchen

International

C3

4800 Third St. (bet. Oakdale & Palou Aves.)

Phone: 415-420-2486 Lunch & dinner Tue – Sat
Web: www.radioafricakitchen.com
Prices: $$

Bayview may be one of the most crime-ridden areas in the city, however, the arrival of hot spots like Radio Africa & Kitchen strutting a unique bill of fare and bright setting, have been hugely sought-after.

This well-received haunt features Ethiopian-born Chef Eskender Aseged's unique style of Afro-Mediterranean food mingled with Cali flair—the ingredients come from a local community garden. A healthy dish of green lentils is topped with roasted red beets, dollops of goat cheese, arugula, and shredded red cabbage; and baked white fish is deliciously seasoned with a fragrant spice blend and crowned with tomato confit. Heartier appetites will return time and again for the leg of lamb massaged with *berbere* spices and coupled with roasted vegetables.

Range

Contemporary XX

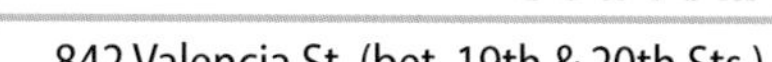

A2

842 Valencia St. (bet. 19th & 20th Sts.)

Phone: 415-282-8283 Dinner nightly
Web: www.rangesf.com
Prices: $$

Sequestered in a block freckled with small Mission boutiques, Range is just what every neighborhood place should be. This minimally decorated, narrow space is cozy with close-knit tables, attractive candlelight, a tiny bar crowded with foodies, and just a few floral arrangements lending a splash of color to dark furnishings and chocolate leather banquettes. Guests are focused on their conversations–which can get loud–and, of course, the enticing food.

Contemporary American meals might begin with a plate of creamed nettles paired with a poached farm egg, black truffles, and buttery, toasty croutons; or entrées like coffee-rubbed pork shoulder with silky hominy and braised greens. People-watchers vie for tables overlooking vivacious Valencia Street.

Regalito

Mexican X

A1

3481 18th St. (at Valencia St.)

Phone: 415-503-0650 Lunch Sat – Sun
Web: www.regalitosf.com Dinner nightly
Prices: $$

Spanish for "little gift," Regalito Rosticeria has a polish unique to the Mission, where Mexican food is synonymous with humble taquerias and markets. Here, Regalito is *the* neighborhood spot for market-driven fare in a stylish atmosphere, clean and bright with chartreuse accent walls and vibrant art.

A long wood counter peeks into the open kitchen, where seasonal food is carefully crafted from mostly organic produce and free range meats. A roasted half chicken is sublimely tender and smothered in nutty *mole negro*, while habanero salsa and fresh avocado garnish smoky, grilled *carnitas*. Flavors are more refined than bold, but these premium ingredients are prepared with skill, as if to enhance the pure tastes and complement the contemporary space.

Saison ✿✿

Californian XX

B1

2124 Folsom St. (bet. 17th & 18th Sts.)

Phone: 415-828-7990 Dinner Tue – Sat
Web: www.saisonsf.com
Prices: $$$$

Mark Leet

Thankfully, the entrance to Saison is in the back covered patio, alongside the cooking hearth and dining counter that faces its embers. Stopping here to sip a glass of sparkling wine is de rigueur. Inside, the small, white dining room has vaulted ceilings, blue-cushioned banquettes, and a wall of windows overlooking that warming hearth. Still, its real focal point is the view into the exhibition kitchen, and perhaps the lucky few who reserved far enough in advance to score that chef's table amid the action.

The service staff is not only polished but has a pleasant sense of humor that adds to the enjoyment of every affluent, well-dressed foodie here.

The talented kitchen makes every dish a near-masterpiece through superb ingredients and precise technique. Memorable meals here may awaken the palate with a shooter of wheatgrass soda with sour oxalis root and leaves, perhaps followed by a wow-inducing base of creamy cauliflower mousse topped with a custardy lobe of Fort Bragg sea urchin and quenelle of smoked sturgeon caviar. Expect that cooking hearth to appear on the plate, as in the hearth-smoked tuna belly with tangy caper berries, earthy artichokes, and zesty Meyer lemon vinaigrette.

Serpentine

C2 — Californian XX

2495 3rd St. (at 22nd St.)

Phone: 415-252-2000 — Lunch daily
Web: www.serpentinesf.com — Dinner Mon – Sat
Prices: $$

Located in the Dogpatch, Serpentine is typically SF: an urban-industrial space with worn wood floors, loft-like ceilings, and exposed ductwork. The setting coupled with Californian fare that features fresh, local, and seasonal ingredients, equals a very popular spot among locals for a business lunch, dinner, or weekend brunch.

Sociable servers may bring you an arugula salad tossed with crunchy sugar snap peas, shaved carrots, Easter egg radishes, sliced almonds, and *ricotta salata* in a tangy red wine vinaigrette. The relaxed atmosphere is ideal for enjoying fresh food prepared with skill—that might even include a fluffy pork *rillette* sandwich heaped with deliciously griddled crispy pork and topped with a tangy shaved fennel- and pepper-relish.

Skool

B1 — Seafood XX

1725 Alameda St. (at De Haro St.)

Phone: 415-255-8800 — Lunch & dinner daily
Web: www.skoolsf.com
Prices: $$

The “k” is just the first indication that Skool is no old-fashioned seafood restaurant. Located in the SF Design Center, this sunny, contemporary interior has no nautical knickknacks to speak of. Rather, high ceilings, reclaimed materials and industrial-chic lines welcome the well-heeled sort to refuel as they peruse their fabric swatches; on gorgeous days, there’s no better spot to dine than on Skool’s garden patio.

Both Californian and Japanese inflections are to be found in the light, bright fare turned out from the open kitchen. Nosh on house-cured salmon pastrami Benedict with yuzu-hollandaise sauce; a modern Niçoise salad with sesame-crusted tuna and cucumber-anchovy vinaigrette; or mussels and smoked bacon in Point Reyes blue cheese broth.

Slow Club

Californian

2501 Mariposa St. (at Hampshire St.)

Phone: 415-241-9390 Lunch daily
Web: www.slowclub.com Dinner Mon – Sat
Prices: $$

Slow Club is one of those Mission restaurants that makes you work for it. But you'll want to score that parking spot, or wait for brunch, because a meal at Slow Club is worth it. The restaurant itself is minimally dressed and industrial, with a small open kitchen and sidewalk patio for sun-soaked days. While the food is not contrived or pretentious, it shows consistent and delicious Californian fare crafted from fresh and local ingredients. A seasonal menu may reflect grilled flatbread with sheep's milk mozzarella, roasted tomato sauce, and applewood-smoked ham; followed by *berbere*-spiced marinated beef skewers served over fluffy quinoa with caramelized turnips and carrots. A yummy butterscotch pecan pie with whipped cream makes for a stellar finale.

Taqueria Guadalajara

Mexican

4798 Mission St. (at Onondaga Ave.)

Phone: 415-469-5480 Lunch & dinner daily
Web: N/A
Prices:

Sitting at a carved wood table inside this Outer Mission favorite, imagine yourself at the center of a Guadalajaran town square: Mexican architectural façades loom in floor-to-ceiling murals on three walls, while the aromas of flavorful grilled meats waft from the open kitchen.

Queue up at the counter and order the inexpensive, fresh, and generously portioned menu. Tacos may be filled with adobo-marinated pork or grilled carne asada along with minced white onion and cilantro. Intrepid eaters should dare to try the chicken super burrito, overloaded with the works. With a focus more on grilled meats than on accoutrement, the self-serve salsa bar is a popular stopover. Complement meals with perhaps the city's best *horchata*, redolent with cinnamon and rice.

Tokyo Go Go

A1 Japanese

3174 16th St. (bet. Guerrero & Valencia Sts.)

Phone: 415-864-2288
Web: www.tokyogogo.com
Prices: **$$**

Dinner nightly

Welcome to Tokyo Go Go, where blazing lights, thumpin' techno beats, and palate-pleasing bites draw in a hip and stylish set from around the Mission. Toss aside any expectations of traditional Japanese and get motoring for innovative flavorsome fusion instead. Sure, you can have your beloved nigiri, but opt for one of the splendid specialty rolls too, like the *kamikaze* (spicy tuna and crunchy asparagus rolled and topped with albacore tuna, scallions, and tangy ponzu), or the fish taco roll (battered fish, avocado, cilantro, onion, tomato, jalapeño, and chipotle aïoli).

Brought your battalion of buddies? Fill the table with "shared plates" like smoky miso-marinated black cod; tempura sweet onion rings; Tokyo garlic shrimp; or the Kobe beef *tataki*.

Universal Cafe

B1 Californian

2814 19th St. (bet. Bryant & Florida Sts.)

Phone: 415-821-4608
Web: www.universalcafe.net
Prices: **$$**

Lunch Wed – Sun
Dinner Tue – Sun

Universal Cafe is one of those contagiously cute places where everyone seems mellow and cheerful. The sunny dining room has a swarming open kitchen, a few counter seats for solo diners, and a rustic urban aura that suits its "Richly Organic" tagline and industrial-cum-residential neighborhood. This friendly haunt has a definite Euro feel, but, with a market-driven menu that rotates daily, it is also *très* Californian.

Brunch is Universal's true claim to fame, so bring your paper and enjoy the wait outdoors. First rate ingredients shine in plates of poached eggs with Creole-shrimp sauce; or the popular Moroccan-marinated roast goat and merguez with saffron rice and a yogurt-mint sauce. A ginger lemonade is especially refreshing with grilled flatbreads.

Woodward's Garden

American

1700 Mission St. (at Duboce St.)

Phone: 415-621-7122 Dinner Tue – Sat
Web: www.woodwardsgarden.com
Prices: $$$

Woodward's Garden may sit on the site of San Francisco's first amusement park in a location that, frankly, has little curb appeal–views to the 101!–but this hidden gem somehow manages to retain a vintage charm that lures a coterie of locals questing a quiet meal on the town. The mainstay feels just a bit like your grandma's house, with peeling paint, comfortable worn furnishings, and an antique chandelier.

The old-fashioned ambience sets a sweet stage for home-style fare that changes with the season. Savor farmer's market-fresh ingredients in dishes such as herbed polenta served in an iron crock with tender mushrooms, fresh thyme, and oozing Taleggio; and red wine-braised Sonoma duck leg aromatic with stewed Bing cherries and earthy turnips.

The sun is out – let's eat alfresco! Look for .

Peter L. Wrenn / MICHELIN

Nob Hill

Chinatown · Russian Hill

In company with the Golden Gate Bridge and Alamo Square's "Painted Ladies," Nob Hill is San Francisco at its most iconic. Historic cable cars chug up the dramatic grades that lead to the top, with familiar chimes tinkling in the wind, and brass rails checking tourists who dare to lean out and take in the sights. The Powell-Mason line offers a peek at Alcatraz; and the California Street car stops right at the gilded doors of Grace Cathedral.

Once a stomping ground for Gold Rush industry titans, this urbane quarter–sometimes dubbed "Snob Hill"–echoes of mighty egos and ancestral riches. It is home to white-glove buildings, ladies who lunch, and opulent dining rooms. Named for the 1800s railroad magnates, the **Big Four** is a stately hermitage known for antique memorabilia and nostalgic chicken potpie. Extravagant **Top of the Mark** is beloved for bounteous brunches and panoramic vistas. **Bacchus Wine Bar** is an elegant and alluring Italian-style hideaway lauded for its stylized interiors and incredible wine, beer, and sake selections. For a total departure, kick back with a Mai Tai (purportedly invented at Oakland's Trader Vic's in 1944) at the **Tonga Room & Hurricane Bar**, a tiki spot with a live thunderstorm inside the Fairmont Hotel.

Russian Hill

Slightly downhill, toward Polk Street, the vibe mellows as heirloom splendor gives way to Russian Hill, chockablock with boutiques, dive bars, and casual eateries that cater to regular groups of mostly twenty-something singles. Good, affordable fare abounds at popular haunts like **Rex Cafe** and **Street**. **Nick's Crispy Tacos**, the tacky taqueria turned nighttime disco, is a perennial favorite. And, for dessert, try the sinful chocolate earthquake from **Swensen's Ice Cream** flagship parlor, which is still *so* 1948. A handful of haute foodie shops fortuitously whet the palates of resident young professionals. **Cheese Plus** showcases more than 300 international cultures, artisan charcuterie, and chocolate. Across the street, the **Jug Shop** is a mecca for micro-brew beers and southern hemisphere wines. Dining at the eternally delish and inexpensive **House of Nanking** is a rare experience. Don't bother ordering from the menu—the owner often takes menus out of diner's hands and orders for them.

Chinatown

For a change of pace, head to Chinatown, whose authentic markets, dim sum palaces, and souvenir emporiums spill down the eastern slope of Nob Hill in a wash of color and Cantonese characters. Here you'll find some of the city's finest and crave-worthy barbecue pork buns at the area's oldest dim sum house, **Hang Ah Tea Room**, and a bevy of quirky must-sees. Fuel up on oven-fresh, 95-cent creamy custard tarts at **Golden Gate Bakery**, but also save room for samples at **Golden Gate Fortune Cookie Company**, where you can watch the prophetic little sweets in the making. The Mid-Autumn Moon Festival brings mooncakes, a traditional pastry stuffed with egg yolk and lotus seed paste. Gastronomes should unwind (and take home a taste of Chinatown) at the family-owned and operated Wok Shop for unique Asian cookware, linens, and tools. Their stock of rare products encompasses nearly every facet of Asian cooking.

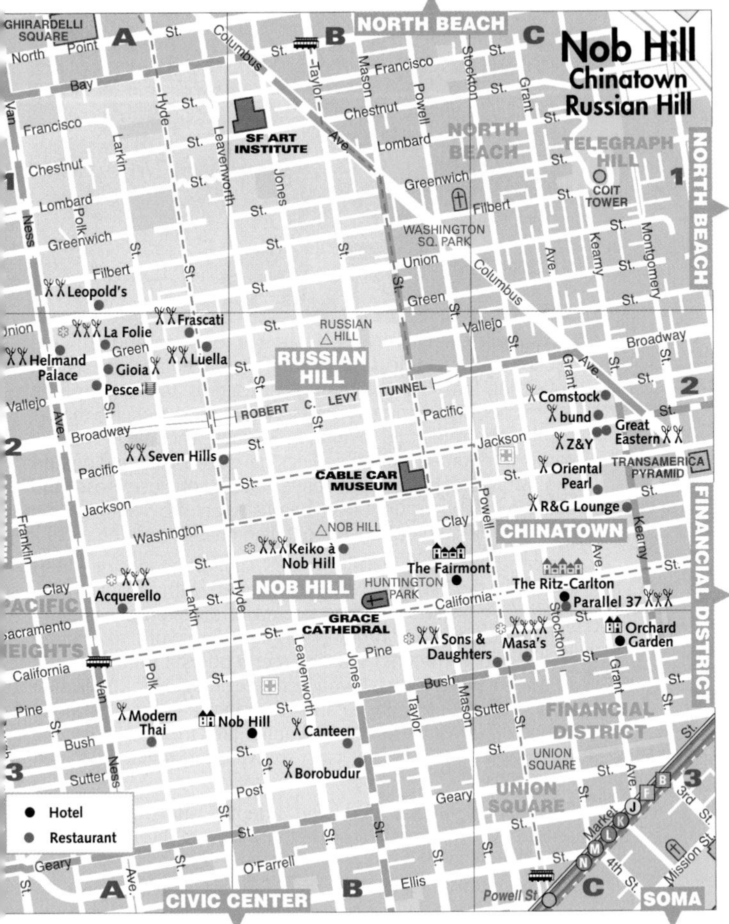

Acquerello ✿

Italian 

A2

1722 Sacramento St. (bet. Polk St. & Van Ness Ave.)

Phone: 415-567-5432 Dinner Tue – Sat
Web: www.acquerello.com
Prices: **$$$$**

Marty Kelly

Acquerello is well-tread by power brokers and affluent locals, so be sure to slip on your finest to dine here. Upon reflecting that this restaurant is housed in an old chapel, it seems perfectly fitting to drop to your knees and give thanks for this charming and inviting holy place. The magic is saved for its interiors—vaulted ceilings have elaborate gilding and the walls are painted in gentle shades of dusty rose and salmon. Two wrought-iron beams span the width of the dining room and enhance the Italian chapel countenance.

Dazzled by its Italian-by-way-of-California cuisine, feast on a classic Parmesan *budino* tangled with "black truffle caviar." A *bavette* of Kobe beef with an intensely fragrant sunchoke purée and Brussels sprouts is, in a word, revelatory. Furthermore, the chef's tasting menu offers a front row seat to the kitchen's fortes. If you're not regaling over a Valrohna chocolate mousse with candied orange, or crème fraîche panna cotta with strawberry granita, take the time to peruse the impressive cheese cart showcasing regional Italian selections.

The expert black-suited staff adeptly offers suggestions and delivers seamless service that elevates the exceptional experience.

Borobudur

Indonesian

B3

700 Post St. (at Jones St.)

Phone: 415-775-1512 Lunch & dinner daily
Web: www.borobudursf.com
Prices:

Named for a Javanese Buddhist monument, Borobudur is an appropriately obscure San Francisco eatery specializing in Indonesian cuisine. Walking down Post Street, just look for the sheer orange draperies and potted orchids in the windows.

Once you do manage to find this hidden gem, you'll be treated to an inviting little dining room where white cloths top the tables and comfortable cushioned booths line the quiet room. You're likely to dine in the company of few, but rest assured they are connoisseurs of the cuisine. Settle in for spicy-sweet flavor profiles in such dishes as sautéed tempeh and tofu in delicate soy sauce, or barbecue chicken in decadent coconut milk. Particularly hungry? Try the *rijsttafel*, which is Dutch for an Indonesian smorgasbord.

bund

Chinese

C2

640 Jackson St. (bet. Kearny St. & Wentworth Pl.)

Phone: 415-982-0618 Lunch & dinner daily
Web: N/A
Prices:

While Chinatown flourishes with some terrific Cantonese options, if you're yearning for delicious, flavorsome Shanghainese food, head on over to bund. The restaurant may be basic, but rest easy as it's clean, attended to by prompt waiters, and the food consistently good. Park at nearby Portsmouth Square Garage because street parking is insufficient.

The place is celebrated for its *xiao long bao* (soup dumplings)—the hot broth is filled with tender meatballs (pork and crab) and served with shredded ginger. Other house faves feature succulent salt & pepper shrimp stir-fried with chilies; and tender bamboo shoots sautéed with pork.

Desserts are coveted, so save room for a taste of soft black sesame paste-filled *mochi* balls served in rice wine soup.

Canteen

Californian

817 Sutter St. (bet. Jones & Leavenworth Sts.)

Phone: 415-928-8870 Lunch Sun
Web: www.sfcanteen.com Dinner Tue – Sat
Prices: $$

Despite first impressions, Canteen is much more than a dinner counter. Set in the nexus called the Tender Nob, locals know Chef/owner Dennis Leary is no slouch. His cuisine continually lures folks to his deep red counter or one of the few booths—note limited seating may mean lengthy waits.

The kitchen is 100% visible and the choreographed chaos can be mesmerizing. Parker House rolls are a staple, but the menu is ever-changing and may highlight sea bass ceviche set beneath cucumber ribbons, sliced jalapeño, and a green tomato aïoli; or potato-crusted sole over sautéed spinach and stewed artichokes, balanced by a briny sauce. It's nothing too fancy, just good cooking and flavors. Try the vanilla soufflé; it's been a treasure for nearly a decade!

Comstock

Gastropub

155 Columbus Ave. (at Pacific Ave.)

Phone: 415-617-0071 Lunch Fri
Web: www.comstocksaloon.com Dinner nightly
Prices: $$

Named for the legendary Henry Comstock and his Lode–the precious metal discovery that sparked the 19th century Gold Rush–this 1907 saloon is a historically correct homage to Americana with its tin ceilings, antiques, old-time portraits, and carved wood bar reflecting the dawn of the Barbary Coast. Enjoy a classic Sazerac or Manhattan and declare yourself Emperor, as Joshua Norton did, but don't call the town "Frisco." Comstock is a bar mainly but, in the SF foodie tradition, also serves quite good pub grub. Soak up such thrilling items as red pepper jelly and cream cheese on cheddar crackers; crispy pork and homemade biscuits; or beef shank and bone marrow pot pie.

The mezzanine above the bar is reserved for live piano and jazz artists in the evening.

Frascati

Mediterranean XX

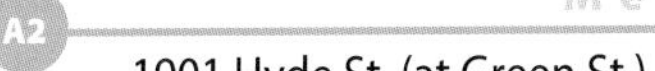

A2

1901 Hyde St. (at Green St.)

Phone: 415-928-1406 — Dinner nightly
Web: www.frascatisf.com
Prices: $$

Named for a bucolic hilltop town overlooking Rome, Frascati is a charming and friendly neighborhood treasure. Sidewalk tables enjoy the chimes of passing cable cars, while lovers prefer romantic mezzanine seating on cooler nights. The interior bursts with boisterous Russian Hill regulars who nosh on seasonal Mediterranean fare paired with wines from California and Italy.

Begin with plump and tender russet Potato gnocchi mingled with leeks, peas, mushrooms, and white truffle oil; or sample a hearty Italian sausage risotto brimming with roasted tomatoes, spinach, and Parmesan. Other faves include pan-seared Bluenose bass with sweet corn, asparagus, and black olive butter; followed by a warm black-and-white chocolate bread pudding with hazelnut ice cream.

Gioia

Pizza X

A2

2240 Polk St. (bet. Green & Vallejo Sts.)

Phone: 415-359-0971 — Lunch & dinner Tue – Sun
Web: www.gioiapizzeria.com
Prices: $$

This San Francisco newbie is the sibling to its very popular and petite Berkeley location. The décor is stylish and blends rustic with contemporary elements—a long marble dining counter, reclaimed barn wood wainscoting, and shiny metal lanterns and light fixtures. Guests can walk-in and order takeout...pizza by the slice? But the majority of diners choose to settle down amid this bustling scene of local business groups and cheery residents.

Start with a salad of arugula with almonds, pecorino, and Banyuls vinaigrette. Then it's pie time: a thin, chewy pizza slathered with *prosciutto cotto,* chili flakes, and minced garlic layered in tangy aged provolone; or thin-crust topped with savory sliced asparagus, red onion, clouds of ricotta, and melted pecorino.

Great Eastern

Chinese

649 Jackson St. (bet. Grant Ave. & Kearny St.)

Phone: 415-986-2500 Lunch & dinner daily
Web: www.greateasternsf.com
Prices: ⓈⓈ

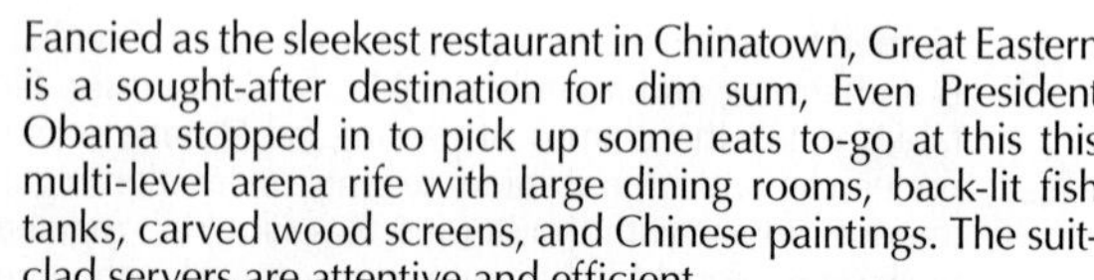

Fancied as the sleekest restaurant in Chinatown, Great Eastern is a sought-after destination for dim sum, Even President Obama stopped in to pick up some eats to-go at this this multi-level arena rife with large dining rooms, back-lit fish tanks, carved wood screens, and Chinese paintings. The suit-clad servers are attentive and efficient.

And while dim sum may be where its capability lies, the à la carte menu is equally remarkable with dishes like crispy skinned half Peking duck strutting a silky fat layer and smoky meat, paired with steamed, fluffy buns—*hao chi*! Chicken sautéed with cashews in a fragrant garlic sauce is delectable; and you can finally enjoy your veggies with perfectly cooked Chinese broccoli glazed in a salty-and-smoky oyster sauce.

Helmand Palace

Afghan

A2

2424 Van Ness Ave. (bet. Green & Union Sts.)

Phone: 415-345-0072 Dinner nightly
Web: www.helmandpalace.com
Prices: $$

In a neighborhood where appearances are everything, Helmand Palace is a reminder that beauty is more than skin deep. On a bus-choked stretch of Van Ness Avenue behind a non-descript façade, this local favorite serves Afghan recipes in an interior as rich as the food. Exotic red carpets and royal blue-cushioned armchairs make a cozy atmosphere for warming up with spicy fare. Newbies can trust that the murals depicting Afghani life are a promise of authenticity.

Here meals begin with hearty oven-fresh bread served with a trio of dips, then go on to include traditional appetizers such as *kaddo*, baked pumpkin with spicy ground beef and yogurt-garlic sauce; or tasty *seek kabab*, a charbroiled leg of lamb with sautéed eggplant, tomato, and raisins.

Keiko à Nob Hill ✿

French XXX

B2

1250 Jones St. (at Clay St.)

Phone: 415-829-7141 — Dinner Tue – Sun
Web: www.keikoanobhill.com
Prices: $$$$

Timothy Gordon

Dining here is stepping back to a time when eating was an event, and settings exceeded expectations. The classic and historic façade atop residential Nob Hill and elegantly dressed guests lend this spot the ambience of a private club. Expect to feel transported to turn-of-the century San Francisco, where romance meets luxury in spacious tabletops draped with thick linens, dark rattan chairs, and cushioned banquettes lining the mirrored walls.

The suit-clad servers are professional, attentive, and well paced, which is key when the nightly fixed-price menu consists of seven or more courses. The masterful wine list is a point of pride, so go for the pairings.

The menu of contemporary French cuisine with Japanese touches and Californian ingredients is as serious and wonderful as everything else before your eyes. Meals may reveal supremely fresh Hokkaido scallops blanketed in foam with sea urchin and chanterelles; a decadent rabbit galette with woodsy morels, butter beans, fiddlehead ferns, and truffles; or a nicely seasoned Black Angus rib eye with *gratin dauphinois* and black garlic sauce. Desserts may prompt swooning, especially when presented with a dark, rich, and custard-like *canelé*.

La Folie 

French 

A2

2316 Polk St. (bet. Green & Union Sts.)

Phone: 415-776-5577 Dinner Mon – Sat
Web: www.lafolie.com
Prices: $$$$

Dan Peak

La Folie is a serious restaurant, discreet and smart, that puts forth a sense of happy romance as timeless and pleasing as the popping of a champagne cork. Even the dining room itself has the feel of well-established elegance with high ceilings, rich colors, and polished woods.

The closely spaced tables are dressed with sophistication and populated by couples young and old who seem to be planning or remembering their milestones. This is the kind of place where the chef goes table to table and chats with guests.

Meals here might begin with a series of canapés, like pork rillettes with diced apple or smoked salmon roulade lollipops with pickled vegetables. Entrées may reveal the kitchen's elaborate skills in a perfect butter-poached lobster served with flavorful pumpkin ravioli and strong, silky truffle fondue. Their desserts can demonstrate modernity with surprising success. The peanut butter opera cake is freshly layered with chocolaty peanut butter and caramel mousse, salt crystals, and a scoop of curry ice cream—a fantastically unexpected complement to crisp bits of nougatine beneath. Traditions are again celebrated in the madeleines, *pâtes de fruits*, and very authentic *canelés*.

Leopold's

Austrian XX

A1

2400 Polk St. (at Union St.)

Phone: 415-474-2000
Web: www.leopoldssf.com
Prices: $$

Lunch Sat – Sun
Dinner nightly

Beer lovers are saying *Prost*! to Leopold's, an authentic Austrian *gasthaus* that opened in 2011 and is already the toast of the town. And it's no wonder: two-, three- and five-liter beer steins and boots hold lots of liquid to cheers with. Word to the wise: non-diehards coming for the food should slip in before it gets too crowded. Reservations? *Nein*.

With Alpine décor and all manner of fried, cheesy, and meaty fare, Leopold's is an honest restaurant ideal for the genuinely hungry. Dinner might include rich *kasespatzle* gratin seasoned with nutmeg, garnished with crisp onions, and served with a warm cabbage and bacon salad; and the extra-hearty *choucroute garnie* platter laden with smoky pork and bratwurst with sauerkraut and caraway-roasted potatoes.

Luella

Mediterranean XX

A2

1896 Hyde St. (at Green St.)

Phone: 415-674-4343
Web: www.luellasf.com
Prices: $$

Dinner nightly

While the parking in this nabe can cause heartburn, the food and service at Luella make it worth the frustration. Better yet, hop aboard the Powell & Hyde Street cable car for a little old-fashioned and stress-free commute.

Ben and Rachel de Vries run the show at this charming, if often raucous, place. From Coca-Cola-braised pork shoulder and salt cod *brandade* with lemon aïoli, to duck confit imperial rolls with a spicy pomegranate sauce, and lamb tortellini with favas, tomato, and Parmesan, this menu covers it all. But, casual pizzas, pastas, and a children's menu prove that Luella doesn't take itself too seriously. Desserts like banana cream pies with Valrhona chocolate sauce are worth saving room; and the three-course prix-fixes are a real deal.

Masa's ✿

C3 **Contemporary**

648 Bush St. (bet. Powell & Stockton Sts.)

Phone: 415-989-7154 Dinner Tue – Sat
Web: www.masasrestaurant.com
Prices: **$$$$**

Salim Sayani

This is among the city's few restaurants where jackets are strongly suggested for men, and everyone seems inclined to dress for the occasion of eating here. The ambience is quiet and reserved, though this may be a whispering homage to the excellent contemporary cuisine—never fussy and always flavorful. The sunken dining room feels slightly subdued, though enlivened by bronze sculptures. The black-suited service staff operates as a single, smooth brigade.

Fixed menus are offered with a range of options and enhancements, such as the seasonal white truffle tastings. The four-course dinner might begin with a neat oval of finely chopped beef with cracked salt, sour blood sorrel, and Meyer lemon *citronette* for a very local take on classic tartare. Moist and flaky pan-seared halibut might be placed on a woodsy mushroom purée dotted with *piment d'Esplette* oil. Slow-cooked chicken takes a brilliant turn when served skinless, then topped with crisped, salted skin chips, with thigh meat roulade, poached apples, and roasted chestnuts.

Desserts sing of the seasons, as in the very autumnal pumpkin panna cotta served atop spicy gingerbread cake, streaked with thick and buttery caramel sauce.

Modern Thai

Thai

1247 Polk St. (at Bush St.)

Phone: 415-922-8424 Lunch & dinner daily
Web: www.modernthaisf.com
Prices: 

In the cheery, colonial-style dining space, shades of raspberry sherbet and lime vivify stark white walls, while colorful Gerber daisies adorn glass-topped tables. An enclosed porch affords sunny street side views and a great spot to tuck into some cheap and tasty Thai. Pumpkin lovers rejoice—this gourd is prepared in all kinds of delicious ways, whether shredded and deep-fried with sesame and coconut, or cubed in a luscious, creamy curry. Specialties like crispy calamari with cashews or roasted duck with lychee curry are equally worthy, as are the fishcakes—golden crispy pancakes of minced fish, silver rice noodles, and shiitake mushrooms.
Exotic desserts like blueberry *roti* or the MT sundae with purple yam and coconut ice cream are a perfect finale.

Oriental Pearl

Chinese

760 Clay St. (bet. Grant Ave. & Kearny St.)

Phone: 415-433-1817 Lunch & dinner daily
Web: www.orientalpearlsf.com
Prices: 

Named to honor Hong Kong "The Pearl of the Orient," Oriental Pearl is more elegant than its Chinatown brethren: white tablecloths, intricately carved chairs, and polite servers make for a pleasant atmosphere. Street parking is at a premium, so park at Portsmouth Square Garage across the street.
This sparkling "pearl" offers an array of dim sum, à la carte, and set combo menus. Lauded as a signature for good reason, meatballs of minced chicken, mushrooms, and ham are wrapped in egg white crêpes and tied at the top with chive slivers—like tasty little beggar's purses. Wide, chewy *chow fun* are tossed with tender beef in a savory black pepper-black bean gravy; while flash-fried string beans with tofu doused in a chili-garlic sauce is a fab veggie option.

Parallel 37

C2 — Californian

600 Stockton St. (bet. California & Pine Sts.)

Phone: 415-773-6168 — Lunch & dinner daily
Web: www.parallel37sf.com
Prices: $$$

The formal Dining Room at the Ritz-Carlton has been transformed into Parallel 37. Rustic meets retro in this sleek and contemporary establishment fitted with roughly hewn wood planks, stone accent walls, and a mod-inspired lounge with backlit glass panels. The bar is popular with the hotel's business patrons, but has yet to catch on with the locals—ironic, as it's named after the latitude line crossing the Bay Area.

Matching Cali's food philosophy, the kitchen aims to source its ingredients locally. The menu uncovers chilled Dungeness crab mixed in light vinaigrette and topped with frisée, shiso, and avocado; or pan-seared snapper rested atop artichoke ravioli in a foamy Parmesan broth, and joined with honey-glazed carrots tossed with fragrant tarragon.

Pesce

A2 — Seafood

2227 Polk St. (bet. Green & Vallejo Sts.)

Phone: 415-928-8025 — Dinner nightly
Web: www.pescesf.com
Prices: $$

Long a mainstay on this bustling stretch of Polk Street, Pesce is an easygoing seafood bar where the locals get along swimmingly. Serving Italian small plates known as *cicchetti*, the restaurant is particularly beloved among neighborhood types who like to catch up over a quick glass of wine and a snack–think plump grilled sardines with pickled root vegetables–at the long zinc bar.

For those who've come to stay a while, simple wood furniture, penny tile floors, and that ever-friendly service make for a comfortable vibe in the narrow ambient space. Look for popular dishes like grilled Monterey calamari with caramelized fennel and spicy *pomodoro* sauce; Dungeness crab with cucumber and avocado; squid ink risotto; and fresh oyster shots spiked with horseradish.

R & G Lounge

Chinese

C2

631 Kearny St. (bet. Clay & Sacramento Sts.)

Lunch & dinner daily

Phone: 415-982-7877
Web: www.rnglounge.com
Prices: $$

R & G Lounge has been a longtime Chinatown fave for Cantonese food. The space is clean, while the service is a bit better than mediocre. Sure the décor is dated and the dropped ceiling of beige ribbons is rather strange, but really who's looking up when delicacies (like tender, falling-off-the-bone honey spare ribs glazed in a sweet and tangy sauce) await down, on your plate?

Tanks of fish signal fresh seafood and fittingly, their signature dish is salt & pepper crab. At lunch, the wood-paneled den downstairs is crammed with families and businessmen. Find them chowing on fresh mixed vegetables delicately stir-fried in garlic sauce; or lamb sautéed with leeks in a mildly-spiced, aromatic gravy of ginger and garlic, teamed with steamed *bao*.

Seven Hills

Italian

A2

1550 Hyde St. (at Pacific Ave.)

Dinner Tue – Sun

Phone: 415-775-1550
Web: www.sevenhillssf.com
Prices: $$

Shrouded by the rustling trees of Hyde Street and the ding-ding of the passing cable car, Seven Hills is an obscure Italian eatery that has become a local favorite. And how could locals not flock to this bambino-sized *ristorante* where a cozy vibe, jovial staff, and just four seats at the bar make Seven Hills a perfectly low-key neighborhood haunt.

Two petite wood-clad dining rooms host a consistent crowd where those in the know opt for pasta, the specialty of the house, in either half- or whole portions. Seasonal recipes might include delish scallop ravioli with sweet corn and English peas. Other delightfully unembellished fare may include seared calamari with tangy caponata to start, and house-made ricotta studded with candied pistachios to finish.

Sons & Daughters ✿

C3 Contemporary XX

708 Bush St. (bet. Mason & Powell Sts.)

Phone: 415-391-8311
Web: www.sonsanddaughterssf.com
Prices: $$$$

Dinner Tue – Sat

Tracey Hymen

Sons & Daughters ushers in a new era of hip dining. The foodie-focused design orients the small dining space around the central exhibition kitchen; while a downstairs lounge, sultry purple-painted ceiling, brass-studded leather chairs, and glass jars complete the trendy setting. Obscure photos present a pop quiz for culinary aficionados whose every whim is catered to by a relaxed yet responsive staff.

Well-dressed groups mingle with casually chic clusters in this cool, atmospheric haven where brilliantly gifted chefs gracefully put out sophisticated fare.

The nightly prix-fixe menus (one is vegetarian) may unfold stories about the delicate yet bold curls of kampachi crudo dressed with lime *kosho* and quail bush leaf; while savory meat courses of spiced and braised wild boar medallions served over streaks of apple and hay purée with a dusting of pink peppercorns may result in memoirs on floral flavors. The creative presentations and combinations present in a caramelized pork belly posed atop blanched English peas sweetened with verjus; or refined dessert of bloomy Osmanthus-infused cake paired with candied beets and rose-vanilla ice cream, will have foodies snapping pictures.

Z & Y

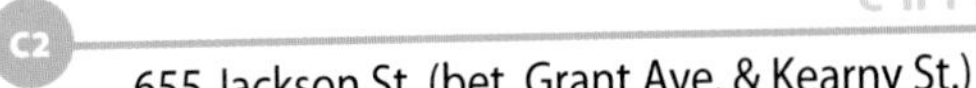

Chinese

655 Jackson St. (bet. Grant Ave. & Kearny St.)

Phone: 415-981-8988
Lunch & dinner daily
Web: www.zandyrestaurant.com
Prices: $$

This precious Chinatown pearl is loved and lauded for its bold-flavored, tasty Chinese food. Attention spice addicts: when Z & Y's menu indicates that a dish will be chili-hot, *trust* them—fiery flavors aren't toned down for gun shy American palates. By virtue of its tempting Chinese, this long and slender restaurant with tight-knit tables aglow with red Chinese lanterns, is forever packed.

Nailing the red-hot motif are brusque servers robed in red and carrying savory dishes like golden brown scallion pancakes sprinkled with sesame seeds; tender pork strips bathing in a garlic sauce pungent with dried Sichuan chilies; and Mongolian beef flavored with oyster and soy sauce. Also joining the fan faves is a deliciously sticky black sesame rice ball soup.

Look for **red** symbols, indicating a particularly pleasant ambience.

North Beach

Fisherman's Wharf · Telegraph Hill

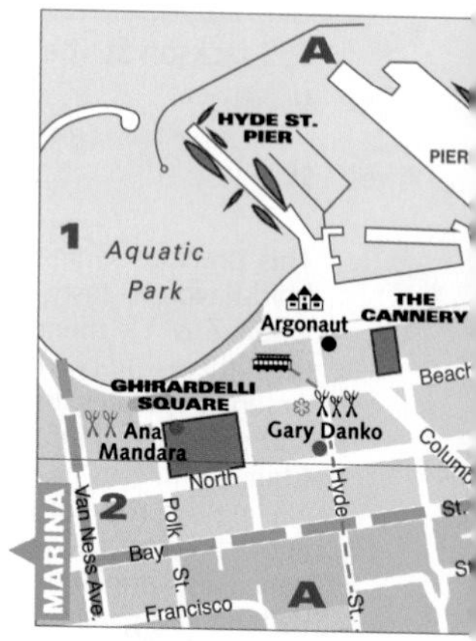

Nestled between bustling Fisherman's Wharf and the steep slopes of Russian and Telegraph Hills, North Beach owes its lively nature to the Italian immigrants who settled here in the late 1800s. Many of these were fishermen from the Ligurian coast; the seafood stew they made on their boats evolved into the quintessential San Francisco treat, cioppino—a must-order in this district. Though Italians may no longer be in the majority here, dozens of pasta places, pizzerias, coffee shops, and bars in North Beach attest to their idea of the good life. At the annual North Beach Festival in mid-June, a celebrity pizza toss, Assisi Animal Blessings, and Arte di Gesso (chalk art) also nod and pay homage to the neighborhood's Italian heritage. **Fog City Diner** remains a popular stop for tourists after a ferry to Alcatraz, or a walk along The Embarcadero.

Today the majority of North Beach's restaurants and bars lie along Columbus Avenue. Be sure to check out the quarter's Italian delis, like **Molinari**'s, whose homemade salami has been a local institution since 1896. Pair some imported meats and cheeses with a bottle of wine for a perfect picnic in nearby Washington Square Park. Hanging out in North Beach can be a full-time job, which is what attracted a ragtag array of beret-wearing poets to the area in the 1950s. These so-called beatniks–Allen Ginsberg and Jack Kerouac among them–were eventually driven out by busloads of tourists. Bohemian spirits linger on at such landmarks as the City Lights bookstore, and next door at **Vesuvio**, the original boho bar.

Feasting in Fisherman's Wharf

You won't find many locals here, but Fisherman's Wharf, the mile-long stretch of waterfront at the foot of Columbus Street, ranks as one of the city's most popular tourist attractions. It may teem with souvenir shops, street performers, rides, and other attractions, but you should go—if only to feast on a sourdough bread bowl soaked in clam chowder, and fresh crabs cooked in huge steamers right on the street. Sample a piece of edible history at **Boudin Bakery**. This old-world respite may have bloomed into a large modern operation–complete with a museum and bakery tour–but they still make their

sourdough bread fresh every day, using the same mother first cultivated here from local wild yeast in 1849. Nearby on North Point Street, Ghirardelli Square preserves another taste of old San Francisco. This venerable chocolate company, founded by Domingo Ghirardelli in 1852, now flaunts its delectable wares at the noteworthy **Ghirardelli Ice Cream and Chocolate Manufactory**. Here you can ogle the original chocolate manufacturing equipment while you enjoy a decadent yet heart-warming hot fudge sundae. Don't leave without taking away some sweet memories in the form of their chocolate squares.

Albona

B2 Italian XX

545 Francisco St. (bet. Mason & Taylor Sts.)

Phone: 415-441-1040
Web: www.albonarestaurant.com
Prices: $$

Dinner nightly

Named after the picturesque town that is perched high on a cliff overlooking the Adriatic Sea, Albona specializes in Istrian cuisine borrowing influences from Italy, Austria, Hungary, Greece, and other parts of Central Europe. Set in a discreet building, the atmosphere inside feels old-fashioned yet charming with a scattering of closely-spaced tables, low lighting, and smiling servers.

A beloved spot for date nights, watch couples devour such interesting and flavorful dishes as *capuzi garbi con prosuto e luganega* (braised sauerkraut fragrant with onions, apples, and prosciutto); *strudel con pasta fatta in casa* (fresh pasta filled with prosciutto, cheese and baked in a casserole with breadcrumbs and béchamel); or braised veal shank with soft polenta.

Ana Mandara

A1 Vietnamese XX

891 Beach St. (at Polk St.)

Phone: 415-771-6800
Web: www.anamandara.com
Prices: $$

Lunch Mon – Sat
Dinner nightly

Any restaurant that can keep its wheels churning for over a decade must be doing something right. Such is the case of Ana Mandara, housed in the kinetic Ghirardelli Sq. As the names suggests, this "beautiful refuge" comes alive in her Southeast Asian temple dressed with silk lanterns, rattan furnishings, leafy palms, and fountains. On weekends, visit the Cham bar & lounge upstairs for live jazz and a lovely perspective of the scene below.

Servers in traditional silk gowns are polite and adept, delivering an array of items with soothing names. Whether you're consuming Silken Baskets (edamame dumplings with pea sprouts and truffle oil); or pieces of gold, spicy caramelized claypot fish with ginger, garlic, and snow peas, you will leave gratified.

Bix

American

D3

56 Gold St. (bet. Montgomery & Sansome Sts.)

Phone: 415-433-6300 — Lunch Fri
Web: www.bixrestaurant.com — Dinner nightly
Prices: **$$$**

Follow the covert entry located off an alley, pass through a nondescript brick façade, and find yourself in the bygone supper club era, paying tribute to jazz great Bix Beiderbecke. This wide-open, bi-level dining room exudes fanciful charm with lofty columns, mahogany paneling, and a baby grand. Lull at the bar where tenders sate with much shaking and stirring. Then sweep up the stairs and into a picturesque booth.

Tuxedo-clad servers enhance the throwback tone, reciting–maybe to the backdrop of jazz music–a carte of revived classics like steak tartare; homemade mozzarella wrapped in prosciutto; and local albacore tuna with fried green tomatoes, Padron pepper relish, and *tonnato* sauce. For all their highbrow efforts, they still make a great burger.

Café Jacqueline

French 

1454 Grant Ave. (bet. Green & Union Sts.)

Phone: 415-981-5565 — Dinner Wed – Sun
Web: N/A
Prices: **$$$**

This petite bistro specializes in soufflés—and what incredibly light and flavorful creations they are. Her space may not dazzle with tables packed like sardines, but Café Jacqueline's faithful French treats certainly will.

Not ideal for large gatherings or groups-on-the-go (meals here may take hours), the café is patronized by those who have time on their hands—and delicious, fluffy soufflés on their mind. Start with the staple French onion soup, but with such a surfeit of savory soufflés on display, it seems only right to follow suit with a towering chanterelle mushroom rich with Gruyère; or lobster soufflé that is at once decadent and fresh. Moving on—the warm dark chocolate soufflé is so plush and moist, you may wonder how you lived before it.

Coi ✿✿

Contemporary XXX

373 Broadway (bet. Montgomery & Sansome Sts.)

Phone: 415-393-9000 Dinner Wed – Sat
Web: www.coirestaurant.com
Prices: **$$$$**

Dwight Eschliman

A slightly sexy, even lurid, sense of velvet-roped nightclubs and limousines pervades this changing neighborhood home to Coi. Within the small, elegant dining room, find earth-toned banquettes strewn with pillows and rice paper panels diffusing natural light and appearing to glow against moodier walls. Overall, this newly refreshed Zen-chic look is clean and clearly Asian-inspired. Servers are professional and mod—even the surrounding conversations seem casually cool as the room fills up. That said, everyone halts to admire each dish.

The fare is creative and eclectic, made from impeccable ingredients, and often has a cerebral spin. Meals might reveal an extraordinarily delicious inverted tart of "beets roasted in hay" with alternating layers of dill pesto and airy goat cheese *espuma*, topped with thin rye wafers. Or, expect a beautifully conceived dish of sliced, medium-rare lamb loin and braised neck set upon a potent purée of bright wheatgrass and raw almond, finished with crunchy grains and bright green shoots.

Desserts pair flavors that verge on celestial, as in the slightly bitter chicory coffee with chocolatey malted-milk foam layered with hidden accents that will have you smitten.

Cotogna

Italian XX

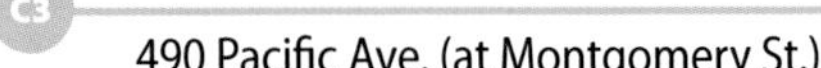

C3

490 Pacific Ave. (at Montgomery St.)

Phone: 415-775-8508 — Lunch Mon – Sat
Web: www.cotognasf.com — Dinner nightly
Prices: $$

Lack the funds to fork over for dinner at Quince? Head to Chef Michael Tusk's latest, less expensive outpost just next door. Cotogna is a rustic Italian eatery aimed at the Roman heart. Here you'll find straightforward, well-prepared fare such as salt-and-pepper Monterey squid over chopped *puntarella* salad; pillowy beet *tortelloni* with poppy seeds in butter; and skirt steak with grilled radicchio and balsamic.

Grab a $10 glass of *vino* at the copper-topped bar and swirl while you spy the goings-on in the kitchen. Here find the pizza furnace and green enamel oven fired by almond wood where the staff labors over grilled meats and esoteric Neapolitan pies (like sea urchin and cauliflower). Take a seat at one of the communal tables for a quieter experience.

the house

Asian X

C3

1230 Grant Ave. (bet. Columbus Ave. & Vallejo St.)

Phone: 415-986-8612 — Lunch Mon – Sat
Web: www.thehse.com — Dinner nightly
Prices: $$

At the heart of Italian North Beach stands a tiny Asian eatery revered for colorful fusion flavors and known simply as the house. Blond wood furnishings and a minimalist décor create a pleasant vibe without detracting from the cuisine, while efficient servers recount the daily specials. Listen closely before making hasty decisions.

The meal begins with tangy marinated cucumbers and appetizers like steamed shrimp-and-chive Chinese dumplings on a vibrant bed of carrots, beets, and radishes. Slurp an udon bowl with grilled chicken and toasted nori or sample more unique fare: wasabi noodles topped with teriyaki-glazed grilled salmon are a house specialty and worth the wait for a table. The house also offers a nice choice of tea, beer, and wines by the glass.

Gary Danko ✿

Contemporary 

A1

800 North Point St. (at Hyde St.)

Phone: 415-749-2060 Dinner nightly
Web: www.garydanko.com
Prices: $$$$

Gary Danko

Gary Danko is a beloved institution and tourists congregate here for all things San Franciscan while locals adore it for special occasions. Perched on a hill above Fisherman's Wharf, cable cars whiz past the front door of this longstanding spot. And did we mention celebrated California chef, Gary Danko? He presents a perfect little package of homegrown love tied with a golden (gate) ribbon.

While this is a great place to be seen (but blackened windows keep things intimate), it is their consistently good food that forms the true bait. An ultimate date place, find pretty pairs coddling a crispy farm egg quivering with polenta and mushrooms. But, business sorts also love it for impressing clients—the staff is old-school professional, trained to the hilt, and work as a well-oiled machine.

Besides an extensive chef's tasting menu, three-, four-, and five-course menus showcase Danko's culinary abilities and contemporary flair. Masterful and refined plates include herb-crusted lamb loin beautifully joined with cannellini beans and cumin-mint yogurt. Those missing a sweet tooth (for macaron ice cream sandwiches?) shouldn't forsake the artisanal cheeses presented with a variety of fruit compotes.

Kokkari Estiatorio 

Greek

D3

200 Jackson St. (at Front St.)

Phone: 415-981-0983 — Lunch Mon – Fri
Web: www.kokkari.com — Dinner nightly
Prices: $$

Praise the Greek Gods as Kokkari is one of those places that consistently serves delicious food—no wonder this ample arena is forever packed. Roaring fireplaces, wood accents, and iron light fixtures give the tavern an old-world feel that complements its fresh and flavorful carte.

In keeping with its spirit, warm servers cradle such exquisite Greek dishes as a mixed green salad mingling apple shavings, golden beets, and salty feta with oregano-infused vinaigrette; or large chunks of grilled yogurt- and herb-marinated chicken souvlaki and red bell peppers served with cool, creamy *tzatziki* and warm homemade pita strewn with herbs and sea salt. End with a filo shell filled with sweet semolina custard, topped with tangy blood orange segments.

Maykadeh

Persian

C2

470 Green St. (bet. Grant Ave. & Kearny St.)

Phone: 415-362-8286 — Lunch & dinner daily
Web: www.maykadehrestaurant.com
Prices: $$

At Maykedeh–a name referring to Persian taverns of yore where poets and mystics converged to dine and drink–gracious service and generous portions abound. A burgundy-and-gold awning crowns the entrance; while inside, Middle Eastern songs and scents linger amid banquettes and linen-draped tables that accommodate crowds savoring the foods of their homeland.

Meals start with a plate of raw onion, fresh basil, and feta cheese—trust in these new refreshing combinations, salads, and dips laced with alluring Middle Eastern flavors. Sample the rich *kashke bademjan,* an eggplant and garlic spread with warm pita, then a tender skewer of *koobideh,* fresh ground lamb and beef with warm Persian spices. Valet the car to avoid the Telegraph Hill parking conundrum.

Park Tavern

American XXX

C2

1652 Stockton St. (bet. Filbert & Union Sts.)

Phone: 415-989-7300 — Lunch Sat – Sun
Web: www.parktavernsf.com — Dinner Wed – Mon
Prices: $$$

From the team behind popular Marlowe in SoMa arrives Park Tavern, a welcome respite from the bustle of North Beach. The see-and-be-scene crowd is almost always packed with affluent locals, young professionals, and power brokers plus their trophy wives. The voluminous tavern is equally sophisticated with beamed ceilings, mosaic floors, and leather banquets.

Start with appetizers like smoked deviled eggs topped with caramelized bacon and jalapeños; or try some Brussels sprouts chips. Tender Cornish game hen is all heart and soul coated with harissa and presented whole on the stand surrounded by wilted spinach and peewee potatoes. A successful combination of lemon cheesecake parfait layered with sweet huckleberries completes this tasty experience.

Piperade

Basque XX

D2

1015 Battery St. (bet. Green & Union Sts.)

Phone: 415-391-2555 — Lunch Mon – Fri
Web: www.piperade.com — Dinner Mon – Sat
Prices: $$

Piperade is still going strong in North Beach with a crowd of locals at lunch and business types appreciating its arched bar rife with tasty libations at dinner. The pleasant interior décor of worn wood floors, brick walls, ruddy-painted ceilings, and interesting chandeliers crafted from inverted wine bottles make dining here a comfortable affair brought to you at the hands of welcoming and amicable servers.

The Basque menu may reveal items such as flaky puff pastry topped with a mélange of wild mushrooms and fresh thyme; and a juicy herb-marinated roasted rack of lamb joined with garlicky lamb sausage and a fennel bulb. For a special finale, plunge into a *gateau Basque*—creamy custard surrounded by puff pastry and covered with plump Amarena cherries.

Quince

Italian

C3

470 Pacific Ave. (bet. Montgomery & Sansome Sts.)

Phone: 415-775-8500 Dinner Mon – Sat
Web: www.quincerestaurant.com
Prices: $$$$

Paul Dyer

Quince lives on as one of the city's hot spots and whoever the scenesters may be, expect to see them dining here. And yes, those are their limos lined up in front of the kitchen's picture window. The stylish clientele matches the restaurant's atmosphere which features a trendy lounge and soft gray dining room with plush banquettes, Murano glass chandeliers, vivid floral displays, and archways leading to a ritzy bar rife with pre-dinner cocktails. This is all overseen by an extraordinary service team that continues to be among the best in San Francisco.

Expense accounts and stiletto-clad sophisticates wash down lavish meals with expensive bottles of wine. Speaking of which, the Italian menu may offer a springtime starter of garlic *vellutata* bobbing with Kusshi oysters and potatoes that once combined with bacon brings smoky richness to the entire plate. However, pastas are the highlight here, as in *casoncelli verdi* excellently mingled with Barinaga Ranch *baserri* cheese and winter greens glossed with *olio verde*.

A cheese course makes a lovely finale, although you must save room for a Tainori chocolate tart caressed with milk chocolate ganache, crispy caramel rice, and praline ice cream.

Rose Pistola

Italian XX

532 Columbus Ave. (bet. Green & Union Sts.)

Phone: 415-399-0499 — Lunch & dinner daily
Web: www.rosepistolasf.com
Prices: **$$$**

Settle into classy and comfy Rose Pistola to relish a menu inspired by North Beach's original Northern Italian (Ligurian) residents. The wood-fired oven plus sleek open kitchen run the length of the dining room, whereas cheery yellow walls and friendly service add to the warmth of this diner.
The menu is skewed towards seafood featuring products from independent farmers and fishermen. Patrons come in droves to revel in flavorful seafood-stuffed calamari set upon a tomato-rich *puttanesca*. Chicken *al mattone* is grilled under a brick and served tender and moist with a dollop of shallot- and herb-butter. Pair this with deep-fried potato wedges infused with Marash chile and...smile.
Dog owners favor the table-lined sidewalk for sneaking focaccia to Fido.

Tommaso's

Italian X

1042 Kearny St. (bet. Broadway St. & Pacific Ave.)

Phone: 415-398-9696 — Dinner Tue – Sun
Web: www.tommasosnorthbeach.com
Prices: **$$**

California pizza kitchens love to celebrate the bounty of the season, turning out pies with toppings that would boggle a red-blooded Italian (snow peas and sauerkraut?). Not so at Tommaso's, the family-friendly North Beach mainstay where the wood-fired pizzas hail straight from the old country. The chewy thin-crust pies are heaped with sausage, meatballs, salami, and *Prosciutto di Parma*. Fancy pants can sample garlic and clams or chicken and artichoke.
Set against a bright mural depicting the Bay of Naples, dinners at Tommaso's might also include a meaty antipasto plate loaded with rosemary ham and *bresaola*, or classic tiramisu. A fixture in the neighborhood since 1935, this fortress is a refreshing escape from seedy North Beach nightlife.

Tony's Pizza Napoletana

Pizza

1570 Stockton St. (at Union St.)

Phone: 415-835-9888
Web: www.tonyspizzanapoletana.com
Prices: $$

Lunch & dinner Wed – Sun

Tony's is a North Beach institution that churns out a large menu of Neapolitan-, Sicilian-, and American-style pizzas; it is also well-liked by locals and tourists who flock here not just for the pizza, but also for the buzzing social scene. You may think you've done well by arriving early, yet find herds waiting for a coveted seat in this casual pizzeria.

The bar is fair game and flanked by crowds hungry for the prized Margherita, a wood-fired crust slathered with San Marzano tomatoes, mozzarella, and basil. Tony's boasts a pizza for every palate, so come with friends to sample selections like the coal-fired New Yorker (pepperoni, sausage, and ricotta); or Californian style: "Fear and Loathing" with tamarind-glazed pork, jalapeños, and agave drizzles.

Trattoria Contadina

Italian 

1800 Mason St. (at Union St.)

Phone: 415-982-5728
Web: www.trattoriacontadina.com
Prices: $$

Dinner nightly

This old-school charmer dispenses Italian-American dishes in a quaint trattoria donning a faux-balcony overhead. Rife with a nostalgic vibe (framed photos of celebs hang throughout), it's no wonder that this homey tavern has such a loyal following. But, don't be surprised if the occasional visitor wanders in looking for an escape from the Italian tourist traps nearby.

The rustic menu is concise, but the portions are hearty. Start with *rigatoncelli* swirled with caramelized pancetta, porcini mushrooms, and sun-dried tomatoes in a tomato-cream sauce; before tucking into a juicy chicken breast covered with smoked mozzarella, prosciutto shavings, and served in a pool of Madeira wine sauce. Still need a drop of sweet? The lemon cheesecake is exemplary.

Richmond & Sunset

Here in the otherworldly outer reaches of San Francisco, the foggy sea washes up to the historic Cliff House and Sutro Baths. In spring, cherry blossoms blush at the breeze in Golden Gate Park; and whimsical topiaries wink at pastel row houses in need of fresh paint. Residents seem inspired by a sense of Zen not quite found elsewhere in town, whether you happen upon a Japanese sushi chef or a Sunset surfer dude. A melting pot of settlers forms the culinary complexion of this quiet urban pocket. The steam wafting from bowls of piping hot *pho* is nearly as thick as the marine layer, while many of the neighborhoods' western accents hail from across the pond.

New Chinatown

The Richmond District, however, has earned the nickname "New Chinatown" for a reason. A big bazaar for the adventurous cook, Clement Street bursts with cramped sidewalk markets where clusters of bananas sway from the awnings and the spices and produce are as vibrant as the nearby **Japanese Tea Garden** in bloom. While the Bay Area mantra "eat local" doesn't really apply here, sundry international goods abound—think kimchi, tamarind, eel, live fish, and pork buns for less than a buck. Curious foodies find global delicacies: This is *the* place to source that 100-year-old egg. A gathering place for sea lovers, **Outerlands** is perfect when in need of warmth, food, shelter, and "community." Here, there is a mom-and-pop joint for every corner and culture. The décor is nothing to write home about and, at times, feels downright seedy, but you're here for the cuisine, which is usually authentic: Korean barbecue at **Brothers Restaurant**; Burmese at **B Star Bar**; *siu mai* at **Shanghai Dumpling King** and **Good Luck Dim Sum**; as well

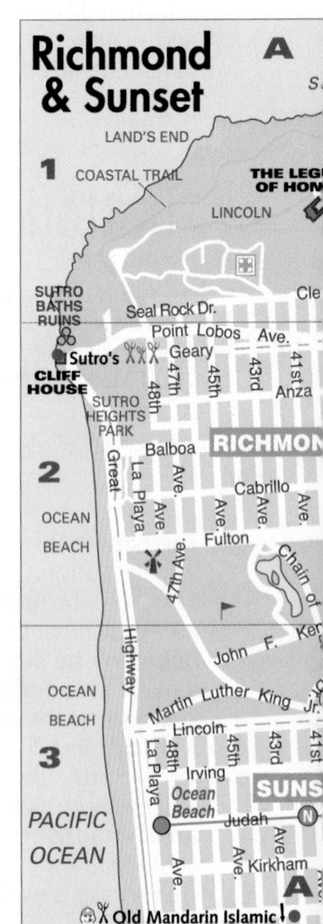

as an intoxicating offering of tequila and mescal at **Tommy's Mexican Restaurant**. For a bit of sweet, it's Asian kitsch: **Polly Ann Ice Cream** has served such flavors as durian, jasmine tea, and taro for years; while young club kids nibble Hong Kong–style delights late night at **Kowloon Tong Dessert Cafe**.

Sunset

A touch more gentrified than neighboring Richmond, Sunset–once a heap of sand dunes–retains a small-town vibe that's groovy around the edges. In the early morning, locals line up for fresh bread and pastries at **Arizmendi Bakery**, then wash down their scones at the **Beanery** around the corner. Asian-devotees flock to **Izakaya Sozai** for their gratifying yakitori specialties, sashimi, and other faithful Japanese treats. While tourists taking in the sights at the DeYoung Museum or the Academy of Sciences, might grab a bite at the **Academy Café**, loyalists to **L'Avenida Taqueria** take their burritos to the park. Finally, don't miss dinner at the **Moss Room**, boasting a plethora of unique and delicious dishes made with local, seasonal, and healthy ingredients.

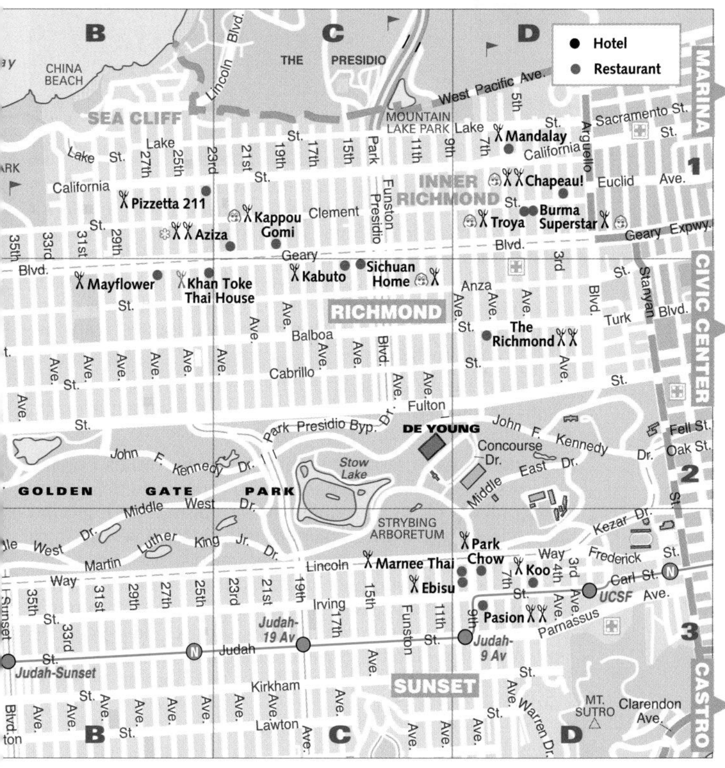

Aziza ✿

Moroccan XX

C1

5800 Geary Blvd. (at 22nd Ave.)

Phone: 415-752-2222 Dinner Wed – Mon
Web: www.aziza-sf.com
Prices: $$$

Amy Snyder

The rather nondescript, cream-colored building that houses Aziza couldn't be more surprising from within. The interior is divided into a front dining room fringed with inlaid tables tucked into attractive archways and intimate niches, all glowing with soft red light. Beyond this, find another long and slender dining room clad in rose-tinted walls and cushy banquettes, as well as a Moroccan-style lounge with low seating and tiny tabletops.

However, the side bar under metal lanterns is where the magic begins, as bartenders invent those signature exotic cocktails, like the red currant-thyme Pisco.

Arriving on each table are white porcelain dishes holding the likes of golden brown *basteeya* surrounding a deliciously moist filling of duck confit, sweet raisins, and ground almonds spiced with cinnamon and ginger. Creamy farro mingled with a brunoise of tender carrots, sweet scallops, and a generous mound of Himalayan truffles shows first-rate skill; while roasted quail roulade paired with potato purée is enticingly enriched with a lusciously silky slow-poached egg. Anyone with a heart will fall for caramelized chocolate brioche French toast topped with a scoop of fragrant cardamom ice cream.

Burma Superstar

Burmese

309 Clement St. (bet. 4th & 5th Aves.)

Phone: 415-387-2147 Lunch & dinner daily
Web: www.burmasuperstar.com
Prices: ⚭

Any foodie worth their cilantro in San Francisco has made the trek to Clement Street to jot their name on a clipboard and wait it out at Burma Superstar, the now cult classic with everything going for it. Seriously, Chinatown restaurants wish they were this cool.

The massive menu wants for large parties that like to share—narrowing down the options can be a bit of a task. Have faith, an uber-friendly staff is on hand to help. You'll find a mix of Asian flavors, but seek out the genuine Burmese recipes noted by asterisks on the menu. Mild-mannered fare includes a tea leaf salad with roasted peanuts and fish sauce. The star of Superstar is the *mohinga*—a divine noodle soup with ground catfish and Asian veggies spiked with lemon and lemongrass.

Chapeau!

French 

126 Clement St. (bet. 2nd & 3rd Aves.)

Phone: 415-750-9787 Dinner Tue – Sat
Web: www.chapeausf.com
Prices: $$

Upon alighting at Chapeau! stylish disciples are welcomed with a kiss-kiss from Monsieur and Madame Gardelle, the husband-wife team that runs this strictly French ship. A long banquette and close-knit tables span the clamorous dining room that, with an ambient amber glow, is equally romantic and spirited for date nights.

Chef/owner Phillipe Gardelle is as often shaking hands in the room as he is in the kitchen, where he prepares such classic Gallic dishes as *escargots de Bourgogne*; salmon gravlax, tartare, and caviar with all the accoutrements; and lavender honey- and Dijon-glazed *petit poussin*. At the end, the chef may turn up tableside for a round of applause.

On weekdays, early birds tip their hats for the under $30 prix-fixe from 5:00 - 6:00 P.M.

Ebisu

Japanese

D3

1283 9th Ave. (at Irving St.)

Phone: 415-566-1770 Lunch & dinner Tue – Sun
Web: www.ebisusushi.com
Prices:

Steps away from Golden Gate Park, the well-tread Ebisu is run by Steve Fujii and his wife Koko. This *sushi-ya* (in business for nearly 30 years) is loved both for its chic and contemporary style (featuring a long, sleek sushi bar and wood accents throughout), as well as its creative maki. While some purists are wary, fresh fish fans know this is the place to experiment. With names like Potato Bug (cucumber and freshwater eel inside-out roll); Tootsie Roll (deep-fried halibut wrapped in soybean paper); and deliciously innovative starters (scallop carpaccio with blood orange vinaigrette or steamed monkfish liver), these inventions clearly push the limits of tradition. To get your slurp on, sip on a premium sake from their impressive collection.

Kabuto

Japanese 

C2

5121 Geary Blvd. (bet. 15th & 16th Aves.)

Phone: 415-752-5652 Lunch Mon – Sat
Web: www.kabutosushi.com Dinner nightly
Prices: $$

Named for a helmet worn by the noble samurai, Kabuto is dead serious about sushi. Here, seafood arrives from Tokyo's Tsukiji Fish Market daily to land beneath the deft blade of these expert *itamae*. For the day's freshest catch, check the whiteboard and watch quietly at the blonde wood counter as the chef transforms simple fish into an artful sushi experience. Each bite is flavor-full, so do heed the occasional "no soy sauce" decree—sushi is best enjoyed without a scowl from the chef. The advice is worth obeying with such clever concoctions as yellowtail sushi topped with sliced pear and Kabuto's fruity mustard sauce; or the 16-20 Kiss, a wild ride with black tiger shrimp wrapped in avocado wrapped with marinated radish and kissed with chocolate sauce.

Kappou Gomi

Japanese

C1

5524 Geary Blvd. (bet. 19th & 20th Aves.)

Phone: 415-221-5353 Dinner Tue – Sun
Web: N/A
Prices: $$

Kappou Gomi feels a world away from the city's popular Japanese eateries and, as a sign in the window makes clear, seekers of bento boxes and trendy maki need not apply. This is one of San Francisco's rare *kappou* restaurants, which specializes in more delicate and authentic food.

The small, subdued space features an extensive menu organized by ingredients and intricate preparations that draw a house full of Japanese diners. Look for such exotic dishes as *namayuba*, a salad of fresh favas in creamy soy skin; raw *tai* with pickled celery in chrysanthemum blossom dressing; and whole *aji tataki*. Once you've finished the fillets, the kitchen will deep-fry the head, bones, and tail for a crunchy finish. You won't find that at your local sushi hot spot!

Khan Toke Thai House

Thai

B2

5937 Geary Blvd. (bet. 23rd & 24th Aves.)

Phone: 415-668-6654 Dinner nightly
Web: N/A
Prices:

Word on the street is that Khan Toke offers *the* most unique Thai in SF. Surely this isn't a stretch given that guests relinquish their shoes at the door as is customary; and the "House's" décor screams authenticity by way of low carved tables frilled with diners seated on floor cushions, dangling their legs in sunken wells beneath. Wood paneling and carvings adorn the walls and faithful artifacts complete the exotic backdrop. In the same vein, diners can look forward to classic, shareable fare like *sur rong hai* (deliciously tender beef tips marinated in tamarind and finished with cilantro); *gaeng kheaw wan* (spicy green chicken curry with potatoes, sweet basil, and lush coconut); and *moo ga prou* (pork sautéed with scallions and splashed with chili sauce).

Koo

D3 — Japanese

408 Irving St. (bet. 5th & 6th Aves.)

Phone: 415-731-7077 — Dinner Tue – Sun
Web: www.sushikoo.com
Prices: $$

Koo is praised and preferred for its delicate tempura and pristine nigiri, but this local darling also advertises an array of maki which, although mighty innovative, are created for an American palate. Enter the pleasant wood-trimmed dining room, dotted with tight-knit tables and hints of classic Japanese architecture, to find a cool Richmond set engrossed in their traditional nightly specials.

Take your cue from here, and order off of the list of fresh fish before the droves in line deplete such specials as *saba tataki*, thin slices of mackerel dressed with scallion and ponzu; top-notch nigiri topped with expertly cut and sourced fish; and an U2 roll filled with lacy shrimp tempura, creamy avocado, and crowned with spicy tuna and tobiko beads.

Mandalay

D1 — Burmese

4348 California St. (bet. 5th & 6th Aves.)

Phone: 415-386-3895 — Lunch & dinner daily
Web: www.mandalaysf.com
Prices: ⊜

Mandalay lays claim to being the oldest Burmese restaurant in the city. The cuisine draws inspiration from the country's borders with China and India; and their flavors will leave you wholly fulfilled. Crowding a large, kitschy dining room (picture a range of holiday decorations that hang year-round) are familiar fans, so be prepared to wait for a table.

An expansive menu puts you in the mood for similar food. Lovers of the subcontinent will find plenty to please their palates here, reveling in such tantalizing creations as a tea leaf salad—a virtual cacophony of flavor with tea leaves, toasted lentil seeds, ground shrimp, garlic, peppers, and peanuts. For something completely unique, try the Rainbow salad made up of twenty intriguing ingredients.

Marnee Thai

Thai

1243 9th Ave. (bet. Irving St. & Lincoln Way)

Phone: 415-731-9999 Lunch & dinner daily
Web: www.marneethaisf.com
Prices: $$

The city's food field may be packed, but Marnee Thai stands tall with its authentic array of affordable, fresh, and creative Thai tidbits. Within an earshot of Golden Gate Park, stroll past the anonymous façade and into a snug dining room coupled with gracious service and creative food. Dodge the rumbling open kitchen by grabbing a seat in the back where curvy orange tabletops with dainty orchids evoke a bit of Siam.

The exotic menu includes mildly spiced angel wings with a chili-garlic sauce; golden triangles laden with pumpkin, potato, and curry in crispy wrappers; and palate-pleasing *pad kee mao*, pan-fried noodles tossed with thinly sliced beef, chili, garlic, tomato, and basil. Vegetarians frolic in the inventive and tasty selection of dishes.

Mayflower

Chinese 

6255 Geary Blvd. (at 27th Ave.)

Phone: 415-387-8338 Lunch & dinner daily
Web: www.mayflower-seafood.com
Prices: $$

Take a hint from the hungry hoards lining the sidewalk for early morning weekend dim sum—they know what's what. Scrumptious Cantonese, speedy service, and densely packed quarters are how it's done here at Mayflower, one of three locations in the Bay Area.

Super fresh seafood is their specialty, so settle into closely spaced banquet tables and dig into steamed surf clams flavored with green onions and soy; or salt- and pepper-crusted shrimp so fresh they still may be quivering. Not in the mood for ocean gems? Roll up your sleeves for an array of meaty bites like steamed buns packed with roasted sweet-and-salty pork; sticky rice noodle rolls stuffed with beef, ginger, cilantro, and splashed with soy; or plump and hearty black sesame dumplings.

Old Mandarin Islamic 

Chinese

3132 Vicente St. (bet. 42nd & 43rd Aves.)

Phone: 415-564-3481
Web: N/A
Prices:

Lunch Fri – Mon & Wed
Dinner nightly

At first glance, Old Mandarin Islamic may seem like a generic Chinese mainstay with a no-frills décor of carpeted floors and mirrored walls. With further scrutiny, you will find that it is in fact anything but average. This little sanctum dedicates itself to Halal Chinese food, following the Islamic dietary code, yet there is no lack of flavor in these boldly seasoned and truly delicious Mandarin dishes.

Lamb is clearly a favorite here and plays the lead in their signature lamb stir-fried in hot oil with cumin seeds and fresh chili paste. True spice-heads will relish the extremely hot pepper chicken with pickled chilies, garlic, and scallions; while flour dumplings sautéed with vegetables in silky garlic sauce are uniquely chewy and deeply flavored.

Park Chow

American

1240 9th Ave. (bet. Irving St. & Lincoln Way)

Phone: 415-665-9912
Web: www.chowfoodbar.com
Prices: $$

Lunch & dinner daily

Welcome to Park Chow, the inner Sunset neighborhood joint where you can truly have it your way. In the mood for spicy Thai noodles tossed with cilantro and peanuts? You got it. Wild mushroom *pizzette* with chewy crust and thyme? Sure thing. Pork chops, deviled eggs, and home-baked coconut cream pie? (You get the picture.)

With such a diverse menu and an equally eclectic staff, Park Chow succeeds at pleasing everyone. A crackling fire warms the homey, two-story spot where a retractable roof lets the sunshine in. Daily sandwiches come with soup or fries for just $10 at lunch, and healthy salads are bountiful. There's even a menu of pint-sized burgers and chicken strips for the kiddos to fuel up before a walk in Golden Gate Park, just a block away.

Pasion

D3

737 Irving St. (bet. 8th & 9th Aves.)

Phone: 415-742-5727 — Lunch Sat – Sun
Web: www.pasionsf.com — Dinner nightly
Prices: $$

In a neighborhood loved for authentic international flavors, Pasion is causing a stir with Latin American ingredients and an ambience as fiery as the food. But while the name suggests a sultry vibe, couples seeking romance may be met with a boisterous after-work scene: squeeze into the bar for an alluring drink and get ready to make a night of it. Luckily, the kitchen has just the thing to pair with that pisco sour.

Helmed by Chef/owner Jose Calvo-Perez of the popular Peruvian restaurant Fresca, Pasion serves zesty ceviches alongside more creative items. Belly up to bold lamb *albondigas* with Manchego cheese and chilies in a savory foie gras broth, or a double-cut pork chop in mango-cilantro sauce. Duck confit empanadas are ideal for sharing at the bar.

Pizzetta 211

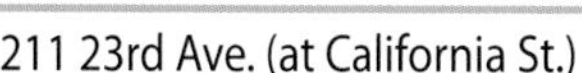

B1

211 23rd Ave. (at California St.)

Phone: 415-379-9880 — Lunch & dinner daily
Web: www.pizzetta211.com
Prices: ⊜

Thin-crust devotees continue to pack this quaint, stripped-down pizzeria hideaway with limited indoor seats at a premium on a cool day—though a few sidewalk tables help accommodate the overflow. No one is pampered here: place an order at the counter, pick up your utensils, napkins, and grab a seat during the five short minutes before the pizza arrives.

The serious staff is "pie-sexual," their focus exudes Neapolitan pheromones. *Pizzettas* change almost as quickly as they cook and reveal specials like butternut squash, sage, brown butter, and ricotta; or farm egg, pancetta, fontina, and green tomato. The menu takes pride in supporting local farmers and its stalwart pies may reveal rosemary, *fiore sardo*, and pine nuts; or tomato, mascarpone, and *olio verde*.

The Richmond

American

D2

615 Balboa St. (bet. 7th and 8th Aves.)

Phone: 415-379-8988 — Dinner Mon – Sat
Web: www.therichmondsf.com
Prices: $$

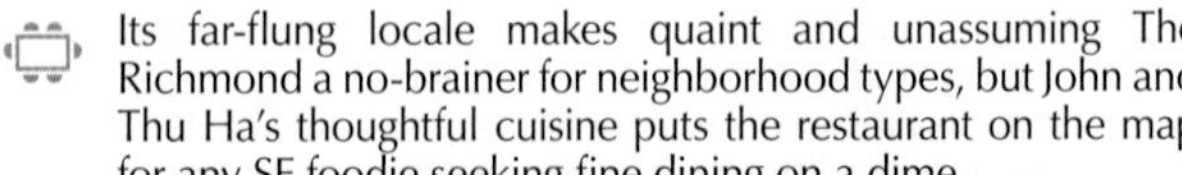

Its far-flung locale makes quaint and unassuming The Richmond a no-brainer for neighborhood types, but John and Thu Ha's thoughtful cuisine puts the restaurant on the map for any SF foodie seeking fine dining on a dime.

After visiting the de Young Museum or Academy of Sciences in Golden Gate Park a few blocks south, head to The Richmond for a five-course tasting menu for less than $50. À la carte offerings are available for those who prefer to steer their own course, including crab cakes with smooth avocado purée or poached yellowfin tuna. A highball of coffee semifreddo is a sweet and speedy cap to the meal. Pine wine crates that double as wall panels and bar tops remind of the rewards of dining here: good wines by the glass start around $7.

Sichuan Home

Chinese

C2

5037 Geary Blvd. (bet. 14th & 15th Aves.)

Phone: 415-221-3288 — Lunch & dinner daily
Web: N/A
Prices: $$

This no-frills Chinese "home" is a cherished sanctum among locals craving flavorful Sichuan food. The décor may be basic and a touch dated, yet the place is packed and guests are willing to wait it out for a table—they know the food is always worth it.

Meals start with spicy pickled cabbage and proceed to dishes copiously sized and boldly flavored. If on offer, try the chef's special fish: flaky fillets stewed in a tangy, garlicky broth filled with mustard greens and noodles. Then move onto stir-fried lamb infused with toasted cumin and numbingly delicious dried red chilies; or spicy beef short ribs imbued with caramelized garlic. You can't miss the excellent duck swimming in a beer sauce fragrant with smoky chili oil, star anise, and sliced rice cakes.

Sutro's

A2

Californian

1090 Point Lobos Ave. (at Ocean Beach)

Phone: 415-386-3330 Lunch & dinner daily
Web: www.cliffhouse.com
Prices: $$$

Care to dine while gazing at the glorious Pacific? Make your way to Sutro's during daylight hours and snag any seat—tables are arranged to face a serene wall of windows, offering stunning views of the ocean. Housed on the lower level of the Cliff House, reservations are necessary here, so plan in advance. Dine on Dungeness crab cakes generously filled with fresh meat, over Cara Cara oranges and shaved fennel salad dressed in tangy vinaigrette; or pistachio-crusted scallops and orange-glazed pork belly with parsnip purée, butternut squash, and red wine syrup.

Be sure to save room for one (or two) of the outstanding desserts, as in the divinely rich butterscotch *pot de crème* garnished with a lacey and buttery tuile, inflused with *garam masala*.

Troya

D1

Mediterranean

349 Clement St. (at 5th Ave.)

Phone: 415-379-6000 Lunch & dinner daily
Web: www.troyasf.com
Prices: $$

The face that launched a thousand ships also inspired one of the city's great Mediterranean eateries. Troya is named in honor of the fabled city Troy and the icons that perished in her wake. Although she lives in a locale largely overrun by East Asian cuisine, Troya excels in simple Greek and Turkish mezes.

This window-lined sanctum is perfect for people-watching. Relax with beautifully golden and flavorful falafel set atop hummus, *tzatziki*, and spicy tomato sauce; tender lamb *shish* kebabs; or, on a foggy day, a steaming crock of moussaka crowned with a béchamel brûlée. In lieu of the expected baklava, try the flaky nightingale's nest: a walnut-stuffed phyllo pastry with vanilla ice cream, pistachios, and honey. Check out Troya's new sib on Fillmore.

SoMa

Peek behind the unassuming doors of the often-gritty façades prevalent in SoMa, the neighborhood South of Market, and discover a trove of creative talent. While you won't find a flood of sidewalk cafés and storefronts ubiquitous to more obviously charming enclaves, SoMa divulges gobs of riches (from artistic diamonds in the rough to megawatt culinary gems) for the tenacious urban treasure seeker.

Residential Mix

A diverse stomping ground that defies definition at every corner, SoMa is often labeled "industrial" for its hodgepodge of converted warehouse lofts. Or, with a mixed troupe of artists, photographers, architects, dancers, and designers now occupying much of SoMa's post-industrial real estate, you might also call it "artsy." In reality, dynamic SoMa wears many faces: Youths in concert tees navigate their skateboards around the pitfalls of constant construction, fueled by "Gibraltars" from cult classic **Blue Bottle Café**. Sports fans of a different sort converge for Giants baseball and sandwiches at **Crazy Crab'z** in AT&T Park. In the Sixth Street Corridor, an immigrant population enjoys tastes of home at such authentic dives as **Tu Lan**, the Vietnamese hole-in-the-wall favored by the late Julia Child. Just blocks away, a towering crop of luxury condominiums draws a trendy yuppie set keen to scoop up modern European furnishings at the SF Design Center and dine at equally slick restaurants—think of **Roe**, which doubles as an after-hours nightclub.

Arts and Eats

Since SoMa is perhaps most notable for its arts scene, this is also home to the San Francisco Museum of Modern Art, countless galleries, Yerba Buena Center for the Arts, and the unique Daniel Libeskind-designed Contemporary Jewish Museum. Thus, neighborhood foodies crave stylish culinary experiences to match their well-rounded worlds. Art and design play a key role in the district's most distinctive dining and nightlife venues; and naturally, the neighborhood is fast welcoming new and avant-garde restaurant concepts. Not far from the Jewish Museum, is **Mint Plaza**—step into this charming gathering spot for a bite, perhaps a respite, or to simply read a book. Post-dinner, art evangelists hit **111 Minna**, a gallery turned late-night DJ bar, or the chic wine lounge **Press Club** for its first-rate array of Californian wines and beers. Down the street, **Ducca** plays on a Venetian theme with a luscious lounge and whimsical paintings of the ducal couple. Speaking of Ducca, the restaurant inside the Westin Market Street, hip hotel restaurants and bars are supremely prolific in SoMa, in part because of its proximity to the Moscone Convention Center. While there are a number of upscale watering holes to choose from, a batch of casual joints has sprung up of late. **Custom Burger/Lounge**, at Best Western Americana, piles gourmet toppings such as Point Reyes Blue Cheese and black olive tapenade onto patties of Kobe beef, salmon, and lamb. **Perry's**, the "meet market" made famous in Armistead Maupin's *Tales of the City*, is enjoying a second home in the upscale boutique Hotel Griffon on Steuart Street. On the lobby level of the InterContinental San Francisco, **Bar 888** pours more than 100 *grappe* to taste. SoMa is also home to a veritable buffet of well-known restaurants with famous toques at the helm. But the fact that these boldface names can also be found in the food court at the mall is testament to the area's democratic approach to food: There is high-quality cuisine to be had here at workaday prices. Likewise, wondrous things can be found between two slices of bread. Tom Colicchio's **'wichcraft** is a popular lunch spot among area professionals, and former Rubicon star Dennis Leary can actually be spotted slinging sandwiches at **The Sentinel**. Take a break from shopping at the Westfield San Francisco Centre to fuel up at **Buckhorn Grill**. This mini-chain was launched in the Bay Area and specializes in aged and marinated tri-tip, deliciously charred over a wood fire. For budget gourmands, SoMa brims with cheap eats. Westfield Centre houses an impressive food court with plenty of international options. Nearby, museumgoers can refuel with a fragrant cup of tea at **Samovar** or try a micro-brew beer at **Thirsty Bear Brewing Company**. Take a peaceful stroll around South Park, and make sure you stop by **Mexico au Parc**, where the *sopes* run out by noon. Ballpark denizens get their burger fix at brewpub **21st Amendment**, and **Citizen's Band** is renowned for its casual vibe and seasonal American fare.

Nightlife

This is all to say little of SoMa's buzzing nightlife, whose scene traverses the red carpet from sports bars to DJ bars, hotel lounges to ultra-lounges, and risqué dinner theater—think drag (at **AsiaSF**) to Dutch (the Amsterdam import **Supperclub** that serves a racy mixed plate of performance art and global cuisine in bed.) Oenophiles should definitely swing by **Terroir**, the witty little wine bar on Folsom that stocks more than 700 organic and old-world varietals. And, for more rowdy imbibing, **Bossa Nova** bursts with the flavors of Rio. Soak up your *cachaça*, SoMa-style, with a Nutella banana pancake from the 11th Street trailer, **Crêpes a Go-Go**.

SoMa
Hotel
Restaurant
NOB HILL
MARINA
CIVIC CENTER
MISSION
CHINATOWN
UNION SQUARE
TENDERLOIN
CIVIC CENTER
ASIAN ART MUSEUM
CITY HALL
UN PLAZA
SF PUBLIC LIBRARY
SF WAR MEMORIAL & PERFORMING ARTS CENTER
OLD MINT
Four Seasons
Bluestem Brasserie
Palomar
Fifth Floor
The Moss
Lark Creek Steak
54 Mint
Luce
AQ
Heaven's Dog
Una Pizza Napoletana
Basil Canteen
Bar Agricole
Manora's Thai Cuisine
Cathead's BBQ
Sushi Zone
Powell St
Civic Center
Van Ness
TUNNEL
MUNI
Jackson
Washington
Clay
Sacramento
California
Pine
Bush
Sutter
Post
Geary
O'Farrell
Ellis
Eddy
Turk
Golden Gate Ave.
McAllister
Fulton St.
Grove
Hayes
Fell
Oak
Page
Duboce Ave.
Polk
Larkin
Hyde
Leavenworth
Jones
Taylor
Mason
Powell
Stockton
Grant
Franklin
Gough
Van Ness Ave.
Octavia
Market
Mission
Howard
Folsom
Harrison
Bryant
Division St.
Valencia
McCoppin St.
Otis St.
Plum St.
Stevenson
Jessie
Minna
Natoma
Tehama
Clementina
Russ
Langton
Rausch St.
Dore
Brady
Kissling

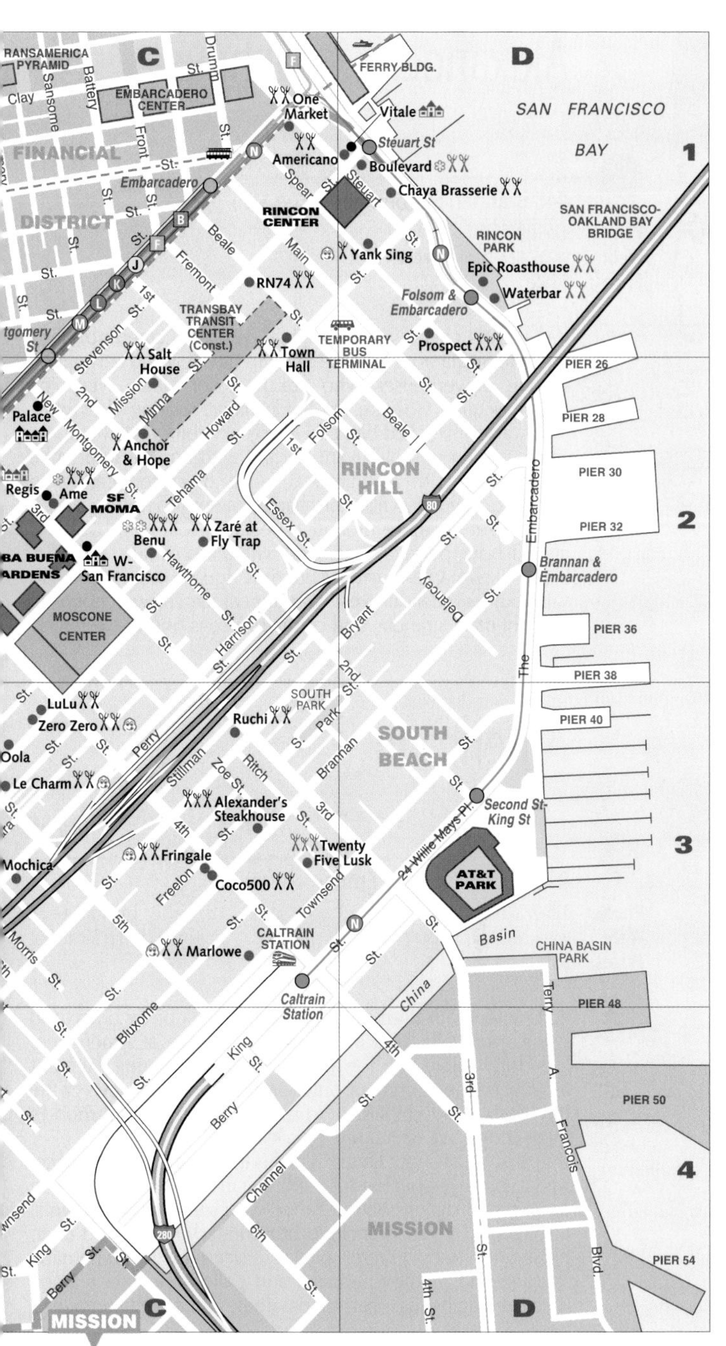

C
D
1
2
3
4
FERRY BLDG.
SAN FRANCISCO
BAY
FINANCIAL
DISTRICT
EMBARCADERO CENTER
RINCON CENTER
One Market
Vitale
Americano
Boulevard
Chaya Brasserie
Steuart St
Embarcadero
SAN FRANCISCO-OAKLAND BAY BRIDGE
RINCON PARK
Yank Sing
Epic Roasthouse
Waterbar
RN74
Folsom & Embarcadero
TRANSBAY TRANSIT CENTER (Const.)
TEMPORARY BUS TERMINAL
Prospect
Town Hall
Salt House
Palace
Anchor & Hope
RINCON HILL
Regis
Ame
SF MOMA
Benu
Zaré at Fly Trap
W-San Francisco
MOSCONE CENTER
Brannan & Embarcadero
PIER 26
PIER 28
PIER 30
PIER 32
PIER 36
PIER 38
PIER 40
PIER 48
PIER 50
PIER 54
LuLu
Zero Zero
Oola
Le Charm
Ruchi
SOUTH PARK
SOUTH BEACH
Alexander's Steakhouse
Twenty Five Lusk
Second St-King St
AT&T PARK
Fringale
Coco500
Mochica
Marlowe
CALTRAIN STATION
Caltrain Station
CHINA BASIN PARK
MISSION

Alexander's Steakhouse

448 Brannan St. (bet. 4th & Zoe Sts.)

Phone: 415-495-1111 Dinner nightly
Web: www.alexanderssteakhouse.com
Prices: $$$$

If you can't check out the original down in Cupertino, don't miss this SoMa sib. The three-level arena is a primo destination among powerhouses who are here for steak. Matching this masculine vibe are loft-like ceilings, soaring glass wine racks, a well-stocked bar, and a large exhibition kitchen.

Meals are an upscale event starting with an amuse-bouche and ending with a whimsical touch of cotton candy. In between, savor the likes of charred, smoky octopus, plated with sweet Japanese mountain peaches; followed by a wet aged T-bone perfectly balanced with a trio of salts and acid. Sides like maple-roasted butternut squash are known to sate, but a winter "harvest" of oatmeal ice cream, chocolate fondant cake, granola, and crème brûlée is bound to delight.

Americano

8 Mission St. (at The Embarcadero)

Phone: 415-278-3777 Lunch Mon – Fri
Web: www.americanorestaurant.com Dinner Mon – Sat
Prices: $$$

Follow the path from frat pack to the FiDi corner office and you'll eventually land in the circular lounge at Americano, the Hotel Vitale hub for happy hour-loving young execs. A lengthy bar and gorgeous outdoor patio boasting views of the Bay Bridge and Embarcadero make this the neighborhood's most conducive restaurant for cocktailing.

But, it isn't just about libations at this trendy, au courant space. Keep your eyes peeled for solid Italian fare presented in an earth-toned dining room. Crafted with seasonal ingredients, tasty crowd pleasers include bruschetta with roasted pear, prosciutto, and *burrata*; pizza *salsiccia* with homemade sausage and piquillo peppers; and grilled ahi tuna teamed with shelling beans, charred tomatoes, and olive tapenade.

Ame ✿

Contemporary

C2

689 Mission St. (at 3rd St.)

Phone: 415-284-4040 Dinner nightly
Web: www.amerestaurant.com
Prices: $$$

Joe Fletcher

It is no surprise that most diners here enter through the St. Regis Hotel lobby entrance—Ame is understandably popular among hotel guests. Beyond the small sashimi bar, find the main dining room and long exhibition kitchen framed by a deep red accent wall and high, dramatic ceilings. Soft lighting and floor-to-ceiling windows dressed in gauzy striped curtains complete the agreeable setting. It may have a corporate edge, but this is balanced by a smattering of couples enjoying a romantic meal out.

The professional (but not overly formal) staff is friendly and shows clear knowledge of each menu item. In addition to the two tasting menus–one for the sashimi bar and the other a broader "Taste of Ame"–the ample feast may begin with such starters as superbly seasoned triangles of *za'atar*-spiced flatbread toast points with a sprinkle of fresh mint sprigs and a mound of chopped yellowfin tuna tartare. This can be followed by pan-roasted halibut over potato gnocchi sauced with a red wine nage and outrageously delicious little mushroom crisps.

To finish, try the rich and flavorful pumpkin crème caramel; or perhaps the creamy, wonderfully nutty, and subtly sweet white sesame blancmange.

Anchor & Hope

Seafood

C2

83 Minna St. (bet. 1st & 2nd Sts.)

Phone: 415-501-9100
Web: www.anchorandhopesf.com
Prices: $$$

Lunch Mon – Fri
Dinner nightly

A maritime theme hangs in the salty air and conjures an east coast seaside shack at Anchor & Hope, sister restaurant to Salt House and Town Hall. This converted early 1900's auto shop now echoes a warehouse on the wharf, with thick ropes hanging from the high-pitched ceiling while a mounted garfish keeps a watchful eye. Like any bustling pier, Anchor & Hope is a boisterous place to dock.

Still, everyone is here for seafood. Blackboards boast the day's fresh oysters and shellfish, while a classic shrimp cocktail or apple-ginger cured salmon tartare are tasty starts. At lunch, try a tuna melt with Gruyère and tomato confit or Smithwicks beer-battered cod with rosemary potato wedges. Finish with a caramel mousse bar with chewy nougat.

AQ

Contemporary

B3

1085 Mission St. (bet. 6th & 7th Sts.)

Phone: 415-341-9000
Web: www.aq-sf.com
Prices: $$$

Lunch Sun
Dinner Tue – Sun

The much-hyped AQ continues to thrive as a popular spot for foodies in the 'hood. It may have a loft-like appearance with large windows draped in green curtains and an open kitchen, but this spot reinvents itself seasonally in design, décor, and menu. Even the staff undergoes a dress change.

High-topped tables are usually heaped with a spring menu of fresh chive blossoms presented with brioche croutons, and a slow-poached egg drizzled with pea purée. If that doesn't delight you, venison tartare layered like a Jenga tower with toasted bread strips, pickled mustard seeds, and coffee grounds; or an updated take on braised lamb shoulder with roasted heirloom carrots will do the trick. To close, caramel popcorn and sponge cake make for a winning combo.

Bar Agricole

Californian

355 11th St. (bet. Folsom & Harrison Sts.)

Phone: 415-355-9400 — Lunch Sun
Web: www.baragricole.com — Dinner nightly
Prices: $$

Bar Agricole is coveted, especially for Sunday brunch. Settled in SoMa, this warehouse-like set features rough concrete surfaces, stacked plank walls, and skylights framed by sculptural glass "curtains" that hang like art installations.

Revered as a foodie haven for its menu of shareable small plates, diners come in droves to sample crispy rye toast points layered with rich salmon gravlax, horseradish crème fraîche, and shallots, finished with a tasty micro herb garnish; or tender lamb shoulder laid beside roasted eggplant, crumbled feta, and a fried egg trickled with an herb-rich pesto. Dinner unveils an *agri-cool* spread of roasted chicken with squash blossoms and tomatillo, thrillingly finished with a lavender meringue-capped lemon-ricotta tart.

Basil Canteen

Thai XX

1489 Folsom St. (at 11th St.)

Phone: 415-552-3963 — Lunch Mon – Fri
Web: www.basilthai.com — Dinner nightly
Prices: $$

Basil Canteen is a pioneer of sorts in the former Jackson Brewery landmark building. This voluminous Thai restaurant keeps company with its surrounds by sporting an industrial look through brick walls, oversized windows, metal stairs, and rising ceilings. Find a communal table downstairs and a smattering of smaller seats on the upstairs mezzanine.

Groups of suits at lunch and locals by night come for the likes of *pau pia yuan*, paper-thin rolls of crunchy cucumber, bean sprouts, herbs, and shrimp in lime vinaigrette; and sizzling drunken beef with Kaffir lime, chili, and lemongrass. The *kang kua goong*, sweet prawns and tender chunks of Japanese pumpkin stewed in red coconut curry, is at once spicy, creamy, tangy, and absolutely delicious.

Benu ✿✿

C2

22 Hawthorne St. (bet. Folsom & Howard Sts.)

Phone: 415-685-4860 Dinner Tue – Sat
Web: www.benusf.com
Prices: $$$$

Benu

Benu is a restaurant that flaunts its distinct aesthetic and personality: everything here is angular, modern, and minimalist. Decorative accents seem to explore the grayscale, from the dark laminated tables to low-backed seats and banquettes. Even the teapots and columns have angles. Still, the lively crowd is hip yet sophisticated, and well-managed service is pleasant and approachable.

The creative, Asian-influenced menu follows suit with its offering of gorgeous, modernist, and minimalist dishes. Hand-pulled mozzarella might be bathed in a spicy, viscous, and dynamic house-made XO sauce, then topped with crispy ham and micro-basil—sublime and yet bold. An extraordinary fermented red pepper sauce again captures the palate when served with a Hokkaido sea cucumber stuffed with shrimp farce, cucumber balls, and onion purée. Other dishes might highlight Cantonese style, as in the blue crab rice porridge with truffles, layers of pickled ginger, and a quartered "thousand year-old quail egg" all enriched with egg white sauce and ringed with red vinegar.

Desserts are equally ambitious, as in a creamy strawberry sorbet over tangy yuzu *espuma* and crumbles of flash-frozen white chocolate.

Bluestem Brasserie

American XX

B2

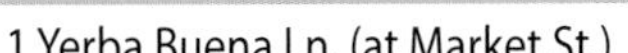

1 Yerba Buena Ln. (at Market St.)

Phone: 415-547-1111 — Lunch & dinner daily
Web: www.bluestembrasserie.com
Prices: $$

Bluestem Brasserie is a pleasant haunt that welcomes a blend of business folk and wandering tourists from nearby Market Street. The voluminous space features loft-like ceilings, a sweeping staircase, and a lounge frequented for after-work cocktails.

The somewhat bumbling service doesn't quite match the classy vibe, but it's nothing that a menu rife with the best of Californian ingredients can't fix. Start with an arugula salad with grilled sweet corn, fresh apricots, and goat's milk cheese, tossed in a Meyer lemon *citronette*. Barbecue-spiced chicken is super juicy bathed in a fragrant garlic-rosemary jus; while dessert is a successful pairing of butterscotch-tapioca pudding with a salty-smoky bacon butter cookie shaped like a...you guessed it...pig!

Cathead's BBQ

Barbecue X

A4

1665 Folsom St. (bet. 12th & 13th Sts.)

Phone: 415-861-4242 — Lunch & dinner Wed – Mon
Web: www.catheadsbbq.com
Prices: ⊜

A bright red building as bold as its barbecue and as fiery as its habanero sauce could only be Cathead's. This hot spot has already generated quite a buzz, so expect to wait in line. After ordering and paying, take a seat—preferably at the counter which offers the best views of the brick smokers. The space is small, making takeout big business here.

The menu features barbecue delights, plus locally inspired items like cornmeal-crusted tofu, or a creamy dandelion-and-potato salad. But really, you're here for the meat combo starring St. Louis ribs, slow-smoked pulled pork, delicious sweet tea BBQ chicken, and Coca-Cola-smoked brisket. Sides (purple cabbage-habanero slaw or pimento mac and cheese) are so tasty you'll wish they were a meal on their own.

Boulevard ✿

Californian XX

D1

1 Mission St. (at Steuart St.)

Phone: 415-543-6084 — Lunch Mon – Fri
Web: www.boulevardrestaurant.com — Dinner nightly
Prices: **$$$**

Boulevard

An historic building, waterfront dining, and years of local admiration are just a few of the hallmarks of this stalwart restaurant. Embracing a unique décor, Boulevard feels like something of a Belle Époque beauty capable of making the most of each handsome detail. Head-spinning accents include pale brick-arched ceilings, iron beams, stained glass, and banquettes booked by those in the know. From the warm welcome to your attentive departure, the staff is swift and ensures an extraordinary experience at this true SoMa destination.

On the menu, Boulevard is widely appealing with a distinctively Californian, ingredient-driven fare that manages brilliant consistency. Many creations are both classic and smart, like a risotto daintily sweetened with butternut squash, salty with *guanciale*, and earthy with pine nut relish. Chef Nancy Oakes' refined hand is delightfully evident in the herb-flavored and wood oven-roasted flat-iron pork, teamed with lightly fried shavings of Brussels sprouts and an ultra-smooth chestnut purée.

Desserts can be playful, interesting, and downright nostalgic renditions of rich *caramello* brownies with *sasparilla* ice cream, root beer sorbet, and bits of salted honeycomb.

Chaya Brasserie

Fusion XX

132 The Embarcadero (bet. Howard & Mission Sts.)

Phone: 415-777-8688 — Lunch Sun – Fri
Web: www.thechaya.com — Dinner nightly
Prices: $$$

Few evening views can top these of the twinkling Bay Bridge, so grab a table at the front of the dining room against the window to secure this picturesque scene. Inside, find steel beams and leather banquettes fashioning a perfectly comfortable ambience for their crowds of local business people gathering here. Contemporary Asian art reflects the Japanese-influenced fare.

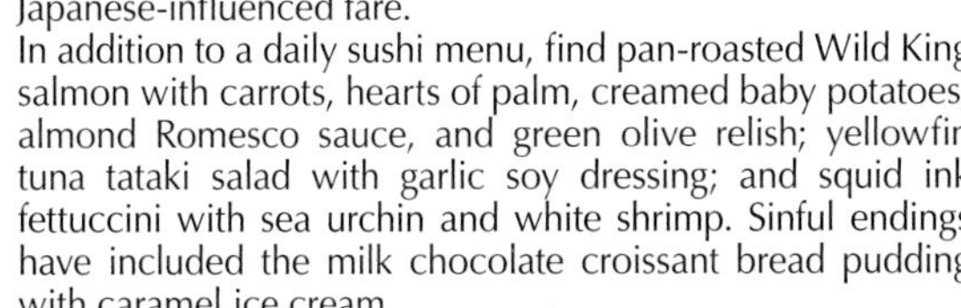

In addition to a daily sushi menu, find pan-roasted Wild King salmon with carrots, hearts of palm, creamed baby potatoes, almond Romesco sauce, and green olive relish; yellowfin tuna tataki salad with garlic soy dressing; and squid ink fettuccini with sea urchin and white shrimp. Sinful endings have included the milk chocolate croissant bread pudding with caramel ice cream.

Coco500

Californian XX

500 Brannan St. (at 4th St.)

Phone: 415-543-2222 — Lunch Mon – Fri
Web: www.coco500.com — Dinner Mon – Sat
Prices: $$

In an area that abounds with grab-and-go spots, Coco500 remains a cherished establishment. With a light-filled dining room decorated with a blue-tiled bar, modern accents, and friendly service, this place attracts a classic blend of Blackberries by day and local residents for dinner.

The kitchen cobbles a Californian menu rife with local, seasonal ingredients, homemade pastas, and wood-fired pizzas. There are small dishes for sharing, like flatbread topped with grated Parmesan melted into mushroom *duxelles* and drizzles of truffle oil; or a memorable ricotta cavatelli tossed in a herb-rich lamb bolognaise studded with fresh peas and torn mint leaves. A Meyer lemon semifreddo served with poppy seed-studded shortbread begs the question, one spoon or two?

Epic Roasthouse

D1 **Steakhouse** XX

369 The Embarcadero (at Folsom St.)

Phone: 415-369-9955 Lunch Wed – Sun
Web: www.epicroasthousesf.com Dinner nightly
Prices: $$$

With a name like Epic, it's a safe bet that this ravishing roasthouse is a thrilling endeavor. Situated on the iconic Embarcadero with matchless views of the Bay Bridge, Epic is a massive and pricey tourist attraction. Exposed pipes and ductwork are inspired by a saltwater pump house that battled the fires of the 1906 quake; however, leather banquettes, plush carpets, and a fireplace lend an air of classic comfort. This is just the ambience you'd want for imbibing a full-bodied merlot with your filet of beef, seasoned with salt and pepper and garnished with glazed baby carrots. Don't forget the sides! Garlic oil and red chili flakes add smoke to grilled *broccolini*, and the scent of truffle adds that *je ne sais quoi* to buttery whipped potatoes.

Fifth Floor

B2 **Contemporary** XXX

12 4th St. (at Market St.)

Phone: 415-348-1555 Dinner Tue – Sat
Web: www.fifthfloorrestaurant.com
Prices: $$$$

Elegantly set on the fifth floor of Hotel Palomar, it seems only fitting that beautiful Fifth Floor's bar and lounge is well-loved by corporate barons and other ritzy revelers. The adjacent dining room is sedate and outfitted with drum lights casting a sultry glow on inlaid wood floors, leather armchairs, and a lavish wine cellar.

A casual dining experience can be had amidst the refined servers and wood tables dressed with sparkling silverware. Such flush accessories keep fine company with contemporary plates of oysters done five ways (béarnaise, caviar, rouille, cucumber, chowder, and mignonette); Mendocino uni flan wth Dungeness crab "fondue" and saffron; lamb married with rye berries, pickled raisins, and yogurt; and a milk chocolate mousse bombe.

54 Mint

Italian

16 Mint Plaza (at Jessie St.)

Phone: 415-543-5100 — Lunch Mon – Fri
Web: www.54mint.com — Dinner Mon – Sat
Prices: $$

On the patio at 54 Mint, suspend all disbelief and imagine yourself on a Roman piazza, shaded by historic architecture and ginkgo trees—that is, if you can get past the sketchy surrounds on Fifth and Mission streets. Named for the Old Mint building, Mint Plaza is an outdoor expanse showcasing fresh flowers, artisanal coffee and, of course, homemade pastas to savor with a glass of *vino*.

This casual trattoria serves rustic fare made from primo ingredients: organic potato gnocchi are tossed in a hearty and aromatic beef ragù ; while a char-grilled skirt steak is served with sauteed broccoli rabe and a drizzle of olive oil. Those impressed with the ingredients may take some home; the space is stocked with mouthwatering Italian groceries for purchase.

Fringale 

French

570 4th St. (bet. Brannan & Bryant Sts.)

Phone: 415-543-0573 — Lunch Tue – Fri
Web: www.fringalesf.com — Dinner nightly
Prices: $$

Housed in a cheery yellow building on SoMa's restaurant-lined Fourth Street, unassuming Fringale is just the sort of intimate bistro this neighborhood needs: petite, hospitable, utterly charming, and delicious every time. The menu satisfies with authentic Basque cuisine and a decidedly French accent. A perfect beginning is found in the spicy Monterey calamari grilled *a la plancha* with *piment d'espelette* and briny olives. Other bistro favorites might include crispy duck confit paired with French lentils, salty bacon, and drizzled with a tangy red wine sauce; sautéed prawns in Pastis; and heart-warming daily specials like bœuf Bourguignon.

For dessert, try Mme. Angèle's gâteau Basque, a buttery almond torte filled with custard cream.

Heaven's Dog

Chinese 

B3

1148 Mission St. (bet. 7th & 8th Sts.)

Phone: 415-863-6008 Dinner nightly
Web: www.heavensdog.com
Prices: $$

This somewhat desolate stretch of Mission Street may seem an odd destination for happy hour, but Heaven's Dog brings it with a quirky vibe–think sleek banquettes and canine art–and inventive alcoholic creations such as the Shanghai Buck, a piquant concoction of Pompero Aniversario rum with fresh pressed ginger.

Cocktailers, of course, will need a bite to eat and few will complain about the contemporary Asian fare dreamed up by Chef/owner Charles Phan—that's right, of Slanted Door fame. Phan's clever take on Chinese cooking brings wonderfully sticky-salty, hoisin-glazed pork tossed in a steamed bun, as well as sweet-and-sour-and-spicy tiger prawns with Thai basil and a fresh twist of pineapple. On warm nights, check out the street-front patio.

Lark Creek Steak

Steakhouse

B2

845 Market St. (bet. 4th & 5th Sts.)

Phone: 415-593-4100 Lunch & dinner daily
Web: www.larkcreeksteak.com
Prices: $$$

Easily the best steak you will find in a mall, Lark Creek Steak is set off the rotunda on the fourth floor of the Westfield Centre, and allures savvy shoppers who come to splurge on sales and great steak. Farm-fresh American fare and a wine list add up to this perfect respite from rifling through the racks at Nordstrom.

Local farms and ranches provide many of the ingredients for the kitchen's seasonal à la carte menu, among which the hearty grass-fed beef and free-range chicken are best. Items like oxtail consommé bobbing with wild mushroom tortellini lead to heartier mains like a Porterhouse for two with roasted baby carrots. The "Famous" butterscotch pudding with Chantilly cream will furnish the sugar rush needed for a few more hours of shopping.

Le Charm

French

315 5th St. (bet. Folsom & Shipley Sts.)

Phone: 415-546-6128 Dinner Tue – Sun
Web: www.lecharm.com
Prices: $$

Le charm of this high-ceilinged spot featuring walls lined with trellised vines; a mini copper bar set off the foyer; and large, wiry chandelier is truly everlasting. Butcher paper-topped tables cluster together in a dining room dressed with persimmon and caramel walls, and the open kitchen offers a perfect respite to both French expats on a budget and novices to the cuisine that everyone will appreciate.

Ubiquitous offerings include a pan-seared Loch Duarte salmon served with French green lentils and a fennel-watercress salad; and profiteroles—crème puffs filled with vanilla ice cream and served with chocolate sauce.

For more variety, opt for the 3-course dinner for $32. Live jazz on the patio every Thursday night merely adds to the allure of Le Charm.

LuLu

Mediterranean 

816 Folsom St. (bet 4th & 5th Sts.)

Phone: 415-495-5775 Lunch & dinner daily
Web: www.restaurantlulu.com
Prices: $$

Visitors traveling to SF in packs or locals hosting the whole family for a weekend on the town should head to this SoMa mainstay with enough space (and an ample bar) to accommodate an entire army. Arched ceilings cap a voluminous interior that is as amenable to business lunches as large scale celebrations, and the Provençal fare is served family style to guarantee a convivial good time.

A roaring rotisserie and wood-burning pizza oven draw the eye into the exhibition kitchen, where seasonal ingredients are king. Thin-crust pizzas may be topped with slices of spring asparagus, while fresh field greens with tangy vinaigrette accompany a bison burger on a green onion bun. Don't miss out on such hearty side dishes as earthy, roasted *kabocha* squash.

Luce ✿

Contemporary XXX

888 Howard St. (at 5th St.)

Phone: 415-616-6566 Lunch & dinner daily
Web: www.lucewinerestaurant.com
Prices: $$$

Mark Leet

Native San Franciscans may eschew Luce for its sharp looks, thinking that this ground-floor dining room is best left to guests sequestered in the soaring glass and steel tower that is the Hotel Intercontinental, but that would mean missing out on the truly exemplary cuisine, especially at dinner.

Make your way through the lobby and bypass Bar 888's buzzing scene for Luce's more modern setting that combines marble inlaid floors, filtered light, a neutral palette, and spherical, smoky glass chandeliers. The service members are proper yet refreshingly engaging.

Under the helm of Chef Daniel Corey, Luce's menu weaves together classic French technique with international influences while giving serious attention to seasonality. Dinner has yielded succulent diver scallops paired with Monterey abalone afloat in Meyer lemon-zested duck consommé; and slow-roasted guinea hen fashioned into a gorgeously crisp-skinned roulade accompanied by strawberries–unripe, garnet, and powdered–with sea spinach, capped by an uni emulsion. Desserts can be daringly impressive, as in the extraordinary slate of ebony-dark chocolate olive oil génoise cubes, white chocolate-olive oil ganache, and chocolate ice cream.

Manora's Thai Cuisine

Thai

A4

1600 Folsom St. (at 12th St.)

Phone: 415-861-6224 — Lunch Mon – Fri
Web: www.manorathai.com — Dinner nightly
Prices: 

Large appetite, small budget? Grab your loose change and get your growling belly to Manora's, where bountiful portions of tasty Thai keep locals coming in herds. Quick service and super cheap specials (soup, fried rice, and two main courses for under 9 bucks) make this a go-to spot for lunch, though dinner lingers in this league. Start off with a bowl of creamy *gai tom ka*, a tangy, traditional Thai soup of coconut milk, lemon, and cilantro quivering with tender chunks of stewed chicken. Next, order up a plate of scrumptious garlic pork–marinated and char-grilled to tender perfection–or the *gai kraprao*, a stir-fry of ground chicken, chili, garlic, and fresh basil.

Quench your thirst with a tall glass of creamy Thai iced-tea—a cool remedy for a warm day.

Marlowe

Californian

330 Townsend St., Ste. 230 (bet. 4th & 5th Sts.)

Phone: 415-974-5599 — Lunch Mon – Fri
Web: www.marlowesf.com — Dinner Mon – Sat
Prices: **$$**

This attractive little SoMa spot is known and loved for its scene. In other words, reservations are a must, though with some luck you may find a few open seats at their small "communal table." Marlowe's urban style has a rustic demeanor evident in its cozy arrangement of dark wood tables. The pleasant staff lends extra warmth to this lively haunt.

The menu is fun, creative, and has wide appeal with a lot of California and a bit of France. Starters may reveal Dungeness crab and rock shrimp in a *louie* bath. Most tables have a basket of fries that pair perfectly with the Marlowe burger crowned with cheddar, onions, and bacon. Desserts here are all the rage and layer on the decadence as in a silky *Tcho* chocolate cream pie, quaintly served in a glass jar.

Mochica

C3 Peruvian XX

937 Harrison St. (bet. 5th & 6th Sts.)

Phone: 415-278-0480 Lunch & dinner Wed – Mon
Web: www.mochicasf.com
Prices: $$

Mochica is the first of Chef Carlos Altamirano's three prized and popular Peruvian eateries in the Bay Area. Rich hues, slate floors and well-set communal tables offer a tasty glimpse through over-sized windows.

The belly-sating cuisine is nearly always perfectly prepared and flavorful, with tastes of authenticity in each bite. Meals here may begin with dishes such as the buttery corn cake, *pastelito choclo,* made with potato, *queso fresco,* and crunchy bits of Peruvian corn alongside salsa blanca and *sarsita d'choclo*; or *causa limena,* a ring of creamy mashed potatoes flavored with *aji amarillo* and lime juice topped with cilantro-marinated tiger shrimp. Tasty endings include a sweet *arroz con leche* drizzled with a deliciously dark purple fruit sauce.

One Market

C1 Californian XX

1 Market St. (at Steuart St.)

Phone: 415-777-5577 Lunch Mon – Fri
Web: www.onemarket.com Dinner Mon – Sat
Prices: $$

This appealing American brasserie sits on a corner opposite the Ferry Building with streetcars gliding past. Retro-feeling décor and high ceilings make this a loud and bustling place attractive to businessmen and tourists alike. Sit at the popular bar to view the lively kitchen or score one of the banquettes in the raised center area for optimal seating.

The large menu of seasonal fare, made with comfort in mind, may feature the signature dish of delicately flavored, smoked Tasmanian trout atop a crisp and golden brown potato cake with pancetta and a runny egg. Entrées such as thin links of house-made duck sausage in soy-based sauce with carrots may be followed by buttery chestnut torte with brown sugar and slices of Reisling-poached pear.

Oola

Californian

860 Folsom St. (bet. 4th & 5th Sts.)

Phone: 415-995-2061 Lunch Sun – Fri
Web: www.oola-sf.com Dinner nightly
Prices: $$

Long and narrow Oola is hugely sought after by corporate groups and after-work revelers for its stellar combo of tasty treats and quenching cocktails. Furnished with delightful bar seating in the front and an elevated dining area at the back, the restaurant is further beautified by sultry, low lighting, exposed brick walls, white bar stools, and contemporary-chic suede banquettes.

The food is the real draw here and may uncover a fresh salad of arugula, baby spinach, walnuts, and apple with tangy blue cheese dressing; and soy-glazed baby back ribs garnished with cilantro and served over a zesty red cabbage-apple slaw. Even a small plate of Swiss chard sautéed with salty pancetta, or a well-prepared vanilla crème brûlée will have you going *oo la la*!

Prospect

American

300 Spear St. (at Folsom St.)

Phone: 415-247-7770 Lunch Sun
Web: www.prospectsf.com Dinner nightly
Prices: $$$

Prospect is still living up to all the hype. Its large bar and lounge is always humming with well-dressed, young, professional clusters; the dining room attracts power brokers; while the private room is forever hosting a fete. The restaurant is as sophisticated and stylish as the food, so dress suitably.

Interpretations of American dishes are prepared with skill and may reveal perfectly seasoned fried green tomatoes served with frisée, plump white prawns, and a streak of red pepper aïoli. A crisp-skinned roasted chicken breast and confit thigh placed over a bed of farro dotted with crunchy cauliflower florets is stunningly trailed by an elegant version of strawberry shortcake—buttery, thin biscuits sandwiched with jam and tangy Greek yogurt.

RN74

Californian XX

C1

301 Mission St. (at Beale St.)

Phone: 415-543-7474
Web: www.rn74.com
Prices: $$$

Lunch Mon – Fri
Dinner nightly

Named for the Burgundy region "Route Nationale 74" in France, RN74 is part restaurant and part wine bar. At the base of the Millennium Tower, set amidst office buildings, it draws a large corporate crowd, particularly for lunch and after-work drinks. Architectural basics like high ceilings and concrete pillars are balanced with unique design elements like train station-style boards that list available wine bottles.

There is also large bar-lounge area, but most flock here for the Californian menu infused with French accents. Expect such flavorful and harmonious preparations as *garganelli* tossed with artichoke hearts, peas, and wild nettles; and supremely moist fried chicken paired with foraged mushrooms—a dish as solid and stylish as the place itself.

Ruchi

Indian XX

C3

474 3rd St. (bet. Bryant & Stillman Sts.)

Phone: 415-392-8353
Web: www.ruchisf.com
Prices:

Lunch & dinner Mon – Sat

The name literally means "taste," so it's not surprising that Ruchi delivers a powerful lip-smacking punch to the taste buds. The focus is on Southern Indian flavors at this SoMa newcomer. *Dosas*, those thin, lacy, crispy little tastes of heaven, are a "don't miss." Try the Mysore masala *dosa* with crushed potato filling and spicy chutney on the side—yum! Stews and curries account for most of the menu, but this isn't anything like your *nani* used to make. Instead, the stews are pungent and flooded with rich flavors and tender, juicy meats.

Nab a table in the back and watch the action in the open kitchen. With all of those bubbling pots of curries and other concoctions, it may look a bit more like a coven, but there's nothing evil about these tasty treats.

Salt House

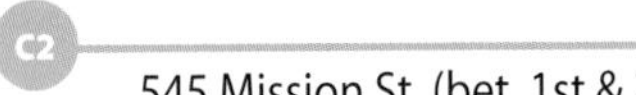

American

C2

545 Mission St. (bet. 1st & 2nd Sts.)

Phone: 415-543-8900
Web: www.salthousesf.com
Prices: $$

Lunch Mon – Fri
Dinner nightly

It's a little bit country, a little bit rock and roll here, where amusing yet chic provincial touches abound (milk bottles are used for water and jars in place of dessert plates) and everyone seems to be having fun. From the communal counter and energetic bar to the bustling open kitchen, Salt House wears a palpable energy. It is ever packed, so reservations are a good idea.

Adept servers and a good mix of citified comfort food make the crowds feel cosseted. Even your country cousin will be appeased by such popular dishes as a *poutine*, SF's take on the Canadian classic with Kennebec fries and Vermont cheddar. Also pleasing is the house burger with blue or cheddar cheese; or petrale sole frilled with king trumpet mushrooms and a mint salsa verde.

Sushi Zone

Japanese

A4

1815 Market St. (at Pearl St.)

Phone: 415-621-1114
Web: N/A
Prices: $$

Dinner Mon – Sat

Sushi connoisseurs looking for the city's best aren't likely to find it at Sushi Zone, but that doesn't stop locals from lining the sidewalk to wait for one of a handful of tables or an old chrome stool at the counter. Situated at the spot where SoMa, the Mission, and Hayes Valley collide, Sushi Zone is a convenient spot for dinner after work.

Check the board for nightly specials, which may include hot items like baked mussels with spicy mayo and scallions or baked seabass with mango. Sushi meanwhile is fresh and simple: albacore, yellowtail, mackerel and salmon nigiri are above average and served over well-prepared rice; sweet papaya balances smoky *unagi* in a simple roll; and a spicy hamachi maki is studded with avocado, jalapeño, and lime.

Town Hall

American 

342 Howard St. (at Fremont St.)

Phone: 415-908-3900 Lunch Mon – Fri
Web: www.townhallsf.com Dinner nightly
Prices: $$

If the town hall is an American tradition, then this SoMa mainstay is a culinary institution. A spacious patio is your first sign of the conviviality one can expect at this large dining hall. The dining room downstairs is outfitted with a communal table while the upstairs is reserved for private events. With exposed brick walls, burnished metal chandeliers, and giant windows, Town Hall is a casual spot that gratifies all and sundry.

The flavor of the kitchen is approachable American with simple yet crave-worthy fare like cornmeal-coated fried oysters with bacon and preserved lemon; and grilled flat iron steak with fingerling potato purée and pickled ramps. Butterscotch and chocolate *pot de crème* beg you to order dessert—even when you couldn't possibly.

Tropisueño

Mexican 

75 Yerba Buena Ln. (bet. Market & Mission Sts.)

Phone: 415-243-0299 Lunch & dinner daily
Web: www.tropisueno.com
Prices: ⊗⊗

Shaded by the dramatic, blue steel wing of the Contemporary Jewish Museum, Yerba Buena Lane is fast becoming a foodie destination for local art junkies and tourists alike. Tropisueño has something for everyone. At lunch, a taqueria-style counter serves tacos and tortas to professionals on the run; for those with time for a knife and fork, the super burrito *mojado* is a saucy siesta-inducer.

The restaurant dresses up a bit for dinner, delivering Latin American dishes like ceviche and tender chicken with *mole poblano*. A small salsa bar brims with jalapeños, sliced radishes, and tangy tomatillo salsa to pile on the mercifully thin chips.

But that's nothing compared to the expansive mahogany bar that oozes fine tequila and top-shelf margs.

Twenty Five Lusk

Contemporary 

25 Lusk St. (bet. 3rd & 4th Sts.)

Phone: 415-495-5875 — Lunch Sun
Web: www.25lusk.com — Dinner nightly
Prices: $$$

As one of the sleekest and chicest respites in town, Twenty Five Lusk is *the* scene for the well-dressed, well-connected, and well-to-do. An after-work cosmo crowd quickly fills in the lower-level bar and lounge decked with rounded settes surrounding hanging fireplace orbs. Upstairs, slick modern surfaces meet brick-and-timber warehouse.

A glassed-in kitchen returns the focal point to cooking which may include dishes like tomato and fennel bisque poured over lobster morsels; grilled prawns posed atop carrot purée and a mound of grits sprinkled with *togarashi*; or a hearty braised pork shoulder served over wilted kale and sided with cornbread and green tomato salsa. Try the classic *baba* inventively soaked in strawberry syrup and coupled with basil sorbet.

Una Pizza Napoletana

Pizza 

210 11th St. (at Howard St.)

Phone: 415-861-3444 — Dinner Wed – Sat
Web: www.unapizza.com
Prices: $$

You get what you pay for at Una Pizza Napoletana, the New York to SoMa transplant that serves purely authentic pies at import prices. But, a bevy of regulars who race in to claim their tables clearly believe that Una Pizza is worth the premium.

There is no decor to speak of unless you count the assemblage of pizzas a product of high design. Make do with white walls and concrete floors, and don't expect your pizza to get any fancier. Just a few choices of 12-inch rounds come fire-licked and lightly topped. Try the Margherita with San Marzano tomatoes, basil, and buffalo mozzarella; or the smoky Ilaria, topped with arugula and cherry tomatoes, and named for the chef's own wife. Finish with an intense Neapolitan coffee served with a hunk of dark chocolate.

Waterbar

Seafood

399 The Embarcadero (at Harrison St.)

Phone: 415-284-9922 Lunch & dinner daily
Web: www.waterbarsf.com
Prices: $$$

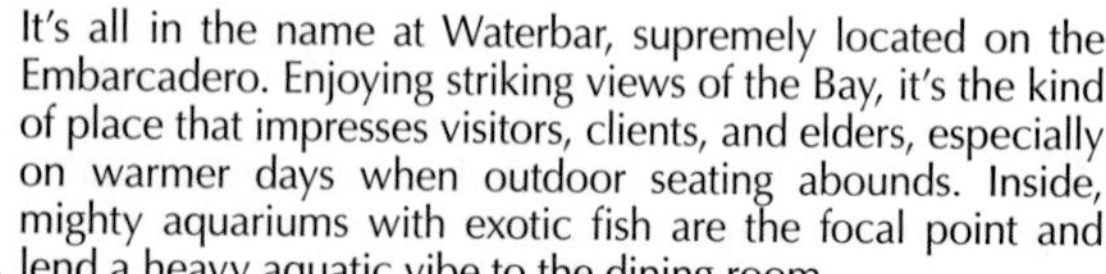

It's all in the name at Waterbar, supremely located on the Embarcadero. Enjoying striking views of the Bay, it's the kind of place that impresses visitors, clients, and elders, especially on warmer days when outdoor seating abounds. Inside, mighty aquariums with exotic fish are the focal point and lend a heavy aquatic vibe to the dining room.

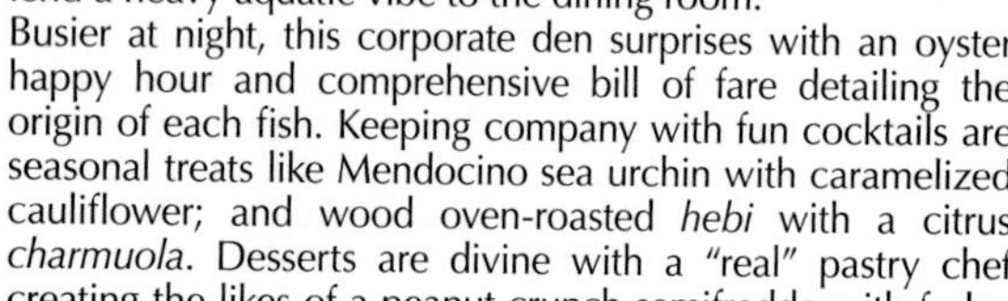

Busier at night, this corporate den surprises with an oyster happy hour and comprehensive bill of fare detailing the origin of each fish. Keeping company with fun cocktails are seasonal treats like Mendocino sea urchin with caramelized cauliflower; and wood oven-roasted *hebi* with a citrus *charmuola*. Desserts are divine with a "real" pastry chef creating the likes of a peanut crunch semifreddo with fudge sauce.

Yank Sing

Chinese

D1

101 Spear St. (bet. Howard & Mission Sts.)

Phone: 415-957-9300 Lunch daily
Web: www.yanksing.com
Prices: $$

Two tiny words will rouse any San Franciscan on Saturday morning: dim sum. The city's soup dumplings are legendary, and no one does them quite like Yank Sing, where Shanghai dumplings are stuffed with moist ground pork and a burst of juicy broth. Lengthy weekend waits are testament to each morsel's yummy goodness.

In the airy urban space, carts manned by servers wired with earpieces and mikes are loaded with steamed and fried delights then wheeled up to tables in rapid fire. Barbecue pork buns are smoky and tender; caramelized pot stickers are a standout; and sesame balls filled with sweet mung paste are a sticky, lovely finish. Over-ordering is a hazard here; mind that prices add up quickly.

Take heart in validated parking in the subterranean garage.

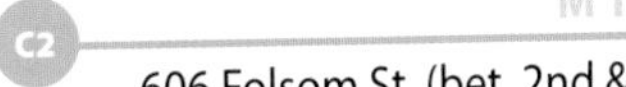

Zaré at Fly Trap

Middle Eastern XX

C2

606 Folsom St. (bet. 2nd & 3rd Sts.)

Phone: 415-243-0580 — Dinner Mon – Sat
Web: www.zareflytrap.com
Prices: **$$**

Nearly 20 years since Hoss Zaré emigrated from Iran and found a job at the Fly Trap to help pay for medical school, the chef/owner is still pursuing his passion in the kitchen he has long called home. A red awning marks the SoMa favorite where the spice-hued interior is as warm as the food.

Zaré himself can be found in the dining room nearly every evening, often serving his flavorful Mediterranean-infused Middle Eastern fare himself, much to the delight of his regulars. The chef's kitchen turns out such mouthwatering dishes as a salmon-and-lentil salad studded with roasted bell peppers, fennel, and endive; braised duck with walnuts and pomegranate; or lamb shank with black-eyed peas. Conclude with the best baklava in San Francisco.

Zero Zero

Pizza XX

C3

826 Folsom St. (bet. 4th & 5th Sts.)

Phone: 415-348-8800 — Lunch & dinner daily
Web: www.zerozerosf.com
Prices: **$$**

A modish neighborhood pizza newcomer, Zero Zero is named for the imported Neapolitan flour that gives these crusts their character. But for a taste of these bubbling Italian masterpieces, be prepared to wait and brave the din: reservations are elusive; and the bar (known for creative and carefully crafted drinks) is inevitably packed.

If you make it to a table beneath the colorful mural in the close-knit upstairs dining room, take advantage of the opportunity to feast. Start with antipasti or local squid à la plancha, then meander through a range of pies, many of which are named after San Francisco streets. The Margherita "Extra" is heaped with buffalo mozzarella, while the Fillmore forgoes the sauce in favor of leeks, fontina, and garlic.

MICHELIN

East Bay

East Bay

Berkeley is legendary for its liberal politics and lush university campus that launched the 1960s Free Speech Movement. Among foodies, this is a Garden of Eden that sprouted American gastronomy's leading purist, Alice Waters, and continues to be a place of worship. Waters' Chez Panisse Foundation has nurtured the Edible Schoolyard, an organic garden and kitchen classroom for students. She also founded Slow Food Nation, the country's largest festival of slow and sustainable foods. Since Waters is credited with developing Californian cuisine, her influence can be tasted in myriad restaurants.

But, one needn't look much further than Berkeley's "gourmet ghetto." The North Shattuck corridor successfully lures with fresh and meticulously-prepared food and/or takeout from **Grégoire** and **Epicurious Garden**. This strip also houses Co-ops like the **Cheese Board Collective**; the **Cheese Board Pizza Collective**; and the **Juice Bar Collective**. On Thursday afternoons, the **North Shattuck Organic Farmers Market** is crammed with local produce. **La Note**'s brioche *pain perdu* is lovely; **Tomate Café** proffers a Cuban breakfast on a pup-friendly patio; and **Caffe Mediterraneum** is the SF birthplace of the caffe latte. Berkeley is also home to **Acme Bread Company** and Chef Paul Bertolli's handcrafted **Fra'Mani Salumi**. Oakland doesn't quite carry the same culinary panache of neighboring Berkeley, but the workaday city has seen a revival of its own with new businesses and condos. **Jack London Square** has stunning views of the bay, and crows the area's chief tourist destination for dining, nightlife, and a **Sunday Farmers and Artisan Market**. **Fentons Creamery** has served ice cream for 115 delicious years. Taco junkies congregate on International Boulevard for a taco feast; while **Tacos Sinaloa** and **Mariscos La Costa** are known for their chorizo and fish tacos, respectively. Downtown, crowds nosh on Po'boys at **Café 15**; and in Temescal, **Bakesale Betty** serves crispy chicken sandwiches atop ironing board tables. After work, the **Trappist** pours over 160 Belgian and specialty beers.

On Sundays, oyster mongers line up at **Rudy Figueroa's** in the **Montclair Farmer's Market** for bivalves shucked to order. In August, the Art & Soul Festival brings a buffet of world flavors, as does the Chinatown Streetfest with curries galore and barbecue meats. In Rockridge, the quaint shopping district between Oakland and Berkeley, boutiques and eateries abound.

Tara's Organic Ice Cream serves unique flavors (imagine chile pistachio or basil) in compostable cups. **Market Hall** is lauded as a gourmet shopper's paradise with sustainable catch at **Hapuku Fish Shop**, specialty groceries at the **Pasta Shop**, a bakery, produce market, and coffee bar.

East Bay
Lafayette
Metro Lafayette
Artisan Bistro
Lafayette Park
Chevalier
Walnut Creek
Élevé
Prima
Walnut Creek Yacht Club
Sasa
Va de Vi
WALNUT CREEK
ALBANY
Vanessa's Bistro
Rivoli
Hamro Aangan
Bangkok Jam
Lalime's
César
Chez Panisse
UNIVERSITY OF CALIFORNIA BERKELEY
ALAMEDA
CONTRA COSTA
North Berkeley
Corso
Bistro Liaison
Comal
La Rose Bistro
Tacubaya
Zut!
Slow
Ippuku
O Chamé
FIVE
Gather
Downtown Berkeley
BERKELEY
Anchalee
Kirala
Claremont Resort & Spa
BERKELEY AQUATIC PARK
900 Grayson
Ashby
Café Colucci
Wood Tavern
Riva Cucina
SAN FRANCISCO BAY
EMERYVILLE
Zachary's Chicago Pizza
Rockridge
Oliveto
À Côté
Uzen
Chu
ROCKRIDGE
Pizzaiolo
Doña Tomás
Hong Kong East Ocean
Sahn Maru
Adesso
MacArthur
Ohgane
Dopo
Bay Wolf
Commis
Hotel
Restaurant
Brown Sugar Kitchen
Camino
PIEDMONT
Boot & Shoe Service
Picán
Hawker Fare
Ikaros
Plum
Grand Avenue Thai
Sidebar
OAKLAND
19 St-Oakland
Lake Merritt
Bellanico
Marzano
West Oakland
Cosecha
Oakland City Center-12 St
Tamarindo
Legendary Palace
Battambang
Champa Garden
Encuentro
Lake Merritt
Miss Pearl's
Haven
Bocanova
Inner Harbor
ALAMEDA NAVAL COMPLEX
COAST GUARD I.
LAFAYETTE, WALNUT CREEK, DANVILLE
DANVILLE
Danville
Thai House
The Peasant & The Pear
Bridges
Esin
DANVILLE
BLACKHAWK MUSEUM

À Côté

B3 Mediterranean

5478 College Ave. (bet. Lawton & Taft Aves.), Oakland

Phone: 510-655-6469 Dinner nightly
Web: www.acoterestaurant.com
Prices: $$

With a convivial communal table, semi-open kitchen, and blazing wood-fired oven, few can find fault with this Rockridge haunt. The small tables are close but comfy, and the patio–sunny in the summer, heated in winter–guarantees a party year-round. Reservations are accepted but there is often a wait. Don't fret as the area's cheeky shops are a pleasant way to pass the time. Singles might score seats at the bar.

Seasonal Mediterranean plates are both simple and satisfying and may reveal a duck liver crostini with pickled shallots; wood oven-treated mussels infused with Pernod; prosciutto and nectarine flatbread with *stracchino* and arugula; or *fior di latte* panna cotta with prosecco-poached nectarines.

New Latin American sib, Rumbo al Sur is worth a visit.

Adesso

B3 Italian

4395 Piedmont Ave. (at Pleasant Valley Rd.), Oakland

Phone: 510-601-0305 Dinner Mon – Sat
Web: www.dopoadesso.com
Prices: $$

Strictly for flesh fiends, Adesso's parade of salty delights (charcuterie, *salumi*, or...ahem...cold cuts) sets tongues wagging. Here, carnivores gather to ogle their different varieties of *salumi* which in turn may arrive sliced tissue-thin, thick, or in crocks. This is truly an ode to cured meats with gifts like *diavolo* made with Sicilian hot chili and white wine; *crespone* with Lambrusco and black pepper; or whipped *lardo* with rosemary.

A relative of nearby Dopo, Adesso successfully attracts an after-work bunch with its wraparound bar (pouring original cocktails), flat-screens, and foosball table. In addition, this cool watering hole also offers a nice selection of small plates including antipasti and panini all quickly served and priced to please.

Anchalee

Thai

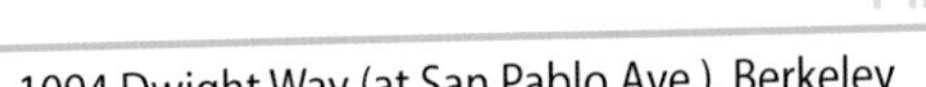

A2

1094 Dwight Way (at San Pablo Ave.), Berkeley

Lunch & dinner daily

Phone: 510-848-4015
Web: www.anchaleethai.com
Prices: ©©

A casual dining room with olive green walls, wood floors, exposed brick, and paintings of the Buddha himself (whose eyes are set in deep meditation) gives Anchalee an air of authenticity that sets it apart from other ethnic eateries crowding Berkeley. Stay clear of the lonely tables by the door—for what you gain in breeze, you lose in ambience. Instead make your way towards the cozy gas fireplace which cuts the chill on foggy days.

Tiny pendant lights cast a flattering glow on Anchalee's fresh, flavorful food. The ample selection of vegetarian choices keeps hungry herbivores (and Berkeley's college set) happy; while creative Thai entrées like basil, squid, and salmon fried rice make for exciting picks alongside trusty standbys like pad Thai and *satays*.

Artisan Bistro

French

B1

1005 Brown Ave. (at Mt. Diablo Blvd.), Lafayette

Lunch & dinner Tue – Sun

Phone: 925-962-0882
Web: www.artisanlafayette.com
Prices: $$

Hearts carved into the exterior shutters are your first clue that this Craftsman cottage is an ideal hideaway for canoodling lovers. Duck into the cluster of cozy dining rooms where warm Dijon walls, local artwork, and a stone hearth work together to set the mood; or, on sunny days, bask on the umbrella-shaded patio.

No matter the season, Chef/owner John Marquez's Cal-French cuisine is right on cue. At lunch, roasted lamb shoulder and grilled portobello mushrooms make for fancy sandwiches; dinners are swankier. One might begin with a creamy corn soup or vibrant baby beets, endives, and apples made decadent with herbed goat cheese. Entrées are hearty—think rabbit three ways or roasted chicken with a terrine of leg, apples, and mustard.

Bangkok Jam

B1 — Thai XX

1892 Solano Ave. (bet. Fresno Ave. & The Alameda), Berkeley

Phone: 510-525-3625
Web: www.bangkokjamberkeley.com
Prices: $$

Lunch & dinner daily

Taking up residence in Boran Thai's former digs, this ritzy replacement kicks it up a notch with fresh, creative twists on classic Thai. Vibrant paintings and vivid photos brighten the walls, while milky glass chandeliers illuminate a chic, modern space. If those luscious scents of coconut, basil, and lemongrass don't have your mouth watering, sate your buds with a "wrap and bite"—roasted coconut, peanuts, lime, ginger, and diced shrimp cradled in lettuce leaves, served with a savory ginger sauce. Alternatively, tuck into crispy shrimp and cream cheese "wontons," dress up prawns aside pineapple sweet and sour sauce.

Fresh produce and organic fixings weave their way into a menu of salads, curries, noodle, and rice dishes with affordable prices to boot.

Battambang

B4 — Cambodian X

850 Broadway (bet. 8th & 9th Sts.), Oakland

Phone: 510-839-8815
Web: N/A
Prices: $$

Lunch Mon – Sat
Dinner nightly

Surrounded by a collection of Chinese restaurants, markets, and grocers, this unassuming spot sings to its own tune. It's all about authentic Cambodian here at Battambang, where true-blue ingredients like *prohuk* (fermented fish paste) and savory lime-based sauces make their way into the dishes.

Golden hues, wood wainscoting, and glass-topped tables outfit the diminutive space, swarming with local families relishing a good meal at great price. To get your appetite going, watch them load up *bangkair aing*, fresh jumbo prawns grilled and served with a pickled veggie relish and lime juice; *saramann*, sliced beef, green beans, sweet potato, and fresh coconut floating in a fragrant red curry; or spicy baked eggplant stuffed with diced prawns and ground pork.

Bay Wolf

Californian XX

B3

3853 Piedmont Ave. (at Rio Vista Ave.), Oakland

Dinner nightly

Phone: 510-655-6004
Web: www.baywolf.com
Prices: $$

Bay Wolf has been a Bay Area icon since the mid 1970's. As the restaurant approaches its 40th birthday, the kitchen is still successfully preparing food the way it always has—excellent ingredients are treated with simplicity and care. True to the local philosophy, this oft-changing menu spotlights seasonal and local ingredients.

Set in a converted house with a small bar and dining rooms on either side, patrons can be seen nibbling on fried ricotta-stuffed squash blossoms, before proceeding to a pork loin roulade with toasted pistachios spiraling through it, deliciously paired with wild rice pilaf. But, the real scene is on the front porch where local artists, intellectuals, and retirees spend hours lingering over buttery apricot upside down cake.

Bellanico

Italian XX

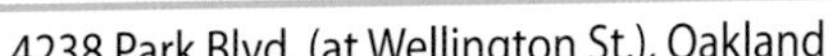

C4

4238 Park Blvd. (at Wellington St.), Oakland

Lunch & dinner daily

Phone: 510-336-1180
Web: www.bellanico.net
Prices: $$

Neighborhood favorite Bellanico serves up consistently good, rustic Italian fare. Large windows overlook Park Boulevard, while inside, persimmon-colored walls, wood furnishings, and an open kitchen welcome foodies. Lunches are low-key, frequented by business people. Dinners are filled with local couples and families appreciative of the "bambino" dishes-apropos in a place named for the owners' daughters.

As at its sister, Aperto, this seasonal, ingredient-driven menu features local, organic products. Start with a selection of *cicchetti* and antipasti of cauliflower fritters with garlic *aglioli* before moving on to other items including spicy *tagliolini pepati* with smoked bacon. Salt fiends adore the grilled pork chop adorned with Umbrian lentils.

Bistro Liaison

B2 French XX

1849 Shattuck Ave. (at Hearst Ave.), Berkeley

Phone: 510-849-2155
Web: www.liaisonbistro.com
Prices: $$

Lunch Sun – Fri
Dinner nightly

Pleasing droves for over a decade now, Bistro Liaison paints the very picture of a bistro with its handsome curved bar, open kitchen, luxurious banquettes, and a dining room done in yellow walls and burgundy accents highlighted by French posters and paintings.

Aluminum vats of fresh produce are a sign of what to expect from Chef Todd Kniess, a former protégé of Roland Passot. His forte lies in creating Fench food for the soul and includes classics like *crevettes antibes* (sautéed prawns with garlic, cherry tomatoes, chilies, and arugula); or petrale sole stuffed with crab and licked with a shrimp- and Cognac-cream—sure to lift the spirits of any expat.

Dessert and cocktail choices are rubber-stamped on the white butcher paper that covers each table.

Bocanova

B4 Latin American XX

55 Webster St. (at Jack London Square), Oakland

Phone: 510-444-1233
Web: www.bocanova.com
Prices: $$

Lunch & dinner daily

Located in lively Jack London Square, everything is big at Bocanova—several dining rooms, a massive (and admired) bar, and the spacious patio overlooking the harbor. The industrial-chic space highlights soaring ceilings, funky light fixtures, and stained glass accents amid fine wood furnishings. Adding to the allure is an open kitchen starring a competent lineup of chefs.

Unlike mere mortals, Bocanova aces the art of compartmentalizing. Whether *From the Pantry, From the Raw Bar,* or *From the Feidora,* dishes are sure to gratify. Expect the likes of a *huarache* topped with crumbled Oaxaca and ghost chili salami; grilled Pacific cod tacos capped with a zesty tomato-avocado relish; and chicken enchiladas smeared with an aromatic tomatillo salsa.

Boot and Shoe Service

Pizza

3308 Grand Ave. (bet. Lake Park Ave. & Mandana Blvd.), Oakland

Phone: 510-763-2668 — Lunch & dinner Tue – Sun
Web: www.bootandshoeservice.com
Prices: $$

Can't get a table at Oakland's popular Pizzaiolo? Well, you may not have much luck at sister pizzeria, Boot and Shoe Service, either. Nevertheless, it's still well worth the wait. On a bustling stretch of Grand Avenue, this crammed casual eatery is also a favorite among East Bay locals looking for a quality pie in a low-key, family-friendly atmosphere.

Here you'll find exposed brick walls, laid-back service, and seats at a counter or bare tables that provide unassuming space for comforting Italian meals. Get your greens on in the form of tender asparagus with poached farm egg; then dig into signature seasonal pizzas topped with rapini and house-made fennel-pork sausage, or black olive and tomato with spicy arugula and shaved Grana Padano.

Bridges

International

B5

44 Church St. (at Hartz Ave.), Danville

Phone: 925-820-7200 — Lunch & dinner daily
Web: www.bridgesdanville.com
Prices: $$

Robin Williams' fans may remember Bridges' cameo appearance in the 1993 hit *Mrs. Doubtfire*, but this Danville starlet stakes its true claim to fame in a consistent appeal to an East Bay audience. The cinematic setting is geared to special occasions with tangled vines and a trickling waterfall weaving romance on the patio. Inside, a mural of grand bridges spans one of the few walls not occupied by soaring windows.

Neighborly hospitality lends a small town vibe. The cuisine however, explores the globe from Europe to Asia and back home again. Start with a hearty salad or a shrimp and avocado quesadilla; then, journey on with sautéed mahi mahi dressed in tangy pineapple salsa. The creamsicle parfait is a dressed-up end to a most enjoyable ride.

Brown Sugar Kitchen

American

2534 Mandela Pkwy. (at 26th St.), Oakland

Phone: 510-839-7685 — Lunch Tue – Sun
Web: www.brownsugarkitchen.com
Prices: $$

Southern folks looking for a taste of home will find it in an unlikely spot: the industrial park that Chef Tanya Holland calls "Sweet West Oakland." In her Brown Sugar Kitchen, the French-trained chef whips local, organic ingredients into down-home goodness—think buttermilk fried chicken atop cornmeal waffles with brown sugar butter and apple cider syrup.

Grab a counter seat overlooking the kitchen and let the hunger seep in. Soulful breakfasts include cheddar grits with poached eggs, while lunches offer fried oyster Po'boys or baby back ribs glazed with brown sugar and pineapple. Wash it all down with a glass of wine from one of their many African-American producers. Don't miss the dessert counter brimming with snickerdoodle cookies and red velvet cake.

Café Colucci

Ethiopian

6427 Telegraph Ave. (at 65th St.), Oakland

Phone: 510-601-7999 — Lunch & dinner daily
Web: www.cafecolucci.com
Prices: ⊜

Looks can be deceiving and such is the case with Café Colucci, an Ethiopian eatery with an Italian name. First-timers will find another world where red wall coverings and colorful tables carry the fragrance of foreign spices, many blended in house. Novices need not fret: a friendly, all-Ethiopian staff has your back.

The menus also offer a glossary of sorts, chock-full of enticing delicacies: *shouro fitfit,* or shards of crêpe-like *injera* bread with tomato and jalapeño in olive oil and spicy dressing; *kitfo,* lean raw beef with cardamom in spicy *mitmita*; and *doro wot,* delicate chicken simmered in a classic and delicious *berbere* sauce. Vegetarians and meat lovers can put aside their differences: with no utensils to speak of, we're all in this together!

Camino

Californian

B3

3917 Grand Ave. (at Sunny Slope Ave.), Oakland

Phone: 510-547-5035 — Lunch Sat – Sun
Web: www.caminorestaurant.com — Wed – Mon dinner only
Prices: $$

Escape from Oakland's Grand Avenue into Camino, a lofty Basque-style dining hall where pressed-tin ceilings and wrought-iron chandeliers hang above exposed brick and salvaged redwood communal tables lit by candles and lined with vintage church pews.

Mammoth bowls laden with fresh produce are a clue to what's on the menu: with 20-year Chez Panisse vet Russell Moore at the fire, you can count on perfectly rustic, seasonal fare. The menu is concise but has something for everyone. Watch from the butcher-block counter as cooks in flannel shirts grill Dungeness crabs; bake Tomales Bay oysters in absinthe; and turn out juicy duck breast from the wood-fired oven. Finish with moist bread pudding crowned by huckleberries, almonds, and crème fraîche.

César

Spanish

B1

1515 Shattuck Ave. (bet. Cedar & Vine Sts.), Berkeley

Phone: 510-883-0222 — Lunch & dinner daily
Web: www.cesarberkeley.com
Prices: $$

Sitting comfortably in the gourmet ghetto next to notable Chez Panisse, the name (César) is a fictional character from Marcel Pagnol's trilogy of movies. These Chez Panisse alumni serve tasty Spanish-style tapas with a wink from California. *Patatas rellenas* (potatoes stuffed with spicy chorizo) may start the meal. *Bocadillos* like tuna and egg, or *croque senor* promises to sate carb addicts as will the open-face version—*montaditos*, toasted bread topped with white anchovies and aïoli.

A minimal list of simple, seasonal, and sweet *postres* is worth a look. There are ample libations available at the bar, but be sure to request the black book for a list of spirits, sherries, Ports, and madeiras. A second and much larger César is on Piedmont in Oakland.

Champa Garden

Asian

2102 8th Ave. (at 21st St.), Oakland

Phone: 510-238-8819 Lunch & dinner daily
Web: N/A
Prices:

Attention Ivy Hill area residents: curious about the sumptuous scents wafting about the 'hood? Follow them straight to Champa Garden, where Thai, Vietnamese, and Laotian cuisines are served with authenticity. Inside, a small bar replete with an awning serves inexpensive beer and a full menu, while the deep rust dining room is equipped with a disco ball and TV monitor in the corner (karaoke anyone?).

Those overwhelmed by the options can begin with the fried rice ball salad–a tasty pile of crispy fried rice, crumbled pork, green onions, dried chilies, and lime juice, served with romaine lettuce, mint, and cilantro–just wrap 'em up and enjoy the symphony of textures and flavors. Or rely on tasty dishes of old favorites, like the classic pad Thai.

Chevalier

B1

French

960 Moraga Rd. (at Moraga Blvd.), Lafayette

Phone: 925-385-0793 Dinner Tue – Sun
Web: www.chevalierrestaurant.com
Prices: **$$**

Chevalier radiates French charm from the flowers in its patio, to the beautifully manicured hedges. Additionally, the dining room feels wonderfully European with chic inflections like drapes set across walls of windows. Adding to this lure is a cadre of friendly servers—even the chef circulates for a chat with guests, both old and new.

The three-course prix-fixe menu is the only way to go here. *Par exemple*, start with mixed greens topped with a warm, pastry-wrapped square of goat cheese sprinkled with *herbes de Provence* and a lemon-thyme vinaigrette. Next comes *poulet rôti fermier à la Tropezienne*, perfectly seasoned, crispy skinned chicken draped over a ragout of tomato, squash, olives, and rosemary. Float away on a lovely cloud of *île flottante*.

Chez Panisse

Californian XX

1517 Shattuck Ave. (bet. Cedar & Vine Sts.), Berkeley

Phone: 510-548-5525 Dinner Mon – Sat
Web: www.chezpanisse.com
Prices: **$$$$**

For Californian cuisine, Chez Panisse has been the mother of invention for over 40 years now. The culinary icon, opened by Chef/owner Alice Waters in 1971, launched a cuisine as well as the careers of many top Bay Area chefs. The jewel of Berkeley's gourmet ghetto is shiny as she ever was: mature vines cover her wooden façade and patio, while antiqued mirrors and copper accents lend her interior a golden hue.
Chez Panisse is still packed to the hilt with masses eager to devour dishes made from farm-fresh produce. Curious eaters may spy the open kitchen for a view of shellfish-and-tomato ragout with green olives and chickpeas; followed by spit-roasted pork loin with roasted peppers and cannellini beans. Finish with honey ice cream crêpes with peaches.

Chu

5362 College Ave. (bet. Bryant & Manila Aves.), Oakland

Phone: 510-601-8818 Lunch Mon – Sat
Web: www.restaurantchu.com Dinner nightly
Prices: **$$**

With black furnishings, a dramatic staircase leading to a second-level dining room, and modern Asian art creating a chic atmosphere, this is the rare Chinese restaurant that features a décor as contemporary as its menu. At lunch, the restaurant attracts a decent business crowd; come evening, find tony Rockridge couples sharing pots of fragrant jasmine green tea and refined renditions of Manchurian beef.
The menu combines bold flavors in such dishes as pork *mu shu bao bing*, with tender, stir-fried strips of meat, wood-ear mushrooms, and Chinese spinach ready for wrapping in delicate crêpes. Try the fresh and tasty combo *chow fun* noodles mingling garlic-soy sauce with fresh mussels, sliced calamari, plump prawns, and tender chicken morsels.

Comal

Mexican

B2

2020 Shattuck Ave. (bet. Addison St. & University Ave.), Berkeley

Phone: 510-926-6300 Dinner nightly
Web: www.comalberkeley.com
Prices: $$

The word is out—Comal is excellent! Jam-packed since day one, the new kid on this (Berkeley) block serves delicious Mexican dishes in an industrial space outfitted with soaring ceilings. Within this lofty lair, the dress is casual and the staff gracious.

The regional food (mostly small plates) is elevated by seasonal Californian ingredients and is great to share. The menu may change frequently, but the flavors are consistently spectacular in dishes like fresh, tangy, and zesty halibut ceviche; tender corn tortillas filled with wood-grilled rock cod, spicy pickled cabbage, and avocado aïoli; or rich duck enchiladas smothered with delicious *mole coloradito*. Everything is made from scratch here—from the griddled tortillas to the wonderful *moles* and salsas.

Corso

Italian

B2

1788 Shattuck Ave. (bet. Delaware & Francisco Sts.), Berkeley

Phone: 510-704-8004 Dinner nightly
Web: www.trattoriacorso.com
Prices: $$

Wining and dining her way through Tuscany was hard work for Wendy Brucker, who now shows off the fruits of her labor at Corso in Berkeley. Mementos of her Florentine travels can be found in framed souvenir menus, an all-Italian wine list–poured by taste, glass, or carafe–and in the traditional *bistecca alla Fiorentina*, named for the Renaissance city's Trattoria Sostanza. Nosh on Dungeness crab toast; butternut squash and potato gnocchi; then perhaps panna cotta for dessert. Most menu items are under $20.

True to Tuscany, Corso's dining room is simply set. The best seats may be at the granite kitchen counter where meat lovers will enjoy the view of dangling, house-cured *salumi*. Movie buffs will dig the black-and-white Italian films over the bar.

Commis ✿

Contemporary XX

B3

3859 Piedmont Ave. (at Rio Vista Ave.), Oakland

Phone: 510-653-3902 Dinner Wed – Sun
Web: www.commisrestaurant.com
Prices: **$$$**

Aaron Stienstra

This simple façade has no obvious signage (check building numbers) and that may be a harbinger of the meal to come. With no printed menu, Commis is a "trust the chef" type of place where the kitchen is deserving of your faith, as those studious foodies packing it nightly already know.

The six-seat counter is ideal for viewing the chefs, hard at work and a world away. Yet even the room's rather stark blond woods, black seats, and white walls accent the same focal point: the exhibition kitchen. Intent and serious, these chefs do not break their focus to chat with diners, though the polished service staff offers thorough and earnest descriptions of each course. Extreme attention is paid to precise details. That fine chiffonade of ginger and micro-dill fronds, bead of tangy yogurt, and small pieces of caramelized sunchoke surrounding four sweet shrimp were positioned with great thought and purpose.

The parade of courses may reveal a velvety-soft egg yolk in rich onion-infused cream, vibrantly enhanced with smoked date paste and crunchy bits of toasted malt-granola. While some may find their meals to be a rather cerebral experience, superb ingredients and skill make everything enjoyable.

Cosecha

Mexican

B4

907 Washington St. (at 9th St.), Oakland

Phone: 510-452-5900 — Lunch Mon – Sat
Web: www.cosechacafe.com — Dinner Thu – Sat
Prices:

This Mexican café is housed in Old Oakland's historic Swan's Market, a great spot for die-hard foodies. Guests order at the counter and sit at one of the communal tables in the warehouse-like space. Note that they serve dinner but close early, so arrive in time to nibble your way through a menu featuring local ingredients infused into flavorsome Mexican fare.

Everything is homemade from the tortillas to the *horchata*. Discover a quesadilla filled with sweet yam and Oaxaca cheese, served with a wonderfully zesty salsa verde. Both achiote-marinated chicken and braised pork tacos are explosively flavorful, topped with pickled onion and cilantro, but save room for *mole verde con pollo*—chicken breast steeped in a delish pumpkin seed-green chile *mole*.

Doña Tomás

Mexican

B3

5004 Telegraph Ave. (bet. 49th & 51st Sts.), Oakland

Phone: 510-450-0522 — Lunch Sat – Sun
Web: www.donatomas.com — Dinner Tue – Sat
Prices: $$

Fresh, seasonal, organic ingredients from the Bay Area are fused with Mexican flavors and preparations resulting in a successful hybrid at Doña Tomás. The restaurant has two dining areas and a bar frequented by locals who come to chat with the friendly bartenders, mingle with friends, and dive into the flavorful Cal-Mex food.

Speaking of which, expect dishes like corn tortilla chips with well-seasoned guacamole; followed by slow-roasted pork layered in homemade tacos and matched with *pico de gallo*, pinto beans, and red rice. Pan-fried petrale sole joined with a luscious corn and zucchini pudding keeps fish fans elated.

The happy hour set return time and again for discounted drinks featuring a good selection of Mexican tequila, mezcal, and cerveza.

Dopo

4293 Piedmont Ave. (at Echo St.), Oakland

Phone: 510-652-3676 — Lunch Mon – Fri
Web: www.dopoadesso.com — Dinner Mon – Sat
Prices: $$

With California in the heart and Italy on the mind, Chef/owner Jon Smulewitz, a veteran of nearby mainstay Oliveto, relies on fresh ingredients grown close to home for simply satisfying spreads at Dopo. On sunny afternoons, if the sidewalk seating is full, rest assured that an ample skylight will illuminate the Mediterranean colors inside: mustard and terra-cotta coat the walls; azure tiles glint from the horseshoe bar; and tables are carved from platinum blonde pine.

Start a meal (the menu changes daily) with *crudi* like local halibut with favas and radish. Antipasti such as swordfish with pine nuts, currants, and lemon; or pastas including agnolotti of lamb with mint and pecorino are not to be overlooked, even if you are a die-hard thin-crust fanatic.

Élevé

1677 N. Main St. (1677 N. Main St.), Walnut Creek

Phone: 925-979-1677 — Lunch Tue – Fri
Web: www.eleverestaurant.com — Dinner Tue – Sun
Prices: $$

Across from City Hall in Walnut Creek, Élevé has broad portrait windows that invite the hungry wanderers strolling these streets. Inside, where natural light and a stunning quartzite bar lend a welcoming and modern vibe, cocktail hounds appreciate such creative pours as the "Sleepy Head," a thrilling concoction of brandy, ginger, and mint; while burled wood tabletops are a warm surface for family-style Vietnamese meals.

The fusion cuisine is laden with crisp flavors in entrées such as a spicy steak salad with fresh watercress, daikon radish, and jalapeños; and chicken *zao lan* featuring a yellow coconut curry with mushrooms and sweet onion. Vegetarians will find plenty of dishes to satisfy them, including garlic tofu and spicy root curry.

Encuentro

Vegetarian X

202 2nd St. (at Jackson St.), Oakland

Phone: 510-832-9463 — Dinner Tue – Sat
Web: www.encuentrooakland.com
Prices:

While many Bay Area restaurants go hog wild for meaty menus showcasing charcuterie and *porchetta*, the chef's club at Encuentro continues to practice the art of high vegetarian cuisine. Lauded in San Francisco as a vegetarian's haven, this is a welcome addition to the burgeoning neighborhood of Jack London Square.

Natural light fills the tiny corner spot where rugs warm the concrete floors and a handful of tables and wine counter seating yield a cozy getaway from the din of the square. Amidst a simple yet welcoming setting, vegans may feast on pâtés made from nuts and truffled mushrooms, while others take their time and their tomato bread pudding with a regal crown of Humboldt Fog cheese. The wine bar is a mellow spot for deviled eggs and roasted nuts.

Esin

Mediterranean XX

750 Camino Ramon (at Sycamore Valley Rd. W.), Danville

Phone: 925-314-0974 — Lunch & dinner daily
Web: www.esinrestaurant.com
Prices: $$

From its plot in Danville's Rose Garden marketplace, Esin feels fresh with soft yellow walls and dark wood trim, as if it just sprouted yesterday. In fact, Esin is actually a transplant that flourished for 10 years in San Ramon.

Here, it continues to please crowds with well-executed, homey fare that takes a cue from the Turkish roots of Chef/owner Esin deCarion, whose name means "inspiration." Working together with her husband and co-owner, this kitchen team turns out such Cal-Med dishes as apple-cured gravlax with grilled bread and caperberry butter; and a fillet of petrale sole cooked meunière-style with lemon-caper beurre blanc. Desserts are tasty and homemade, like the rich and subtly sweet banana cream pie with a dark chocolate cookie crust.

FIVE

American XX

2086 Allston Way (at Shattuck Ave.), Berkeley

Phone: 510-225-6055 Lunch & dinner daily
Web: www.five-berkeley.com
Prices: $$

Set on the main level of the Shattuck Plaza, FIVE caters to hotel guests and stylish suits. Yet, it is an equally cherished destination among locals and families too. The boldly patterned walls and massive chandelier lend a sense of drama, while service is welcoming and friendly.

The menu of well-prepared American fare is as wonderful as the décor itself. Expect items where every element oozes deliciousness as in rich duck confit enchiladas crowned with tangy salsa verde, avocado purée, lime crème fraîche, and *queso fresco*. Add to it an elegant side of "mac" and cheese (piping-hot orzo with smoked Gouda and tangy organic tomato jam), and finish with an excellent butterscotch pudding with peanut brittle and whipped cream that simply must *not* be missed.

Gather

XX

2200 Oxford St. (at Allston Way.), Berkeley

Phone: 510-809-0400 Lunch & dinner daily
Web: www.gatherrestaurant.com
Prices: $$

For organic omnivorous fare and biodynamic wines, set off to Gather, just a stone fruit's throw from UC Berkeley. From the open kitchen, skilled cooks boldly master the humble vegetable with a dexterity that can make even the most self-assured carnivore begin to question himself. These conversions begin with the vegan charcuterie platter (served at dinner only).

This is campus territory where a festive collegiate vibe rules and the cocktails flow freely. Herbivores may opt for roasted brassicas with chanterelles, artichokes, Red Flint polenta, and hazelnut breadcrumb; while meat lovers relish crispy cardoons with frisée, chopped duck egg, and potatoes. The fig cake may be a crowd-pleaser, but the Redwood Hill Farms goat milk semifreddo is a revelation.

Grand Avenue Thai

Thai XX

B4

384 Grand Ave. (bet. Perkins St. & Staten Ave.), Oakland

Phone: 510-444-1507 Lunch Mon – Sat
Web: www.grandavenuethai.com Dinner nightly
Prices: $$

Dying to appease your hunger pangs after a jog around Lake Merritt? What's better than Grand Avenue Thai with its chic and cheery décor of bright walls, splashes of color from fresh flowers on every table, and evocative artwork created by the chef's friend?

A comfy space for sampling contemporary Thai cuisine, Grand Avenue fills daily with the Oakland workaday crowd looking for a lunchtime pick-me-up. Spice lovers may be disappointed (the kitchen turns down the heat to suit Western palates), but dishes are nonetheless packed with flavor. House favorites include roast duck in red coconut curry studded with basil and veggies; grilled marinated rack of lamb gleaming with a spicy garlic sauce; and a tasty array of Thai noodle and barbecue dishes.

Hamro Aangan

Nepali X

A1

856 San Pablo Ave. (bet. Solano & Washington Aves.), Albany

Phone: 510-524-2220 Lunch & dinner daily
Web: www.hamroaangan.com
Prices: $$

Hamro Aangan is not your routine Indian spot with Nepali accents thrown in for good measure. Instead, this trinket parades an excellent mix of Indian and Nepali dishes that are as spicy as they are addictive. Housed within a spacious room, pretty peach tones contrast rather lyrically with a brick wall canvassed in scenes of Nepal and Tibet.

Matching its fiery flavor-profile, tabletops are also dressed in bright woven fabrics. Add this to the lure of Indian hospitality, and it's no wonder Hamro is so adored for its substantial portions of chicken *momo,* steamed chicken dumplings splashed with mint chutney; *khashi ko masu,* goat curry infused with smoky *garam masala*; and a delightfully crispy *masala dosa* served with a creamy coconut chutney.

Haven

B4 — Contemporary XX

44 Webster St. (at Jack London Sq.), Oakland

Phone: 510-663-4440
Web: www.havenoakland.com
Prices: $$$

Dinner nightly

Daniel Patterson of Coi fame is responsible for this wonderful arrival in Jack London Square. Haven's ample space, with its floor-to-ceiling windows and harbor-facing views, has an airy feel, and is styled in warm woods, shiny steel, and pristine white tiles.

The best seats in the house reside at the kitchen-facing counter, so snag one and get things started with smoked pasta—ribbons of al dente goodness bursting with pancetta and cracked black pepper in a decadent cream sauce. Next, try the tender lamb braised in coffee liquor and paired with carrots, onions and shallots. Pan-roasted Brussels sprouts tossed with mint and lime juice are bound to elevate any experience, thrillingly chased by baked California, an almond cookie topped with yuzu sorbet.

Hawker Fare

B4 — Asian X

2300 Webster St. (at 23rd St.), Oakland

Phone: 510-832-8896
Web: www.hawkerfare.com
Prices: ⊜

Lunch Mon – Fri
Dinner Tue – Sat

Street carts often dole out some of the tastiest food you can find, but who wants to stand on a street corner as you nibble and nosh? Salvation can be found at Hawker Fare. This Oakland newcomer brings the flavors of Southeast Asian street carts inside to a funky, but friendly, space filled with graffiti-decorated walls and stained concrete floors.

Mostly Thai in influence, the inexpensive menu features appetizers and main course rice bowls topped with everything from lemongrass chicken and pork belly to *Issan* sausage and beef short ribs. Tasty salads like the beef *larb* with grilled beef and fish sauce-lime vinaigrette; and the Hawker *affogato*, made with condensed milk-flavored soft-serve ice cream and a shot of Thai coffee, are especially refreshing.

Hong Kong East Ocean

Chinese XX

3199 Powell St., Emeryville

Phone: 510-655-3388 Lunch & dinner daily
Web: www.hkeo.us
Prices: $$

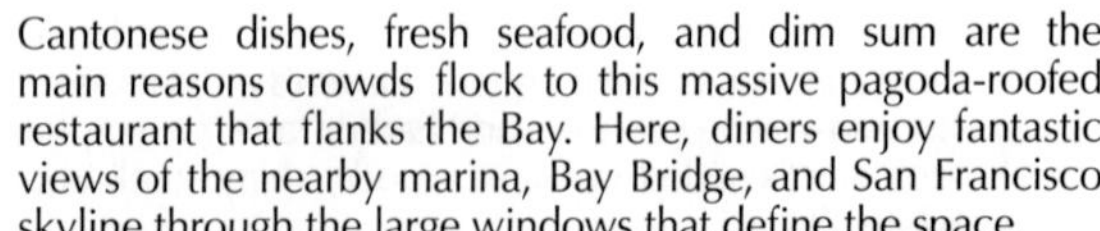

Cantonese dishes, fresh seafood, and dim sum are the main reasons crowds flock to this massive pagoda-roofed restaurant that flanks the Bay. Here, diners enjoy fantastic views of the nearby marina, Bay Bridge, and San Francisco skyline through the large windows that define the space.

This place is meant for family-style dining, so bring a few relatives or friends and try the special set menu available for four, six, or eight. Or choose from the regular bill of fare, which includes fish from the massive tanks along one wall. At lunchtime, opt for dim sum; check off a sampling of items from the written list, and moments later they parade from the kitchen one by one.

Plenty of banquet rooms accommodate groups from business meetings to birthday parties.

Ikaros

Greek XX

3268 Grand Ave. (bet. Mandana Blvd. & Santa Clara Ave.), Oakland

Phone: 510-899-4400 Lunch & dinner daily
Web: www.ikarosgr.com
Prices: $$

While there are no white, sandy beaches here, the soothing Grecian vibe, Greek patrons, and scrumptious bites will take you at least part of the way to the Greek Isles. Inside, Mediterranean blues and whites color the high-arched ceiling, where a long skylight evokes that sublime island feel; framed photos of the coast, white stone sculptures, and Greek music seal the deal.

Sit down to an order of tangy *dolmades* (stuffed grape leaves), packed with rice and fresh herbs, served with a thick yogurt sauce. Next sink your teeth into a gyros stacker—chunks of seasoned lamb and chicken, served with pita, thick steak fries, sliced red onion, tomato, and *tzatziki*. The classic spanakopita filled with spinach, dill, and feta, is crispy and delicious.

Ippuku

2130 Center St. (bet. Oxford St. & Shattuck Ave.), Berkeley

Phone: 510-665-1969 — Lunch Mon – Fri
Web: www.ippukuberkeley.com — Dinner nightly
Prices: $$

Ippuku is not just tasty but a wholly fun experience. The hidden gem, just steps from UC Berkley, thrives in a strip of restaurants and bars. Its traditional entrance leads to the slim room outfitted with low tables over floor cut-outs, booths, and a dining counter situated before a grill in the back. However, the front is really where the chefs meticulously work their magic.

The décor is a stunning display of urban Japan with wood and cement accents. Ippuku is also an ace date place, secreted away from the bustle outside even though it sees a routine roster of students and locals. Lit sake bottles cast a gentle glow upon plates of yuba dolloped with wasabi; *tsukune* with yakitori sauce; and skewered Brussels sprouts with *shichimi*-Kewpie mayo.

Kirala

2100 Ward St. (at Shattuck Ave.), Berkeley

Phone: 510-549-3486 — Lunch Mon – Fri
Web: www.kiralaberkeley.com — Dinner nightly
Prices:

Situated only steps away from the original Berkeley Bowl, Kirala is a treasured local haunt. Named for "Mother Nature," Kirala's dining room is fittingly restrained and echoes such eclectic beats as reggae, jazz, and Latin. The bona fide décor and pristine spread make her a natural selection for Japanophiles around the Berkeley way.

Nature plays a pivotal role in the form of superbly fresh seafood; daily market specials are displayed on a whiteboard staffed by experts who also take great care while preparing perfectly steamed sticky rice topped with hamachi or crimson *maguro*; bowls of steaming soba and udon; and grilled *robata* items like skewered baby lobster tails, lamb chops, smoky bacon-wrapped asparagus, and chicken-stuffed mushrooms.

Lalime's

International 

A1

1329 Gilman St. (bet. Neilson & Peralta Aves.), Berkeley

Phone: 510-527-9838 Dinner Wed – Sun
Web: www.lalimes.com
Prices: $$

Owners Haig and Cindy Krikorian still know how to throw a party. Their first-born, Lalime's, open for over a quarter century, is a local favorite drawing an affable crowd of regulars who congregate upstairs for lively meals near the bar, fireplace, and semi-open kitchen. The downstairs dining room, preferred by couples and lone souls, is larger with citrus walls and storefront windows offering a view of bright, blaring cars.

The staff is attentive and knowledgeable of the cuisine, which leans Italian with Californian vibrancy and a seasonal-organic philosophy. Dishes may include butter beans with tuna confit, kale, and lemon zest; roasted king trumpet and porcini pappardelle with smoked ricotta and melted leeks; and a chocolate-blackberry bombe finale.

La Rose Bistro

French 

B2

2037 Shattuck Ave. (at Addison St.), Berkeley

Phone: 510-644-1913 Lunch Tue – Fri
Web: www.larosebistro.com Dinner Tue – Sun
Prices: $$

Painted with pastel hues and pastoral murals, La Rose is equally good for a casual lunch, family get-together, or romantic evening out. This laid back bistro is located in Berkeley's theater district (on the one way, northbound bit of Shattuck), attracting drama lovers as well.

A meal here begins with fresh-baked French bread and an herbaceous cilantro pesto for dipping. Then come consistently well-prepared French classics, such as *entrecôte frites* and duck confit with Madeira sauce. Californian touches stand out in succulent roasted medallions of pork with honeyed apples and rosemary jus.

Lunch may offer sandwiches such as the *pain bagnat* stuffed with tuna, olives, anchovies, and egg, as well as a full complement of main courses.

Legendary Palace

Chinese

708 Franklin St. (at 7th St.), Oakland

Phone: 510-663-9188 — Lunch & dinner daily
Web: N/A
Prices:

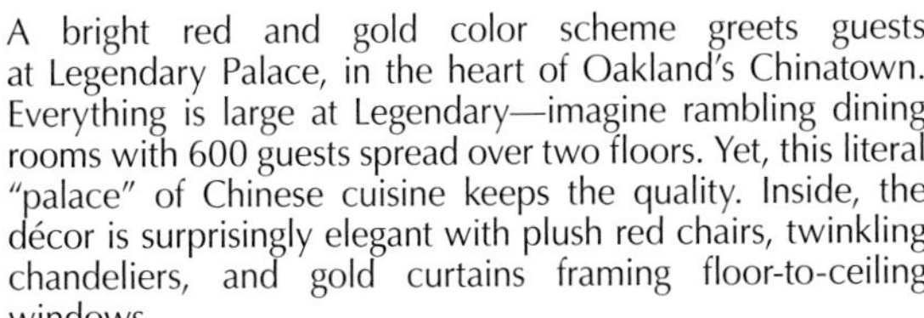

A bright red and gold color scheme greets guests at Legendary Palace, in the heart of Oakland's Chinatown. Everything is large at Legendary—imagine rambling dining rooms with 600 guests spread over two floors. Yet, this literal "palace" of Chinese cuisine keeps the quality. Inside, the décor is surprisingly elegant with plush red chairs, twinkling chandeliers, and gold curtains framing floor-to-ceiling windows.

During dim sum hour, carts circulate amid close-knit tables unveiling a treasure trove of tasty gems including shrimp and water chestnut dumplings; chicken feet with black bean sauce; sliced barbecued pork; and egg custard tarts. An à la carte selection spotlights Cantonese specialties and seafood fresh from the aquarium tanks in the back.

Marzano

Pizza 

4214 Park Blvd. (at Glenfield Ave.), Oakland

Phone: 510-531-4500 — Lunch Sat – Sun
Web: www.marzanorestaurant.com — Dinner nightly
Prices: $$

This Oakland eatery takes its name from the town located on the volcanic slopes that produce the world's best tomatoes, and Marzano strives to honor this legacy. Gothic chandeliers and hand-blown glass wine casks illuminate the timber beams and brick walls, while an 800-degree fire in the wood-burning pizza oven casts a glow on the kitchen. Tip your hat to the *pizzaiolo*: his blood and sweat are your tears of joy.

Charred and chewy Neapolitan pies are pure perfection whether you choose the simple Margherita or a specialty topped with calamari, pecorino, and spicy tomato. Begin with *gnocchi alla Romana* set on goat cheese and wilted spinach or fire-roasted winter squash with *burrata* and marjoram. The close-knit bar is ideal for antipasti and *vino*.

Metro Lafayette

Californian

3524 Mt. Diablo Blvd. (bet. 1st St. & Oak Hill Rd.), Lafayette

Phone: 925-284-4422 Lunch & dinner daily
Web: www.metrolafayette.com
Prices: $$

If Lafayette boasts a scene, then the patio at Metro Lafayette is *the* place to see and be seen. With an affluent clientele, relaxed atmosphere, and straightforward cuisine, this is the type of spot where families, couples, and groups of all ages gather. The tree-shaded patio is a lovely nook on warm days, but power-brokers pack the modern dining room and jovial bar area up front.

A Californian menu that relies on global influences is the name of the game here. Also spotlighted is a raw bar displaying oyster flights and seafood *crudi*. Bolder bites include duck confit tortelloni with cherry tomatoes and Alba mushroom and game jus; beef short ribs with saffron risotto and gremolata; or tempura prawns with a smoky aïoli, cucumber salad, lime, and sea salt.

Miss Pearl's

Southern 

1 Broadway (at Jack London Sq.), Oakland

Phone: 510-444-7171 Lunch & dinner daily
Web: www.misspearlsoakland.com
Prices: $$

A minor revamp has made Miss Pearl's a little more contemporary (in design) and Southern (in cuisine). Housed in Jack London Square and adjoining the Waterfront Hotel, its fresh interior features well-worn wood floors, bright white and grey walls, comfy cushioned chairs, and large framed black-and-white photos of jazz musicians. By virtue of its locale, Miss Pearl's sees a mix of tourists, hotel guests, and local business types.

Expect soulful Southern dishes like well-spiced creole gumbo with shrimp, pulled chicken, ham, okra, and Andouille sausage steeped in a flavorful roux. Watch the boats in the harbor as you munch on a catfish Po'boy layered with coleslaw and served with sweet potato fries. Save room for a side of delicious black-eyed peas.

900 Grayson

American

900 Grayson St. (at 7th St.), Berkeley

Phone: 510-704-9900 — Lunch Mon – Sat
Web: www.900grayson.com
Prices:

On the corner of a commercial stretch of Berkeley is a colorful cottage with decorative tile trim that practically shouts, "Chicken and waffles." Good thing, too, since 900 Grayson is only open for breakfast, lunch, and weekend brunch. But the little spot has a dedicated following of regulars who don't mind waiting for a table during the busy brunch time.

See what the fuss is about with a Caesar salad of gem lettuce and rustic croutons showered with Manchego and tossed in a classic dressing with a hint of anchovy; or a "piggy" sandwich of milk-braised pulled pork shoulder slathered onto an Acme bun with barbecue sauce, caramelized onions, and tangy red cabbage slaw, served with herb-dusted fries. Top it off with an artisanal root beer float. Ah, weekends.

O Chamé

Asian 

1830 4th St. (bet. Hearst Ave. & Virginia St.), Berkeley

Phone: 510-841-8783 — Lunch & dinner daily
Web: www.ochame.com
Prices: $$

The piping hot bowls of soba and udon soup at this high-end noodle house are a go-to treat for shoppers in Berkeley's Fourth Street neighborhood. On sunny days, the patio is an ideal perch for people watching; those on the go will takeout a bento box, although it may have lost some of its caché when it officially became a menu item and no longer the exclusive domain of in the know foodies.

Inside, peaceful scenes of the Orient are etched into honey-hued walls, and earthenware dishes are heaped with the likes of sweet corn and green onion pancakes, grilled local sardines, and seared tuna sashimi with braised leeks and horseradish sauce. Try the tender beef tongue with grilled artichoke hearts or save room for a unique dessert, like sherry custard.

Ohgane

3915 Broadway (bet. 38th & 40th Sts.), Oakland

Phone: 510-594-8300 — Lunch & dinner daily
Web: www.ohgane.com
Prices:

Buffet? Do-it-yourself table-top grilling? À la carte menu? Dining options abound at this sprawling Oakland retreat, where families and company folk convene for the tasty Korean eats.

Featuring faux-granite, grill-top tables under stainless steel ventilation hoods, blond wood floors, and sunny yellow walls, this airy space also struts an excellent assortment of *banchan*. Begin each meal with deliciously tangy pickled vegetables and kimchi, before letting the kitchen indulge your grilling, steaming, and sautéing needs. Have a go at smoky short ribs marinated in garlic-soy; Korean sausage coupled with sweet potato noodles; or spicy *jhap chae*—noodles stuffed with veggies, wrapped in seaweed, dunked in tempura batter, then deep-fried to golden precision.

Oliveto

5655 College Ave. (at Shafter Ave.), Oakland

Phone: 510-547-5356 — Lunch Mon – Fri
Web: www.oliveto.com — Dinner nightly
Prices: **$$$**

Sandwiched between a gourmet market and bud-sized flower shop in impossibly charming Rockridge, Oliveto is just the sort of secluded spot that's perfect for a mid-afternoon glass of *vino*. The café downstairs serves a mean oven-licked pizza, but for real culinary action, wind your way up the polished spiral staircase and into the well-loved dining room. Here, guests have reserved early for tables by large windows overlooking College Avenue; foodies prefer the view of the central wood-burning oven that's fired up to churn out pan-roasted pigeon with grilled porcini mushrooms. A shaved root vegetable salad with almond pesto provides just the right amount of crunch before a hearty plate of saffron *chitarra* with Monterey squid ragù infused with hot peppers.

Picán

Southern XXX

B4

2295 Broadway (at 23rd St.), Oakland

Phone: 510-834-1000 — Lunch Sun – Fri
Web: www.picanrestaurant.com — Dinner nightly
Prices: $$

Picán is all business in Oakland—jamming with a business set at lunch and after-work cocktail clusters at dusk. The large space has a sidewalk patio (dreamy when the weather is warm), a bar and lounge (where you can order off the menu), and elegant dining areas with soaring ceilings and stately columns. Servers are friendly if a bit scattered during busy meal times.

A recent chef change has brought a few bumps in the road, but the dishes are smoothing out nicely. Look for braised pork belly with buttery white beans and thick toast; signature buttermilk fried chicken with decadent smoked Gouda mac 'n cheese and a tangy side of cabbage- and pickled red onion-slaw; or hushpuppies with mustard dipping sauce. Also, check out their fantastic Bourbon selection.

Pizzaiolo

Pizza X

B3

5008 Telegraph Ave. (bet. 49th & 51st Sts.), Oakland

Phone: 510-652-4888 — Dinner Mon – Sat
Web: www.pizzaiolooakland.com
Prices: $$

Couples and small groups descend upon Pizzaiolo's main room (set with wood floors and whitewashed brick walls) while solo diners line the polished wood bar at this lasting East Bay pet. All come for the blistered, thin-crust pizzas, coupled with wine or a signature cocktail. Piled with toppings that personify California, pizza creations may pair eggplant, *ricotta salata*, and mint; or earthy chanterelles and gremolata. Peek into the open kitchen to find colorful wall tiles, a wood-burning oven that turns out those mesmerizing pies, and a spunky staff. Outside, two spacious patios are perfect for basking before antipasti plates of spicy wood oven-roasted clams with tomato and saffron; or a beet salad tossing celery root and mustard-crème fraîche.

Plum

Californian

B4

2214 Broadway (at 22nd St.), Oakland

Phone: 510-444-7586 Dinner nightly
Web: www.plumoakland.com
Prices: $$

More than two years after its debut, Plum is still going strong. This minimalist darling spins out contemporary Californian fare that is beautiful both in its presentation and taste. The space is long and narrow, but the walls–painted a dark plum and hung with oversized prints of the fruit–exude warmth. Against this restful set, find a stylish crowd sipping and savoring a delicious starter combining the sweetness of peaches with the earthiness of roasted porcini and trumpet mushrooms, all perfectly balanced by salty olives and crunchy fennel. Veggie lovers yearn for squash cubes arranged with green beans and smoked *coppa*; whereas pork freaks adore the slow-cooked *porchetta* served with a spicy salad of peppercress, sweet plums, cashews, and onions.

Prima

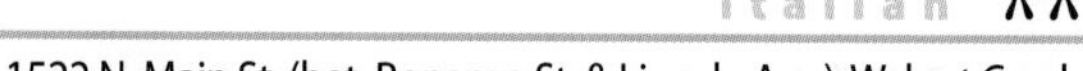

Italian

C1

1522 N. Main St. (bet. Bonanza St. & Lincoln Ave.), Walnut Creek

Phone: 925-935-7780 Lunch Mon – Sat
Web: www.primawine.com Dinner nightly
Prices: $$$

Prima's prized location–in Walnut Creek's shopping district crowded with boutiques and cafés–makes it a pearl among the Italian-loving locals. Whether you linger in the front area anchored by a wood-burning oven, next to the wine cellar reveling in Italian reds, or at the back bar, sultry touches like fireplaces, skylights, and candles are sure to lure.
Try an item from the "Salumeria" (maybe *finocchiona salame* with fennel and black pepper; or *mortadella* studded with pistachios) to understand what all the fuss is about. A market-fresh menu unveils the likes of risotto with braised chicken, pomegranate, and Taleggio; roasted *tagliata* of lamb with cranberry beans and artichoke *gratinado*; or ahi tuna *conservato crostino* with avocado and Calabrian chilies.

Riva Cucina

Italian

800 Heinz Ave. (at 7th St.), Berkeley

Phone: 510-841-7482 — Lunch Tue – Fri
Web: www.rivacucina.com — Dinner Tue – Sat
Prices: $$

Riva Cucina has all of the charm you'd expect from a restaurant specializing in what is ostensibly, Italy's culinary soul—Emilia Romagna, where Chef Massimiliano Boldrini is from. Most of the kitchen action is on view from the tables or bar in the airy room, but for a private repast make your way behind those red velvet panels. The walls are bare, but the colors are deep and warm.

Locals are lucky to partake of their regional cooking. From a small but appealing menu, pick an artichoke soup before moving on to cloud-light knobs of gnocchi in a creamy sauce of smoked salmon; and finish with an excellent pork loin scaloppini trickled with capers and verdant spinach. With just one bite of the *torta della nonna* you'll notice the kitchen's attention to detail.

Rivoli

Californian

1539 Solano Ave. (bet. Neilson St. & Peralta Ave.), Berkeley

Phone: 510-526-2542 — Dinner nightly
Web: www.rivolirestaurant.com
Prices: $$

Recycled cork wainscoting and parchment lanterns lend an earthy, Japanese vibe to Rivoli, which backs up to a lush "secret" garden framed by dramatic windows. The potted plants, climbing ivy, and fronds are a pretty, natural contrast to the interior's white linen-topped tables, which provide a clean backdrop for northern Californian fare with a shake of Italian seasoning.

Start with a purée of summer squash and potato soup crowned with crème fraîche and rouille; pork roast braised with chocolate, pine nuts, and chilies and served with corn spoonbread soufflé; then dive in deeper with Dungeness crab- and ricotta-cannelloni dressed in a Nantua sauce. Save room for the light, tasty, and warm bread pudding with a drizzle of brandy sauce and whipped cream.

Sahn Maru

B3

Korean

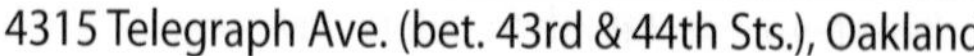

4315 Telegraph Ave. (bet. 43rd & 44th Sts.), Oakland

Phone: 510-653-3366 — Lunch & dinner Wed – Mon
Web: www.sahnmarukoreanbbq.com
Prices: $$

In Korean, Sahn Maru means "top of the mountain" and literally, this paragon of Korean cuisine towers over the rest for her unique and quality food. She may be pricey, but homey Sahn Maru captivates with a fine assortment of *banchan* (think dried fish in chili sauce, and bean sprouts in sesame oil) that is served faithfully with every meal.

Impressing locals are the quality ingredients and singular recipes—proof is in the soft tofu served in a stoneware pot topped with oysters, shrimp, and clams; and black goat stew paired with a pungent dipping sauce. Further proof lies in the fact that most diners converse with the servers in Korean; and, as if to finally reinforce her authenticity, local TV plays in the background, and Korean trinkets adorn the walls.

Sasa

C1

Japanese

1432 N. Main St. (bet. Cypress St. & Lincoln Ave.), Walnut Creek

Phone: 925-210-0188 — Lunch & dinner daily
Web: www.sasawc.com
Prices: $$

For a stylish, contemporary Japanese retreat in the heart of Walnut Creek, Sasa is a true find. Sleek furnishings, stone accents, water streams, and a lovely garden patio give this respite its flair and feel. Not to be outdone, the crowd here is as chic as the space itself and gathers for delicious sake sips alongside small plates of modern Japanese fare.

While avid Japanophiles and purists might cry foul, the rest of us can enjoy the creative interpretations of traditional ingredients and flavors, evident in such sushi and *makimono* as the N. Main filled with tuna, crab, and a spicy aïoli. Other dishes might include smoky kalbi beef lettuce wraps crested with pickled vegetables or fluffy popcorn chicken *kara-age* finished with sea salt and lemon juice.

Sidebar

Gastropub

542 Grand Ave. (bet. Euclid Ave. & MacArthur Blvd.), Oakland

Phone: 510-452-9500 — Lunch Mon – Fri
Web: www.sidebar-oaktown.com — Dinner Mon – Sat
Prices: $$

Waft into Sidebar along with the breeze from Lake Merritt for artisanal cocktails (need a Corpse Reviver?) and Mediterranean-inspired gastropub dining in a quirky space. Photographs of life on the road add character to the pumpkin-spiced interior, anchored by a U-shaped copper bar. Go with friends and belly up to the communal table or score a seat at the dining counter with views of the open kitchen.

Lunchtime focuses on sandwiches, such as a meaty Cuban with roast pork, Gruyère and jalapeño relish; or the Monte Cristo panini with lighter options including a smoked trout salad. Dinners are hearty and wholesome, featuring the likes of baked pasta dishes or a Basque seafood stew. Wine lovers will find varietals from California, France, and Spain.

Slow

1966 University Ave. (bet. Martin Luther King Jr. Way & Milvia St.), Berkeley

Phone: 510-647-3663 — Lunch & dinner Mon – Sat
Web: www.slowberkeley.com
Prices: 

Slow lives up to its credo of presenting gourmet food crafted from local ingredients at judicious prices. Once inside this slightly sized refuge, place your order at the counter, and then take a seat at one among a handful of tables in the jovial, yellow-walled front area featuring an open kitchen. Note—for those looking to linger, dine out back in the pretty rose garden.

The roster of Californian dishes spins to the season and expectedly gushes with flavor. While some may start with a chilled beet and savoy salad tossed with tangy goat cheese and a refreshing Meyer lemon *citronette*; others may opt to dive straight into meaty ox tail braised until falling off the bone and coupled with caramelized pieces of sunchoke, heirloom carrot, and cauliflower.

Tacubaya

Mexican

1788 4th St. (bet. Hearst Ave. & Virginia St.), Berkeley

Phone: 510-525-5160 Lunch & dinner daily
Web: www.tacubaya.net
Prices: $$

Don't let the crowded patio and long line deter you from this Fourth Street neighborhood favorite: good frijoles come to those who wait. But truly, once you reach the register at this go-to Mexican, your order will arrive faster than you can correctly pronounce Tacubaya.

Sister to Oakland's Doña Tomas, Tacubaya has all the trimmings of a beloved taqueria—festive color scheme, wrought-iron chandeliers, and a communal vibe. But the colorful chalkboard is the object of everyone's focus. Here, find the likes of *tacos al pastor*; seasonal chile relleno; and mushroom quesadillas. Open at 10:00 A.M. for *desayuno,* arrive here early for the *revueltos Norteños*, or scrambled eggs with *nopales*, tomatoes, and black beans. Wash it down with a blood orange aqua fresca.

Tamarindo

Mexican

468 8th St. (at Broadway), Oakland

Phone: 510-444-1944 Lunch & dinner Mon – Sat
Web: www.tamarindoantojeria.com
Prices: $$

Gather a gang of amigos and pop into this sunny spot for a banquet of mouthwatering *antojitos*—small plates, or "little whims." These sharable bites may be small, but they're big on flavor, so park it on the wooden communal table and prepare for a feast. Munch on the likes of Oaxacan tamales steamed in banana leaves; smoky chipotle meatballs; crispy shrimp tacos; or *torta poblana*, a pile of grilled chicken, melted cheese, avocado, and roasted poblano in a fresh torpedo roll spread with black beans and aïoli.

In a space styled in whitewashed walls and tin ceilings, the relatively new Miel tequila bar pours a wealth of *coctels* made with the beloved liquor. Hospitality is first-rate, thanks to Gloria Dominguez and her family, who run the place with heart.

Thai House

Thai

254 Rose Ave. (bet. Diablo Rd. & Linda Mesa Ave.), Danville

Phone: 925-820-0635 — Lunch Mon – Fri
Web: www.thaihousedanville.net — Dinner nightly
Prices:

Want to feel like you're dining in the home of your Thai friends? Visit Thai House, a quaint restaurant just off the beaten path in Danville. This retreat is sheltered within a tranquil cottage filled with blooming flowers, antique chandeliers, and hand-carved wood details. The smiling staff makes guests feel warm and comfy in this appropriately named place.

How spicy can you take it? Hopefully a bit more than usual because they have a one- to four-star system, and the heat kicks in at level 2. The menu is huge and can be a bit overwhelming, but just ask for help and you'll be steered in the right direction. Some of the highlights include tender shrimp in a flavorful hot and sour soup, and juicy chicken simmered in coconut milk and *Massaman* curry.

The Peasant & The Pear

International 

267 Hartz Ave. (at Linda Mesa Ave.), Danville

Phone: 925-820-6611 — Lunch & dinner Tue – Sun
Web: www.thepeasantandthepear.com
Prices: $$

Located in the Danville Clock Center, this warm and hospitable bistro nods to the original Parisian aesthetic where simple, slow-cooked foods are served to you in a modest setting. Within these cozy buttery walls adorned with framed photos, beautiful candle sconces, and pendant lamps, regulars get their fill of bacon-wrapped shrimp over cheddar cheese grits with red eye gravy.

The Peasant & The Pear feels as proverbial as the well-worn dining room of a favorite relative. The zinc bar is an easy perch to sip and gab with the friendly staff. Disciples appreciate the kitchen's love for pears in dishes like *burrata* with pear-honey compote, and a quesadilla with Brie and spiced pear chutney. Sunday dinners feature a three-course meal for $25.

Uzen

Japanese

5415 College Ave. (bet. Hudson St. & Kales Ave.), Oakland

Phone: 510-654-7753 — Lunch Mon – Fri
Web: N/A — Dinner Mon – Sat
Prices: $$

Small Uzen may have a blink-and-you-missed-it façade, but really, you wouldn't want to pass up this very popular sushi restaurant. There isn't much in terms of décor, but the space gets flooded with natural light from a front wall of windows. The best seats in the house are at the sushi bar where you can chat with the friendly chefs who will share their recommendations.

The à la carte menu is ideal for less exploratory palates, but the best way to enjoy Uzen is via their list of fresh nigiri personally handled by the chefs. Traditional flavors come alive in a crispy vegetable roll with toasted nori; firm slices of albacore tuna, rich silky slivers of mackerel, and tender fresh water eel, each presented over neat mounds of sushi rice. It's all so *oishi-so*!

Va de Vi

Fusion

1511 Mt. Diablo Blvd. (near Main St.), Walnut Creek

Phone: 925-979-0100 — Lunch & dinner daily
Web: www.vadevi.com
Prices: $$

When on the prowl for fine wine and globally-inspired eats, Walnut Creek denizens head for the hugely hip Va de Vi. The restaurant has an oak-barrel ceiling, dining tables which run its length, and a front bar packed with stylish locals. And with more than 16 wine varietals available by the glass, the taste, or in flights of three, this über popular (yet relaxed) bistro's focus on wine is true to its Catalan moniker.

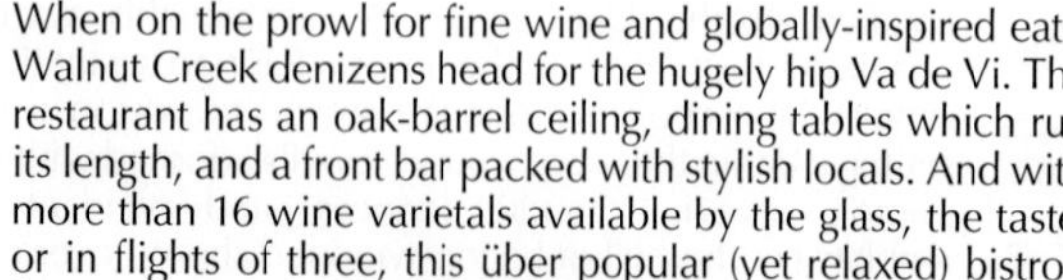

Dishes like English pea bruschetta spread with house-made ricotta, mint, and lemon oil; roasted mushrooms with a slow-poached egg, fennel soubise, and bacon marmalade; or yakitori-style pork meatballs with a soy-sake glaze further demonstrate the menu's international tone and scope. Outdoor seats are near majestic when the sun shines.

Vanessa's Bistro

Vietnamese XX

1715 Solano Ave. (at Tulare Ave.), Berkeley

Phone: 510-525-8300 Dinner Wed – Mon
Web: www.vanessasbistro.com
Prices: $$

There may be no sexier pairing of words than French-Vietnamese, the culinary temptress behind wonders like duck strudel with wild mushrooms and basil risotto. For this tasty fix, head to Vanessa's Bistro, the packed Berkeley spot, run by Chef Vanessa Dang, and begin the night with wicked specialty cocktails at the bamboo-topped bar.

Creative types are wise to listen for the specials; or, go all the way with a four-course tasting menu at just $40. Of course, ordering à la carte does have its perks—small plates are perfectly suited for sharing. Tease your palate with crispy salt-and-pepper prawns with chili-lime dipping sauce, green papaya salad, and banana-raisin-peach bread pudding for dessert. Also look for Vanessa's Bistro in Walnut Creek.

Walnut Creek Yacht Club

Seafood XX

1555 Bonanza St. (at Locust St.), Walnut Creek

Phone: 925-944-3474 Lunch & dinner Mon – Sat
Web: www.wcyc.net
Prices: $$

Keys to a yacht are not required at this marine-themed restaurant in Walnut Creek, with mahogany and teak fixtures and a boatload of sailing tchotchkes. America's Cup pennants and an authentic jib add to the nautical vibe; if that's not enough, grab a seat at the raw bar for a lesson in oyster shucking.

Chef/owner Kevin Weinberg takes seafood seriously—as did the Mako shark now hanging over the bar. Fish is fresh, never frozen, with nearly a dozen daily selections ready to be grilled and served with simple sides. Other aquatic fare may include seafood cocktails; lobster macaroni and cheese gratin; mahi mahi tacos; or an Idaho trout BLT on ciabatta. Few can resist the Commodore's sundae or warm triple chocolate brownie with vanilla bean ice cream.

East Bay

Wood Tavern

B2

Phone: 510-654-6607
Web: www.woodtavern.net
Prices: $$

Lunch Mon – Sat
Dinner nightly

On a stretch of road missing only a candlestick maker, Rebekah and Rich Wood have given the term "tavern" a deliciously new meaning. Wood Tavern is the ultimate salt lick where artisanal charcuterie and cheese boards are divine for soaking up a glass. Here, find many a foodie indulging in happy hours. And why not? With lofty ceilings, sage walls, streetfront windows, and mismatched flatware, Wood Tavern is a charming model of an up-market local spot.

Nab a seat at the counter for a view of the kitchen, where Mediterranean comfort is the fare du jour. Nosh on creamy corn and jalapeño soup; scallops over fennel and spring onion risotto; or crispy confit pork shoulder with puréed garbanzos. If rushed, give their sib sandwich shop "Southie" next door a try.

Zachary's Chicago Pizza

B3

Pizza

5801 College Ave. (at Oak Grove Ave.), Oakland

Phone: 510-655-6385
Web: www.zacharys.com
Prices:

Lunch & dinner daily

In keeping with their reputation of being East Bay's pizza aficionados for over 25 years, Zachary's ensures that their pie is presented with pride at this employee-owned pizzeria. Both locals and lovers of Chicago-style deep dish know that the long wait is part of the deal, and they rest assured in anticipation of the cheesy, calorie-laden Nirvana that is Zachary's signature stuffed pie. Many of the toppings slathered over their tangy tomato sauce are also available on a thin cornmeal crust—though not the favorite spinach and mushroom.

Great for families, this simple spot is always busy (other locations are in Berkeley and San Ramon). To cut down the wait, consider calling ahead to place an order, or take home a "half-baked" pizza to cook in your oven.

Zut!

A2

1820 4th St. (bet. Hearst Ave & Virginia St.), Berkeley

Phone: 510-644-0444 Lunch & dinner daily
Web: www.zutonfourth.com
Prices: **$$**

For ladies looking for a light lunch that won't bog them down while shopping Berkeley's Fourth Street district, Zut! answers the call with tuna Niçoise salads, sandwiches, and wraps. But the warm, cherry and pine wood interior sates heartier palates too, serving oven-baked flatbreads and artisanal pizzas all day—try the cremini mushroom pie with bits of Brie and thyme.

Short for *zut alors*, or "shucks" in French slang, Zut! is a cozy little spot with copper mirrors, billowing textiles, and a backlit bar. At dinner, the Mediterranean café resembles its mural of a bustling restaurant scene as tables are loaded with the likes of lamb meatballs in tangy tomato sauce; falafel with red pepper and yogurt; and chèvre cheesecake on a gingersnap cookie crust.

Bib Gourmand indicates our inspectors' favorites for good value.

San Francisco Travel Association photo by Phil Coblentz

Marin

Marin

Journey north of the Golden Gate Bridge and entrée the sprawling Marin County. Draped along the breathtaking Highway 1, coastal climates hallow this region with abounding agricultural advantages. Snake your way through this gorgeous, meandering county, and find that food oases are spread out. But when fortunate to 'catch' them, expect fresh and luscious seafood, oysters, and cold beer...slurp! Farm-to-table cuisine is the par in North Bay and they boast an avalanche of local food purveyors.

Begin with the prodigious cheese chronicles by visiting the quaint and rustic **Cowgirl Creamery** where "cowgirls" make delicious, distinctive, and artisan cheeses. As a result of focusing and producing only farmstead cheese, they help refine and define artisan cheesemaking...respect! The cheese conte continues at **Point Reyes Farmstead Cheese Co.** For a more lush and heady blue cheese, dive into their decadent 'Original Blue.' These driving and enterprising cheesemakers live by terroir. Restaurants here follow the European standard and offer cheese before, or in lieu of a dessert course. The ideal is simply magical...end of story! Not sweet enough? Get your candy fix on at **Munchies** of Sausalito; or you can opt for a more sinful (and creamy) affair at **Noci**'s gelato. From tales of cheese to ranch romances, **Marin Sun Farms** is at the crest. A magnified butcher shop, their heart, hub, and soul lies in the production of local and natural-fed livestock for a sweeping nexus of establishments—from farmers and grocery stores, to a plethora of restaurants. Speaking of marvelous meats, a visit to **Bryan's Fine Foods** is a must. Although petite in comparison, this Corte Madera haunt is an excellent butcher shop.

If ravenous after hours of scenic driving and the ocean waft, rest at **The Pelican Inn**. Their hearty stew of English country cooking and wide brew of the English 'bar' will leave you craving more of the bucolic. Carry on your hiatus and stroll into foodie paradise, otherwise known as **Spanish Table**. Settled in Mill Valley, gourmand's revel in their selection of Spanish cookbooks, cookware, specialty foods, and rare, palate-pleasing wines. Like most thirsty travelers, let your desire lead the way to **Three Twins Ice Cream**. A lick of their organically-produced creamy goodness is sure to bring heaven to earth.

Waters off the coast here provide divers with exceptional hunting ground, and restaurants across the country seek the same including fresh oysters, fleshy clams, and mussels. The difficulty in obtaining a hunting permit, as well as the inability to retrieve these large savory mollusks, makes red abalone a treasured species, especially in surrounding Asian restaurants. Yet, despite such hurdles, seafood is the accepted norm and form at most restaurants in Marin County. One such gem is **Sam's Anchor Café** known for their glorious views and superbly fresh, well-prepared seafood. Turn the leaf to **Western Boat & Tackle** seafood market. Admired greatly by the fishing community in San Rafael, this seafood shop is outfitted with all things fishy, including a fantastic menu and marine supply store. Not a fan? Entice your palate with authentic and sumptuous Puerto Rican flavors at **Sol Food**. Marin County is known for its deluge of local and organic ingredients carried in the numerous farmers' markets. This marriage of food and wine is best expressed at Sausalito's own "Tour de Cuisine" and The Marin County Tomato Festival. Magnificent Marin, with its panoramic vistas, is one of the most sought after locales and celebrities abound. Thus, some diners may have a touristy mien; however, it is undeniable that restaurants and chefs here are blessed with easy access to the choicest food, produce, and local food agents.

Arti

A1 Indian

7282 Sir Francis Drake Blvd. (at Cintura Ave.), Lagunitas

Phone: 415-488-4700 Lunch & dinner Tue – Sun
Web: www.articafe.com
Prices: $$

If Indian cuisine is about aromas, flavors, and textures, then Arti is an idyllic incarnation. Settled in a surreptitious shopping center in sleepy 'lil Lagunitas, this *desi* den is all charm and cheer—a yellow dining room is propitiously chaperoned by an ample outdoor patio. Befitting its delicate disposition, a handful of tables spaced along wood benches are embellished with colorful pillows and flowering vases.

Arti tantalizes all callers with her inventive food. Tour your way through the fiery south with tangy Goan shrimp *vindaloo*. Then journey north for a beautifully spiced and creamy chicken *tikka masala*. If fish and fowl don't fit the bill, tender lamb cubes in a rich cashew-coconut *korma* served with fragrant basmati rice are bound to hit the spot.

Arun

B1 Thai

385 Bel Marin Keys Blvd. (near Hamilton Dr.), Novato

Phone: 415-883-8017 Lunch Mon – Fri
Web: www.arunnovato.com Dinner nightly
Prices: $$

Nestled in an area void of Thai treats, Arun's is a fresh little find in meandering Marin. This neighborhood dwelling is beloved by businessmen, software suits, and local families alike who can't help but smile at the sight of such large portions of boldly flavored, well-prepared Thai food.

It may reside in a commercial park, but Arun's handsome floors and furnishings, vibrant accents, Thai relics, and friendly staff ooze oodles of warmth. Strutting a variety of dishes, the menu might also unveil tasty Thai finds like *larb gai*, that tasty plate of ground chicken spiked with fish sauce, lime juice, and chilies; and pumpkin curry lush with prawns, potatoes, and coconut milk. The ginger ice cream is spicy, but a perfect palate-cleanser.

Bar Bocce

Pizza

A3

1250 Bridgeway (bet. Johnson & Turney Sts.), Sausalito

Lunch & dinner daily

Phone: 415-331-0555
Web: www.barbocce.com
Prices: $$

The only view in Sausalito to rival Bar Bocce's boat-dotted harbor vista is that of its own wood-burning pizza ovens in the exhibition kitchen. Locals and tourists alike are happy to wait for a seat at a simple wooden table, particularly on weekends, for a taste of the artisanal pies.

Bar Bocce finds inspiration both here and there: while a turn at the bocce court is a tribute to Italy, Dungeness crab and Meyer lemon piled atop an avocado and crème fraîche pizza tastes distinctly like home. Additional pies include calamari and clam sprinkled with spicy chili oil, or pork sausage with fennel pollen and onion. Light salads of artichoke, fennel, celery, and pecorino; roasted chicken with lemon and herbs; and fudgesicles (even winesicles) complete the menu.

Boca Steak

Steakhouse

B1

340 Ignacio Blvd. (bet. Alameda Del Prado & Enfrente Rd.), Novato

Lunch Mon – Fri
Dinner nightly

Phone: 415-883-0901
Web: www.bocasteak.com
Prices: $$

Hidden in plain sight in downtown Novato, Boca Steak evokes a lodge more likely found in Texas or Montana. However, true to his roots, founding chef George Morrone, had this spot designed to evoke the Argentinian ranches of his childhood—featuring comfortable banquettes, "country" tables, and high-pitched ceilings. With so much art around, this is definitely a fresh take on a steakhouse.

Wood-oven roasted prawns in a spicy garlic sauce are best before the steak, which may be a rosemary- and balsamic-marinated ribeye, grilled to a nice char, and served with chimichurri and garlic-smashed potatoes. Be sure to sample the four flavors of empanadas (maybe chicken with *mole*?) before filling up on a banana-mascarpone cake trickled with caramel sauce.

Brick & Bottle

American 

C2

55 Tamal Vista Blvd. (bet. Council Crest Dr. & Chicksaw Ct.), Corte Madera

Phone: 415-924-3366 Dinner nightly
Web: www.brickandbottle.com
Prices: **$$**

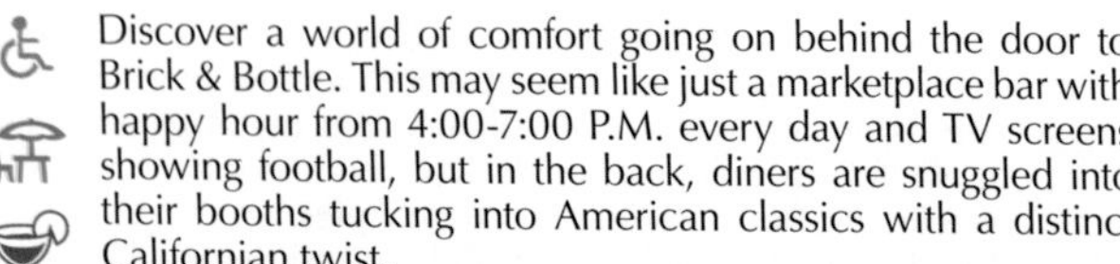
Discover a world of comfort going on behind the door to Brick & Bottle. This may seem like just a marketplace bar with happy hour from 4:00-7:00 P.M. every day and TV screens showing football, but in the back, diners are snuggled into their booths tucking into American classics with a distinct Californian twist.

The pizzas and sandwiches take center stage, as in a pulled pork sandwich with cider-vinegar barbeque sauce. Dinners may include Maine diver scallops with herb risotto, or petrale sole with Dungeness crab and Yukon potato purée. Don't miss the noteworthy side of orzo mac & local goat cheese with tomato jam, or grandmother's lovely recipe for butterscotch pudding. It may not seem the trendiest spot, but the food here is all-American good.

Buckeye Roadhouse

American

A2

15 Shoreline Hwy. (west of Hwy. 101), Mill Valley

Phone: 415-331-2600 Lunch & dinner daily
Web: www.buckeyeroadhouse.com
Prices: **$$**

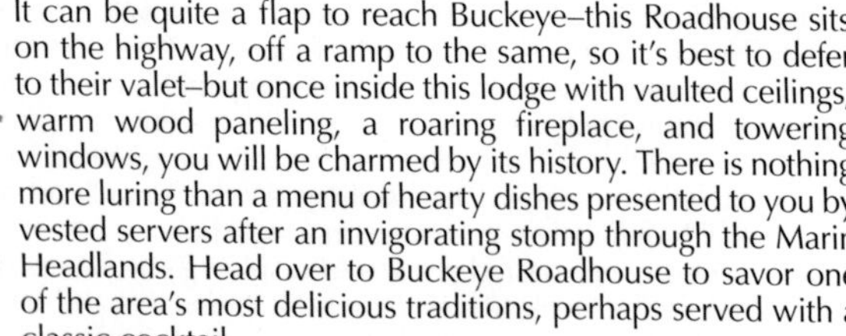
It can be quite a flap to reach Buckeye–this Roadhouse sits on the highway, off a ramp to the same, so it's best to defer to their valet–but once inside this lodge with vaulted ceilings, warm wood paneling, a roaring fireplace, and towering windows, you will be charmed by its history. There is nothing more luring than a menu of hearty dishes presented to you by vested servers after an invigorating stomp through the Marin Headlands. Head over to Buckeye Roadhouse to savor one of the area's most delicious traditions, perhaps served with a classic cocktail.

Dishes may unveil seared scallops with piquillo pepper risotto and mâche; beef brisket with horseradish cream and garlic mashed potatoes; or grilled nectarines and mushroom-goat cheese pudding.

Bungalow 44

American

44 E. Blithedale Ave. (at Sunnyside Ave.), Mill Valley

Phone: 415-381-2500 Dinner nightly
Web: www.bungalow44.com
Prices: $$

Applauded for its fab drinks and delicious food and housed in little Mill Valley, resplendent with chic boutiques and great restaurants like this local fave, Bungalow 44 is heaving with young, trendy couples. Huddled by the bar, their lively chatter and raucous demeanor (blame it on the drinks) can overwhelm the space, but images of crunchy artichoke fritters with tarragon aïoli should resume the calm.

On Wednesday nights they molt into a bit of a supper club, so those seeking a quieter evening should aim for a table in the tented dining area or in the main room past the open kitchen. The menu plays with American dishes, so mouths drool for kickin' fried chicken as well as a surfeit of seafood, pork, and beef specialties from the wood-burning grill.

Copita

Mexican

739 Bridgeway (at Anchor St.), Sausalito

Phone: 415-331-7400 Lunch & dinner daily
Web: www.copitarestaurant.com
Prices: $$

One of Sausalito's newest additions is this breezy Bridgeway bar and kitchen owned by cookbook author Joanne Weir. The congenially attended room is a lovely spot to while away an afternoon amid sienna-glazed walls and vivid tile accents. A wall of tequila bottles behind the bar and a prominently positioned wood-burning rotisserie arouse the desire to drink, eat, and relax.

Headed by two Mexican-born chefs, the kitchen produces south-of-the-border fare dressed with a distinctly Californian sensibility. Munch on crisp jicama batons sprinkled with chile, lime, and salt before delving into a bowlful of tart halibut ceviche studded with ripe mango, or house-made tortillas stuffed with plump shrimp, strips of roasted poblano, and early corn.

Cucina

Italian XX

510 San Anselmo Ave. (at Tunstead Ave.), San Anselmo

Phone: 415-454-2942 Dinner Tue – Sun
Web: www.cucinarestaurantandwinebar.com
Prices: $$

For a case of the warm fuzzies along this quaint main strip of San Anselmo, try this charming and welcoming trattoria. Sunny walls, terra-cotta floors, and a blazing wood-burning oven warm the family-friendly dining room, where the staff greets regulars by name and everyone with a smile. Garlicky tomato bruschetta is a tasty start, compliments of the house.

The ever-changing menu may feature rustic dishes such as *carpaccio di zucchini* dotted with almonds and pecorino; *spaghetti all'Amatriciana* with sautéed pancetta, onions, garlic, and chili flakes; or *tortellini al forno,* meat-filled pasta floating in a creamy prosciutto-and-mushroom sauce studded with generous layers of mozzarella and Parmesan.

The wine bar at back is a perfect post-dinner spot.

El Huarache Loco

1803 Larkspur Landing Circle (near Sir Francis Drake Blvd.), Larkspur

Phone: 415-925-1403 Lunch & dinner daily
Web: www.huaracheloco.com
Prices:

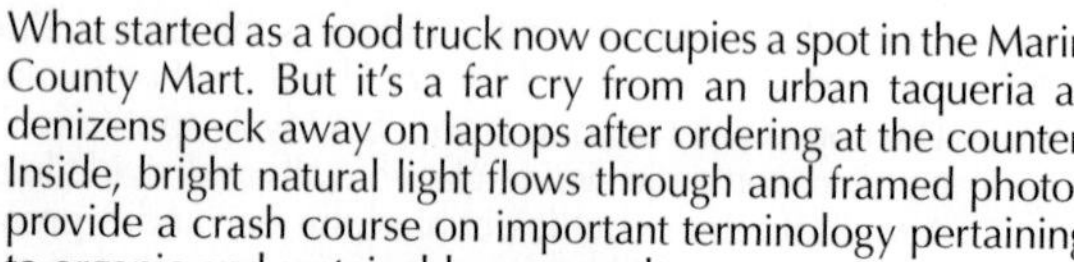

What started as a food truck now occupies a spot in the Marin County Mart. But it's a far cry from an urban taqueria as denizens peck away on laptops after ordering at the counter. Inside, bright natural light flows through and framed photos provide a crash course on important terminology pertaining to organic and sustainable permaculture.

Here, atop a decorative tiled floor, patrons peruse a menu focused on the delicious street foods of Mexico City. Start with crispy fried chicken *taquitos* topped with guacamole and *queso fresco,* or mini *sopes* overflowing with potatoes and chorizo. Try a *huarache* in one of eight versions–perhaps steak or smoky chorizo–crowned with salsas (from a station that covers every level of heat) and nirvana will follow.

El Paseo

American XX

B2

17 Throckmorton Ave. (bet. Blithedale & Sunnyside Aves.), Mill Valley

Dinner nightly

Phone: 415-388-0741
Web: www.elpaseomillvalley.com
Prices: $$$

El Paseo House of Chops isn't cutting any corners when it comes to romancing its diners with a warm and inviting atmosphere. Tucked inside a secluded courtyard that will woo even the most hard-core urbanite with its country appeal, it is also a go-to spot for date night.

If the Smithsonian had a museum of American cuisine, it would certainly include a good portion of this menu. It has all the hits—Parker House rolls with garlic butter sauce, served in a cute cast-iron dish; BLT deviled eggs with caviar for a spruced up version of that family picnic favorite; even chocolate soufflé (borrowed from the French, but perfectly at home state-side). Of course, as the name suggests, El Paseo specializes in meat, and the 38-day, dry-aged sirloin steak is a winner.

Fish

Seafood 

350 Harbor Dr. (off Bridgeway), Sausalito

Lunch & dinner daily

Phone: 415-331-3474
Web: www.331fish.com
Prices: $$

To sate a hankering for sustainable seafood and family-friendly feasts served in a bright and airy space overlooking a picturesque Sausalito harbor, go to Fish. Order at the counter and then pick your perch—broad window walls flood the interior with sunlight and aquatic views, while outdoor picnic tables beckon with toe-dipping proximity to the water.

This casual, cash-only joint serves generous portions composed of organic ingredients to satisfy the whole family. Tangy homemade lemonade is a refreshing companion to grilled tilapia tacos with a mound of fresh cilantro or Anchor Steam-battered cod with rustic wedge "chips."

On your way out, check out the small fish market counter where various raw goods are just waiting to be cooked at home.

Frantoio

Italian XX

152 Shoreline Hwy. (Stinson Beach exit off Hwy. 101), Mill Valley

Phone: 415-289-5777 — Dinner nightly
Web: www.frantoio.com
Prices: $$

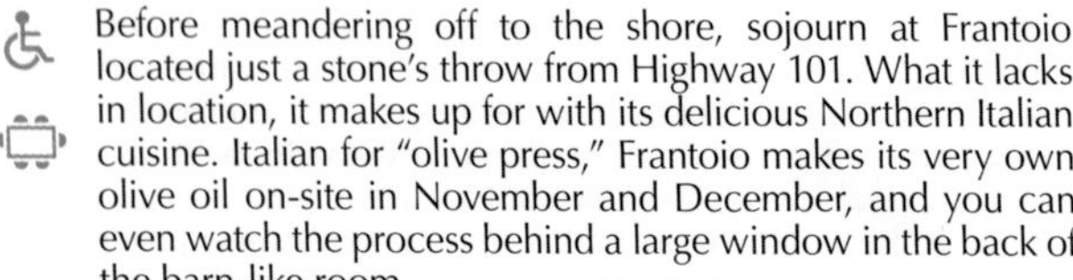

Before meandering off to the shore, sojourn at Frantoio located just a stone's throw from Highway 101. What it lacks in location, it makes up for with its delicious Northern Italian cuisine. Italian for "olive press," Frantoio makes its very own olive oil on-site in November and December, and you can even watch the process behind a large window in the back of the barn-like room.

While lingering at the bar, pick up their floppy leather menu and ogle the ample and fine selection of Italian food. It can get frantic here as high ceilings reverberate with animated conversations over spreads like *pizza salsiccia* with San Marzano tomatoes, sweet Italian sausage, and smoked mozzarella; or homemade pappardelle with pulled braised local rabbit and wild mushrooms.

Hawk's Tavern

American XX

B2

507 Miller Ave. (bet. Reed St. & Camino Alto), Mill Valley

Phone: 415-388-3474 — Lunch & dinner daily
Web: www.hawkstavern.com
Prices: $$

Chef Tyler Florence can't seem to get enough of Mill Valley. His "tavern's" décor underlines a bit of the old west-meets-farmhouse and is furnished with a flagstone gas fireplace, deer antler chandelier, and homey inflections like drinks served in Mason jars. Despite the snug interior, some of the best seats are on the sun-shaded patio.

The menu takes inspiration from British gastropubs—pork sausage and buttermilk mashed potatoes get the title of bangers and mash. A freshly baked pretzel and prawns-and-peppers sautéed with chili and cilantro go hand-in-hand with a salmon BLT comprised of ciabatta stuffed with applewood-smoked bacon and herb aïoli. Plates are too small to share, but a crisp list of wines and craft beers can be enjoyed by one and all.

Insalata's

Mediterranean XX

B2

120 Sir Francis Drake Blvd. (at Barber Ave.), San Anselmo

Phone: 415-457-7700 Lunch & dinner daily
Web: www.insalatas.com
Prices: $$

In Italy, cooking is a family affair. And so it is at Insalata's, the charming Sausalito hangout named for Chef/owner Heidi Krahling's late father, Italo Insalata. Today, Krahling pays homage to her beloved *babbo* by mixing tender loving care with Mediterranean fare and local, seasonal ingredients.

Insalata's dining room is spacious and perpetually packed yet somehow remains snug with wood furnishings and art that depicts nature's bounty. Expect Middle Eastern specialties and meze plates of eggplant fries with *tzatziki*, crispy spanakopita, and duck confit cigars; or heartier fare like a roasted honey- and pomegranate-glazed duck breast with couscous and Moroccan tomato jam. In the spotlight every Tuesday to Thursday night is a prix-fixe for under $30.

Left Bank

French XX

B2

507 Magnolia Ave. (at Ward St.), Larkspur

Phone: 415-927-3331 Lunch & dinner daily
Web: www.leftbank.com
Prices: $$

Next time you're in Larkspur, wing over to Left Bank where pressed-tin ceilings, wood accents, a slender bar, and wraparound dining porch are clues that this is no typical chain restaurant. Tucked inside the town's historic Blue Rock Inn, this authentic French brasserie is one of three Bay Area locations.

Following the Inn's pleasant and calm vibe, Left Bank is a low-key spot to enjoy French comfort foods. On chilly days, the rich onion soup with Emmental gratinée is a must, perhaps paired with a *salade Lyonnaise* tossing frisée, bacon, and a warm poached egg. Fish fans die over *truite Grenobloise*, roasted trout with brown butter, lemon, and capers; while *magret de canard* with spätzle, Brussels sprouts, and huckleberry-Port jus will sate fowl fiends.

Le Garage

French

85 Liberty Ship Way, Ste.109 (off Marinship Way), Sausalito

Phone: 415-332-5625 — Lunch daily
Web: www.legaragebistrosausalito.com — Dinner Mon – Sat
Prices: $$

There may be no other picturesque (and tough to find) place for a Gallic lunch than Le Garage, the Sausalito restaurant at the tip of Liberty Ship Way with a bay breeze and view of bobbing yachts and dinghies. Housed in, yes, a real converted garage, the stark and stylish space features crimson retractable doors thrown open to the waterfront air, making this a serene spot for an aperitif and light lunch.

Servers keep with the service station theme in classic mechanics' uniforms, though the accent is French, of both the staff and food. Pull up a wooden bistro chair and order such delights as shrimp Napoleon with avocado mousse and lobster oil, or Tasmanian pepper-crusted steak with house-cut frites. French and Californian wines make for perfect pairing.

Marché aux Fleurs

Mediterranean

B2

23 Ross Common (off Lagunitas Rd.), Ross

Phone: 415-925-9200 — Dinner Tue – Sat
Web: www.marcheauxfleursrestaurant.com
Prices: $$$

You have not died and gone to the South of France, so don't let your taste buds fool you. It may seem like it, but you are still firmly planted in Marin County in the town of Ross. Named for the celebrated farmer's market in Provence, this French restaurant charms the pants off locals with its farm-fresh cuisine and attractive setting.

Aptly named as the kitchen works exclusively with products sourced from local farmers, this place turns out consistently delicious Mediterranean-inspired dishes. Witness a bit of cheer on every plate from tagliatelle with La Quercia proscuitto, Lacopi peas, and pecorino; grilled fisherman's daughter prawns with Gypsy and Padron peppers; and crispy Sonoma duck with Mission and Kadota figs alongside grilled Torpedo onions.

Marinitas

Latin American XX

218 Sir Francis Drake Blvd. (bet. Bank St. & Tunstead Ave.), San Anselmo

Lunch & dinner daily

Phone: 415-454-8900
Web: www.marinitas.net
Prices: $$

Nothing is free in the posh enclave of Marin. Well, except for those delicious and warm homemade tortilla chips with peppery red and green salsas at Marinitas, Heidi Krahling's local tribute to Mexican and Latin American culinary traditions. The lofty cantina makes everyone feel at home with sports on the big screen and a large stone fireplace to keep the taxidermy warm.

Fresh-squeezed juices and sweet-and-sour mixes made in-house highlight the focus on bright flavors and complement a major tequila selection. Sip one of Marinita's killer margaritas and relax while perusing the menu. With options like grilled Atlantic cod tacos, chile relleno stuffed with butternut squash, and daily specials like savory slow-braised carnitas, choosing can be brutal.

Murray Circle

Californian XX

601 Murray Circle (at Fort Baker), Sausalito

Lunch & dinner daily

Phone: 415-339-4750
Web: www.murraycircle.com
Prices: $$

Winding headlands lead to Murray Circle—the restaurant at Fort Baker's Cavallo Point, also a lodge with dramatic views of the Golden Gate Bridge and SF city. A nostalgic sense of history flows through this charming arena with its pressed-tin ceilings, wagon wheel light fixtures, and front porch dotted with rocking chairs—Murray Circle's colonial spirit entertains guests as well as the general public.

A meal features crispy squid mixed with fried jalapeños; then parcels of Parmesan *gnocchetti* blended with asparagus, fava beans, and hearts of palm. You must not pass up on an excellent torte layering lemon chiffon and key lime curd, garnished with a mango and mint brunoise.

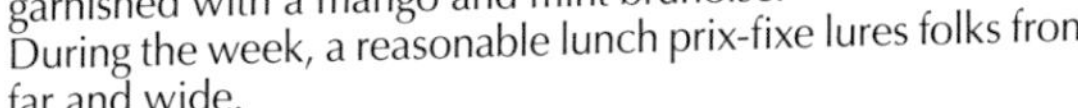

During the week, a reasonable lunch prix-fixe lures folks from far and wide.

Nick's Cove

American XX

23240 Hwy. 1, Marshall

Phone: 415-663-1033
Web: www.nickscove.com
Prices: $$

Lunch & dinner daily

Keep an eye out for the red 1940s pickup truck and ancient green gas pump. Nick's Cove on scenic Hwy 1 is an attraction on its own, but truly it's the food inside that makes this a worthy stop. The bar-cum-lounge is divine; while the main dining room, dotted with taxidermy, maritime plaques, and large tables is coveted by boisterous groups of all ages.

An enclosed patio offers stunning views of Tomales Bay where noisy clusters can be seen enjoying a Dungeness crab *Louis* laden with cucumber, avocado, and a perfect pink "Louis" dressing; or "Nick-erfellers," grilled oysters topped with butter and tarragon-Pernod sauce. Juicy meatballs enhanced with Rossotti Ranch goat cheese are not-to-be-missed, as is the warm gingerbread with Comice pears and sabayon.

Osteria Stellina

A1 — Italian XX

11285 Hwy. 1 (at 3rd St.), Point Reyes Station

Phone: 415-663-9988
Web: www.osteriastellina.com
Prices: $$$

Lunch & dinner daily

Point Reyes Station feels like a mythical Western town with barns, weathered clapboards, and the wholesomeness of an area dominated by cheese-making farms. It's all very restful and sitting on a prominent corner is Stellina. This "little star" sports a lively room within which easygoing patrons enjoy wonderful artwork, and tables graced with tiny vases of fresh flowers.

The menu is impressively listed with places from where ingredients are derived, and expectedly all the items are bursting with flavor. Let the informed staff guide you toward an enjoyable penne with cannellini beans and braised greens; or delicate petrale sole laced with fingerling potatoes and baby carrots. Seal this unforgettable meal with a velvety milk chocolate panna cotta.

Picco

320 Magnolia Ave. (at King St.), Larkspur

Dinner nightly

Phone: 415-924-0300
Web: www.restaurantpicco.com
Prices: $$

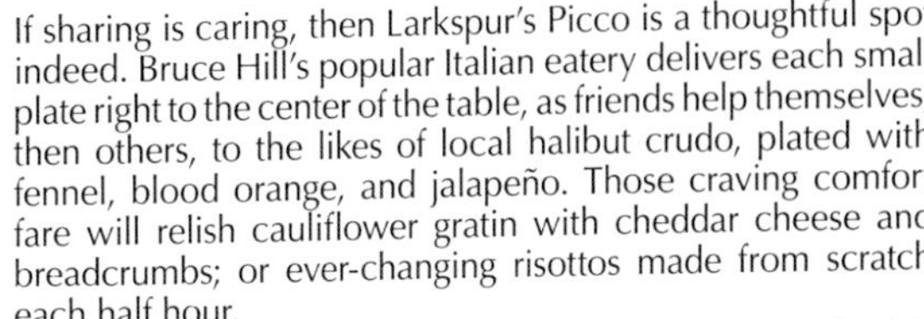

If sharing is caring, then Larkspur's Picco is a thoughtful spot indeed. Bruce Hill's popular Italian eatery delivers each small plate right to the center of the table, as friends help themselves, then others, to the likes of local halibut crudo, plated with fennel, blood orange, and jalapeño. Those craving comfort fare will relish cauliflower gratin with cheddar cheese and breadcrumbs; or ever-changing risottos made from scratch each half hour.

Exposed brick, dim lighting, and redwood accents make this a romantic date-night spot. Before heading home, cap the meal with a selection of artisanal cheeses. Locals love Marin Mondays, which showcase the best of North Bay produce. City dwellers can get a taste of Picco at Hill's SoMa outpost, Zero Zero.

The Plate Shop

Californian

39 Caledonia St. (bet. Johnson & Pine Sts.), Sausalito

Lunch Sun
Dinner Tue – Sun

Phone: 415-887-9047
Web: www.plateshop.net
Prices: $$

From the barely-there signage on a large window pane, The Plate Shop doesn't aim for sexy, but it is! Ensconced in a 100-year-old building that opened as the Gold Dust Bar in 1937, this is a large and charming respite. For all its hard surfaces, there are many soft touches—elusive lighting, cream-colored banquettes, and striking deep red walls.

All the perfect backdrop in which to savor the standout fare that might bring about freshly baked bread and house-churned butter to dunk into grilled local squid slathered with salsa verde, fresh cranberry beans, and smoky chorizo. Tender-seared rabbit braised in a pimento- garlic- and white wine-enhanced broth is deliciously gamey; while maple syrup tart with crème fraîche ensures that you will be back again.

Poggio

Italian XX

777 Bridgeway (at Bay St.), Sausalito

Phone: 415-332-7771

Web: www.poggiotrattoria.com

Prices: $$

Lunch & dinner daily

This "special hillside place" settled on the ground level of Casa Madrona Hotel & Spa, successfully whips out an array of Northern Italian indulgences. Having cooked in the regions of Tuscany and Lombardy, Chef Peter McNee brings authenticity to this menu filled with the freshest Californian products.

Mahogany archways, plush booths, terra-cotta tiles, and a lively bar make dining here quite a thrill, especially in the warmer months when French doors swing open to views of the serene Sausalito yacht harbor across the street. Start with antipasti like wood-fired lamb meatballs before moving on to *primi* such as *strozzapreti* with wild boar sausage, beans, and pecorino; or oak-grilled swordfish with roasted artichokes and potatoes sauced with tapenade.

R'Noh Thai

B2

Thai XX

1000 Magnolia Ave. (bet. Frances & Murray Aves.), Larkspur

Phone: 415-925-0599

Web: www.rnohthai.com

Prices: ⓢⓢ

Lunch Mon – Sat
Dinner nightly

A small back deck overlooking a marshland and bird sanctuary adds to the tranquility of the "Rising sun," a fitting translation for this Thai spot where a soothing vibe, cheery service, and robust flavors uplift and satisfy. The bi-level space rocks with rich red walls and a cozy fireplace on one level, and billowing white fabric under a sunny skylight on the other.

Get your caffeine fix with a creamy Thai iced coffee. When you're ready to chow, choose from any number of delightful curries, salads, soups, noodles, or rice dishes, many of which are prepared with local and organic ingredients. Promising to quench regulars, who are all on a first-name basis with the owner, is a savory affair that includes chicken with coconut rice and spicy salmon curry.

Sushi Ran

Japanese XX

107 Caledonia St. (bet. Pine & Turney Sts.), Sausalito

Phone: 415-332-3620 — Lunch Mon – Fri
Web: www.sushiran.com — Dinner nightly
Prices: $$

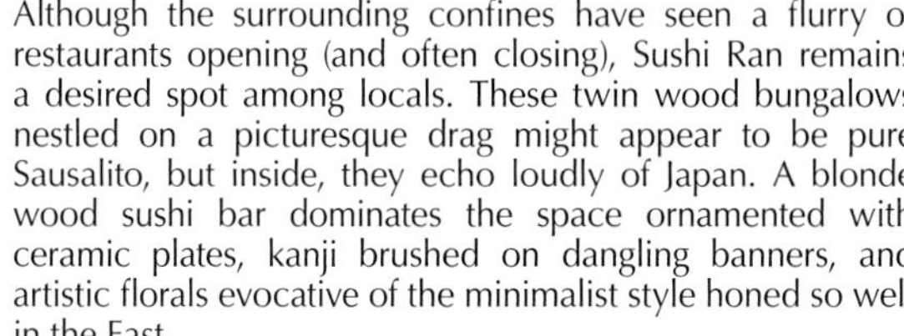

Although the surrounding confines have seen a flurry of restaurants opening (and often closing), Sushi Ran remains a desired spot among locals. These twin wood bungalows nestled on a picturesque drag might appear to be pure Sausalito, but inside, they echo loudly of Japan. A blonde wood sushi bar dominates the space ornamented with ceramic plates, kanji brushed on dangling banners, and artistic florals evocative of the minimalist style honed so well in the East.

Of course, most admired are their lunchtime bento boxes, tempura, and superior maki reflecting Californian and Pacific Rim influences. But, do save room for charred baby octopus with long beans and Thai basil; grilled hamachi *kama* with ponzu; and Wagyu beef carpaccio with *kaiware* and wasabi oil.

Tavern at Lark Creek

American XX

B2

234 Magnolia Ave. (at Madrone Ave.), Larkspur

Phone: 415-924-7766 — Lunch Sun
Web: www.tavernatlarkcreek.com — Dinner nightly
Prices: $$

At Tavern at Lark Creek, a lone dartboard (tucked behind flowers) carries the flag for more traditional taverns inside this redwood-shaded Victorian home with a somewhat misleading name. Valet your wheels and roll up to the spacious bar where wine, not beer, awaits on tap. Order by the glass, half, or full bottle, and congratulate yourself on money well saved.

Another bargain may be found in the fab three-course prix-fixe menu, which changes according to the season. Look for delights such as blue cheese soufflé with arugula, walnuts, and grapes; panko-crusted macaroni and cheese croquettes; and lemon cheesecake brûlée. On weekends, greet the day with brunch at the communal table beneath a massive skylight, or imbibe creative cocktails at dusk.

tavola

Italian 

5800 Nave Dr. (near Roblar Dr.), Novato

Phone: 415-883-6686 Lunch & dinner daily
Web: www.tavolaitaliankitchen.com
Prices: $$

This newcomer to Novato has welcoming service, a casual atmosphere, and streams of light (envision large arched windows) that families will enjoy. Located merely steps from the Hamilton Marketplace shopping center, tavola offers an attractive respite to weary shoppers amidst its stylish space featuring a gleaming exhibition kitchen, concrete floors, and soaring ceilings.

This is the place to refresh with a starter of über creamy *burrata* served with thinly sliced rustic toast spread with a tangy tomato-herb-garlic jam. Refuel with a thin-crust *aglio verde* pizza topped with shaved asparagus, vibrant green garlic, melted asiago, and speck, before splurging on a decadent, rich chocolate ganache tart in an olive oil shell sprinkled with fleur de sel.

Look for the symbol for a brilliant breakfast to start your day off right.

Jay Graham

Peninsula

Peninsula

The Peninsula may not be internationally heralded for its celebrity chefs and groundbreaking Californian cuisine but, with such a diverse population rich in Asian cultures, the area is laden with neighborhood eateries and bountiful markets that appeal to locals craving authentic cuisines. Those seeking a taste of the East can scoop up inexpensive seafood (and links of *longaniza*) alongside the Filipino population at Daly City's **Manila Oriental Market** as well as **Kukje Super Market**, replete with prepared Korean food. If not, they can practice the art of chopstick wielding at one of the many Japanese sushi bars, ramen houses, and *izakayas*. Chinese food fans tickle their fancies with traditional sweets such as assorted mooncakes and yolk pastries at San Mateo's cash-only **Sheng Kee Bakery**; while sugar junkies of the western variety chow on authentic Danish pastries at Burlingame's **Copenhagen Bakery**, also lauded for its special occasion cakes.

In addition to harboring some of the Bay Area's most impressive and enticing Cantonese and dim sum houses, Millbrae is a lovely spot to raise one last toast to summer. The Millbrae Art & Wine Festival is a cornucopia of wicked fairground eats—think gooey cheesesteak, Cajun-style corndogs, and fennel-scented sausages. Wash it all down with a glass of wine or a cold microbrew, and kick up your heels to the tune of a local cover band. Speaking of which, **Back A Yard** (in Menlo Park) may be a total dive, but it offers some über flavorful Caribbean food. If, however, it is cooking classes that you require, head to **Draeger's Market** in San Mateo and sign up for "Indian Cooking Boot Camp" or a lesson in baking "Rustic Italian Breads." While here, also sample artisan and specialty goods (maybe at **Suruki Japanese Market**?), or pick up some wine and cheese to-go. In keeping with take-home deliciousness, Half Moon Bay is a must-stop for insanely fresh and seasonal ingredients. Load up on gorgeous fruits and vegetables at the many roadside stands on Route 92; and don't miss the town's **Coastside Farmers Market** where you'll find local bounty including Harley Farms goat cheese (from Pescadero), and organic eggs from **Green Oaks Creek Farm** up in the Santa Cruz Mountains.

If seafood is more your speed, **Barbara's Fish Trap**, just north in Princeton by the Sea, serves fish 'n' chips by the harbor. And after all that piscine, pork ribs are in order, so join locals at **Gorilla Barbeque** for their meaty combos and down-home sides, served out of an orange railroad car on Cabrillo Highway in Pacifica.

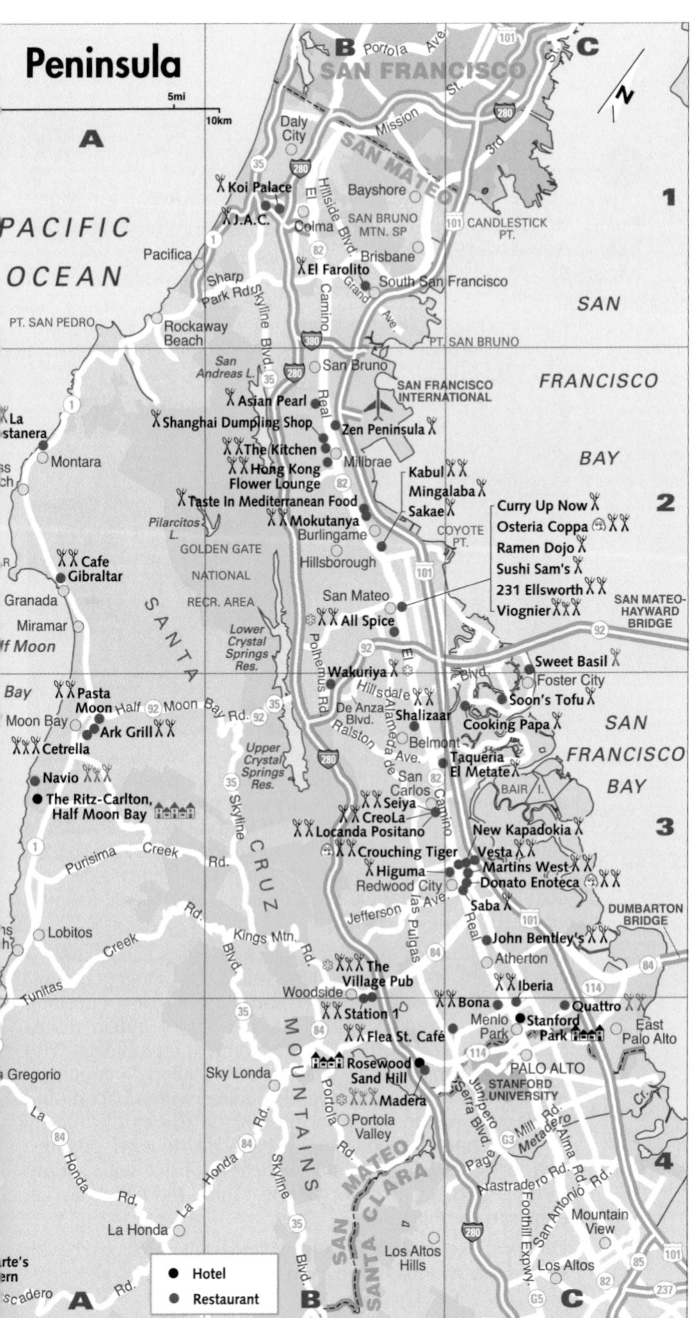
Peninsula
5mi
10km
A
B
C
1
2
3
4
PACIFIC OCEAN
SAN FRANCISCO BAY
SAN FRANCISCO
SAN MATEO
SANTA CRUZ MOUNTAINS
SAN MATEO
SANTA CLARA
Koi Palace
J.A.C.
El Farolito
La Costanera
Shanghai Dumpling Shop
Asian Pearl
Zen Peninsula
The Kitchen
Hong Kong Flower Lounge
Taste In Mediterranean Food
Mokutanya
Kabul
Mingalaba
Sakae
Curry Up Now
Osteria Coppa
Ramen Dojo
Sushi Sam's
231 Ellsworth
Viognier
Cafe Gibraltar
All Spice
Sweet Basil
Wakuriya
Soon's Tofu
Shalizaar
Cooking Papa
Pasta Moon
Ark Grill
Cetrella
Navio
The Ritz-Carlton, Half Moon Bay
Taqueria El Metate
Seiya
CreoLa
Locanda Positano
New Kapadokia
Crouching Tiger
Vesta
Higuma
Martins West
Donato Enoteca
Saba
John Bentley's
The Village Pub
Iberia
Bona
Quattro
Station 1
Stanford Park
Flea St. Café
Rosewood Sand Hill
Madera
Hotel
Restaurant

All Spice ✿

B2 Indian XX

1602 El Camino Real (bet. Barneson & Borel Aves.), San Mateo

Phone: 650-627-4303 Dinner Tue – Sat
Web: www.allspicerestaurant.com
Prices: $$

Hardy Wilson

Blink and you'll miss the sign for this sweet, snug little bungalow, set back from the historic El Camino Real. This is a charming spot with a distinctly warm personality, courtesy of the gracious staff who are truly passionate about the cuisine. Comprised of three quaint rooms with close-spaced tables that are somehow never cramped, All Spice's décor is cozy but has modern accents that lend an upscale feel; the vibe is busy, never chaotic.

Personal touches thrive in the form of soft lighting, a crackling fireplace, windows veiled by sheer curtains, and iridescent wallpaper. Yet one thing remains constant: the kitchen adeptly churns out a roster of Indian dishes that mesh deliciously with Californian ingredients. You may expect the likes of three buttery scallops, intriguingly infused with cumin and lavender, paired with a bacon- and cardamom-potato sauce; or the unique flavors of a crispy *dosa* wrapped around smoky eggplant, toasted peanuts, and tart goat cheese. Butter-poached lobster with shrimp mousse and a drizzle of saffron-vanilla reduction are an exquisite combination.

Desserts like a dark chocolate and sticky-rich *kulfi* with spiced macadamia brittle are perfectly playful.

Ark Grill

 A3

 Indian 

724 Main St. (bet. Correas & Filbert St.), Half Moon Bay

Phone: 650-560-8152
Web: www.arkgrill.com
Prices: $$

Lunch & dinner Tue – Sun

This North Indian newbie offers a lunch buffet and à la carte dinner experience that is worth the trek to Half Moon Bay. Set in a converted old house that has a front bay window and small porch, Ark Grill is flooded with natural light and exudes a homey ambience.

In fact, you may as well be sitting in your *nani*'s kitchen with their roster of boldly spiced and flavored fare. Begin with tasty and crispy-fried samosas stuffed with spiced potatoes and peas, before moving on to entrées like plump, succulent prawns and potatoes stewed in a well-spiced *vindaloo*; or tender chunks of marinated chicken in a creamy *tikka masala*—both the perfect foil for a charred the chewy garlic-cilantro *naan*. Need to turn the heat down? Check in with the obliging staff.

Asian Pearl

 B2

Chinese 

1671 El Camino Real (at Park Pl.), Millbrae

Phone: 650-616-8288
Web: N/A
Prices: 

Lunch Wed, Sat – Sun
Dinner nightly

Asian Pearl is lauded for its dim sum, but the dinner menu of mostly Cantonese-style dishes is really where the restaurant shines. The large banquet style tables are perfect for groups, while smaller rooms can be portioned off for private parties. The staff is curt, but the food is worth it. A back wall lined with tanks full of crustaceans, fish, and mollusks will get your appetite going.

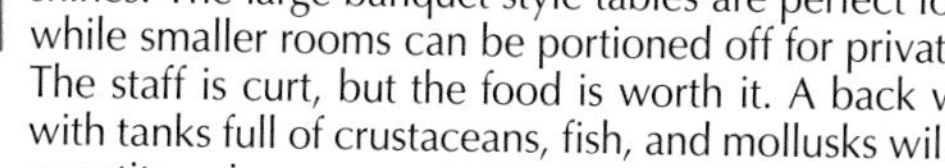

Start with a superbly crisp and crackly-skinned duck that was brined before roasting; then a clay pot filled with tender slices of braised beef in a thick soy- and oyster-sauce—enoki mushrooms are tossed in tableside as if to further tease your taste buds. Can't move? Tender pieces of pumpkin and taro root simmered in creamy coconut milk are also served over the burner.

Bona

Polish XX

651 Maloney St. (bet. Chestnut Ln. & Oak Grove Ave.), Menlo Park

Phone: 650-328-2778 Lunch Tue – Fri
Web: www.bonasrestaurant.com Dinner Tue – Sun
Prices: $$

On an easy-to-miss lane in Menlo Park, Bona's authentic fare is just like your Polish grandmother used to make (or good enough to make you wish you had one). Expect delicious sourdough soup, or *zurek*, made from fermented starter for a fabulously tangy broth laden with potatoes, pork sausage, carrots, and herbs; potato and cheese *pierogis* drizzled in melted butter; and stuffed cabbage rolls smothered in mushroom sauce.

This relative newcomer is already packed with Polish and Eastern European families who appreciate the concise menu and taste of home; but its casual vibe, with wood furnishings and burgundy linen-topped tables, is more than welcoming to foreigners.

And if the food sounds heavy, just wear loose pants, skip dessert, and allow time for a nap.

Cafe Gibraltar

Mediterranean XX

425 Avenue Alhambra (at Palma St.), El Granada

Phone: 650-560-9039 Dinner Tue – Sun
Web: www.cafegibraltar.com
Prices: $$$

The world is small and delicious at Café Gibraltar, the coastal San Mateo county kitchen that melds French, Italian, Persian, and Moroccan flavors all in one big pot—plus a dash of Turkey, Greece, and Spain. Watch the cuisine come to life over the wood-fired oven in the open kitchen, or sink into a floor cushion beneath a tented table tucked away for a sexy North African vibe.

Wherever you sit, prepare to be charmed. Sunny hues and Moorish accents set the scene for Chef/owner Jose Luis Ugalde's aromatic Mediterranean fare. Begin with an ample meze platter laden with flatbread, roasted garlic, olives, and spreads; then meander on to a slow-braised lamb shank in harissa-date-red wine broth. For dessert, indulge in a velvety lavender crème brûlée.

Cetrella

A3

845 Main St. (at Spruce St.), Half Moon Bay

Phone: 650-726-4090
Web: www.cetrella.com
Prices: $$$

Lunch Sun
Dinner Tue – Sun

In the beach town of Half Moon Bay lives stylish and sophisticated Cetrella. Decorated like a Mediterranean villa with stucco walls and vaulted ceilings, there is even a temperature-controlled cheese room bound to gratify those dairy fanatics. The best seats in the house are those in the private wine cellar or around the roaring fireplace in the main dining room, making this a beloved destination for celebrations, groups, and date night.

The enticing *carte du jour* is produced with skill, and may reveal such delights as a velvety green garlic soup, enriched with cream and delicately garnished with a prosciutto chip; or a braised lamb shank with tender root vegetables. Cardamom panna cotta with strawberry salad is the best way to seal this lovely meal.

Cooking Papa

Chinese 

C3

949 Edgewater Blvd., Ste. A (at Beach Park Blvd.), Foster City

Phone: 650-577-1830
Web: www.mycookingpapa.com
Prices: ©©

Lunch & dinner daily

Cooking Papa is a totally casual and deliciously straightforward addition to the Foster City's food scene. Clearly, they are doing something right, as residents routinely line up for a table here. Set in the Edgewater Shopping Center and tucked behind some buildings on the pier, Cooking Papa brags pretty views. Inside it is simply dressed with dark furnishings, a glass-enclosed kitchen, and granite-like tabletops packed with families from grandmothers to babies in strollers.

Weekend dim sum can get wild, so opt for a less crazy weekday lunch or dinner where the staff may deliver pure joy in juicy Peking duck assembled into steamed buns with hoisin and scallions; salty pork with a rich honey-barbecue glaze; or a piping-hot black sesame sweet soup.

CreoLa

Southern XX

344 El Camino Real (bet. Harbour Blvd. & Holly St.), San Carlos

Phone: 650-654-0882 — Lunch Fri
Web: www.creolabistro.com — Dinner Tue – Sun
Prices: $$

Cravin' Cajun? Head on down to this San Carlos favorite for a taste of New Orleans-style heaven where authentic, hearty dishes are fired up with a whole lotta love. Jazz tunes pep up the space, decked in brick and yellow walls, funky art prints, and white wood-planked ceilings.

Loyal locals pack the place, as does a business crowd at lunchtime. Start the feast with delectable crawfish hushpuppies, perfectly spiced and cooked to a tender crunch, served with tasty remoulade sauces for dipping. The Cajun jambalaya is a sure bet comprised of spiced rice chock-full of sliced andouille, plump prawns, shredded chicken, and scallions, served with a quarter of smoky chicken, and grilled slices of sausage and tasso ham. Service is relaxed but responsive.

Crouching Tiger

Chinese XX

2644 Broadway St. (bet. El Camino Real & Perry St.), Redwood City

Phone: 650-298-8881 — Lunch & dinner daily
Web: www.crouchingtigerrestaurant.com
Prices:

A word of warning to the chili-intolerant: this fiery cat will pounce. These Sichuan and Hunan signature dishes ain't for the faint, humming with chilies, chili oil, chili paste, fearlessly kicking up that painful-but-heavenly heat (though tamer options do exist). A popular spot for inexpensive business lunches and family-style dinners, the inviting space sports dark wood furnishings, vibrant touches, and large round tables with lazy Susans.

Get your spice on with a number of delicious goodies, like silky *mapo* tofu with ginger and garlic; flaky white fish filets with sautéed zucchini, carrot, and bamboo shoots braised in red chili sauce; succulent Sichuan prawns; and tender wok-fried Mongolian beef with caramelized onions and oyster sauce.

Curry Up Now

Indian

129 S. B St. (bet. 1st and 2nd Aves.), San Mateo

Phone: 650-477-3000 Lunch & dinner Tue – Sun
Web: www.curryupnow.com
Prices: ⊜

Curry Up Now has settled into its brick and mortar house, though the food truck itself continues to turn its wheels. Having mastered operations, this Indian favorite now capably handles its lunchtime rush with ease. Inside, the colorful chalkboard menu presides by outlining the exotic preparations of the day.

Place your order, pay at the counter, get a number, and wait amid a troop of loyal young professionals. Curry Up Now keeps Indian street food (delivered in biodegradable disposable dishes) inspired and interesting with the likes of a tender *aloo tikki,* potato cake stuffed with farmer's cheese and served with an onion-tomato-cilantro relish; or Punjabi by Nature burrito wrapped with *chicken tikka masala, methi pulao,* and spicy *chana masala.*

Donato Enoteca

C3

Italian

1041 Middlefield Rd. (bet. Jefferson Ave. & Main St.), Redwood City

Phone: 650-701-1000 Lunch & dinner daily
Web: www.donatoenoteca.com
Prices: $$

Donato Enoteca, settled in the heart of Redwood City, oozes with rustic northern ambience from the wood-beamed dining room, to the alfresco patio, to the private wine cellar room. The counter facing the busy open kitchen is perfect for solo diners or those wanting to watch the cooks up close.

The seasonally inspired menu might begin with such wonderfully simple pasta courses as *spaghetti alle vongole* tossed with spicy Calabrian chilies. Expect mains like *controfiletto scalogno*–tender steak served with roasted shallots and fresh rosemary–and sides of organic *fagiolini* flavored with caramelized *guanciale.* Tiramisu layered with espresso-soaked ladyfingers makes a luscious finale. The wine list features a good selection of Italian varietals.

Duarte's Tavern

American

A4

202 Stage Rd. (at Pescadero Creek Rd.), Pescadero

Phone: 650-879-0464 Lunch & dinner daily
Web: www.duartestavern.com
Prices: $$

Duarte's is a longtime favorite of the food media who are perpetually extolling the virtues of this old-time place with amazing American staples. Naturally, die-hard foodies and tourists pack the 115-year-old family-run tavern, but pulling up to its Pescadero locale, it's easy to wonder if you're in the wrong place: Duarte's surrounds resemble the Wild West, and that's part of the charm.

The legendary duo of artichoke and green chile soups (that locals like to mix) is worth all the hype, but instead of a slice of the overrated olallieberry pie focus on the simply prepared seafood and specials. Coastal proximity means superior swimmers so don't miss outstanding baked oysters, pan-seared abalone, lightly fried calamari, or an aromatic bowl of cioppino.

El Farolito

Mexican

B1

394 Grand Ave. (at Maple Ave.), South San Francisco

Phone: 650-737-0138 Lunch & dinner daily
Web: www.elfarolitoinc.com
Prices: 

San Franciscans are welcome to wait in line at the Mission's location of El Farolito, where super burritos are a tasty cult classic. But, just minutes south of town, this San Francisco locale serves the same satisfying fare to a local working class that is happy to walk right up to the counter and order their hearts' content.

Cleaner than most of El Farolito's outposts, the dining room (if you can call it that) is all about cheap, yummy eats. If the massive grilled chicken burrito packed with black beans, rice, and cheese isn't enough to satiate you, take a gander at shrimp ceviche tostadas; slightly spicy green chile pork tacos; or crispy *taquitos* with smoky carne asada. Cinnamon *horchata* is a sweet addition to a meal—never mind the Styrofoam cup.

Flea St. Café

Californian

C4

3607 Alameda de las Pulgas (at Avy Ave.), Menlo Park

Phone: 650-854-1226 Dinner Tue – Sun
Web: www.cooleatz.com
Prices: $$$

Beloved Flea St. Café in Menlo Park fills up early and stays packed until closing time with professor-types and well-to-do couples dressed up for date night. Located on a sloping hill, the homey bungalow features tiered dining areas, pastel walls, white moldings, and cozy candle-lit tables. One of the few bar tables may be open, but reservations are necessary for the dining room.

Flea St. delivers in-season, local, and sustainable ingredients, as in a smooth and earthy roasted pumpkin soup topped with pork belly. Expect the professional service staff to bring the likes of Dungeness crab and sweet potato cake; pan-roasted black cod with nutty wild rice, butternut squash, and crispy leeks; or honey-sweet and gently floral lavender panna cotta.

Higuma

Japanese

C3

540 El Camino Real (bet. Hopkins & Whipple Aves.), Redwood City

Phone: 650-369-3240 Lunch Mon – Fri
Web: www.higuma-restaurant.com Dinner Mon – Sat
Prices:

Easygoing and intimate Higuma is housed in a quaint little bungalow on El Camino Real, and is adored by suits and regulars for its honest Japanese preparations. The small cottage is cloaked in wood and wooden accents (Japanese brown bears, *higumas*, dot the space), and feels rustic and cozy. And nothing says cozy better than steaming, comforting bowls of ramen noodles or a miso soup.

The chef's sushi assortment emerges as an ungarnished array of neat packages of fresh fish placed atop rice. Also featured is a large lineup of specialty rolls, sashimi, and donburi. Seats at the tiny sushi bar are at a premium here, but small tables hug each other in the dining room where you will be greeted with friendly service, pretty prices, and top-notch ingredients.

Hong Kong Flower Lounge

B2 — Chinese XX

51 Millbrae Ave. (at El Camino Real), Millbrae

Phone: 650-692-6666 — Lunch & dinner daily
Web: www.mayflower-seafood.com
Prices: $$

When in Millbrae, do as the local Chinese do and go directly for dim sum at Hong Kong Flower Lounge. No need to look hard—its dramatic, multi-level pagoda-style façade is immediately recognizable. On weekends, bring your morning paper and wait among the crowds craving sticky rice noodle rolls with tender beef and scallions; smoky-salty-sweet sliced barbecue pork; and Wushi–style spareribs infused with rice wine, soy, and ginger.

Luckily, 400 seats give Hong Kong Flower Lounge the upper hand; like the namesake city itself, it is a veritable mob scene. Look for the servers in pink jackets if you don't speak Cantonese. Crowds aren't your thing? Forgo the whirling rolling carts at lunch and come for seafood and traditional à la carte fare at dinner.

Iberia

C4 — Spanish XX

1026 Alma St. (at Ravenswood St.), Menlo Park

Phone: 650-325-8981 — Lunch Mon – Sat
Web: www.iberiarestaurant.com — Dinner nightly
Prices: $$

Spain has landed in Menlo Park, in the form of a fetching brick bungalow on Alma Street. It's a bonanza of bona fide Spanish heart and soul here at Iberia, where traditional tapas, a homey interior, and adjacent food and import shop delight in all things *España*. Seating options range from a gorgeous garden patio; sun-drenched dining room decked in artwork and linen-topped tables; or the impossibly adorable bar set atop hard wood floors.

Beneath the glow of an intricate wine cellar (that hangs overhead), tables are awash with the likes of *tortilla de patatas*, mini pan-fried potato "omelettes;" crispy-fried Dungeness crab fritters; or smoky-sweet chorizo-stuffed dates wrapped in bacon.

Not feeling the tapas? Order the seafood and chicken paella.

J.A.C.

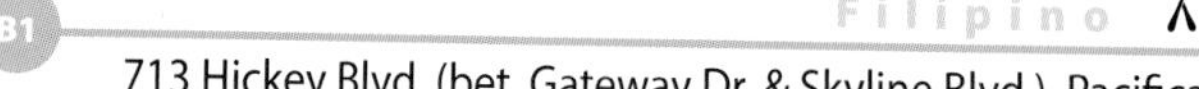

Filipino

713 Hickey Blvd. (bet. Gateway Dr. & Skyline Blvd.), Pacifica

Phone: 650-359-4522 — Lunch & dinner Tue – Sun
Web: www.jacasiancuisine.com
Prices: ⓈⓈ

Try the Fairmont shopping center in Pacifica for some honest to goodness, fresh Filipino treats, and nevermind the slow, spacey service. Inside, J.A.C. (Juan de la Cruz Asian Cuisine) is styled in simple, blonde wood furnishings giving off a casual, clean vibe.

Dishes are authentic, flavorful, and homey, ranging from soups and stews to marinated and grilled pork to deep-fried beef short ribs. Begin with *lumpiang* Shanghai with pork and shrimp—crispy spring rolls stuffed with toothsome ground pork and a single, plump prawn served with a sweet-chili dipping sauce. Look for *"ni Juan"* on the menu, indicating house specialties like the hearty *micehado ni Juan*, with tender beef, carrots, and bell peppers stewed in a tasty tomato, soy, and vinegar broth.

John Bentley's

C3 — Contemporary

2915 El Camino Real (bet. Berkshire Ave. & E. Selby Ln.), Redwood City

Phone: 650-365-7777 — Lunch Mon – Fri
Web: www.johnbentleys.com — Dinner Mon – Sat
Prices: $$$

There's no mistaking a genuine local favorite, and John Bentley's is one such place. Here, you will find all the elements necessary to convert visitors into thorough-bred regulars: a trellised entrance entangled with vines; laid-back ambience; comfortable booths; rustic design; and American fare that is consistently good. Expect a working crowd at lunch and a mix of residents for dinner.

To start, John Bentley's serves a vibrant plate of fresh and spicy tuna tartare frilled with pickled cucumber and wasabi cream. Crispy sweetbreads with smoked bacon, Yukon Gold potatoes, and grain mustard sauce; or grilled marinated ribeye licked with a Gorgonzola-cabernet demi-glace and teamed with roasted garlic mash and broccolini make for exciting courses.

Kabul

Afghan XX

1101 Burlingame Ave. (at California Dr.), Burlingame

Phone: 650-343-2075 Lunch & dinner daily
Web: www.kabulcuisine.com
Prices: **$$**

Sister to the original location in San Carlos, this pleasant Burlingame favorite offers a true taste of Afghanistan amid dark wood furnishings, colorful tapestries, and windowed walls that stream in sunlight. The décor is simple and the service informal, but this local spot is filled with surprises.

The home-style menu may include dishes of *sambosa-e-ghoushti*—fried pastries stuffed with a tender mix of ground lamb and chickpeas infused with garlic and spices. Topped with garlic yogurt, the large, sweet, and silky chunks of pumpkin in *challaw kadu* may actually melt in your mouth. The *kabal-e-gousfand*, skewers of tender marinated lamb, is charbroiled and perfectly completed with fragrant basmati rice and fluffy flatbread sprinkled with poppy seeds.

The Kitchen

Chinese XX

279 El Camino Real (at La Cruz Ave.), Millbrae

Phone: 650-692-9688 Lunch & dinner daily
Web: www.thekitchenmillbrae.com
Prices:

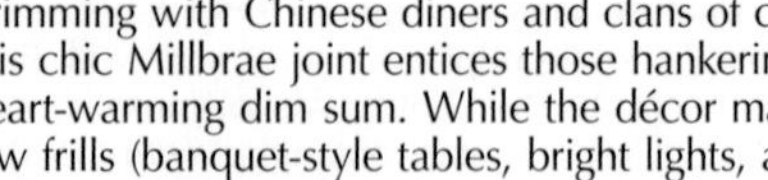

Brimming with Chinese diners and clans of corporate types, this chic Millbrae joint entices those hankering for tasty and heart-warming dim sum. While the décor may boast only a few frills (banquet-style tables, bright lights, and white walls with grey wainscoting), the menu is replete with specialties starring fresh seafood—note the wall of fish and crustacean tanks.

Once inside the airy space, start demolishing sure bets like caramelized, crispy roasted duck folded into steamed *bao* with hoisin; or spareribs glazed in a Sichuan chili sauce. But we suggest taking a hint from the crowd and digging into some dim sum. Try the cold jelly fish and seaweed salad tossed in a rice wine dressing; or go for golden perfection in crispy pork dumplings.

Koi Palace

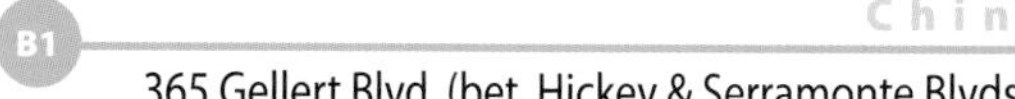

Chinese

365 Gellert Blvd. (bet. Hickey & Serramonte Blvds.), Daly City

Phone: 650-992-9000 — Lunch & dinner daily
Web: www.koipalace.com
Prices:

Koi Palace can seat 400 guests, and the ample parking lot often overflows with cars having to be stationed on the surrounding streets. This phenomenon bespeaks the restaurant's popularity—mostly with a local Chinese clientele who flock here for dim sum at appealing prices.

Walk through the moon gate to spot aquarium tanks swimming with the day's catch; koi ponds in the dining room add aesthetic appeal for adults and provide little ones with entertainment. Try to snag a seat on an aisle for the best service. From here, you can more easily hail the servers who hurry by with a staggering array of items. Offerings include everything from familiar *siu mai* with diced mushrooms or barbecued pork, to exotic fare like poached queen's clam and soya duck slices.

Locanda Positano

Italian

617 Laurel St. (bet. Cherry St. & San Carlos Ave.), San Carlos

Phone: 650-591-5700 — Lunch & dinner daily
Web: www.locanda-positano.com
Prices: $$

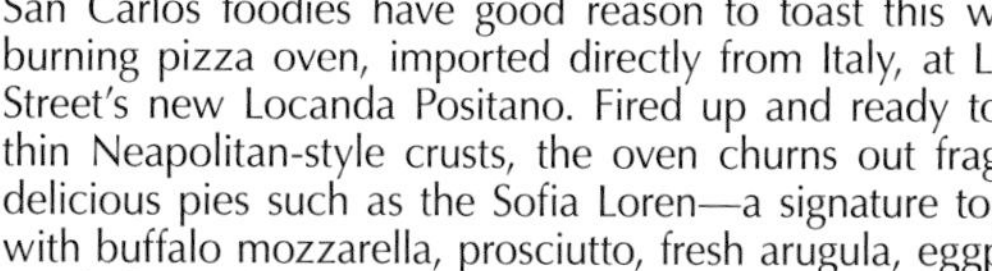

San Carlos foodies have good reason to toast this wood-burning pizza oven, imported directly from Italy, at Laurel Street's new Locanda Positano. Fired up and ready to lick thin Neapolitan-style crusts, the oven churns out fragrant, delicious pies such as the Sofia Loren—a signature topped with buffalo mozzarella, prosciutto, fresh arugula, eggplant, artichoke, and zucchini.

The selection of pizzas, salads, and a menu for *bambini* make this a go-to fave for local families. Amid the chic dining room, find a host of friendly servers buzzing around. Tasty salads like grilled artichokes with arugula in tangy citronette make way for the star of this show, best viewed from a seat at the counter facing the pizza oven.

Visit sister restaurant Limone next door.

La Costanera ✿

Peruvian XX

8150 Cabrillo Hwy. (bet. 1st & 2nd Sts.), Montara

Phone: 650-728-1600 Dinner Tue – Sun
Web: www.lacostanerarestaurant.com
Prices: **$$$**

JFA Images

La Costanera rests on a bluff that overlooks a pristine beach stretching to the Pacific Ocean. Yet this tri-level respite doesn't rest merely on its spectacular, panoramic views. Between the décor (imagine a wall of windows with unobstructed views of the roaring waves, a two-tiered dining room with glass balconies, gleaming skylights) and exquisitely prepared Peruvian fare, La Costanera is a jewel in the crown of coastline dining everywhere.

Inside, the bright and breezy room is dressed with casual style in blond wood floors, small votive lights, and neutral colors.

Friendly servers are attentive and informative in delivering starters like golden-fried yucca balls with salty chorizo, and *cebiche pescado* slathered with spicy *aji rocoto*. The menu goes on to feature such restrained yet flavorful plates as *adobo*—an incredibly moist, slow-cooked pork shoulder wonderfully seasoned with *aji panca* and *aderezo* served atop a lush potato-cheese gratin. Sliced red onions add incredible crunch to saffron-flecked paella brimming with seafood; while *pollo salvaje*, Peruvian roasted chicken coated in a herb-and-garlic paste and coupled with yucca fries, is a tantalizing version of the classic.

Madera ✿

B4

Contemporary XXX

2825 Sand Hill Rd. (at I-280), Menlo Park

Phone: 650-561-1540

Web: www.maderasandhill.com

Prices: $$$$

Lunch & dinner daily

Rosewood Hotels & Resorts

From its spacious home in the sprawling Rosewood Sand Hill Resort, Madera soars with vaulted ceilings, a warming fireplace, and prominent exhibition kitchen. It has a very upscale yet lodge-like ambience, from the polished wood table tops to the shining wood beams overhead, further enhanced by the friendly and efficient service team. An affluent mix of corporate crowds and hotel guests consistently fill the expansive room lined with oversized windows—the views from which are an extraordinary tableau of verdant mountains and evening sky.

The kitchen is undeniably skilled and consistently operates at a high level in creating contemporary dishes with Californian ingredients. The 24-hour braised Wagyu beef stomach is superbly rich with tenderness akin to short ribs, balanced with a deliciously vinegary cabbage-carrot slaw and crisp black rice *arancini* with tangy blood orange flavors. Even humble sides do not disappoint with the likes of roasted and caramelized Brussels sprouts with smoky chestnuts drizzled in Madeira-brown butter.

Sweet poached pears artfully arranged with toasted gingerbread, whipped ginger foam, and refreshing Poire William sherbet combine as a lovely dessert finale.

Martins West

Gastropub XX

831 Main St. (bet. Broadway & Stambaugh Sts.), Redwood City

Phone: 650-366-4366 — Lunch Wed – Sat
Web: www.martinswestgp.com — Dinner Mon – Sat
Prices: $$

This gastropub brings old-world charm to Redwood City with a rich wood bar, wax-dripped candelabras, and exposed brick walls. Yet it shines with new-world edge through brushed aluminum chairs, exposed steel beams, and reclaimed materials.

This is all reflected in a kitchen dedicated to contemporary interpretations of pub classics—think golden-fried Scotch quail eggs, their velvety yolks infused with garlic, fennel, and a touch of pepper. Served with updated farm-to-table fashion, "rarebit" becomes thick slices of toasted artisanal bread with savory fenugreek béchamel and tomato-mozzarella salad.

A subdued lunch crowd walks in from the nearby courthouse and city offices. Cocktail hour and dinner have that deliciously rambunctious vibe, befitting a pub.

Mingalaba

Asian X

B2

1213 Burlingame Ave. (bet. Lorton Ave. & Park Rd.), Burlingame

Phone: 650-343-3228 — Lunch & dinner daily
Web: www.mingalabarestaurant.com
Prices:

Take a break from strolling the shops of Burlingame Ave., and step inside Mingalaba. This quick service hot spot has a loyal and large following, so get here early to avoid a wait. Amidst bamboo wainscoting, modern lighting, and bright walls gilded with Asian artifacts, crowds gather if only to get a whiff of the kitchen's Burmese (and Mandarin) preparations. Most locals know the drill and let cheery servers tempt with bold Burmese fare over more forgettable Mandarin menu options. Begin with a *lap pat dok* (tea leaf salad); move on to a Burmese-style black pepper soup with fish; break at string beans with dried shrimp; and finally, thrill your taste buds with a spicy lamb curry. Cool down at dessert with mango pudding served in a leaf-shaped bowl.

Mokutanya

B2 Japanese

1155 California Dr. (bet. Broadway & Carmelita Ave.), Burlingame

Phone: 650-348-9388 Lunch & dinner daily
Web: www.themokutanya.com
Prices: $$

Newcomer Mokutanya epitomizes sleek modernity, nevermind the little strip mall location. The ultra-cool space is a palette of black surfaces, bright red cushions, and white serving pieces. A red accent wall cuts away to reveal the charcoal grill and an enticing collection of sake bottles. To sit at the sunken, dark wood tables, slip off your shoes and slide onto a red cushion as you rest your legs in the well below. Glass partitions lend an air of privacy.

The charcoal-grilled yakitori and *kushiyaki* specialties are intensely smoky and irresistible here. There are no missteps, from skewers of bacon-wrapped asparagus and Kurobuta pork sausage with a trio of dipping salts, to rich duck breast and well-seasoned chicken meatballs drizzled with spicy aïoli.

Navio

A3 Californian

1 Miramontes Point Rd. (at Hwy. 1), Half Moon Bay

Phone: 650-712-7040 Lunch Sat – Sun
Web: www.naviorestaurant.com Dinner nightly
Prices: $$$$

Housed in the Ritz-Carlton and boasting spectacular ocean views, Navio begins with a level of refinement that carries through to the barrel-vaulted ceilings, tufted chocolate leather banquettes, and internationally inspired Californian fare from the dramatic exhibition kitchen.

This is the Ritz, so elegance is de rigueur; but it's also the Bay Area, so expect a local bent. The menu highlights area producers in dishes like roasted quail with wild rice-orzo pilaf, sherried raisins, and royal trumpet mushrooms; hamachi with grapefruit, yuzu, and taro chips; or a chocolate peanutbar with peanut ice cream.

Not every dish is transcendent here, but a vista of the California sun dripping into dusky Half Moon Bay may be all the epiphany you can handle over dinner.

New Kapadokia

2399 Broadway St. (at Winslow St.), Redwood City

Phone: 650-368-5500 — Lunch Tue – Fri
Web: www.newkapadokia.us — Dinner Tue – Sun
Prices:

This precious mom-and-pop eatery plumb in the heart of Redwood City fires up plates of inexpensive Turkish goodness. The simple, narrow interior is painted mauve with mounted iron sconces, framed pictures, and a lovely mural of a Mevlevi (or Sufi) dancer adorning the back wall.

Warm the belly with a red lentil soup chock-full of mint, cumin, and garlic; followed by *sarma beyti kebab,* skewered ground beef, broiled and wrapped in Turkish flatbread, served in tomato sauce and drizzled with garlic yogurt. Carb fans will adore the *sebzeli güveç* (vegetable and lamb casserole coupled with rice); while the *kunefe,* is a fine way to end—sweet cheese baked between layers of shredded filo dough, drizzled with cherry syrup, and sprinkled with chopped pistachios.

Osteria Coppa

Italian

139 S. B St. (bet. 1st & 2nd Aves.), San Mateo

Phone: 650-579-6021 — Lunch Mon –Fri
Web: www.osteriacoppa.com — Dinner nightly
Prices: $$

Osteria Coppa may not literally mean "pasta," but this house-made specialty is on everyone's mind upon entering. The spacious dining room is rustic, contemporary and relaxed—though hungry hearts are known to skip a beat upon glimpsing those racks of fresh, drying pasta in the kitchen. If available, the *scialatielli* is a rare treat: thicker than spaghetti, it has an alluring texture, perhaps served here in tomato sauce with roasted eggplant and shaved ricotta *salata*.

Whether sitting in the back dining patio or enjoying the windowed tables overlooking B Street, the service is friendly. And if you don't feel like pasta, the thin-crust pizza topped with sausage crumbles, speck, tender cremini mushrooms, and spicy Calabrian chilies is simply delicious.

Pasta Moon

Italian XX

315 Main St. (at Mill St.), Half Moon Bay

Phone: 650-726-5125 Lunch & dinner daily
Web: www.pastamoon.com
Prices: $$

It's definitely *amore* when this (Pasta) moon hits your eye. Located on the main drag in charming Half Moon Bay, Pasta Moon is a sure bet for yup, you guessed it, pasta!

Its design can feel like a haphazard and half-finished mix of spaces that afford views of pasta-making during trips to the restrooms; but after a few bites, you won't care that the owner needs to find an architect—stat. Dreamy pastas along with homemade pizzas and breads are divine. You can't go wrong with anything on this Californian-Italian menu. The lasagna strays from grandma's standard with impressive results and is packed with rich, creamy flavor; while crispy *fritto misto* and a Brussels sprout salad tossed with pancetta and cannellini beans are beloved at all times.

Quattro

2050 University Ave. (at I-101), East Palo Alto

Phone: 650-566-1200 Lunch & dinner daily
Web: www.quattrorestaurant.com
Prices: $$$

Inside the Four Seasons Silicon Valley, Quattro is inspired by the constant revolution of nature. A garden patio is ideal for warmer months while a blaring fireplace in the lounge wards off a winter chill. Amongst its wall of windows, the main dining room feels like a solarium whose lofty ceilings are drenched in natural light, and plush chairs invite businessmen and posh couples to get cozy. Frosted glass panels lend extra privacy to the banquettes.

A casually refined clientele peruse the seasonal menu which may unveil such contemporary Italian treats as a chilled carrot soup with watermelon radish, goat cheese panna cotta, and lavender honey; hand-cut fettucini with Manila clams, lemon, and parsley; or sockeye salmon Marsala with raisins and caponata.

Ramen Dojo

Japanese

B2

805 S. B St. (bet. 8th & 9th Sts.), San Mateo

Phone: 650-401-6568 Lunch & dinner Wed – Mon
Web: N/A
Prices:

Busy office types find plenty of time to catch up on the morning paper while in line for lunch at Ramen Dojo, the popular San Mateo Japanese noodle house that often comes with a half hour wait. Add your name to the clipboard at the door and ponder your soup of choice.

The dining room isn't much to look at, and service is quick and minimal, but everyone is here for the hearty, steaming bowls of ramen. Soups are available with three base options (soy sauce, garlic-pork, and soy bean) and three degrees of heat (mild, regular, and extra spicy). All orders come heaped with roasted pork, fried garlic, kikurage mushrooms, scallions, and hard-boiled quail egg, but a list of extra toppings also includes Napa cabbage, shiitake mushrooms, and Kurobuta pork.

Saba

Vietnamese

C3

823 Hamilton St. (bet. Broadway & Winslow Sts.), Redwood City

Phone: 650-257-3759 Lunch & dinner Mon – Sat
Web: www.sabacaferwc.com
Prices: **$$**

Drop by this downtown Redwood City newcomer, where tasty Vietnamese *banh mi* are served up at lunch and shared small plates showcase at dinner. The interior is polished and contemporary with blond wood chairs, aluminum tables, pale grey walls, and flowers sprinkled about adding a dash of color.

Tuck into grilled, marinated pork rolls packed with mint, lettuce, cucumber, and pickled carrot, served with a chili sauce for dipping; spicy lemongrass chicken stir-fried with green onion and chilies; or plump shell-on prawns tossed in a sweet tamarind sauce fragrant and rich with fresh cilantro, garlic, and butter. Other pleasures uncover grilled quail ambrosial with coriander; or banana leaf-wrapped salmon. A convenient parking lot is available for drivers.

Sakae

Japanese

243 California Dr. (at Highland Ave.), Burlingame

Phone: 650-348-4064
Web: www.sakaesushi.com
Prices: $$

Lunch Mon – Sat
Dinner nightly

Downtown Burlingame may be the last place one would expect to find authentic sushi, but Sakae hits the spot with fish flown in daily from Japan's Tsukiji Market. While it may be surprising, this stylish eatery is certainly no secret—at lunch, the blond wood sushi bar and tables are crammed with local business suits.

For those on the go, affordable combinations are an easy treat; but those with time to savor a meal should first check out the boards listing the daily specials. Sample a nigiri plate of albacore and bluefin tuna, kanpachi, and mackerel; or warm up with a bowl of udon noodle soup with seaweed and spicy *togarashi.*

Weekends feature sake flights and live karaoke for all. Also try Yuzu, their sister restaurant in San Mateo.

Seiya

Japanese

741 Laurel St. (bet. Cherry & Olive Sts.), San Carlos

Phone: 650-508-8888
Web: www.seiyasushi.com
Prices: $$

Lunch Tue – Fri
Dinner nightly

Sleepy San Carlos has awoken to find this mod Japanese respite, Seiya, in its midst. Inside, find an urbane Asian aesthetic in dark wood furnishings, stone accent walls, low lights, and a long sushi bar. Lunch is quiet, but come dinnertime, the handful of tables and sushi counter fill up with locals eager to sample and share the small plates.

And this is what sets Seiya apart: a full range menu–revealing small plates, *robata*, sushi, sashimi, and maki–that has a little something for everyone. Try the beef *tataki* (seared filet mignon with garlic tataki sauce); *ankimo* (monkfish liver with garlic ponzu); or Great Balls of Fire (deep-fried, panko-crusted, spicy tuna roll with spicy mayo). Savor sesame and green tea ice cream on the sidewalk patio on warm days.

Shalizaar

B3 — Persian XX

300 El Camino Real (bet. Anita & Belmont Aves.), Belmont

Phone: 650-596-9000 — Lunch & dinner daily
Web: www.shalizaar.com
Prices: $$

For a taste of Persia on this side of the pond, head to Shalizaar—a large restaurant sleekly attired in wood floors, walls of windows, and French doors that flood the room with light. A central chandelier adorned with leaves sparkles above beautiful wood-wainscoting and a communal table packed with corporate casts and families alike.

An open wood-fired oven in the back is used for baking warm flatbread paired with feta, walnuts, and fresh mint. Served with every meal, this may be chased by ample portions of *tah dig*, crisped rice topped with *gheymeh* (a flavorful stew of ground beef, chickpeas, and Persian spices); *soltani* mingling *barg* and *koobideh* (beef) kabobs with saffron-tinged white rice; and flaky *baghlava* redolent of walnuts and cinnamon.

Shanghai Dumpling Shop

B2 — Chinese X

455 Broadway (bet. Hillcrest & Taylor Blvds.), Millbrae

Phone: 650-697-0682 — Lunch & dinner daily
Web: N/A
Prices: ⊜

They say that good things come to those who wait. At Shanghai Dumpling Shop, the mmm-mmm goodness comes in the form of delectable soup dumplings, or *xiao long bao* to those in the know. Served with black vinegar and bits of ginger, these tender pork-stuffed morsels may be the gateway to Nirvana. Of course, half the town is lining up at the gates of heaven, so prepare to park it on the sidewalk before claiming a table at lunch.

This particular slice of paradise comes with minimal décor, but the place is packed to the rafters with suits looking to cheer up on authentic and soul-warming Shanghainese treats. Other offerings include fluffy steamed pork buns; spicy wontons with peanut-chili sauce; and black sesame dumplings bobbing in a rice wine soup.

Soon's Tofu

Korean

1062 Foster City Blvd. (at Marlin Ave.), Foster City

Phone: 650-286-0860 Lunch & dinner daily
Web: www.soonstofu.com
Prices: 

This Korean newcomer to Foster City is housed in a shopping center. Its industrial-minimal look is painted with concrete floors, exposed ductwork, and hanging pendant lights. Soon's Tofu is casual and caters to local families.

Meals start with a collection of tasty *banchan* like Korean-style potato salad and marinated vegetables in sesame oil. From there, venture into a flavorful tofu stew presented in a stone bowl with spicy kimchi and scallions, topped with a deliciously runny egg. A large bowl of beef *bibimbap* with mounds of daikon and tangy shiitake mushrooms is crowned with a perfectly fried egg; while heaping piles of short-ribs steeped in a sweet-salty sauce and grilled until smoky and caramelized are best for big appetites.

Station 1

Californian

2991 Woodside Rd. (bet. Mountain Home & Whiskey Hill Rds.), Woodside

Phone: 650-851-4988 Dinner Tue – Sat
Web: www.station1restaurant.com
Prices: $$$

Station 1 is a quaint Californian eatery tucked into picturesque Woodside. The restaurant feels homey and familiar, furnished with repurposed barn wood tables, a cozy fireplace, and covered back porch. In other words, head this way with your date night or for a quiet family feast.

The menu spins to highlight local and seasonal ingredients, but a set tasting deal could reveal butter bean and prosciutto soup; a poached farm egg atop buttery black rice garnished with enoki mushrooms and shisito peppers; or tender "pork squared," named for the braised pork shoulder as well as the loin, cooked with black tea and served over a sweet roasted plum purée and pickled cabbage salad. To conclude, savor a sweet absinthe lemon bar with a torched juniper marshmallow.

Peninsula

Sushi Sam's

B2 Japanese

218 E. 3rd Ave. (bet. B St. & Ellsworth Ave.), San Mateo

Phone: 650-344-0888 Lunch & dinner Tue – Sat
Web: www.sushisams.com
Prices: $$

Do not be fooled by the no-frills dining space and nondescript exterior—this San Mateo sushi spot is a treasure. Forget the lunchtime bento box and opt for the luscious omakase, which promises that this very good little *sushi-ya* understands excellence.

On this menu, the chef prepares generous slices of their freshest fish, with garnishes that enhance natural flavors. Expect succulent, sweet blue shrimp; silky butterfish topped with tangy pickled daikon and scallions; ponzu-topped wild Japanese yellowtail; or sweet lobster nigiri with creamy *tobiko* mayo and toasted, sliced almonds. Dessert may include mild and velvety *teh kuan yin* panna cotta, delicately embellished with chrysanthemum syrup, poached goji berries, crispy puffed brown rice, and *mochi*.

Sweet Basil

C2 Thai

1473 Beach Park Blvd. (at Marlin Ave.), Foster City

Phone: 650-212-5788 Lunch & dinner daily
Web: www.sweetbasilfoster.com
Prices: $$

It's no wonder this Thai fave (and Thai Idea, its vegetarian baby sis a few doors down) is forever-packed. Superb ingredients whipped up into irresistible plates of sumptuousness keep folks coming back every time. Chillin' in a shopping center in Foster City, Sweet Basil's casual vibe and chic décor is marked by modern light fixtures, multi-hued wood floors, and black-lacquered chairs.

Atop bamboo tabletops, feast on such delectable offerings as red coconut curry overflowing with juicy prawns, pumpkin, carrots, bamboo shoots, and basil; or *pad see-ew*, wide stir-fried noodles tossed with cabbage, broccoli, egg, and tender slices of beef. The sweet basil chicken speckled with chilies, onions, and crunchy bell peppers is a classic that never fails to sate.

Taqueria El Metate

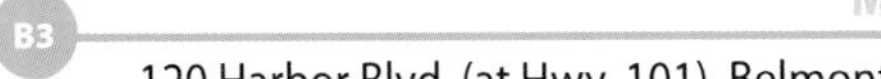

Mexican

B3

120 Harbor Blvd. (at Hwy. 101), Belmont

Phone: 650-595-1110 Lunch & dinner daily
Web: N/A
Prices: $$

Taqueria El Metate will become a personal favorite as soon as you've discovered it. Most everybody here seems well acquainted with this classic hangout and its long lines out the door. From the Harbor Blvd. exit off Highway 101 south, make a sharp right to arrive at their parking lot. Inside, El Metate is roomy with rows of hand-painted local furniture; the wood tables and chairs depict colorful scenes of Mexican food and art.

Long tables laden with chips and salsa feel communal; plan to share these during peak hours. The delicious scent of a pork chili verde burrito filled with rice, beans, and *queso fresco*; and the salty and pineapple-sweet, caramelized *al pastor* "super" taco topped with chopped onion and cilantro have everyone clamoring for more.

Taste In Mediterranean Food

Mediterranean 

B2

1199 Broadway, Ste. 1 (bet. Chula Vista & Laguna Aves.), Burlingame

Phone: 650-348-3097 Lunch & dinner daily
Web: www.tasteinbroadway.com
Prices: $$

Put simply, this unassuming spot spins out the best *shawarma* and falafel on the Peninsula. It's a pay-at-the-counter kind of place, where refrigerator cases display Mediterranean dips, salads, and spreads, while tempting trays of baklava make the mouth water. On a warm day, grab a table on the dog-friendly sidewalk and enjoy their Medi-Middle Eastern goodness.

A vegetarian plate of crispy falafel hits the spot; made with chickpeas, parsley, garlic, spices, and served with tahini sauce, creamy hummus, and a fresh cucumber, tomato, and red onion salad. If craving meat, go for a lamb *shawarma* pita wrap—shaved slices of spit-roasted lamb heaped into a pita with roasted potato, fresh vegetables, and topped with garlicky yogurt and a drizzle of spicy red aïoli.

231 Ellsworth

B2 **Contemporary** XX

231 S. Ellsworth Ave. (bet. 2nd & 3rd Aves.), San Mateo

Phone: 650-347-7231 Lunch Tue – Fri
Web: www.231ellsworth.com Dinner Mon – Sat
Prices: $$$

231 Ellsworth is one of the most popular picks for company junkets in San Mateo. Businessmen adore this contemporary pearl for its reliably good American food served in a classically elegant setting. For those ever-important deals, find refuge in one of many private dining areas. Otherwise, the main room with mauve walls, metallic accents, and a dramatic blue barrel ceiling offers a pretty perspective.

The finest seats in the house are at the cushioned banquettes, but a wine cellar up front is ace for a casual repast that may unveil the likes of roasted vegetables smothered in a rich buttery-cheesy sauce; fresh, seared and flaky king salmon paired with Italian butter beans; and a decadent Valrhona chocolate lava cake crowned with *feuilletine*.

Vesta

C3 **Pizza** XX

2022 Broadway St. (bet. Jefferson Ave. & Main St.), Redwood City

Phone: 650-362-5052 Lunch & dinner Tue – Sat
Web: www.vestarwc.com
Prices: $$

Vesta is a newbie in downtown Redwood City that churns out a roster of artisan pizzas and sumptuous Italian small plates. The restaurant sports a chic dining room with an open kitchen pivoted around a wood-fired oven; whereas a wall of glass-paneled doors opens onto the patio to give the space an exemplary indoor-outdoor feel.

Expect tasty flavor combos like *burrata* with heirloom tomatoes, drizzled with balsamic vinegar and basil-garlic pesto. Share a plate of succulent pork meatballs served with a salad of shaved Parmesan and arugula; or devour a thin-crust, wood-fired pizza slathered with tomato sauce, Italian sausage, spicy chilies, mascarpone, and sweetened with honey for an interesting balance. No surprise that she is already a local gem.

The Village Pub ✿

Gastropub XXX

B3

2967 Woodside Rd. (off Whiskey Hill Rd.), Woodside

Phone: 650-851-9888
Web: www.thevillagepub.net
Prices: $$

Lunch Sun – Fri
Dinner nightly

Ed Anderson

In its picturesque home of Woodside, The Village Pub leads two distinct lives. On the one hand, it is a comfortable pub that flaunts traditional trappings like coffered ceilings with dark wood beams, a roaring fireplace, and low lighting. At the same time, it is a place for fine dining amid elegant table settings, a suited wait staff, and plush velvet banquettes. Expect this pub to be fully packed with an affluent clientele of locals, couples, groups, and a sophisticated, casual-chic bar crowd.

At the bar, peruse the pub menu of charcuterie, cheese, burgers, and refined small plates like a perfectly rich pork pâté, balanced with tangy port-soaked cherries and the traditional accompaniments of cornichons and a bit of frisée salad.

On the full dining room menu, find a delightful combination of earthiness and richness in the tender abalone over a creamy pillow of cauliflower mousseline, topped with a soft-poached egg and fluffy truffle foam. Other highlights include the puff pastry almost overflowing with crispy sweetbreads, root vegetables, porcini mushrooms, and rich Madeira-veal jus. Desserts may show a refined take on classics, such as a creamy white chocolate-and-banana cream tart.

Peninsula

Viognier

Contemporary XXX

B2

222 E. 4th Ave. (at B St.), San Mateo

Phone: 650-685-3727 Dinner Mon – Sat
Web: www.viognierrestaurant.com
Prices: **$$$**

Get gussied up and make your way to this elegant spot, nestled atop Draeger's Market in San Mateo. Spend an afternoon browsing the aisles of the gourmet grocery below, or sneak a peek at the cooking class taught in the kitchen upstairs. It's a full day of foodie heaven! Finally, snag a cushioned banquette next to the fireplace and let the feasting begin.

The menu divides into three- four- or five-course fixed price meals where the following may be featured: a salad of heirloom tomatoes with creamy mozzarella, fresh basil, black olive tapenade, and toasted slices of Levain bread; chased by cuttlefish slices with grilled shrimp posed atop white peaches. Pleasing palates for its unique flavors is grilled Hawaiian walu posed over a square of *pommes fondant*.

Zen Peninsula

Chinese X

B2

1180 El Camino Real (at Center St.), Millbrae

Phone: 650-616-9388 Lunch & dinner daily
Web: www.zenpeninsula.com
Prices: **$$**

It's a dim sum extravaganza here at Zen Peninsula where delicious, steaming hot bites served out of traditional rolling carts keep the crowds a coming. Special event menus and à la carte seafood specialties are also on offer, but that's not why you're here. Tightly positioned, banquet-style round tables fill up with large groups devouring the likes of *har gow*—sticky wrappers stuffed with shrimp, ginger, garlic, and sesame oil; or roasted suckling pig in a smoky-sweet five spice glaze.

Be prepared to wait for a table during peak hours or on weekends. Clearly the never-ending crowds can't get enough of lip-smacking ground beef crêpes drizzled with soy and sprinkled with slices of scallion; or fluffy egg custard buns flavored with a hint of coconut.

Wakuriya ✿

Japanese

B3

115 De Anza Blvd. (at Parrot Dr.), San Mateo

Phone: 650-286-0410 Dinner Wed – Sun
Web: www.wakuriya.com
Prices: $$$$

Wakuriya

Everything here conveys simplicity, from the shopping center location and bare wood décor to the small staff, as if to belie the superb cuisine of Chef Katsuhiro Yamasaki. Reservations are competitive and absolutely necessary—especially for seating along the dining counter facing the chef as he prepares the kaiseki. A shelf of sake bottles provides a bit of visual interest, but even sake becomes more beautiful when poured into the crystal, free-form glasses alongside lacquered trays and delicate Japanese pottery.

A handful of guests include tech types and those aficionados craving an authentic kaiseki experience, which Wakuriya delivers.

This nightly chef's menu is the only option. Highlights might include an appetizer trio of deep-fried pork with daikon-ponzu sauce and cherry, uni with sushi rice and Parmesan sauce, and slow-cooked jade eggplant in a mirin marinade, followed by an exquisite *chawan mushi* with duck and fava beans. The sashimi course will be superbly fresh. Then on to a lightly seared wagyu beef artfully arranged with cherry tomato, *hon shimeji* mushroom, seaweed, and okra. Conclude with the likes of *sake-kasu* (lees) blancmange topped with a subtly sweet strawberry coulis.

Peter L. Wrenn/MICHELIN

South Bay

South Bay

Tech geeks around the world know the way to San Jose, but foodies typically will get lost in San Francisco. It's a shame really as tech money plus an international population equals a dynamic and superb culinary scene. Not to mention the rich wine culture descending from the Santa Cruz Mountains, where a burgeoning vintner community takes great pride in its work. In May, sample over 70 area wines at the **Santa Cruz Mountains Wine Express**, at Roaring Camp Railroad in Felton.

Festive Foods

The Valley may have a nerdy rep, but South Bay locals definitely know how to party. In San Jose, the festival season kicks off in May with music, dancing, drinks, and eats at the wildly adored **Greek Festival**. Then in June, buckets of cornhusks wait to be stuffed and sold at the **Story Road Tamale Festival**, held within the orchards of Emma Prusch Farm Park. In July, Japantown comes alive for the two-day **Obon/Bazaar** and, in August, the Italian-American Heritage Foundation celebrates its yearly **Family Festa**. **Santana Row** also keeps the party going year-round: This sleek shopping village is home to numerous upscale restaurants, and its very own farmer's market. Opened in August 2010, San Jose's newest and noted foodie destination is **San Pedro Square Market**, which houses artisan merchants at the historic Peralta Adobe downtown. Farmers and specialty markets are a way of life for South Bay locals and each city has at least one or more throughout the week.

A Morsel of Vietnam

San Jose is also a melting pot for global culinary influences. Neighborhood *pho* shops and *banh mi* delis sate the growing Vietnamese community, which also heads toward **Grand Century Mall** for hard-to-find authentic snacks. Meanwhile, the intersection of King and Tully streets, is home to some of the area's best Vietnamese flavors: Try **Huong Lan** for its delicious *banh mi* sandwiches; cream puffs at **Hong-Van Bakery**; and crispy green waffles flavored with *pandan* paste at **Century Bakery**, just a few blocks away. And that's not all—**Lion Plaza** is another hub for Vietnamese bakeries, markets, and canteens. If Cambodian noodle soup is more your cup of tea, look no further than **Nam Vang Restaurant** or **F&D Yummy**. The large and lofty **Dynasty Chinese Seafood Restaurant**, on Story Road, is popular for big parties and is also the local dim sum favorite. In the Asian vein, **Nijiya Market** is a Japanese market (in Mountain View) venerated for its specialty goods, fabulous ingredients, and all things

Japanese. Long before it was trendy to be organic in America, Nijiya's mission was to bring the taste of Japan in the form of high-quality, seasonal, and local ingredients to the California crowd. Stop by this Far East sanctum for fresh seafood, meat, veggies, and fruit, as well as an array of sushi and bento boxes. Also available on their website are a spectrum of sumptuous recipes ranging from faithful noodle and rice preparations to ethnic specialties. Moving from Asia to South America, devotees of Mexican cuisine are smitten by the fresh and still-warm tortillas at **Tropicana** or surprisingly good tacos from one of the area's 18 **Mi Pueblo Food Centers**.

A Spread for Students

However, there is more to the South Bay than just San Jose. Los Gatos is home to the sweet patisserie **Fleur de Cocoa** as well as **Testarossa Winery**, the Bay Area's oldest, continually operating winery. Meanwhile, Palo Alto is a casual home base for the countless students and faculty of reputed Stanford University. Here, locals line up for organic, artisanal yogurts (both fresh and frozen) at **Fraîche**; and delish double-decker sandwiches at **Village Cheese House** (perhaps the vegetarian-friendly Italian Veggie-ball spread with tofu, marinara, and mozzarella?). If you're dreaming of Korean food, make your way to Santa Clara where the Korean community enjoys a range of authentic nibbles and tasty spreads at **Lawrence Plaza** food court. And if in urgent need of groceries, shopping along El Camino Real near the Lawrence Expressway intersection is a feast for the eyes. Local foodies favor the caramelized and roasted sweet potatoes at **Sweet Potato Stall**, just outside the Galleria, and **SGD Tofu House** for *bibimbop* or *soondubu jjigae*. Despite the fast pace of technology in Silicon Valley, **Slow Food**–the grassroots movement dedicated to local food traditions–has a thriving South Bay chapter.

Even Google, in Mountain View, feeds its staff three organic square meals a day. For a selection of delicacies, South Bay's eateries and stores dish up gourmet goods and ethnic eats. The rest of us can visit nearby **Milk Pail Market**, known for more than 300 varieties of cheese. Make your pick between such splendid choices as Camembert, Bleu d'Auvergne, Morbier, and Cabriquet. Another haunt favored by meat-loving mortals is **Los Gatos Meats & Smokehouse**. This flesh mecca has been serving the South Bay community for years via a plethora of poultry, fish, and fresh-butchered meat sandwiches. Revered by all, this salt haven also quenches diners with such homey "specialties" as prime rib roasts, pork loin, beef jerky, sausages, corned beef, and bacon...regular, pepper, country-style or Canadian? Pair your charcuterie and cheese with a bottle from Mountain View's famous **Savvy Seller Wine Bar & Wine Shop**—it's a picnic in the making!

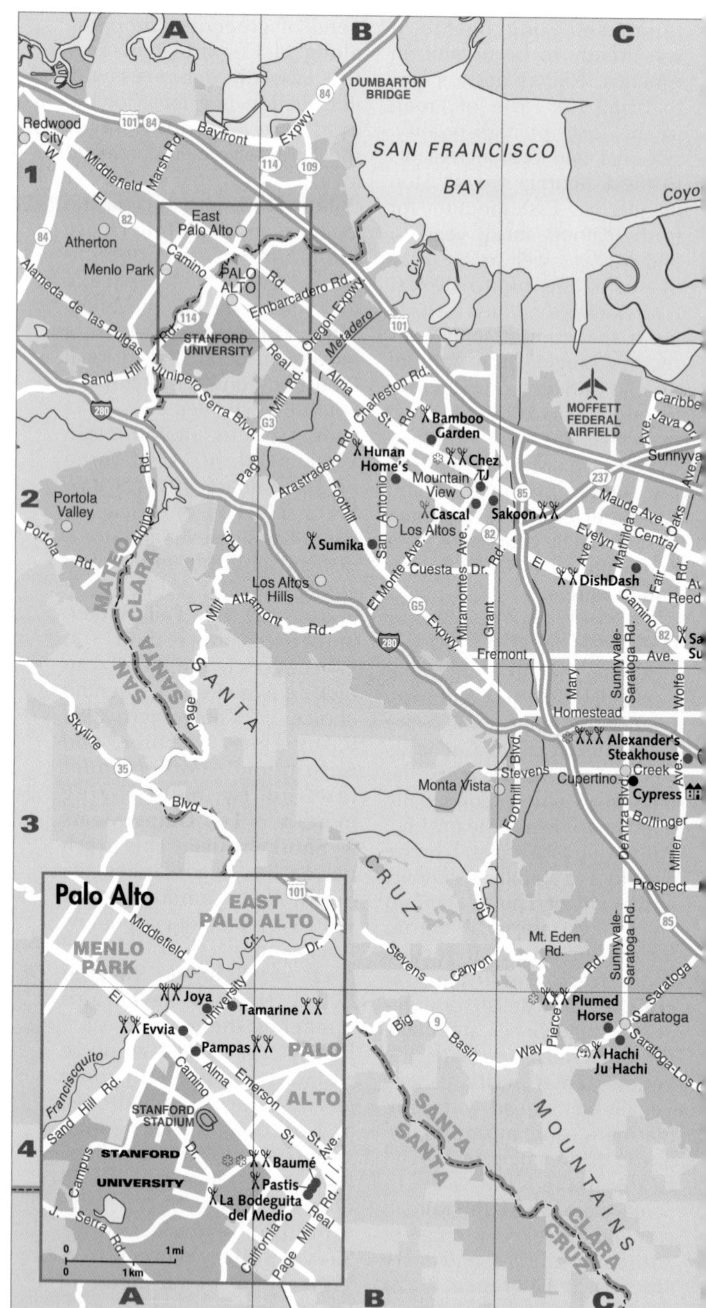

A
B
C
1
2
3
4
DUMBARTON BRIDGE
SAN FRANCISCO BAY
Redwood City
Bayfront Expwy.
Middlefield
Marsh Rd.
El Camino Real
East Palo Alto
Atherton
Menlo Park
PALO ALTO
Embarcadero Rd.
Oregon Expwy.
Metadero
Alameda de las Pulgas
STANFORD UNIVERSITY
Sand Hill Rd.
Junipero Serra Blvd.
Page Mill Rd.
Alma St.
Charleston Rd.
Coyo
Caribbe
Java Dr.
Sunnyva
MOFFETT FEDERAL AIRFIELD
Bamboo Garden
Hunan Home's
Chez TJ
Mountain View
Arastradero Rd.
Foothill
San Antonio
Cascal
Sakoon
Los Altos
Sumika
Maude Ave.
Evelyn Ave.
Central
Mathilda Ave.
Oaks
Portola Valley
Portola Rd.
Alpine Rd.
Los Altos Hills
Altamont Rd.
El Monte Ave.
Cuesta Dr.
Miramontes Ave.
Grant Rd.
DishDash
Fair
Reed
Expwy.
Fremont Ave.
Sunnyvale-Saratoga Rd.
Mary
Wolfe
Homestead
SAN MATEO
SANTA CLARA
SANTA
Skyline Blvd.
Alexander's Steakhouse
Creek
Cupertino
Cypress
Monta Vista
Stevens
Foothill Blvd.
Bollinger
DeAnza Blvd.
Miller
Prospect
CRUZ
Mt. Eden Rd.
Stevens Canyon Rd.
Plumed Horse
Saratoga
Big Basin Way
Pierce Rd.
Hachi Ju Hachi
Saratoga-Los
MOUNTAINS
SANTA CRUZ
SANTA CLARA
Palo Alto
EAST PALO ALTO
MENLO PARK
Middlefield
Cr.
Dr.
University
Joya
Tamarine
Evvia
Pampas
PALO ALTO
Francisquito
Sand Hill Rd.
Camino
Alma
Emerson
STANFORD STADIUM
STANFORD
UNIVERSITY
Campus
Dr.
Baumé
Pastis
La Bodeguita del Medio
J. Serra Rd.
Page Mill Rd.
California
Real
St.
Ave.
0
1 mi
0
1 km

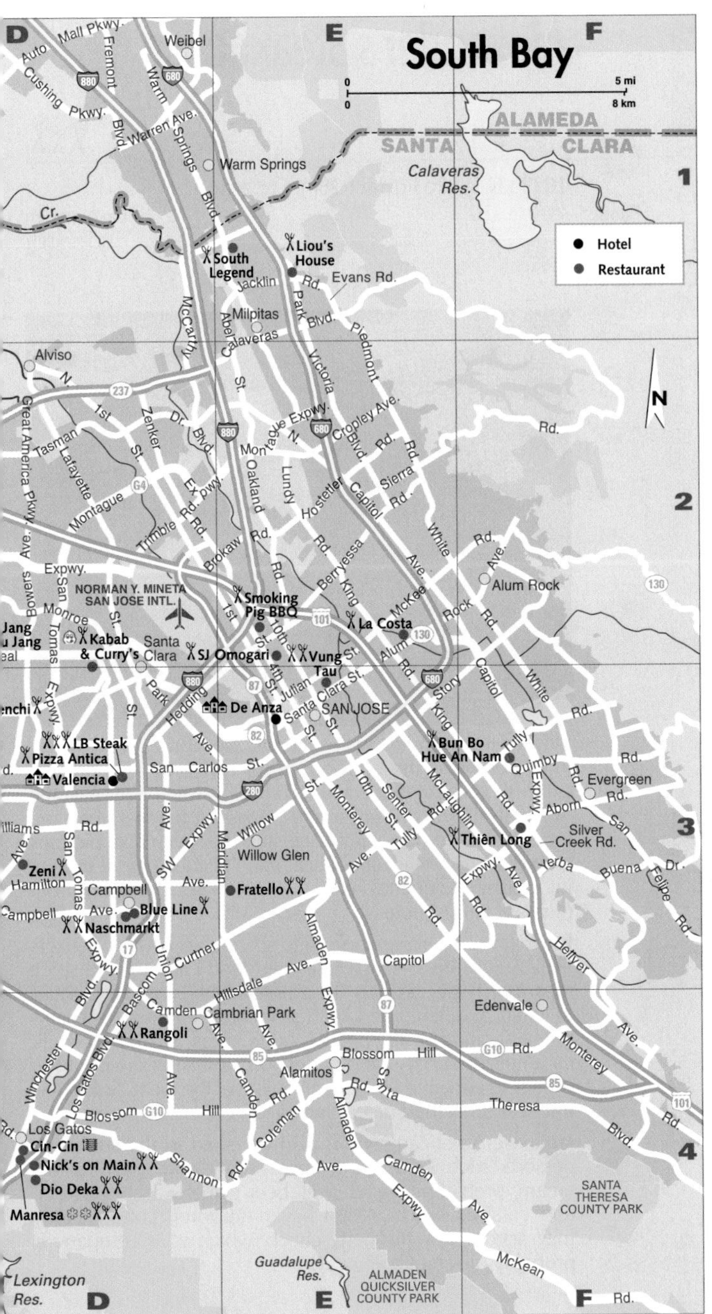

South Bay
0 5 mi
0 8 km
Hotel
Restaurant
ALAMEDA
SANTA CLARA
Calaveras Res.
Warm Springs
Weibel
Liou's House
South Legend
Milpitas
Alviso
NORMAN Y. MINETA SAN JOSE INTL.
Smoking Pig BBQ
La Costa
Alum Rock
Kabab & Curry's
Santa Clara
SJ Omogari
Vung Tau
De Anza
SAN JOSE
LB Steak
Pizza Antica
Valencia
Bun Bo Hue An Nam
Evergreen
Thiên Long
Willow Glen
Zeni
Campbell
Blue Line
Naschmarkt
Fratello
Rangoli
Cambrian Park
Edenvale
Alamitos
Los Gatos
Cin-Cin
Nick's on Main
Dio Deka
Manresa
SANTA THERESA COUNTY PARK
Guadalupe Res.
ALMADEN QUICKSILVER COUNTY PARK
Lexington Res.

Alexander's Steakhouse ✿

Steakhouse XXX

C3

10330 N. Wolfe Rd. (at I-280), Cupertino

Phone: 408-446-2222 — Lunch Tue – Fri

Web: www.alexanderssteakhouse.com — Dinner nightly

Prices: $$$$

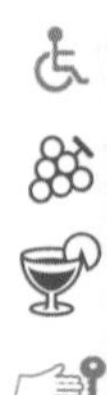

Jeffrey Stout/Alexander's Steakhouse

Despite the shopping mall environs, Alexander's Steakhouse in Cupertino is the go-to place for tech-types conducting expense account dinners. Suited businessmen filter past the steaks in the meat-aging rooms, pause at the front bar and lounge dressed with a fireplace, and may even take pictures with the chef at the central exhibition kitchen before settling into cushy banquettes and large armchairs in this busy but pleasant atmosphere.

Cupertino's clientele appreciate sharing copious appetizers like "Angry Birds"—Japanese-style fried chicken in a spicy *togarashi* batter, kicked up a notch with deep-fried slices of chili, and tempered with a creamy egg sauce. Mains might include a dry-aged T-bone steak seared to well-caramelized, pretty pink perfection, and served with a trio of salts to enhance the rich minerality of the meat. Sides may uncover duck fried rice or mixed sautéed mushrooms.

Japanese-American style is also reflected in the surprising desserts such as a warm apple confit with cheddar ice cream, pretzel-pecan streusel, beer gelée, wasabi powder, and caramel sauce. A fun banana-flavored cotton candy may accompany the hefty check, which your company is probably picking up anyway.

Bamboo Garden

108 N. Rengstorff Ave. (at Central Expwy.), Mountain View

Phone: 650-967-7334 Lunch daily
Web: www.bamboogardenmv.com Dinner Mon – Sat
Prices: ⓈⓈ

Don't let the fuss-free shopping center and well-worn interior deter you. This is the go-to place for real deal Shanghainese cuisine. Just follow the local Chinese residents, who can be found relishing in these fantastically authentic offerings. The menu provides some Americanized fare as well as some Mandarin options, but stay with their traditional items and you will be golden.

The sticky rice–served in a hollowed-out bamboo stalk and studded with tender-braised pork, fatty pork belly, and bamboo shoots–is an outstanding dish. Other notables feature rich and flavorful smoked duck; fresh fish fillets stewed in a thick rice wine sauce with wood ear mushrooms; or Shanghai greens—spinach shoots sautéed with broth, garlic, goji berries, and sesame oil.

Blue Line

415 E. Campbell Ave. (bet. Civic Center Dr. & Railway Ave.), Campbell

Phone: 408-378-2800 Lunch & dinner daily
Web: www.bluelinepizza.com
Prices: $$

Sibling to the ever-popular Little Star pizza, Blue Line is a new recruit to the South Bay that is fast becoming a favorite. This large, casual dining room is mobbed by locals flanking its flat-screens, while families mill about amid exposed ductwork and blue-painted walls.

Named for the Chicago Blue Line, the cornmeal-crusted, deep-dish pizzas are sure to please—perhaps the veggie version with a thick tomato sauce filled with cheese and packed with zucchini, peppers, and mushrooms? For those who don't go deep, the thin-crust Italian combo offers a layer of sauce generously heaped with pepperoni, salami, and olives. Conveniently located on Campbell Avenue steps from the light rail tracks, you can also pick up baked or half-baked pizzas on your way home.

Baumé ✿✿

B4 — Contemporary XX

201 S. California Ave. (at Park Blvd.), Palo Alto

Phone: 650-328-8899 Lunch Fri
Web: www.baumerestaurant.com Dinner Wed – Sun
Prices: $$$$

Peter Giles

Look for the bright orange door of this rather nondescript single-story building, and be rewarded. Inside, the two dining areas are semi-private with dramatic floor-to-ceiling striped orange curtains. Inlaid marble and tile floors enhance the minimal design, though brightly colored triangular plates pop with a dash of whimsy. The pleasant ambience makes Baumé popular among well-dressed business types and special occasion celebrants.

The fixed menu isn't exactly a menu per se, but the list of ingredients that will comprise your meal each night. The black-suited and very adept service team will inquire as to any allergies or aversions, then thoroughly explain each dish as it is presented.

Expect the chef to employ both modernist and classic techniques throughout meals that might begin with a zesty young radish with mint-scented pea purée, followed by cool stalks of poached asparagus topped with a luscious egg-yolk and truffle-oil sabayon beneath a generous shaving of Perigord truffles. An accompanying shot of celery juice further awakens the palate. A silky morsel of poached turbot is served over a fragrant coriander-cumin sauce, with pink peppercorns, fava beans and leaves.

Bun Bo Hue An Nam

F3 — Vietnamese

2060 Tully Rd. (at Quimby Rd.), San Jose

Phone: 408-270-7100
Web: N/A
Prices: ⊜

Lunch & dinner daily

Take a cue from Vietnamese locals and march into this popular San Jose joint for steaming bowls of fantastic *pho*. Soups and stews are the name of the game here, many of which are jazzed up with ingredients like shrimp cake, soft tendon, fat brisket, and tripe. Slurp down the *bún bò hue*—spicy beef soup with tender chunks of flank steak, pork knuckles, shrimp cake, and rice noodles in a fragrant lemongrass broth, presented with a pile of fresh bean sprouts, mint, cilantro, lemon wedges, and green chilies. Or sample the *pho bò áp chao*—piquant pan-fried beef dressed in a garlic-lemongrass chili sauce, tossed over rice noodles with peppers, onions, basil, cilantro, and mint.

This is the second of two locations–the first is also in San Jose–on Story Road.

Cascal

B2 — Spanish

400 Castro St. (at California St.), Mountain View

Phone: 650-940-9500
Web: www.cascalrestaurant.com
Prices: **$$**

Lunch & dinner daily

It's no mystery why Mountain View locals adore Cascal: this vibrant eatery shakes infinite and wickedly tempting variations on the mojito, margarita, and caipirinha for a festive after-work crowd. They also seduce many on a restricted diet with vegetarian, dairy-free, and gluten-free items.

Splashy hues and dressed-up Spanish architectural elements like wrought-iron fixtures and polished wood tables hint at the Latin, tapas-style fare.

Flavorful dishes might include braised oxtail in a Rioja wine and herb sauce; marinated grilled quail stuffed with caramelized shallots; and duck confit *gorditas* paired with a chipotle- chile- and espresso sauce. At lunch, Cascal is a popular escape among the cubicle crowd, while dog lovers enjoy family meals on the patio.

Chez TJ ✿

Contemporary XX

B2

938 Villa St. (bet. Bryant & Franklin Sts.), Mountain View

Phone: 650-964-7466 Dinner Tue – Sat
Web: www.cheztj.com
Prices: $$$$

Mark Leet

Quaint architecture reflects Chez TJ's past as a former home in the heart of Mountain View. Each room is small and unique in wallpaper or paint, but all are colorful with charming details that include bay windows, a roaring fireplace, and hand-blown glass lamps. This is indeed a festive spot for local professionals, but it's also where foodies go for date-night.

Expect polished service with thorough explanations of each dish on the fixed menus ranging from four to eight courses, with wines offered as full- or half-pairings.

There is talent, risk, and reward in many of these dishes, courtesy of a kitchen that dares to verge on being fussy. Starters can be as vibrant as they are unique: the rose and lemon-cured yellowtail begins with eating a menthol candy to awaken the palate to the bright and delicious flavors. This might be followed by fresh scallops cooked until translucent, served with drops of black garlic coulis, tiny broccoli florets, toasted pine-nut powder, and blood orange gelée. As a finale, a chocolate bread pudding is warm and infused with smoky ancho chili, spicy cinnamon, and ground black sesame seeds, alongside supremely nutty *kinako* (roasted soybean paste) ice cream.

Cin-Cin

International

D4

368 Village Ln. (at Saratoga Los Gatos Rd.), Los Gatos

Phone: 408-354-8006 Dinner Mon – Sat
Web: www.cincinwinebar.com
Prices: $$

Sure, enjoy that well-priced Happy Hour (Monday-Saturday from 4:00 - 6:00 P.M.), but just make sure to stick around for the wonderfully diverse range of international small plates. Almost any craving can be quenched here, where Asian, American, Mexican, French, and Italian goodies are available for a sharing showdown.

The lively wine bar is styled in blond woods, pale greens, and low lights, with two adjoining dining spaces and a primo lounge. To start, fill up on lettuce cups piled with cold soba noodles, shaved apple, fried shiitakes, and sauced with chipotle aïoli. Hamburger sliders on silver dollar rolls with grilled onion and aged cheddar fondue; or Korean tacos heaped with kimchi and shaved rib eye are a delightful balance of flavor and texture.

Dio Deka

Greek

D4

210 E. Main St. (near Fiesta Way), Los Gatos

Phone: 408-354-7700 Dinner nightly
Web: www.diodeka.com
Prices: $$$

Dio Deka, housed in the vine-covered Hotel Los Gatos, is perpetually humming with affluent locals. The Greek-tavern setting is rustic yet casually chic with exposed beams, woven seating, and roaring fireplaces. Sprigs of rosemary tucked into each napkin supply that extra Mediterranean touch.

Chef Marty Cattaneo's menu presents an upscale Hellenistic theme and bolsters it with mesquite-grilled steakhouse fare. Start with warm herb-dusted pita triangles, before devouring grilled octopus drizzled with romesco and lemon vinaigrette, served atop hazelnuts, and finished with arugula. Finally, tuck into hearty lamb chops perched beside roasted potato and creamed spinach.

Dessert is a chic affair of sweetened Greek yogurt with strawberries and walnut streusel.

DishDash

C2

190 S. Murphy Ave. (bet. Evelyn & Washington Aves.), Sunnyvale

Phone: 408-774-1889 Lunch & dinner Mon – Sat
Web: www.dishdash.net
Prices: $$

Named after a traditional, cozy piece of Middle Eastern garb, this hoppin' Murphy Street spot captures just that kind of spirit. Notes of sumac and saffron drift through the air, dark wood tables sit against exposed brick walls, and cultural knickknacks dot the dining space. Bold flavors rock a vibrant, pan-Middle Eastern menu, with offerings from tangy chicken *shawarma* salad (spit-roasted chicken atop Romaine, cucumber, tomato, onions, and parsley drizzled with garlicky yogurt) to tasty *beriani dajaj* (potatoes, golden raisins, slivered almonds, and garbanzo beans touched with aged yogurt, alongside saffron rice and garlic-herbed chicken breast).
Sugar craving? Work your sweet way through assorted baklavas: six syrupy choices from cashew to walnut.

Evvia

Greek

A4

420 Emerson St. (bet. Lytton & University Aves.), Palo Alto

Phone: 650-326-0983 Lunch Mon – Fri
Web: www.evvia.net Dinner nightly
Prices: $$

Palo Alto denizens are lucky to have Evvia in their town, and they know it. The warmly lit dining room has the rustic coziness of a Greek *estiatorio*, with a roaring stone fireplace, closely-spaced tables, and an open kitchen adorned with hanging copper pots and pans. A lovely backlit wall of shelves illuminates a colorful array of glass bottles of oils, vinegars, and grains.
Frequently packed, the place is popular among the business crowds at lunch and Palo Alto residents at dinner (reservations are recommended). Fresh, flavorful Greek favorites may include roasted artichoke and eggplant souvlaki, served with fresh strained yogurt and house-made pita; or the tender, perfectly seasoned, herb-roasted lamb with dill-flavored *tzatziki*.

Fratello

Italian XX

1712 Meridian Ave. (bet. Hamilton Ave. & Lenn Dr.), San Jose

Phone: 408-269-3801 — Lunch Thu – Fri
Web: www.fratello-ristorante.com — Dinner Tue – Sun
Prices: $$

Fratello in San Jose might not be fancy-schmancy, but this quaint, casual, and family-friendly spot definitely has its own charm. Its theme is echoed in the terra-cotta-colored walls with paintings of the Italian countryside. The warm-spirited Italian family that runs the show welcomes you and yours with an array of authentic dishes that run the gamut from pastas and panini at lunch to more impressive seafood dishes in the evening.

Twist your fork around the homemade pappardelle topped with veal ragù or savor the charred taste of the tender grilled octopus, drizzled with fresh lemon, olive oil, and a sprinkling of fragrant Sicilian oregano. The crisp-skinned *salmone al brodo*, served in a roasted garlic and lemon broth, is delicious in its simplicity.

Hachi Ju Hachi

Japanese X

14480 Big Basin Way (bet. Saratoga Los Gatos Rd. & 3rd St.), Saratoga

Phone: 408-647-2258 — Dinner Tue – Sun
Web: www.hachijuhachi88.com
Prices: $$

Simple chairs and a blonde wood counter may not be much to look at, but the casual Saratoga interior manages to capture the serene essence of Japan. Wise visitors will take the straightforward space as a sign that Hachi Ju Hachi is focused on cuisine.

Delicate à la carte dishes may include cuttlefish with spicy cod roe and pork belly in white miso marinade, but the real adventure begins with a reservation. Folks with a bit of foresight and extra funds may pull up a chair for an elaborate *kaiseki* where the chef himself will comment on every course. Mouthwatering delights include the likes of kombu-burdock roll; hamachi skin and fragrant shiso; yellowtail sashimi with house-made sea salt; and miso-braised beef with blistered shisito peppers.

Hunan Home's

B2 Chinese

4880 El Camino Real (bet. Jordan Ave. & Los Altos Sq.), Los Altos

Phone: 650-965-8888 Lunch & dinner daily
Web: www.hunanhomes.com
Prices: ⊜

If home is where the heart is, then follow yours to Hunan Home's. Chinese may be the cuisine craze in this city, and this restaurant's name may be lost in translation, yet it continues to seduce business and family circles with its wonderfully authentic food. Set in a bungalow beset with shopping stalls, the elevated dining room is cheery with smiling service.

Groups of all sizes gather to ogle the gamut of Chinese delights—from *kung pao* prawns dressed in silky, spicy oyster sauce, to the house specialty of deeply caramelized Peking duck sandwiched in steamed pancakes with scallions and hoisin, to soft tofu cubes sautéed with chili and fermented black bean paste. The same in any language, a dizzying array of complimentary dishes adds incredible value.

Jang Su Jang

D2 Korean

3561 El Camino Real, Ste.10 (bet. Flora Vista Ave. & Lawrence Expwy.), Santa Clara

Phone: 408-246-1212 Lunch & dinner daily
Web: www.jangsujang.com
Prices: $$

You may as well call this stretch of El Camino in Santa Clara "Little Korea": the plaza brims with Korean-owned businesses whose owners and families congregate at nearby tofu shops and groceries. Jang Su Jang is among the local haunts, serving such authentic recipes as crisp and fluffy pancakes, filled with vegetables and flavored with sesame oil; and spicy beef stew with hand-cut noodles and scrambled egg in bright red broth. Screens offer a bit of privacy between tables, which are equipped with call buttons to summon your server. Cushioned banquettes are comfortable for intimate groups, while scattered private dining areas accommodate large family gatherings and special occasions. DIY-ers should request a grill table to savor homemade barbecue meats.

Joya

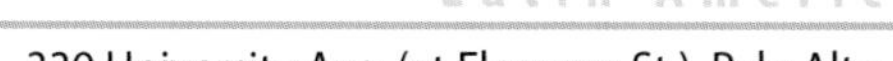

Latin American

A4

339 University Ave. (at Florence St.), Palo Alto

Phone: 650-853-9800 — Lunch & dinner daily
Web: www.joyarestaurant.com
Prices: $$

Come dressed to impress at Joya, the popular downtown Palo Alto hot spot for Latin tapas and sangria. Pose under oversized chandeliers in the stylish dark wood and leather lounge area, and be prepared for the fiesta to spill out onto the sidewalk patio. Lunches are low-key, but the younger crowd kicks the volume up a notch at dinner.

Group dining is the rage, as the extensive menu of seasonal Latin tapas is ideal for sharing. Check out the fresh *masa sopes*, made with tasty roasted chicken in a smoky chipotle sauce finished with pimento crèma; or the plump and sweet crab cakes, perfectly seasoned and drizzled with chipotle aïoli. Pair zesty dishes with refreshing tropical cocktails, such as the creamy-minty coconut mojito, for a mini-vacation.

Kabab & Curry's

Indian

D2

1498 Isabella St. (at Clay St.), Santa Clara

Phone: 408-247-0745 — Lunch & dinner Tue – Sun
Web: www.kababandcurrys.com
Prices:

If you're hanging around the South Bay at lunchtime and wondering where the area's large Indian and Pakistani population goes to eat, follow the crowd of engineers from Intel and Google to Kabab & Curry's, an authentic eatery that literally serves all you can eat.

Expect a line at the door–this place is a zoo at lunch–but be patient: the $10 buffet is worth the wait at Kabab & Curry's. Here, plates are laden with tender lamb cubes in spicy *vindaloo*; tandoori chicken so moist it's falling off the bone; and velvety chicken *tikka masala*. Every dish is hearty and delicious, the atmosphere is easygoing with plain wood furniture and tiled floors, and the naan is warm, bountiful, and always served with a smile. Come hungry, and leave stuffed!

La Bodeguita del Medio

Cuban

463 S. California Ave. (bet. Ash St. & El Camino Real), Palo Alto

Phone: 650-326-7762 — Lunch Mon – Fri
Web: www.labodeguita.com — Dinner Mon – Sat
Prices: $$

La Bodeguita del Medio is both a thriving Cuban restaurant and a separate tobacco shop, frequented by local businessmen at lunch and families for dinner. Welcoming you inside are clay tile floors, vibrant Cuban paintings, and amicable servers. Guests can sip cocktails at the bar and enjoy an authentic Cuban meal, before smoking those rare cigars in the back lounge.

The spread usually involves flaky, golden brown empanadas filled with shredded pork, spiced with chiles and pepper jack, and splashed with a delicious coconut-jalapeño sauce. *Tortillas con pescado* are filled with pan-seared salmon and topped with an herbaceous cilantro-avocado pesto flavored with lime and garlic. Couple that with buttery, caramelized sweet plantains for a *muy sabroso* finale.

La Costa

Mexican

E2

1805 Alum Rock Ave. (bet. Jackson Ave. & King Rd.), San Jose

Phone: 408-937-1010 — Lunch & dinner daily
Web: N/A
Prices:

Is it a taqueria, or is it a taco stand? You be the judge at La Costa, a San Jose hot spot where the décor is, well, the great outdoors. Inside, La Costa 's space features a kitchen with red, green, and white tile floors. But never mind that, because you're not going inside.

Belly up to the cashier's window and order to your heart's content: Perhaps a tender taco *asado* seasoned with spices and chiles and topped with crunchy salsa? Or maybe a burrito stuffed with strips of grilled chicken, avocado, cheese, and spicy condiments. Whatever you order, expect it to come fast and come outside—the only seating at La Costa is on the covered patio. But the food is cheap, tasty, and enjoys a massive following; regulars include foodies and area residents alike.

LB Steak

Steakhouse XXX

D3

334 Santana Row, Ste. 1000 (bet. Olin Ave. & Stevens Creek Blvd.), San Jose

Phone: 408-244-1180 Lunch & dinner daily
Web: www.lbsteak.com
Prices: $$$

Roland Passot's French métier shines at LB Steak, from the opposite end of its tony Santana Row shopping center sister, Left Bank Brasserie. The vibe is upscale and cosmopolitan with high-backed banquettes and chandeliers in the elegant main room; chic, cabana-style front patio; and private dining room with fireplace perfect for celebrations. Behold the immaculate exhibition kitchen behind sleek, automatic glass doors.

The menu includes burgers and some seafood, but showcases a fine selection of juicy and well-marbled USDA prime steaks, including bone-in and dry-aged cuts, served flame-licked, tender, and perfectly caramelized. Complete a meal here with classic steakhouse sides and New York cheesecake with nectarine coulis to end on a sweet note.

Liou's House

Chinese X

E1

1245 Jacklin Rd. (at Park Victoria Dr.), Milpitas

Phone: 408-263-9888 Lunch & dinner Tue – Sun
Web: N/A
Prices: ©©

Trek out to this little restaurant in Milpitas to be rewarded with unique Hunan dishes not easily found elsewhere. Unassuming Liou's House is no-frills with tile floors and faux-granite tables. But note, lunches are filled with business people, and dinners are busy with families and groups, many of whom are Chinese; so rest assured, Liou's is very popular and very authentic.

The wise thing to do is order from the menu of chef's specialties, such as Hunan tofu infused with spicy garlic and fermented black bean sauce, served piping hot with mixed vegetables in a clay pot. Those in the know call ahead to pre-order from a separate listing of dishes needing extra time: honey ham with chestnuts; sea cucumber with ground pork; or spareribs in a kabocha squash.

Manresa ✿✿

Contemporary ✗✗✗

D4

320 Village Ln. (bet. Santa Cruz & University Aves.), Los Gatos

Phone: 408-354-4330 Dinner Wed – Sun

Web: www.manresarestaurant.com

Prices: **$$$$**

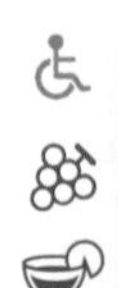

Michael David Rose

Located in a trendy shopping area of Los Gatos yet discreetly shielded from prying eyes with its opaque shades, Manresa seems all the more an old friend. Inside, what once felt rustic is now contemporary with its curvy fireplace, elegant chandeliers, blue mosaic tiles, and couch-filled lounge. An expansion in the back includes soft lighting set above luxurious pillowed banquettes. Servers are sharp and synchronized yet upbeat, never stuffy, and always capable of handling the bustling dining room.

Chef David Kinch helms a kitchen that seems to run best on all cylinders serving two prix-fixe options: one is extensive; while the other "Chef's Spontaneous Menu" is even more detailed but lists only ingredients. Both are rooted in small portions of product-driven cuisine, bring tasty dashes of esoterica, and often impart a deep love for Japanese tastes and subtlety. Picture small, seared Nantucket bay scallops and multi-colored marble potato confit with yarrow butter and an exotic mélange of herbs, mustard flowers, and *mizuna* garnish.

Finales here unveil such grand compositions as pine-nut pudding, candy-cap mushroom ice cream, maple gelatin, and crispy beignets set in white chocolate sauce.

Naschmarkt

D3 Austrian

384 E. Campbell Ave. (bet. Central & Railway Aves.), Campbell

Phone: 408-378-0335 Lunch Tue – Fri
Web: www.naschmarkt-restaurant.com Dinner Tue – Sun
Prices: $$

Named for the large produce market in Vienna known as the "city's stomach," this new spot in Campbell is becoming a gastro-favorite. On weekends, find romantic couples savoring the contemporary space, boasting a wrap-around dining counter, open kitchen, exposed brick walls, and high ceilings. The cuisine captures the true spirit of Austria by preparing its classics with modern style. Familiar traditions are found in Hungarian beef goulash braised in paprika with herbed spätzle; or classic wiener schnitzel with lingonberry sauce and potato salad. Innovations are clear in riesling-steamed black mussels with carrots and celery root. Stay for the sweet, as in a piping-hot and fluffy *salzburger nockerl* with tangy yogurt and stewed blueberry compote.

Nick's on Main

D4 American

35 E. Main St. (bet. College Ave. & Pageant Way), Los Gatos

Phone: 408-399-6457 Lunch & dinner Tue – Sat
Web: www.nicksonmainst.com
Prices: $$$

Nick's on Main is a perpetual favorite among denizens of quaint Los Gatos. It's a place where local couples flock on date night... or any night for that matter. The banquettes lining the cozy room and intimate tables under the spiraling iron chandelier are almost always packed with regulars who chat with the staff (and Nick) like old friends. Reservations are necessary.

The well-prepared American fare highlights local, seasonal ingredients, as in tender pan-roasted pheasant breast with creamy Tuscan white bean puree, grilled corn kernels, and silken sautéed wild mushrooms at dinner. For lunch, try the Kobe burger with braised pork belly and melted blue cheese. Finish with the buttery goodness of banana bread pudding, and you too will "trust the chef."

Orenchi

Japanese

3540 Homestead Rd. (near Lawrence Expy.), Santa Clara

Phone: 408-246-2955 — Lunch & dinner Tue – Sun
Web: www.orenchi-ramen.com
Prices: ₠

There are few bowls of soup worth a several-mile drive to a defunct shopping center only to find a line at the door and an inconvenient cash-only policy. But if you are looking for such a soup, Orenchi serves ramen so authentic that Japanese ex-pats come from all over for a piping hot taste of home.

There is no need for décor in this authentic noodle house—you'll be too busy waiting in line and then slurping down soup to notice. Upon arrival, jot your name on the clipboard and consider your options: Orenchi ramen has a *tonkotsu* base with chunks of pork, soft-boiled egg, and enoki mushrooms; Shio ramen comes with seaweed, leeks, and yuzu zest. Additional menu items include braised pork belly and fish cake tempura. No cash? There's an ATM in the corner.

Pampas

Brazilian

529 Alma St. (bet. Hamilton & University Aves.), Palo Alto

Phone: 650-327-1323 — Lunch Mon – Fri
Web: www.pampaspaloalto.com — Dinner nightly
Prices: **$$$**

With low slung banquettes, cool earth tones, and chic industrial accents, Pampas' urbane, bi-level interior defies common expectations of an all-you-can-eat affair (as do the sophisticated clientele sipping a full-bodied malbec). The sexy décor befits this Brazilian *churrascaria,* which specializes in authentic *rodízio* meals with limitless roasted meats stealing the scene.

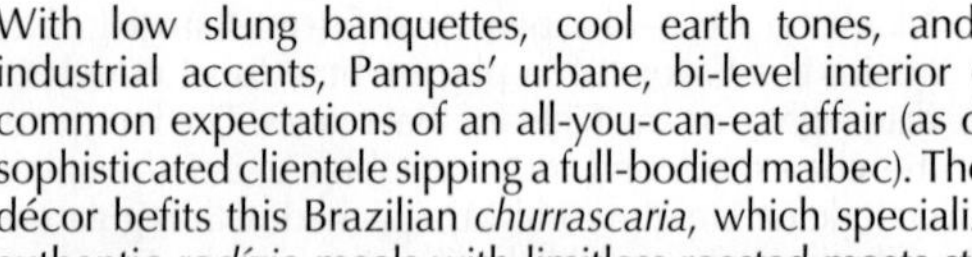

Served on skewers by circulating *passadors,* flavorful highlights include pork loin seasoned with coriander adobo; sirloin filet with garlic and herbs; and spicy linguiça. Try to save room for a trip to the sidebar–not for the faint of appetite–with its heaps of cheese, charcuterie, gazpacho, salads, smoked fish, and hot sides of coconut whipped sweet potatoes or zucchini fritters.

Pastis

447 S. California Ave. (bet. Ash St. & El Camino Real), Palo Alto

Phone: 650-324-1355 — Lunch Tue – Sun
Web: N/A — Dinner Tue – Sat
Prices: **$$**

Amid the cheerful yellow walls and vintage posters at Pastis, you may find yourself practicing your *français* with their French-speaking servers. New to Palo Alto, this cozy bistro has already begun attracting the local French expat community and is quite the brunch-time hit.

Of course, the menu of authentic bistro fare features the likes of *moules frites* and bœuf Bourguignon. Lunch may include a traditional and fresh *salade* Niçoise of mixed greens, tomato, red onion, anchovy, and hardboiled egg tossed in a light mustard dressing; or the ever-classic *croque madame* in a creamy Mornay sauce and topped with a perfectly fried egg. No matter what you order, a sweet sponge cake topped with juicy strawberries and whipped cream is always *très bon*!

Pizza Antica

334 Santana Row, Ste. 1065 (bet. Stevens Creek Blvd. & Tatum Ln.), San Jose

Phone: 408-557-8373 — Lunch & dinner daily
Web: www.pizzaantica.com
Prices: **$$**

The name says it all: thin-crust pizza made in the Roman style. Since this outpost of Pizza Antica is situated in the Santana Row shopping mall, it attracts shoppers in need of refueling as well as families and small groups. This "pizzeria" has a vintage café feel with black-and-white tile floors, pressed-tin ceilings, and an exhibition kitchen pivoted around roaring pizza ovens.

The kitchen lists pizzas with the toppings decided (Our Pizza), or you can assemble your own (Your Pizza). Our Pizza might be covered with crumbled fennel-flavored pork sausage, meaty pieces of portobello, and caramelized roasted onion. Your Pizza might feature a flavorful tomato sauce, oozing slices of mozzarella, fresh basil leaves, and mildly spiced Calabrese sausage. *Buona*!

Plumed Horse ✿

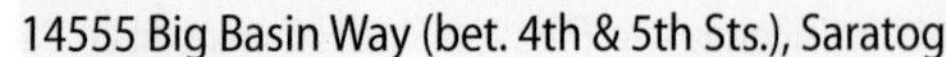

Contemporary XXX

C4

14555 Big Basin Way (bet. 4th & 5th Sts.), Saratoga

Phone: 408-867-4711 Dinner Mon – Sat
Web: www.plumedhorse.com
Prices: **$$$$**

James Fong

Located on a pretty tree-lined stretch, Plumed Horse blends nicely into this quaint town—just as it has for over 20 years. The rooms are elegantly appointed with dark wood trim, white panels, and a very impressive glassed-in wine storage area. (Have fun perusing their broad selection on an iPad.) Arched ceilings, soft lighting, and fresh flowers lend to the calm and tranquility, making this an ideal spot for a romantic evening or special occasion.

The chef blends contemporary French sensibilities with California-fresh panache to highlight the bounty of local ingredients. Expect the menu to reveal an egg white topped with lightly smoked salmon, red tobiko, pumpernickel crumbs, and baby arugula; a demitasse of golden brown soufflé flavored with black pepper and Parmesan, with a beurre blanc "fondue" of Dungeness crab and uni; or tender antelope, nicely seasoned and presented with meatballs and stuffed piquillo peppers in a cabernet and shallot jus. To finish, the B-52 bar layers Kahlua mousse and Bailey's ganache set on a toasted hazelnut sable with caramel and crème anglaise.

The professional staff allows guests to enjoy their evening without feeling rushed. Jackets are appropriate.

Rangoli

Indian XX

3695 Union Ave. (at Woodard Rd.), San Jose

Phone: 408-377-2222 — Lunch Sun – Fri
Web: www.rangolica.com — Dinner nightly
Prices: $$

Located on the edge of San Jose, between Campbell and Los Gatos, Rangoli is a lovely and upscale Indian restaurant. Leagues ahead of its neighboring (read: pedestrian) *desi* diners, it is no wonder that elegant Rangoli is so popular among the local South Asians. The dining areas consist of half-partitions and little alcoves, and tabletops are adorned with pretty votive candles.

The restaurant offers a massive buffet, but the best option is to order à la carte. Try spice-sparked items like a tandoor-smoked eggplant appetizer blended with chilies; followed by lamb Madras—cubes of lamb stewed in a hearty red coconut curry; or juicy chicken in a nutty, creamy, and saffron-infused *korma*. As always, a chewy naan is the best way to sop up any leftover sauce.

Sakoon

Indian XX

357 Castro St. (bet. California & Dana Sts.), Mountain View

Phone: 650-965-2000 — Lunch & dinner daily
Web: www.sakoonrestaurant.com
Prices: $$

For a sophisticated dose of cheer in Mountain View, make haste for Sakoon, a contemporary Indian restaurant dressed in a virtual riot of color and fun. Bright glass fixtures illuminate large mirrors and vibrant striped and polka-dotted furniture. The bar is backlit with neon hues; a fiber-optic light sculpture changes color every few seconds.

It may sound like a circus, but Sakoon is startlingly stylish and its cuisine is refined. Settle into a booth, order a pomegranate gin Kamasutra, and peruse the menu. Dishes include avocado *jhalmuri*, a fresh and flavorful layered salad; *murgh sakoonwala*, chicken curry stewed with Indian spicies, cardamom, and bell pepper; and Punjabi black lentils simmered in a creamy sauce of tomatoes, ginger, and red chilies.

Sawa Sushi

Japanese

1042 E. El Camino Real (at Henderson Ave.), Sunnyvale

Phone: 408-241-7292 Dinner Mon – Sat
Web: www.sawasushi.net
Prices: **$$$$**

At Sawa Sushi, Chef/owner/server Steve Sawa will craft your omakase and then deliver it to you at the sushi bar. Chef Sawa may be deeply dry and his restaurant borders on dingy–the fish cases are empty and plates may be chipped–but you've got to hand it to him: he's made plenty from nothing for over a decade now.

Without a reservation, the chef may question your motives. He may also mention that his super secret recipes come at a premium and are served omakase only. Take a cue from the full house and go with the flow. You'll be treated to the freshest fish even if his sometimes sloppy knife skills leave something to be desired. Expect unique items like slow-poached tuna belly in ponzu, and fresh shrimp topped with creamy uni and sea salt.

SJ Omogari

Korean

154 E. Jackson St. (at 4th St.), San Jose

Phone: 408-288-8134 Lunch & dinner Mon – Sat
Web: www.omogari.biz
Prices:

This homespun, family-owned Korean eatery in San Jose is one to rival any of the cuisine's authentic go-tos in Santa Clara. The traditional *banchan* may be lackluster, but area foodies come anyway for terrific *bi bim bap,* a piping hot stone pot that may be loaded with tender spicy pork, shredded carrot and daikon radish salad, and scallions with an egg on top.

SJ Omogari is a small, simple space with just a few wood tables and little art. And while you won't find the ubiquitous grill-topped tables, you will find most memorable *galbi*–smoky, grilled, and caramelized beef short ribs–from the kitchen. Soft tofu stews arrive with mushrooms or kimchi for vegetable lovers, and all meals end with a complimentary scoop of green tea ice cream.

Smoking Pig BBQ

Barbecue

1144 N. 4th St. (bet. Commercial St. & E. Younger Ave.), San Jose

Phone: 408-380-4784 Lunch & dinner Tue – Sun
Web: www.smokingpigbbq.net
Prices: $$

Leave your diet at home, ignore the neighborhood, and follow your snout to the waft of barbecue coming from the large, black smoker parked alongside the Smoking Pig BBQ. The old building has housed previous restaurants (the worn booths are telling). Still, aficionados run down here for heaping mounds of fingerlickin' good spare ribs and friendly down-home service.

The ribs and pulled pork are delectably, fall-off-the-bone delicious, especially when coupled with the cheekily named homemade sauces: Kansas City Hottie, California Honey, Carolina Sassy. Important points: food here is served on paper-lined aluminum trays with plastic cutlery; secondly, the wolf turds (smoky jalapenos stuffed with molten cheese) and peanut butter pie are not to be missed!

South Legend

Chinese

1720 N. Milpitas Blvd. (bet. Dixon Landing Rd. & Sunnyhills Ct.), Milpitas

Phone: 408-934-3970 Lunch & dinner daily
Web: www.southlegend.com
Prices: $$

South Legend may be located in a shopping center full of markets, Asian-run businesses, and...you guessed it...Chinese restaurants, but ring the alarm as this one stands tall for its bold menu of specialties from China's extra hot Sichuan province. The décor is plain and the service straightforward at this discreet, local haunt; the cooking is anything but and the likes of Chongqing fish fillets with chili, *mapo* tofu, chili-fried eel, and other sizzling platters are not for the faint of heart.

This is food that will leave you blushing from a flavor-packed smack down of chili paste, peppercorns, and red chili oil. Not feeling so brave? The Chengdu-style dim sum, featuring pork crescent dumplings and yam cakes oozing with red bean paste, is sure to satisfy.

Sumika

Japanese

236 Plaza Central (bet. 2nd & 3rd Sts.), Los Altos

Phone: 650-917-1822 — Lunch Tue – Sat
Web: www.sumikagrill.com — Dinner Tue – Sun
Prices: $$

Sumika is first and foremost an *izakaya*. There are just a handful of wood tables and the rest of the guests sit at a counter facing the kitchen, where they gaze longingly at the specialty—*kushiyaki,* skewers on a smoking grill set atop a charcoal fire. Lunch is a mellow meal frequented by local families. A noon spread likely includes fragrant miso soup, followed by a bowlful of white rice topped with crumbled chicken *tsukune* and a soft-cooked egg; or golden-fried chicken *katsu* matched with spicy Japanese mustard and smoky *tonkatsu* sauce.

At dinner, the place fills up with those seeking an easygoing vibe in which to enjoy beer and sake with their skewers of chicken heart or pork cheek. Small plates of deliciously crispy Japanese-style fried chicken anyone?

Tamarine

Vietnamese

546 University Ave. (bet. Cowper & Webster Sts.), Palo Alto

Phone: 650-325-8500 — Lunch Mon – Fri
Web: www.tamarinerestaurant.com — Dinner nightly
Prices: $$$

At Tamarine, contemporary Asian accents, low lighting, and walls showcasing works for sale by Vietnamese artists combine to fashion a swanky atmosphere that reflects the restaurant's modern take on Vietnamese cuisine.

All of this makes chic Tamarine a darling of Palo Alto, drawing a constant crowd. Corporate suits talk business in the large private dining room. Moneyed tech types fill up the front bar and share the likes of tender hoisin, garlic, and rosemary-glazed lamb chops, or *banh mi roti* with spicy coconut Penang curry sauce for dipping those puffy wheat crêpes. In the quieter back dining room, one might find ladies who lunch and couples sharing the outstanding sticky toffee pudding oozing hot caramel, or sipping refreshing Kaffir lime cocktails.

Thiên Long

Vietnamese

F3

3005 Silver Creek Rd., Ste.138 (bet. Aborn Rd. & Lexann Ave.), San Jose

Phone: 408-223-6188 Lunch & dinner daily
Web: www.thienlongrestaurant.com
Prices: 

Don't have cash? No need to stop at the ATM on your way to this San Jose favorite as their cheap eats are easy on the pockets. Thiên Long is located in a shopping center that brims with Asian storefronts and is popular among the area's burgeoning Vietnamese community.

With tile floors and wooden chairs, the interior isn't much. But it doesn't need to be: food is fresh and light, and service is friendly. On chilly days, sop up your *bánh mì bò kho*, a chunky beef stew with jalapeño and Thai basil, with a crusty baguette. Or, opt for a noodle bowl laden with barbecue pork and prawns for the perfect flavor combination of smoky, salty, and sweet. Don't miss the tapioca pearl smoothies, including a coffee rendition or exotic durian, jackfruit, and taro.

Vung Tau

Vietnamese

E3

535 E. Santa Clara St. (at 12th St.), San Jose

Phone: 408-288-9055 Lunch & dinner daily
Web: www.vungtaurestaurant.com
Prices: 

Vung Tau's voluminous space is filled with tables for their hordes of loyal Vietnamese devotees. Despite their rather chaste décor and basic service, the gamut of food offerings keeps these patrons riveted. While the hefty menu can stupefy, rest assured that the home-style food is as authentic as it is tasty.

Imagine a plethora of both unique and classic delights from steaming noodle bowls to seafood and meat dishes. Watch as the faithful order the likes of *bo bia* (soft rolls filled with Chinese sausage and egg); or *tam bi tom cha* (broken rice cloaked with shredded pork and succulent prawns). *Banh khot* are enticingly savory confections, crisp at the edges, depressed at the center to hold a filling of sweet shrimp and minced scallions.

Zeni

Ethiopian

D3

1320 Saratoga Ave. (at Payne Ave.), San Jose

Phone: 408-615-8282 Lunch & dinner Tue – Sun
Web: www.zenirestaurant.com
Prices: $$

Ethiopia's cuisine–while roaming the globe–has cultivated a global following. Zeni is a cultural delight luring natives with a deliciously authentic menu and proper set featuring a thatched bar, exotic artwork, and classic furnishings. Amicability reigns as diners dispel with cutlery and chow in communion. With no utensil in sight, visit the wash basin before diving in...fingers first.

Embodying simple food is the *injera*—a fluffy flatbread used to scoop up flavorful meats and sauces. Chatty servers indulge locals with dreamy collard greens; tangy spiced lentils; split peas with turmeric; and veggies gilded with garlic and ginger. *Kitfo* (ground steak with herb butter and chili powder) is perfectly chased down by black tea swirled with honey-spice syrup.

Feast for under $25 at all restaurants with ☺.

Peter L. Wrenn /

Peter L. Wrenn/MICHELIN

Wine Country

Wine Country

Napa Valley & Sonoma County

Picnicking on artisan-made cheeses and fresh crusty bread amid acres of gnarled grapevines; sipping wine on a terrace above a hillside of silvery olive trees; touring caves heady with the sweet smell of fermenting grapes—this is northern California's wine country. Lying within an hour's drive north and northeast of San Francisco, the hills and vales of gorgeous Sonoma County and Napa Valley thrive on the abundant sunshine and fertile soil that produce grapes for some of North America's finest wines.

Fruit of the Vine

Cuttings of Criollas grapevines traveled north with Franciscan *padres* from the Baja Peninsula during the late 17th century. Wines made from these "mission" grapes were used primarily for trade and for sacramental purposes. In the early 1830s, a French immigrant propitiously named Jean-Louis Vignes (*vigne* is French for "vine") established a large vineyard near Los Angeles using cuttings of European grapevines *(Vitis vinifera)*, and by the mid-19th century, winemaking had become one of southern California's principal industries. In 1857, Hungarian immigrant Agoston Haraszthy purchased a 400-acre estate in Sonoma County, named it Buena Vista, and cultivated Tokaji vine cuttings imported from his homeland. In 1861, bolstered by promises of state funding, Haraszthy went to Europe to gather assorted *vinifera* cuttings to plant them in California soil. Upon his return, however, the state legislature reneged on their commitment. Undeterred, Haraszthy forged ahead and continued to distribute (at his own expense) some 100,000 cuttings and testing varieties in different soil types. Successful application of his discoveries created a boom in the local wine industry in the late 19th century.

The Tide Turns

As the 1800s drew to a close, northern California grapevines fell prey to phylloxera, a root louse that attacks susceptible *vinifera* plants. Entire vineyards were decimated. Eventually researchers discovered they could combat phylloxera by replanting vineyards with disease-resistant wild grape rootstocks, onto which *vinifera* cuttings could be grafted. The wine industry had achieved a modicum of recovery by the early 20th century, only to be slapped with the 18th Amendment to the Constitution, prohibiting the manufacture, sale, importation, and transportation of intoxicating liquors in the United States. California's winemaking industry remained at a near-standstill until 1933, when Prohibition was repealed. The Great Depression slowed the reclamation of vineyards and it wasn't until the early 1970s that California's wine industry was fully re-established. In 1976, California wines took top honors in a blind taste testing by French judges in Paris. The results helped open up a whole new world of respectability for Californian vineyards.

Coming of Age

As Napa and Sonoma County wines have established their reputations, the importance of individual growing regions has increased. Many sub-regions have sought and acquired Federal regulation of the place names as American Viticultural Areas, or AVAs, in order to set the boundaries of wine-growing areas that are distinctive for their soil, microclimate, and wine styles. Although this system is subject to debate, there is no doubt that an AVA such as Russian River Valley, Carneros, or Spring Mountain can be very meaningful. The precise location of a vineyard relative to the Pacific Ocean or San Pablo Bay; the elevation and slope of a vineyard; the soil type and moisture content; and even the proximity to a mountain gap can make essential differences.

Together, Sonoma and Napa have almost 30 registered appellations, which vary in size and sometimes overlap. Specific place names are becoming increasingly important as growers learn what to plant where and how to care for vines in each unique circumstance. The fact that more and more wines go to market with a specific AVA flies in the face of the worldwide trend to ever larger and less specific "branded" wines. Individual wineries and associations are working to promote the individuality of North Coast appellations and to preserve their integrity and viability as sustainable agriculture. In recent decades, the Napa Valley and Sonoma County have experienced tremendous levels of development. Besides significant increases in vineyard acreage, the late 20th century witnessed an explosion of small-scale operations, some housed in old wineries updated with state-of-the-art equipment.

Meanwhile, the Russian River Valley remains less developed, retaining its rural feel with country roads winding past picturesque wineries, rolling hills of grapevines, and stands of redwood trees. With easy access to world-class wines, and organic produce and cheeses from local farms, residents of northern California's wine country enjoy an enviable quality of life. Happily for the scores of visitors, those same products supply the area's burgeoning number of restaurants, creating a culture of gourmet dining that stretches from the city of Napa all the way north to Healdsburg and beyond.

Note that if you elect to bring your own wine, most restaurants charge a corkage fee (which can vary from $10 to as much as $50 per bottle). Many restaurants waive this fee on one particular day, or if you purchase an additional bottle from their list.

Which Food?	*Which Wine?*	*Some Examples*
Shellfish	Semi-dry White	Early harvest Riesling, Chenin Blanc, early harvest Gewürztraminer, Viognier
	Dry White	Lighter Chardonnay (less oak), Pinot Blanc, Sauvignon Blanc, dry Riesling, dry Chenin Blanc
	Sparkling Wine	Brut, Extra Dry, Brut Rosé
	Dry Rosé	Pinot Noir, Syrah, Cabernet
Fish	Dry White	Chardonnay (oaky or not) Sauvignon Blanc, dry Riesling, dry Chenin Blanc, Pinot Blanc
	Sparkling Wine	Brut, Blanc de Blancs, Brut Rosé
	Light Red	Pinot Noir, Pinot Meunier, light-bodied Zinfandel
	Dry Rosé	Pinot Noir, Syrah, Cabernet
Cured Meats/ Picnic Fare	Semi-dry White	Early harvest Riesling or early harvest Gewürztraminer
	Dry White	Chardonnay (less oak), Sauvignon Blanc, dry Riesling
	Sparkling Wine	Brut, Blanc de Blancs, Brut Rosé
	Light Red	Gamay, Pinot Noir, Zinfandel, Sangiovese
	Young Heavy Red	Syrah, Cabernet Sauvignon, Zinfandel, Cabernet Franc, Merlot
	Rosé	Any light Rosé
Red Meat	Dry Rosé	Pinot Noir, Cabernet, Syrah, Blends
	Light Red	Pinot Noir, Zinfandel, Gamay, Pinot Meunier
	Young Heavy Red	Cabernet Sauvignon, Cabernet Franc, Syrah, Grenache, Petite Sirah, Merlot, Blends, Pinot Noir, Cabernet Sauvignon
	Mature Red	Merlot, Syrah, Zinfandel, Meritage, Blends
Fowl	Semi-dry White	Early harvest Riesling, Chenin Blanc, Viognier
	Dry White	Sauvignon Blanc, Chardonnay, Pinot Blanc, dry Riesling
	Sparkling Wine	Extra Dry, Brut, Brut Rosé
	Rosé	Any light Rosé
	Light Red	Pinot Noir, Zinfandel, Blends, Gamay
	Mature Red	Pinot Noir, Cabernet Sauvignon, Merlot, Syrah, Zinfandel, Meritage, Blends
Cheese	Semi-dry White	Riesling, Gewürztraminer, Chenin Blanc
	Dry White	Sauvignon Blanc, Chardonnay, Pinot Blanc, dry Riesling
	Sparkling Wine	Extra Dry, Brut
	Rosé	Pinot Noir, Cabernet, Grenache
	Light Red	Pinot Noir, Zinfandel, Blends, Gamay
	Young Heavy Red	Cabernet Sauvignon, Cabernet Franc, Syrah, Grenache, Petite Sirah, Merlot, Blends
Dessert	Sweet White	Any late harvest White
	Semi-dry White	Riesling, Gewürztraminer, Chenin Blanc, Muscat
	Sparkling Wine	Extra Dry, Brut, Rosé, Rouge
	Dessert Reds	Late harvest Zinfandel, Port

tage	1996	1997	1998	1999	2000	2001	2002	2003	2004	2005	2006	2007	2008	2009
rdonnay **neros**	Above Average	Outstanding	Average	Above Average	Above Average	Outstanding	Outstanding	Outstanding	Outstanding	Above Average	Above Average	Above Average	Above Average	Above Average
rdonnay **sian River**	Above Average	Outstanding	Average	Above Average	Above Average	Outstanding	Outstanding	Above Average	Outstanding	Outstanding	Above Average	Outstanding	Above Average	Above Average
rdonnay **a Valley**	Outstanding	Outstanding	Above Average	Above Average	Average	Above Average	Outstanding	Outstanding	Above Average	Above Average	Above Average	Above Average	Above Average	Outstanding
vignon Blanc **a Valley**	Above Average	Outstanding	Average	Above Average	Average	Outstanding	Outstanding	Above Average	Outstanding	Outstanding	Above Average	Above Average	Above Average	Above Average
vignon Blanc **oma County**	Above Average	Outstanding	Average	Above Average	Average	Outstanding	Above Average	Above Average	Outstanding	Above Average	Outstanding	Above Average	Above Average	Above Average
ot Noir **neros**	Above Average	Outstanding	Average	Above Average	Average	Outstanding	Above Average	Outstanding	Outstanding	Above Average	Above Average	Above Average	Above Average	Above Average
ot Noir **sian River**	Above Average	Outstanding	Above Average	Above Average	Above Average	Above Average	Outstanding	Outstanding	Outstanding	Above Average	Above Average	Outstanding	Outstanding	Above Average
rlot **pa Valley**	Outstanding	Outstanding	Above Average	Outstanding	Above Average	Outstanding	Above Average	Outstanding	Above Average	Outstanding	Above Average	Above Average	Above Average	Above Average
rlot **oma County**	Above Average	Outstanding	Above Average	Above Average	Above Average	Above Average	Above Average	Above Average	Outstanding	Outstanding	Above Average	Above Average	Above Average	Above Average
ernet Sauvignon **pa Valley**	Outstanding	Outstanding	Above Average	Outstanding	Above Average	Outstanding	Outstanding	Above Average	Outstanding	Outstanding	Outstanding	Outstanding	Outstanding	Outstanding
ernet Sauvignon **uthern Sonoma**	Outstanding	Outstanding	Above Average	Above Average	Above Average	Outstanding	Above Average	Above Average	Outstanding	Above Average	Above Average	Above Average	Outstanding	Outstanding
ernet Sauvignon **rthern Sonoma**	Outstanding	Outstanding	Above Average	Above Average	Above Average	Above Average	Outstanding	Above Average	Outstanding	Outstanding	Outstanding	Above Average	Outstanding	Outstanding
fandel **pa Valley**	Outstanding	Outstanding	Above Average	Above Average	Above Average	Outstanding	Outstanding	Outstanding	Outstanding	Above Average	Outstanding	Outstanding	Above Average	Above Average
fandel **uthern Sonoma**	Outstanding	Outstanding	Above Average	Above Average	Above Average	Outstanding	Outstanding	Outstanding	Outstanding	Above Average	Outstanding	Outstanding	Above Average	Above Average
fandel **rthern Sonoma**	Outstanding	Outstanding	Above Average	Outstanding	Above Average	Outstanding	Outstanding	Outstanding	Outstanding	Above Average	Outstanding	Above Average	Above Average	Above Average

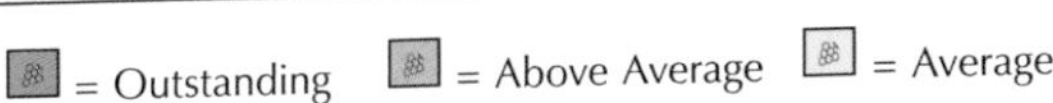

Peter L. Wrenn/MICHELIN

Napa Valley

Wine is the watchword in this 35-mile-long lush valley, which extends in a northerly direction from the San Pablo Bay to Mount St. Helena. Cradled between the Mayacama and the Vaca mountain ranges, Napa Valley boasts some of California's most prestigious wineries, along with a host of restaurants that are destinations in themselves.

A Whirl of Wineries

Reclaimed 19th century stone wineries and Victorian houses punctuate the valley's rolling landscape, reminding the traveler that there were some 140 wineries here prior to 1890. Today, Napa Valley has more than 400 producing wineries (and over 400 brands), up from a post-Prohibition low of perhaps a dozen. They are all clustered along Route 29, the valley's main artery, which runs up the western side of the mountains, passing through the commercial hub of Napa and continuing north through the charming little wine burgs of Yountville, Oakville, Rutherford, St. Helena, and Calistoga.

More wineries dot the tranquil Silverado Trail, which hugs the foothills of the eastern range and gives a more pastoral perspective on this rural farm county. Along both routes, picturesque spots for alfresco dining abound. So pick up some picnic supplies at the **Oakville Grocery** (on Route 29), or stop by either the **Model Bakery** in St. Helena or **Bouchon Bakery** in Yountville for freshly-baked bread and delectable pastries. Throughout the valley you'll spot knolls, canyons, dry creek beds, stretches of valley floor, and glorious mountain

vistas, all of which afford varying microclimates and soil types for growing wine. San Pablo Bay has a moderating effect on the valley's temperatures, while the mountains lessen the influence of the Pacific Ocean. In the valley, powerfully hot summer days and still cool nights provide the ideal climate for cabernet sauvignon grapes, a varietal for which Napa is justifiably famous.

Among the region's many winemakers are well-known names like Robert Mondavi, Francis Ford Coppola, and the Miljenko "Mike" Grgich. Originally from Croatia, Grgich rose to fame as the winemaker at **Chateau Montelena** when his 1973 chardonnay took the top prize at the Judgment of Paris in 1976, outshining one of France's best white Burgundies. This feat turned the wine world

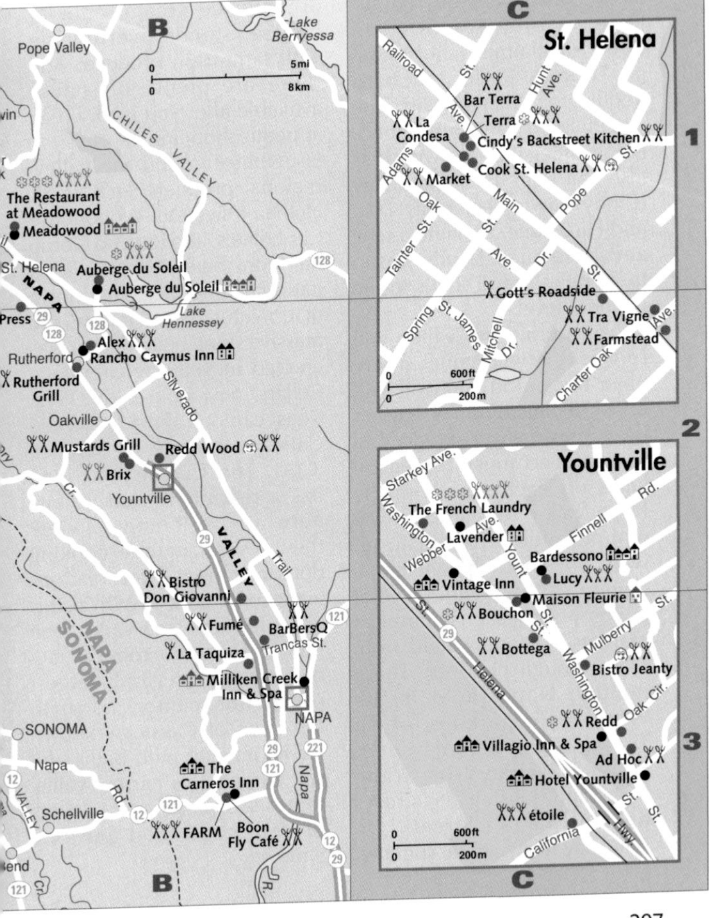

on its ear, and put California on the map as a bona fide producer of fine wine. Since then, Napa's success with premium wine has fostered a special pride of place. Fourteen American Viticultural Areas (AVAs) currently regulate the boundaries for sub-regions such as Carneros, Stags Leap, Rutherford, and Los Carneros. The boom in wine production has spawned a special kind of food-and-wine tourism: Today tasting rooms, tours, and farm-fresh cuisine are de rigueur here. Along Washington Street, acclaimed chefs such as Thomas Keller, Richard Reddington, Michael Chiarello, and Philippe Jeanty rub elbows. Many other well-known chefs also hail from the Napa Valley (Cindy Pawlcyn, Jeremy Fox, and Hiro Sone, to name a few) and have successfully raised their local-legend status to the national level.

Those touring the valley will spot fields of wild fennel, silvery olive trees, and rows of wild mustard that bloom between the grapevines in February and March. The mustard season kicks off each year with the Napa Valley Mustard Festival, which celebrates the food, wine, art, and rich agricultural bounty of the region. Several towns host seasonal farmer's markets, generally held from May through October. These include Napa (held in the Wine Train parking lot on Tuesdays and Saturdays); St. Helena (Fridays in Crane Park); and Calistoga (Saturdays on Washington Street). On Thursday nights in the summer, there's a **Chef's Market** in the Napa Town Center. Opened in early 2008, **Oxbow Public Market** is a block-long 40,000-square-foot facility that is meant to vie with the Ferry Building Marketplace across the bay. Oxbow brims with local food artisans and wine vendors, all from within a 100-mile radius of the market. Within this barn-like building you'll find cheeses and charcuterie; spices and specialty teas; olive oils and organic ice cream; and, of course, stands overflowing with farm-fresh produce. And there are plenty of snacks available after you work up an appetite shopping.

Elsewhere around the valley, regional products such as St. Helena Olive Oil, Woodhouse Chocolates, and Rancho Gordo heirloom beans are gaining a national following. Just north of downtown St. Helena, the massive stone building that was erected in 1889 as Greystone Cellars, now houses the West Coast campus of the renowned Culinary Institute of America (CIA). The Culinary Institute has a restaurant, and visitors here are welcome to view their several unique cooking demonstrations—reservations are recommended. With all this going for the Napa Valley, one thing is for sure: From the city of Napa, the region's largest population center, north to the town of Calistoga–known for its mineral mud baths and spa cuisine–this narrow valley represents paradise for lovers of both good food and fine wine.

Ad Hoc

C3 American XX

6476 Washington St. (bet. California Dr. & Oak Circle), Yountville

Phone: 707-944-2487 Lunch Sun
Web: www.adhocrestaurant.com Dinner Thu – Mon
Prices: $$$

While the world clamors for a taste of Thomas Keller's renowned cooking, lucky Napa locals can make their way down the street from his flagships, to easy-breezy Ad Hoc. Hugely homey, this rustic-chic spot–with wood residing everywhere–is always crammed with locals and tourists.

The set menu is served family-style and may underscore such teasers as an elegant salad of little gem lettuces, romaine hearts, beets, and brioche croutons in a tangy herb vinaigrette. Buttered radishes and pea-and-potato salad are perfect complements to the best fried chicken *ever*—crisp-skinned, briny, moist, and finished with bacon crumbles and dill. For the big win, dive into a cheese course revealing tangy cheddar and crisp puff pastry licked with vanilla-pear compote.

Alex

Italian 

1140 Rutherford Rd. (off Hwy. 29), Rutherford

Phone: 707-967-5500 Lunch Tue – Sat
Web: www.alexitalianrestaurant.com Dinner Tue – Sun
Prices: $$$

This fresh-faced Italian gem is fast becoming a fave in Rutherford. Handsome Alex has a stacked stone fireplace, Carrara marble bar, vaulted ceilings, and arched windows. Similarly, guests are well-styled Napa tourists from the adjacent Rancho Caymus Inn or locals planning their next wine-growing season.

Centering on seasonal ingredients and skillful preparations, the vast Italian menu has included such treats as artichoke- and ricotta-filled *tortelli* served in brown butter dotted with crispy-fried sage leaves and shaved Parmigiano; and juicy roulades of Cornish game hen stuffed with delicious garlicky greens, wrapped in pancetta, and served over a medley of grilled vegetables. Complete the Italian job with an espresso-mascarpone tiramisu...*buono*!

Angèle

A3 French XX

540 Main St. (at 5th St.), Napa

Phone: 707-252-8115 Lunch & dinner daily
Web: www.angelerestaurant.com
Prices: $$

How to be absolutely charming in the heart of an impossibly charming Napa town? Be French, *bien sûr*! Set an orange-and-blue, country-quaint brasserie in a historic ship chandlery from the 1890s, add a romantic wicker-filled patio overlooking the Napa riverfront for outdoor lunches, and proudly serve a classic Gallic menu.

Friendly staff arrives at the linen-laid table to bring crunchy, crackling, suckling pig with mustard spaetzle or a golden croque monsieur. The beautiful people buzz over the local subject (wine) and certainly a vineyard owner is among them. Perhaps he brought his favorite bottle for the corkage fee—you can, too, or order a Napa selection from the list. Finish with the Valrhona chocolate pot de crème because life is *fantastique*!

Azzurro

A3 Pizza X

1260 Main St. (at Clinton St.), Napa

Phone: 707-255-5552 Lunch & dinner daily
Web: www.azzurropizzeria.com
Prices: $$

A blue-and-white tiled gas-fired pizza oven gleams in the center of the sleek open kitchen, where a marble bar at the chef's station offers views of the action. The airy dining space features a long wooden banquette, zinc-topped tables, and glossy black chairs.

Ten tasty varieties of thin crust pizza–with combinations for both purists and gourmands–are the specialty at Azzuro. Try the *funghi*, with roasted cremini and wild mushrooms, Taleggio, and thyme; or the *salsiccia*, with fennel sausage, red onion, and mozzarella. Anyone torn between a salad and a slice can go for the *manciata*—baked pizza dough topped with a choice of salads. Rustic pasta and antipasti dishes like *gamberi* (grilled shrimp, white beans, sausage and arugula) complete the menu.

Auberge du Soleil ✿

B1

180 Rutherford Hill Rd. (off the Silverado Trail), Rutherford

Phone: 707-963-1211 Lunch & dinner daily
Web: www.aubergedusoleil.com
Prices: **$$$$**

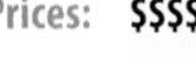

Trinette Reed

From its hilltop home in a light orange Mediterranean villa surrounded by the vineyards of northern Napa, Auberge du Soleil's setting leaves nothing to be desired. The interior dining room conjures rustic Provence, but the heated and covered terrace is the place to be enveloped by spectacular views over the valley floor. The staff wears crisp, gray waistcoats while keeping everything friendly and very smooth for their young, attractive, and discerning clientele sipping their favorite local zinfandel.

Though the view alone seems enough reason to dine here, the accomplished kitchen rivals its environs with delicious food that celebrates local products and California style. Simple and unfussy starters might feature sweet and distinctively fresh shrimp on a bed of crunchy lettuce, supple avocado, and segments of sharp, citrusy orange. Entrées have revealed tender, juicy, and generous pork chops sliced off the bone and served with a fricassee of crisp bacon, soft dates, fennel, and waxy potatoes in a light jus.

Seasonally influenced desserts may highlight classic accompaniments as in caramelized apple tart with peanut butter caramel and a quenelle of beautifully smooth vanilla ice cream.

Bank Café and Bar

Contemporary XX

1314 McKinstry St. (at Soscol Ave.), Napa

Phone: 707-257-5151 Lunch & dinner daily
Web: www.latoque.com/bankbar
Prices: $$

The hotel-like aura at Bank Café and Bar, set off the lobby of the Westin Verasa Napa, does not do this conversation-worthy café any favors. But there is great news: Ken Frank, also of the hotel's La Toque, is notably at the helm here too. Even the casual slant of a Michelin-starred chef tends to inspire, and Chef Frank obliges with upscale bar food and a weekly regional French menu.

Dining in the Languedoc may reveal *brandade de Morue*, chicken with black olives and strawberry *vacherin* for $36. You can also order Cali-flecked items like rock shrimp with a hoisin-lemongrass sauce; or ham-and-cheese sandwiches and pretend that you're gliding along the Seine. Those in the know and with dollars to spare may even pick dishes from the menu at noble La Toque.

BarBersQ

Barbecue 

3900 D, Bel Aire Plaza (at Trancas St.), Napa

Phone: 707-224-6600 Lunch & dinner daily
Web: www.barbersq.com
Prices: $$

Buzzing in Napa is easygoing BarBersQ. This well-liked spot is frequented by families and private parties who adore their copiously sized dishes and relatively inexpensive prices. The urban-rustic décor has concrete floors, brushed aluminum chairs, and cushy banquettes.

Tables are topped with squirt bottles of three different house sauces as well as the ubiquitous hot sauce. Sample all of the meats on the menu with "A Taste of the Q"—an extravagant platter of spice-rubbed and glazed baby back ribs, tender pulled pork, juicy BBQ brisket smothered in a tomato paste-based barbecue sauce, BBQ chicken with an excellent spice coating, and spicy charred sausage. Well-seasoned coleslaw and rustic cornbread served with whipped honey butter complete the effect.

barolo

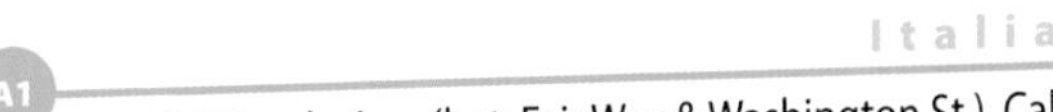

Italian

A1

1457 Lincoln Ave. (bet. Fair Way & Washington St.), Calistoga

Phone: 707-942-9900
Web: www.barolocalistoga.com
Prices: $$

Lunch Tue – Sun
Dinner nightly

More than just a wine bar, barolo is an über hip restaurant complete with a metropolitan vibe. After a day of lolling in the mud, or yes, tasting wine at local vineyards, visit this lounge-like wine country darling for a little city chic in the sleepy 'burb of Calistoga. As might be expected, the wine list has some unique local and small production labels that blend perfectly with their Italian dishes.

Decked with red leather booths, metallic fixtures, and a candy apple red Vespa perched on the wall, this is not your average checkered table cloth, red sauce joint. Instead, look forward to faithful helpings of cast iron skillet mussels with white wine, garlic, and chili butter; spaghetti with meatballs; and salmon with ratatouille and red pepper coulis.

Bar Terra

Contemporary

C1

1345 Railroad Ave. (bet. Adams St. & Hunt Ave.), St. Helena

Phone: 707-963-8931
Web: www.terrarestaurant.com
Prices: $$

Dinner Wed – Mon

Yes, it shares an address with the more formal Terra next door, but Bar Terra is a solid restaurant in its own right. The rustic stone walls, cozy banquette seating, and friendly servers form a charming respite, where locals love to gather around the L-shaped bar rife with thrilling concoctions.

The menu presents a selection of cocktail accompaniments like *chicharrònes* (fried pork rinds) or *bacalao*, salted cod and potato fritters fried to golden brown gratification. For bigger bites, opt for tender braised beef cheeks in an intense tomato sauce, served with sautéed rapini. Desserts are dreamy here so be sure to save room for a flaky *bisteeya*, crispy layers of filo filled with apricot and almond cream and crested with Meyer lemon-rose ice cream.

Bistro Don Giovanni

B2 — Italian XX

4110 Howard Ln. (at Hwy. 29), Napa

Phone: 707-224-3300

Web: www.bistrodongiovanni.com

Prices: $$

Lunch & dinner daily

The stars in Galileo's sky aligned in the making of Don Giovanni. This large room is blessed with gloriously alive floral ensembles and soaring ceilings. If the latter can't contain the din, the garden terrace (which knows no peer on sunny days in the valley) will. At the bar up front, find locals and tourists comparing wine notes; while the communal table, supported by a massive wooden carving of a man, is armed with rattan chairs and food-loving faithfuls.

Gleaming copper cookware dangling above the wood-burning oven hint at the kitchen's rustic bounty of antipasti, seasonal risottos, and pastas. Reviving residents and wine tasters alike are fried green olives with Marcona almonds and roasted pork with garden tomato panzanella and pepper jelly.

Bistro Jeanty 

C3 — French XX

6510 Washington St. (at Mulberry St.), Yountville

Phone: 707-944-0103

Web: www.bistrojeanty.com

Prices: $$

Lunch & dinner daily

This cheery bistro in the heart of the culinary mecca that is Yountville is quintessentially French. Envision yellow walls, antiques, full flower boxes, and those woven café chairs and you will get the picture. And yet it also reeks of wine country charm by virtue of its welcoming staff and casual yet elegant demeanor.

The bistro's quality-ridden menu is exemplary, classic, and expertly prepared. For instance, a perfect and balanced rabbit pâté served with Dijon mustard and cornichons is beautifully chased by a supremely tender, slow-roasted pork shoulder paired with butternut squash gratin, caramelized Brussels sprouts, and bacon. One morsel of the crème caramel with a flaky Palmier on the gorgeous patio and you will be instantly transported.

Boon Fly Café

Californian

4048 Sonoma Hwy. (at Los Carneros Ave.), Napa

Phone: 707-299-4870 — Lunch & dinner daily
Web: www.thecarnerosinn.com
Prices: $$

Set in the Carneros Inn–an agri-chic complex amid 27 pastoral acres off the Old Sonoma Highway–is the rustic, red barn-style of the Boon Fly Café. While the café serves breakfast, lunch, and dinner, it is brunch that is a true standout here with plates of Boon Fly Benedict served with Caggiano ham and jalapeño hollandaise or Poppa Joe's "eggs in a hole."

With corrugated aluminum walls and porch swings to ease brunch time waits, this is a decidedly elegant roadhouse eatery. The same creative spirit shines at lunch and dinner with entrées like Dungeness crab cakes posing beside a poached citrus salad and herb aïoli; flatbread specials (maybe featuring Ohlone smoked salmon); and a classic NY strip with watercress, chimichurrri, and crisp truffle fries.

Bottega

Italian

6525 Washington St. (near Yount St.), Yountville

Phone: 707-945-1050 — Lunch Tue – Sun
Web: www.bottegaanapavalley.com — Dinner nightly
Prices: $$

The crowds flock to the heart of Yountville for a bite of famed Michael Chiarello's signature NapaStyle. Expect striped yellow chairs with lots of stone and wood at the spacious and comfortable Bottega. Reservations are essential.

The menu is Chiarello's take on Cal-Italian cuisine. Plates are oversized, stamped with "bottega," and available for sale. The typically local staff and well-timed kitchen turn out hearty, rustic dishes with big flavors, as in butternut squash *caramelle* with house-made dough; paprika oil-marinated grilled skirt steak with crisp Yukon gold potato chips; and that ubiquitous side of truffle-Parmesan fries. Bring your appetite for his famed tiramisu and sponge cake gelato in a "cocoa puff" of bittersweet dark chocolate sauce.

Bouchon ✿

C3

French XX

6534 Washington St. (at Yount St.), Yountville

Phone: 707-944-8037 Lunch & dinner daily

Web: www.bouchonbistro.com

Prices: $$$

Deborah Jones

It's easy to imagine yourself in France when gazing at Bouchon's burgundy exterior in this picture-postcard town. That authentic and instantly agreeable essence of a Parisian bistro has been captured here through shiny brass details, tile floors, an oyster bar, blackboard specials, and simple luxuries. The ambience attracts a chatty mix of casual business types, ladies lunching, and wine country tourists. It's the sort of place we all wish were local.

The *pain d'epi* (from Bouchon Bakery next door) alone ensures that this is a serious kitchen. Further delights from the accessible French-Californian menu may begin with a deep timbale of *rillettes de lapin*, flash-fried and perfectly seasoned, served with radishes, rich mustardy jus, and the essential sweetness of apples. The *salade de courge* bursts with the flavors and colors of butternut squash, chestnut confit, celery root, Brussels sprouts, and sage emulsion.

Finally, and best paired with an excellent cup of espresso, an amazing *île flottante* is impossibly light atop ultra-smooth crème anglaise, with caramel sauce poured tableside—even the accompanying nut-crusted tuile and sugar-roasted almond show an extraordinary level of finesse.

Bounty Hunter

American

975 First St. (at Main St.), Napa

Phone: 707-226-3976 — Lunch & dinner daily
Web: www.bountyhunterwinebar.com
Prices: $$

Deep in the heart of Napa, a landmark 1888 brick building with worn wood floors and pressed-copper ceilings is just the place for a wine bar-meets-barbecue joint that feels worlds away from the honkytonks of yore. Designer tasting flights and private label wines fit the oenophile locale, but those juicy meats from the grill out back make the Bounty Hunter a real prize.

Majestic mounted game presides over the saloon-style space where locals pair their wines with shredded crab and red pepper bisque; bone-in rib eyes; and hearty barbecue sandwiches. The beer can chicken is a must, even if it does elicit a sophomoric chuckle—the crispy Cajun-skinned fowl stands upright on a Tecate can. The job of carving the bird is all yours, but so is the reward.

Brannan's Grill

American

1374 Lincoln Ave. (at Washington St.), Calistoga

Phone: 707-942-2233 — Lunch Fri – Sun, Dinner nightly
Web: www.brannansgrill.com
Prices: $$

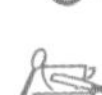

Built on the main drag and heralded for Calistoga's founder and gold rush pioneer, Sam Brannan, this comforting grill is an American standard sating hungry shoppers with familiar food. Beyond the Spanish colonial façade is a mountain lodge-style dining room decorated with a gorgeous, handcrafted bar, wine-country murals, and of course, large screen windows that swing open during warmer months.

Some may start with fresh salads and seafood, while others may opt for the likes of smoked salmon carpaccio topped with rows of finely sieved egg yolks, capers, and chives. Even spa-fiends and hot spring enthusiasts (two of Calistoga's chief draws) can't help but devour the Reuben packed with thick slices of house-cured corned beef, sauerkraut, and melted Swiss.

Brix

B2 

7377 St. Helena Hwy. (at Washington St.), Yountville

Phone: 707-944-2749 — Lunch & dinner daily
Web: www.brix.com
Prices: $$$

When it comes to ingredients in the Napa Valley, there's local–from one of many nearby farms–and then there's *local*, as in straight from your own backyard. At beloved Brix, expect the red radish and pea shoots that adorn your smoked salmon crêpe to hail from the garden patio out back. There may be no fresher salad in Yountville.

The farm-to-table menu is straightforward with both Italian and Asian inflections: braised pork and chestnut ragù warm the orecchiette pasta; while garden pepper linguini is tossed with Laughing Bird shrimp. If weather permits, enjoy a glass of Carneros pinot noir in the gardens, hugged by rolling vineyards and craggy mountain views. Pick up dessert and a wine country memento at the bake shop and gift boutique.

Bui Bistro

A3 — Vietnamese XX

976 Pearl St. (bet. Main St. & Soscol Ave.), Napa

Phone: 707-255-5417 — Lunch & dinner Tue – Sun
Web: www.buibistro.com
Prices: $$

Napa Valley denizens craving the flavors of Vietnam are heading to Chef/owner Patrick Bui's namesake bistro in the wine country where Bui serves the same affordable, flavorful fare for which his former Berkeley location was known.

Inside, gilded mirrors dress up sage green walls and rosewood tables; a small granite bar is well suited to singles lingering over glasses of wine and warm bowls of rice noodles, teeming with delicate prawns, scallops and squid, with plates of condiments. French influences can be found in such dishes as Asian duck confit and beef carpaccio, but the tasty Vietnamese mainstays are also here. Look for shaken beef, pepper tuna, and an array of spicy curries. For dessert, moist tiramisu is both an unexpected and chocolaty surprise.

Ca'Momi

Italian 

610 1st St. (at McKinstry St.), Napa

Phone: 707-257-4992 Lunch & dinner daily
Web: www.camomienoteca.com
Prices: $$

Local, Organic & Italian is the motto at Ca'Momi. If the ingredients aren't local and organic, rest assured that they are imported from Italy. The authenticity here is praiseworthy as the thin-crust pizzas are VPN (Verace Pizza Napoletana) certified—we're talking bona fides. Perhaps small and basic, this Italian treasure also does a large take-out business.

The wood-fired oven turns out thin-crust pizzas capped with super creamy mascarpone, mounds of arugula, and shaved Parmigiano Reggiano; or maybe tomato sauce and smoked buffalo mozzarella, topped with pancetta and sautéed wild mushrooms. Whatever transpires during a meal, save room for the exquisite *bignè* drizzled with hard caramel and filled with honey-sweetened cream...and go...*molto buono*!

Carpe Diem

1001 2nd St. (at Brown St.), Napa

Phone: 707-224-0800 Dinner nightly
Web: www.carpediemwinebar.com
Prices: $$

This wine bar in the heart of Napa has a handful of tables that quickly fill up, so most guests clamor for a spot at the packed bar. With dark stone floors, gleaming wood-covered walls, and a youthful vibe, this is *the* place where thirty and forty-somethings love to hang out in Napa.

Expect a nice selection of wines by the glass and a menu of American dishes that are heavily influenced by global cuisines. Plates may range from wild boar salami to shrimp and grits. Ideal with a glass of *vino* is an Italian Stallion, brick-oven flatbread topped with Meyer lemon mascarpone, salty prosciutto, and caramelized onions; or find a perfect pair in an ostrich burger layered with creamy Brie and a zinfindel reduction. Most can't resist the crispy truffle fries.

C Casa

A3 Mexican

610 1st St. (at McKinstry St.), Napa

Phone: 707-226-7700 — Lunch & dinner daily
Web: www.myccasa.com
Prices:

Bay Area foodies will instantly recognize the Oxbow Public Market, Napa's answer to SF's Ferry Building bursting with kitchen shops and global foodstuffs. Co-owner Catherine Bergen–also former owner of Made in Napa's all-natural pantry products–is translating her taste for healthy gourmet eats to this innovative taqueria.

C Casa is an order-at-the-counter affair, but don't let the casual setting fool you. The market kitchen excels with its made-to-order tortillas topped with spiced lamb and grilled mahi mahi. Dig your compostable fork into a lean ground buffalo taco with goat cheese and chipotle aïoli, or try a grilled shrimp cocktail with tomato and cucumber relish.

Typically, Wednesday's mean live music "Chill'n Wednesdays" and drink specials.

Celadon

A3 International

500 Main St., Ste. G (at 5th St.), Napa

Phone: 707-254-9690 — Lunch Mon – Fri
Web: www.celadonnapa.com — Dinner nightly
Prices: $$

Celadon is one of many businesses in the repurposed and historic Napa Mill along the river. This serene respite is as amicable as it is accessible with two distinct dining rooms—one is a large shaded atrium with a brick fireplace and pitched corrugated ceiling streaming natural light; while the inside feels more quaint with hefty wine bottles, vintage posters, and Celadon ceramics lining the walls.

Soothing grey-green hues coat the space, where butcher paper and white linens dress small tables and a charming bar is best for a glass. Celadon's menu is as worldly as its wine country patronage wandering the globe from Macadamia-crusted goat cheese with Port-poached figs, to Gorgonzola- and spinach-stuffed chicken breast with roasted potatoes and bacon jus.

Cindy's Backstreet Kitchen

International

C1

1327 Railroad Ave. (bet. Adams St. & Hunt Ave.), St. Helena

Phone: 707-963-1200 — Lunch & dinner daily
Web: www.cindysbackstreetkitchen.com
Prices: $$

Cindy's can be found in a historic 1800's house tucked along Railroad Avenue in quaint St. Helena. Locals and families enjoy the welcoming setting—loads of country charm infuses everything from the fruit-motif wallpaper, down to the cushioned banquettes and gracious service.

Under the spin of ceiling fans, a globally influenced menu of small plates, salads, sandwiches, and large plates is divulged. Expect the likes of achiote-roasted pulled pork tacos featuring white corn tortillas, avocado, and kicky red chile salsa; or a delightful duck burger flavored with ginger, topped with a shiitake mushroom reduction, smear of Chinese mustard, and served with crispy fries. But keep room for dessert or just save the homemade honey-glazed cornbread for last!

Cole's Chop House

Steakhouse

A3

1122 Main St. (bet. 1st & Pearl Sts.), Napa

Phone: 707-224-6328 — Dinner nightly
Web: www.coleschophouse.com
Prices: $$$$

An original open truss ceiling and Douglas fir floors attest to the history of the 1886 hand-hewn stone building now home to Cole's Chop House, a classic meat-and-potatoes destination replete with a clubby ambience and spendy cuisine: entrées top out at $69 for a 21-day dry-aged Porterhouse. But don't fret, as there are 20 plus pages of wines, including several luscious Napa cabernets, or classic and seasonal cocktails to take your mind off the bill.

Boozier pleasures aside, Greg Cole's Chop House serves an American-style menu that is dizzying for omnivores. Look for succulent Iowa pork, New Zealand lamb, and sustainable seafood in addition to such classics as oysters Rockefeller topped with Hollandaise and spinach; or a chophouse Caesar.

Cook St. Helena 

Italian

C1

1310 Main St. (bet. Adams & Spring Sts.), St. Helena

Phone: 707-963-7088 — Lunch Mon – Sat
Web: www.cooksthelena.com — Dinner nightly
Prices: $$

On Main Street in chic St. Helena, pull over at Cook where a Carrara marble wine bar awaits with local temptations. This spot reflects its wine country setting with taste and whimsy: antique tin-framed mirrors and black-and-white vegetable prints adorn the walls; dark wood covers the floor; and a playful bovine lantern is mounted like a trophy on the wall.
While solo diners may prefer a spot at the bar, white linen topped with butcher paper make the close-knit tables a cozy place to dine. With pride, the kitchen brings to you reasonably priced Cal-Italian fare, with daily specials on the blackboard. Sample steamed mussels in spicy tomato broth; red trout stuffed with roasted fennel and fingerlings; and a flourless chocolate cake dusted with grey sea salt.

Cuvée

American

A2

1650 Soscol Ave. (at River Terrace Dr.), Napa

Phone: 707-224-2330 — Dinner nightly
Web: www.cuveenapa.com
Prices: $$

In downtown Napa on a Thursday night, head to Cuvée for half-priced bottles of wine and (if lucky) live music. When the evening is warm, find the large retractable doors thrown open to a tree-lined courtyard; when cooler, look for a bit of the outdoors inside, where vine clippings make for rustic wall art beneath contemporary chandeliers.
Next door to the River Terrace Inn, Cuvée is a favorite among hotel guests and locals hungry for American fare such as pinot noir-braised short ribs and Atlantic salmon wrapped in paper-thin potatoes. For a subtle taste of the Orient, try tuna tartare with crunchy Asian slaw and crisp rice crackers. In true old-world style, the wine selection includes several locally made options on tap, as a barrel tasting.

étoile

C3

1 California Dr. (off Hwy. 29), Yountville

Phone: 707-204-7529 — Lunch & dinner Thu – Mon
Web: www.chandon.com
Prices: $$$$

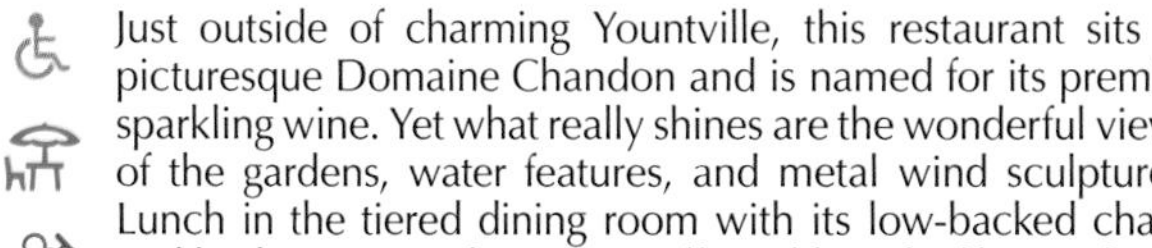

Just outside of charming Yountville, this restaurant sits in picturesque Domaine Chandon and is named for its premier sparkling wine. Yet what really shines are the wonderful views of the gardens, water features, and metal wind sculptures. Lunch in the tiered dining room with its low-backed chairs and bud vases may be a quiet affair, although alfresco diners may take advantage of the gorgeous grounds.

The classically based menu uses local produce and changes daily. It may unveil a trout rillette with dill, celery, orange, and brioche crumbs; or a sliced pork chop served atop sweet pumpkin with butter beans and crunchy apple. Top it all off with a smooth chocolate-hazelnut semifreddo, with morsels of sweet caramel popcorn and peppercorn crème fraîche.

FARM

B3

4048 Sonoma Hwy. (at Old Sonoma Rd.), Napa

Phone: 707-299-4882 — Dinner Wed – Sun
Web: www.thecarnerosinn.com
Prices: $$$

Just off a main road at the Carneros Inn, FARM exudes wine country style with cathedral ceilings, romantic banquettes, trendy fixtures, and the requisite fireplaces. Expect a mixed clientele of fancy locals, tourists, and hotel guests filling the main dining room and watching the chefs through the glassed-in kitchen.

Whether settling into a cushioned wicker seat in the outdoor lounge to sip local wines by the half-glass, noshing at the indoor bar, or going for the tasting menu in the dining room, the gorgeous surrounds will not disappoint. On the menu, expect interesting compositions like lobster risotto with Parmesan and Meyer lemon. Seasonal desserts can be a highlight, as in pumpkin pudding cake with sugar-sweet pumpkin and butternut frosting.

Farmstead

Californian XX

738 Main St. (at Charter Oak Ave.), St. Helena

Phone: 707-963-9181 Lunch & dinner daily
Web: www.thefarmsteadnapa.com
Prices: $$

As its name alludes, Farmstead (the restaurant at Long Meadow Ranch) is praised and preferred for its farm-to-table Californian cooking. Likewise, its surrounds are locally sourced—the wine country-chic barn is clad in wood left over from surrounding redwoods and anchored by a central open kitchen outfitted with a cast-iron grill.

Under airy, vaulted ceilings, dishes are prepared with local and sustainable ingredients and may include Lacinato kale salad tossed with *chile pequin* and *tuiles* of toasted Grana Padano; wonderfully delicate rock bass fillets spread with a creamy aïoli, and posing atop wood-roasted sausages and potatoes in a cioppino broth; and an expert side of buttery flageolet beans fragrant with garlic and fresh herbs.

Fish Story

Seafood XX

790 Main St. (at 3rd St.), Napa

Phone: 707-251-5600 Lunch & dinner daily
Web: www.fishstorynapa.com
Prices: $$

Ahoy, seafood lovers! This is a yarn about a true fish house on the banks of the Napa River, where a heated patio thaws the bones and a nip from the horseshoe bar warms the belly. Never mind the chill cast from the local maritime temperatures posted on the wall—documented local fishing stories and photos posted in the hall do plenty to authenticate the experience.

Fish Story never veers from its course: silver lures and hooks hang from above, and the day's fresh catch is displayed on ice. Those large kettles are used for brewing the namesake beer, perfect for washing down towers of raw seafood from oysters to ceviche; ahi tuna tartare with Asian pear and avocado mousse; plump grilled Florida shrimp; and Half Moon petrale sole swimming in a saffron broth.

The French Laundry ✿✿✿

C2 — Contemporary

6640 Washington St. (at Creek St.), Yountville

Phone: 707-944-2380
Web: www.frenchlaundry.com
Prices: $$$$

Lunch Fri – Sun
Dinner nightly

Deborah Jones

The French Laundry is a venerable destination set in sleepy Yountville. This marvelous structure's rustic and restrained façade seems unassuming, but to better appreciate its celebrated French-country sensibilities, stroll the grounds across the street and get a whiff of the ingredients that will ultimately star on your plate.

Inside, lambent candles, ceiling beams, and wood railings add bucolic touches to an elegant room purged of all stuffy formalities. Meals here are opportunities to dive deeper into the profound culinary knowledge that every server and sommelier must inherently possess. In the kitchen, Chef Timothy Hollingsworth honors the path blazed by Thomas Keller years ago.

Meticulous skill and delight combine with total precision in meals that rouse the palate with the likes of sautéed pompano fillets over Akita Komachi rice, green garlic, and black sesame purée. The delicate hands of an artist are clear in artichokes *"en barigoule"* teamed with mushrooms, petite onions, and extra virgin olive oil powder. Thankfully, multi-course fixed menus are the only dining option, so there is no foregoing the best cheese course of your life.

Book well in advance for the alfresco dining table.

Fumé

International XX

B3

4050 Byway East (bet. Avalon Ct. & Wise Dr.), Napa

Lunch & dinner daily

Phone: 707-257-1999
Web: www.fumebistro.com
Prices: $$

Fumé, situated along Highway 29, has long been a sweetheart among both locals and tourists. With a moderately-priced international carte set alongside a kid's menu, this family-friendly haunt has something for everyone. The setting welcomes all in wine country casual style with a polished wood bar, sunken dining room, and aromatic wood-burning oven.

Try the golden brown duck confit spring rolls filled with radicchio, Napa cabbage, spicy sprouts, and scallions, served with sweet-and-sour sauce; or wood oven-roasted artichokes splashed with tarragon aïoli and herb butter. A massive bowlful of Cajun-spiced rock shrimp fettuccine tossed in a flavorful garlic-chile cream sauce studded with spicy andouille and Asiago is yet another known delight.

Gott's Roadside

American X

C2

933 Main St. (at Charter Oak Ave.), St. Helena

Lunch & dinner daily

Phone: 707-963-3486
Web: www.gottsroadside.com
Prices: ⊖

For a quick burger in wine country, look no farther than this roadside icon that opened in 1949, long before Napa was renowned for wine. A bit of a naming feud led to the hamburger haven's (FKA Taylor's Refresher) name change. At Gott's Roadside Tray Gourmet, while the prices seem high, so is the quality—know that juicy Niman Ranch beef lies between buns, beneath toppings like grilled mushrooms or guacamole. The restaurant also churns out hot dogs topped with hearty homemade chile and sides of sweet potato fries. Gott's refreshes with milk shakes, draft beers, and local wines by the glass, half-bottle, or bottle.

All three locations (San Francisco's Ferry Building and Napa's Oxbow Public Market) have picnic tables perfect for alfresco dining.

Grace's Table

A3 International XX

1400 2nd St. (at Franklin St.), Napa

Phone: 707-226-6200 Lunch & dinner daily
Web: www.gracestable.net
Prices: $$

Named for Mother Nature's fabulous bounty, Grace's Table is just as you might expect: a little earthy. Recycled materials in green and brown hues come together for a low-key vibe, while potted plants breathe life onto wooden tables.

Couples and singles can grab a beer and nosh at the 10-seat bar, while tables are preferred for dinners and weekend brunch. The global menu leans toward European comfort fare like tender pork osso buco with wild mushroom risotto, but it's the seasonal tamale that has become a local legend. If the short rib-stuffed tamale isn't wicked enough, try a slice of the old-fashioned devil's food cake with dark chocolate frosting, Chantilly cream, and a sprinkling of Maldon salt—this dessert is the sweet work of Gaia.

JoLē

A1 Mediterranean XX

1457 Lincoln Ave. (bet. Fair Way & Washington St.), Calistoga

Phone: 707-942-5938 Lunch Sat – Sun
Web: www.jolerestaurant.com Dinner nightly
Prices: $$

Located in the heart of Calistoga, JoLē is owned and operated by a husband (chef)-and-wife (pastry chef) team. The dining room may be simple but it is never silent. Dressed with wood furnishings, a small bar lined with solo diners, and an exhibition prep area, this Mediterranean marvel is always jamming with locals and visitors.

The farm-to-table food is prepared with seasonal and flavorful ingredients. A tasting menu unveils shredded kale stew, salty from ham and creamy from potatoes and a Parmesan fonduta; while bruschetta is topped with fine fixings like wilted spinach, buttery chanterelles, and a quail egg. A glazed duck breast with eggplant and tofu is as tender as the cubes of lamb in a flavorful stew of carrots finished with pillows of gnocchi.

Kitchen Door

International

610 1st St. (at McKinstry St.), Napa

Phone: 707-226-1560 Lunch & dinner daily
Web: www.kitchendoornapa.com
Prices: $$

A novel kid on the Oxbow Public Market block, Kitchen Door preens a roster of internationally-inspired and reasonably priced dishes. Enter this mighty, bright space through swinging red kitchen doors and place your order at the counter. Then fetch your flatware, find a seat in the dining room or on the patio, and await the rest.

Large communal tables face the open kitchen while private booths allow for cozy reunions. Sealing the family-friendly deal are sky-lit ceilings, hanging pots and pans, and shelves of foodstuffs. As if that weren't enough, there is a dish for every palate—from simple beef carpaccio with Himalayan truffle purée, potatoes, and lemon aïoli, to an exhilarating candy cap mushroom bread pudding with golden raisins and maple anglaise.

La Condesa

Mexican

1320 Main St. (bet. Adams St. & Hunt Ave.), St. Helena

Phone: 707-967-8111 Lunch & dinner daily
Web: www.lacondesanapavalley.com
Prices: $$

Housed in the historic Keller Brothers Meats building in quaint St. Helena, the new La Condesa is sibling to a popular Austin outpost. Baby sis' décor is in keeping with its modern (read: Americanized) Mexican food and features robin's egg blue walls, tufted leather banquettes, and molded black-and-white chairs.

Age has no bar at this funky-stylish den, loved by all for its tasty array of guacamole and salsa—the former topped with Dungeness crab while the latter may be infused with blackened, smoky chiles. *Cochinita pibil* crested with pickled jalapeños is hugely gratifying; while spicy guava-glazed *costillas de Puerco* are so tender, they will fall off the bone with little compulsion. A vast tequila and mescal list only elevates the level of fulfillment.

La Taquiza

B3 Mexican

2007 Redwood Rd., Ste. 104 (at Solano Rd.), Napa

Phone: 707-224-2320 — Lunch & dinner Mon – Sat
Web: www.lataquizanapa.com
Prices: ⊜

Wine country zealots on burrito budgets find salvation *con* salsa at La Taquiza, a taqueria whose dining room has an urbane, dressed-up fast food-feel. Large, cool, and colorful paintings penned by a local artist brighten things up; and Baja-style fresh Mex defies its Redwood Plaza locale with lighter, more inventive seafood-driven fare.

Whether fried or grilled, signature fish tacos are a delicious starting point, but the menu's more exotic options whet adventurous appetites. Don't hesitate to sample fresh ceviches, beer-battered oysters, and *pulpo*–grilled, tender octopus ideal for a unique taco–as well as chilled seafood cóctels and bowls known as *tazons*. Swing by the salsa bar for varying degrees of heat and smoke to satisfy all tastes.

Lucy

C2 Californian

6526 Yount St. (bet. Finnell Rd. & Mulberry St.), Yountville

Phone: 707-204-6030 — Lunch & dinner daily
Web: www.bardessono.com
Prices: **$$$**

The Bardessono hotel's restaurant has been revamped as Lucy (named after the Bardessono family's matriarch). This pretty refuge's elegant design combines rustic and urban sensibilities with a beautiful communal table, white sculptural wall, and modern pendant lights. Guests and residents alike have nothing but love for Lucy's ambience and adept service.

The menu features local ingredients (some grown in their own garden) and may uncover plump oysters on the half shell, served with a blood orange-champagne mignonette; or braised lamb cassoulet with *gigante* beans and seasonal vegetables creatively topped with a fried quail egg and lemon-thyme breadcrumbs. A sweet potato pie with Kaffir lime marshmallow and black sesame ice cream crafts a gratifying finish.

La Toque ✿

Contemporary XXX

A2

1314 McKinstry St. (at Soscol Ave.), Napa

Phone: 707-257-5157 Dinner nightly
Web: www.latoque.com
Prices: $$$

La Toque

Discreet and stylish La Toque is situated within Napa's Westin, though it maintains a separate entrance to the side of the hotel. The modern room is fashioned in cream and brown, with a small fireplace and the added entertainment of the kitchen nearby. Booths are the best place to rest amid low lighting, while plenty of floor-to-ceiling windows lend a formal yet agreeable feel to this largely corporate-toned lair. Smartly uniformed staff attends to the local couples and businessmen.

The massive wine list is superb and interesting, with an exceptional selection from Napa Valley (unsurprisingly), in addition to spectacular French and other old-world varietals.

Tasting and à la carte menus boast the likes of a clever and complimentary mix of sweetly marinated Japanese red snapper with chopped ripe avocado and crunchy-sweet pear, salted dashi jelly, and creamy yuzu sauce. Meals might go on to include squash cubes mixed with meaty lobster tail, served warm with chilled crème fraîche; or a hearty Colorado buffalo strip loin with root vegetable terrine finished with a strong reduction of red wine jus. Desserts like peanut parfait with banana ice cream bring all things to a very good end.

Market

C1

1347 Main St. (bet. Adams & Spring Sts.), St. Helena

Phone: 707-963-3799 — Lunch & dinner daily
Web: www.marketsthelena.com
Prices: $$

Chef/owner Eduardo Martinez is sharing his American dream at Market, where classics like mac 'n' cheese, dressed up with aged Fiscalini cheddar, mingle with little tastes from his Mexico City home—think buttermilk fried chicken and peppery cheddar-jalapeño cornbread, or blackened chicken rolls spiced with chipotle chiles.

There are many reasons to love Market, including pristine oysters on the half shell; a $15 lunch comprised of "soup, sandwich and a treat" (think rice krispies); and a sinfully fabulous butterscotch pudding made with real Scotch, ahem, and served in a waffle cone bowl. Slip into a plush brown leather banquette and get comfy with your latest prize from wine tasting: an anomaly in the Valley, Market generously forgoes corkage fees.

Mini Mango Thai Bistro

Thai

A3

1408 W. Clay St. (bet. Franklin and Seminary Sts.), Napa

Phone: 707-226-8884 — Lunch Mon – Sat
Web: www.minimangonapa.com — Dinner nightly
Prices:

This Napa nook may not be the easiest to find, but having overcome its geographical challenges, Mini Mango deserves a pat on its back for thriving in a turf where other restaurants have failed. The snug bistro may be low on tables but they are big on flavor; and the space does double when the sun is out, with a roomy and bustling front patio ringed in olive trees.

Thanks to owners Pornchai and Cherry Pengchareon, Mini Mango offers a tiny slice of Thailand in the wine country with a hint of a Californian accent. Pleasant servers glide amid compact tables to deliver classics like coconut chicken soup; *tom yum* prawns in a consommé fragrant with lemongrass and Kaffir lime; and frilly Indo-Chine corn fritters served with a spicy-sweet *sambal*-plum reduction.

Morimoto Napa

A3 — Japanese XXX

610 Main St. (at 5th St.), Napa

Phone: 707-252-1600 — Lunch & dinner daily
Web: www.morimotonapa.com
Prices: $$$

Beautiful Morimoto draws tourists and locals for its sleek industrial style and contemporary cuisine. The front room is best for groups and sports a sushi bar, stylish lounge, and large communal tables. While the back nook with its smooth wood tables and cushioned banquettes is ideal for a private party.

The innovative kitchen encourages sharing in dishes like sashimi towers (crafted from toro, salmon, eel, and tuna) painted with yuzu juice or barbecue eel sauce. Homemade tofu is prepared tableside and expertly coupled with mushroom sauce and bonito flakes; while a hearty pot pie of stewed abalone is comfort food at its best. Come with friends so you don't miss out on a fantastic sticky toffee pudding made with kabocha and topped with poached Asian pear.

Mustards Grill

B2 — American XX

7399 St. Helena Hwy. (at Hwy. 29), Yountville

Phone: 707-944-2424 — Lunch & dinner daily
Web: www.mustardsgrill.com
Prices: $$

Well before Thomas Keller staked his flag in Yountville, local favorite Cindy Pawlcyn was serving luxe "truckstop" fare at her already iconic Mustards. Opened in 1983, this wine country roadhouse still draws the crowds for new American fare (think oak-smoked barbecue ribs) and bargain sips from the list of Too Many Wines.

Soak up your favorite California varietal with one of the various daily specials scribbled on the blackboard, or try such old favorites as Dungeness crab cakes or grilled quail accented with herbs and vegetables from the restaurant's own gardens. Venture out for a stroll and you just might encounter the chef. If reservations aren't available at Mustards, pick up one of Pawlcyn's many cookbooks and try your hand at home.

Norman Rose Tavern

A3 — Gastropub XX

1401 1st St. (at Franklin St.), Napa

Phone: 707-258-1516 — Lunch & dinner daily
Web: www.normanrosenapa.com
Prices: $$

For everyone who is lagging after the dragging from winery to winery and just wants an ice-cold pint at the end of a hoity-toity day, this place is for you. Those of you who just perked up should cruise over to Norman Rose Tavern, one of the few spots in the Valley with a true-blue penchant for a burger and a PBR (or micro-brew on tap). Plentiful bar seating, walls lined with reclaimed barn wood, and a ceiling of empty "decorative" beer bottles leave no one doubting the theme. Chef Michael Gyetvan gets it—never mind that his resume includes stints at One Market and Tra Vigne. At his approachable American pub, find plump all-beef hot dogs with tangy relish; milk-braised pork shoulder with gravy and sausage grits; and highbrow junk food at its very best.

Oenotri

A3 — Italian XX

1425 1st St. (bet. Franklin & School Sts.), Napa

Phone: 707-252-1022 — Lunch Mon – Fri
Web: www.oenotri.com — Dinner nightly
Prices: $$

The pizza ovens at Oakland's Oliveto have seasoned more than a handful of talented chefs, including Curtis Di Fede and Tyler Rodde who are now blistering their pies in an oven imported from Naples to Napa. Be warned, locals are happy to wait for a taste of that almond- and cherry-wood fire-licked pie.

With sunny textiles, exposed brick, and concrete floors, Oenotri–from an ancient word for "vine cultivator"–is a mix of practicality and pretty. But the design is just a side dish to standout Italian food including the smoky pizza Napoletana; porcini *fidei* pasta with grated tuna heart; and Silverado Trail strawberry *crostata* with Meyer lemon cream. With 30 wines for under $25, Oenotri is ideal for cultivating your palate without breaking the bank.

Pica Pica

Latin American

610 First St. (at McKinstry St.), Napa

Phone: 707-251-3757 Lunch & dinner daily
Web: www.picapicakitchen.com
Prices: ⊜

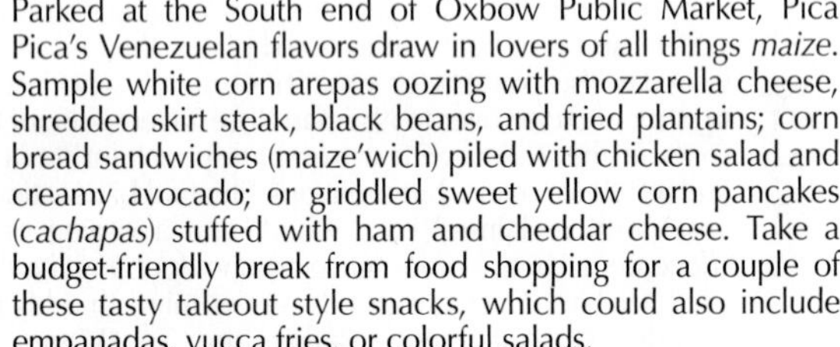

Parked at the South end of Oxbow Public Market, Pica Pica's Venezuelan flavors draw in lovers of all things *maize*. Sample white corn arepas oozing with mozzarella cheese, shredded skirt steak, black beans, and fried plantains; corn bread sandwiches (maize'wich) piled with chicken salad and creamy avocado; or griddled sweet yellow corn pancakes (*cachapas*) stuffed with ham and cheddar cheese. Take a budget-friendly break from food shopping for a couple of these tasty takeout style snacks, which could also include empanadas, yucca fries, or colorful salads.

The tiny space sports a few tables and a small bar area where food orders are taken. Choose between a refreshing brew or sangria while waiting for your order and grab yourself a table.

Press

Steakhouse XXX

587 St. Helena Hwy. South, St. Helena

Phone: 707-967-0550 Dinner Wed – Mon
Web: www.pressstthelena.com
Prices: **$$$$**

Here at Press, there are no sub-par cuts of meat. Those toppings–blue cheese, truffle butter, a fried organic egg–and bounty of tasty sauces may be delicious but are certainly not required on such perfectly prepared beef. Deeper pockets should go for the Wagyu from Idaho.

The gorgeous St. Helena space fashions a bucolic vibe with its black walnut floors, reclaimed from a Midwestern mill, and bar crafted from a trio of walnut trees. A roaring fireplace warms the contemporary yet rustic interior, while a second hearth and candles add to the patio's ambience and make for an ideal spot to sit and sip a rich, steak-worthy cabernet. The raw bar and many seasonal offerings are just as wonderful and will please those who shy away from the main attraction.

Redd ✿

Contemporary XX

C3

6480 Washington St. (at Oak Circle), Yountville

Phone: 707-944-2222 Lunch & dinner daily
Web: www.reddnapavalley.com
Prices: $$$$

Andy Katz

With its welcoming feel, wood-framed windows overlooking the heart of picturesque Yountville, and solid contemporary cooking, Redd has earned its reputation as a dining destination among locals and food tourists alike. The low-rise gray building features a front patio for warm weather alfresco dining amid olive trees with an outdoor fireplace and decorative pool. Inside feels modern, clean, and mid-century with Eames-style chairs, white walls, and votive-adorned tables.

While the kitchen is serious and engrossed, the professional service staff seems intent on ensuring guests' comfort and enjoyment—a lovely and atypical attribute for a restaurant operating at this level.

On the menu, some dishes dare to surprise with crowd-pleasing comforts as in a bowl of thick cheddar cheese polenta surrounded by a pool of *mole*, topped with a deboned and delightfully crisp chicken thigh. This might be followed by an exquisite risotto, lacing Meyer lemon confit through succulent lobster meat drizzled in fragrant truffle oil. Desserts combine wonderful flavors and skill, perhaps layering luscious butterscotch pudding with vanilla anglaise mousse, crumbled toffee, and chocolate-coated pretzel pieces.

Redd Wood

Italian XX

B2

6755 Washington St. (bet. Madison & Pedroni Sts.), Yountville

Phone: 707-299-5030 — Lunch & dinner daily
Web: www.redd-wood.com
Prices: $$

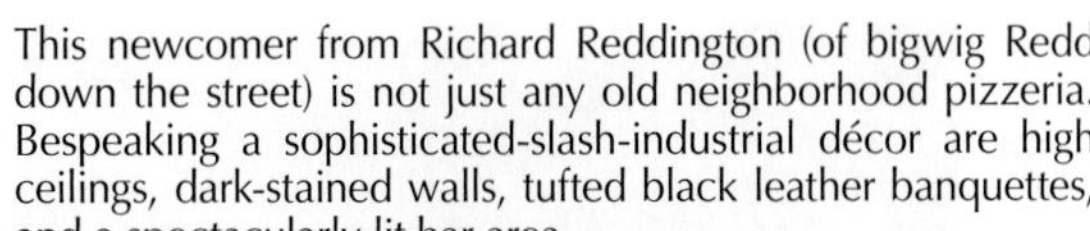

This newcomer from Richard Reddington (of bigwig Redd down the street) is not just any old neighborhood pizzeria. Bespeaking a sophisticated-slash-industrial décor are high ceilings, dark-stained walls, tufted black leather banquettes, and a spectacularly lit bar area.

The Italian roster fulfills your wine country noshing needs. For a super start, indulge in golden brown salt cod fritters served with batons of *panisse* and streaked with harissa aïoli; then move onto a thin-crust pizza topped with taleggio, prosciutto, and a farm-fresh egg. Bookend fluffy potato gnocchi joined by tender pieces of duck meat and caramelized pancetta, with a super sweet butterscotch semifreddo capped in a heady Bourbon sauce. Sleep it off at the adjoining North Block hotel.

Rutherford Grill

American XX

B2

1180 Rutherford Rd. (at Hwy. 29), Rutherford

Phone: 707-963-1792 — Lunch & dinner daily
Web: www.hillstone.com
Prices: $$

Temptation starts in the parking lot at Rutherford Grill, where aromas from the wood-fired rotisserie make impatient bellies growl. Just don't arrive too hungry; this popular hangout nearly guarantees a wait. Sidle up to the bar in the meantime for a glass of something local and you might find yourself rubbing elbows with notable Napa Valley oenophiles.

Once summoned from your barstool, step up to a red leather booth and sink into the warm ambience primed for hearty fare. The open kitchen aces menu staples such as artichoke dip; buttery skillet cornbread; and slabs of fall-off-the-bone pork ribs served with shoestring fries and slaw. Rutherford Grill mingles so well with wine country charm that its chain restaurant roots are all but forgotten.

The Restaurant at Meadowood ✿✿✿

Contemporary XXXX

B1

900 Meadowood Ln. (off Silverado Trail), St. Helena

Phone: 707-967-1205 — Dinner Mon – Sat
Web: www.meadowood.com
Prices: $$$$

Meadowood Napa Valley

Located just a short stroll from the main lobby at the Meadowood resort, down a bucolic garden path with a view of groves, meadows, and quaint cottages, find this recently refreshed dining room. The appearance is now more contemporary, with dramatic flowers, dark accents, and framed mirrors; skylights atop the vaulted ceiling and an arching wall of windows to make the most of any sunset. The suit-clad servers work as a cohesive, welcoming brigade who somehow seem as happy to be here as the affluent locals and resort guests.

The chef's tasting menu–the only dining option here–is ten courses and differs from table to table. This may begin with an assortment of canapés like pillows of *fromage blanc* encased in crisp pastry; geoduck fritters filled with clam chowder and Meyer lemon zest; or stalks of beet greens in tomato water "snow." While each dish can seem truly inspired, highlights include flaky cubes of lightly smoked black cod over a buttery "hash" of rutabaga and fingerling potatoes.

Expect a truly decadent cheese course like whipped triple cream French *L'explorateur* sandwiched between wavy tuiles, topped with freeze-dried and cured cherries, as well as cherry blossoms and young leaves.

Solbar ✿

A1

755 Silverado Trail (at Rosedale Rd.), Calistoga

Phone: 707-226-0850 Lunch & dinner daily
Web: www.solagecalistoga.com
Prices: **$$$**

Every classy, rustic, and polished detail is sure to remind you exactly where you are: The Solage Spa and Resort is nestled amid wineries at the foot of the mountains and has spared no drama in fashioning these grounds with water features, palm trees, and fire pits. The interior is airy and chic with a barn-meets-loft vibe; long velvet curtains and modern wood chairs lend added sophistication. Everything feels effortlessly attractive, from the young staff to the polished tabletops adorned with tiny flowers and a ceramic dish of red Hawaiian sea salt.

While emphasis on beauty may be paramount, the kitchen proves itself increasingly mature, smart, and creative in reflecting spa cuisine with lighter or heartier pleasures. Meals here might begin as a dainty rendition of fluffy gnocchi with crisped Oregon chanterelles and fresh corn kernels enriched with hugely flavorful house-cured pancetta. Comforting and delicious larger dishes have included Petaluma chicken cooked *a la plancha*, served with plump roasted grapes tossed with pickled mustard seeds, sautéed rapini, and tiny, sugar-pie pumpkin-stuffed agnolotti.

Desserts like a warm and sugar-crusted Basque cake are always just right.

Tarla

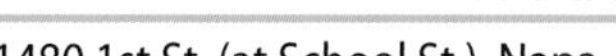

Mediterranean

A3

1480 1st St. (at School St.), Napa

Phone: 707-255-5599 Lunch & dinner daily
Web: www.tarlagrill.com
Prices: $$

A stacked stone façade and orange sign indicate that you've found Tarla. This casual Mediterranean restaurant in Napa's hub boasts a modern décor with hints of rusticity—bright orange barn door panels line the walls. Guests can eat at the bar, or at tables along a banquette. But, when the sun is out, alfresco seats on the sidewalk are most coveted.

Expect to see a mix of local business sorts at lunch and families for dinner devouring items that range in influence from Greek to Turkish. These have included a juicy lamb *kofte* burger layered with fava bean spread and white cheddar cheese, coupled with herb-strewn fries; or tasty beef *doner,* shavings of Turkish spit-roasted beef served on a pita spread with spicy mayonnaise and topped with a sumac salad.

Tra Vigne

Italian

C2

1050 Charter Oak Ave. (off Hwy. 29), St. Helena

Phone: 707-963-4444 Lunch & dinner daily
Web: www.travignerestaurant.com
Prices: $$$

It's impossible not to love Tra Vigne, the St. Helena retreat evocative of Tuscany with its rugged stone building and vineyard surrounds. On balmy nights, head to the garden patio where tables intertwine with olive trees and white lights twinkle overhead. Cooler weather? No matter. The spacious interior is just as cozy for enjoying rustic Italian fare as it makes its way from the exhibition kitchen.

Tra Vigne is best known for its dishes from the wood-burning oven in hearty portions that highlight seasonal ingredients, as in the cracker-crisp fig pizza topped with spicy arugula and Gorgonzola. The signature and über-creamy mozzarella *al minuto* deserves its buzzing popularity. After dinner, join the locals in savoring a cabernet at the bustling bar.

Terra ✿

Contemporary XXX

C1

1345 Railroad Ave. (bet. Adams St. & Hunt Ave.), St. Helena

Phone: 707-963-8931 Dinner Wed – Mon
Web: www.terrarestaurant.com
Prices: **$$$**

Enter this historic stand-alone building in downtown St. Helena and steer left to arrive at Terra where the mood is intimate, the food is classic, and the lighting is dim ("watch your step!"). Inside, the dining room is decked with glossy terra-cotta floor tiles and stone walls; beautiful arched windows cast a sultry and flattering sheen throughout, as if to highlight the decades (or days) of romance that each couple seems to be celebrating. In short, this is a great date place.

On the menu, Asian and Californian cuisines are combined seamlessly, with just a splash of Italian. Tasty starters like cream of green garlic soup with a slow-cooked Jidori egg becomes brilliant when finished with shimmering pearls of lobster that lend a meaty pop to each spoonful. Wonderfully "savory" bites of Ezo abalone bathed in escargot butter with mushrooms and a tangle of roasted fennel make way for exquisitely satisfying desserts that you won't want to split with your date. End with such sweets as a moist chocolate bread pudding fragrant with sour cherries and tucked under fluffy peaks of crème fraîche.

Check out Bar Terra across the foyer for simpler fare pitched alongside perfectly composed cocktails.

Wine Spectator Greystone

Californian

A1

2555 Main St. (at Deer Park Rd.), St. Helena

Phone: 707-967-1010 Lunch & dinner daily
Web: www.ciarestaurants.com
Prices: $$$

This historic château, once home to the Christian Brothers Winery, is flanked by grapevines intertwining like lace through the grounds. Dream up the most idyllic wine country setting imaginable, but know your arrival at Greystone will exceed expectations as olive trees, rosemary, and lavender pave the way to a sunny terrace with a trickling fountain.
Inside, the dining room is grand with stone walls rising to soaring ceilings and a fireplace in the warm lounge. Since Greystone houses the CIA's California campus, the three open kitchens offer a veritable dinner theater starring seasonal Californian acts with Mediterranean flair like sweet corn soup with peekytoe crab and chive oil; or prosciutto-wrapped cod with butter bean relish and Catalan vinaigrette.

Zuzu

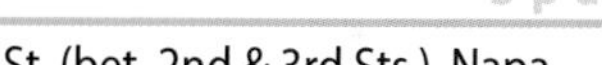

Spanish

A3

829 Main St. (bet. 2nd & 3rd Sts.), Napa

Phone: 707-224-8555 Lunch Mon – Fri
Web: www.zuzunapa.com Dinner nightly
Prices: $$

Don't let the faded tile floors, weathered wood beams, and salvaged tin ceiling fool you—Zuzu is only a decade old and its Mediterranean-style tapas have only become more delicious with age. A self-proclaimed celebration of food, wine, and art, Zuzu's Latin beats are a groovy backdrop for paintings and metalwork courtesy of area artisans; while more than 20 off-the-beaten-path wines are poured at their recycled pine bar.
Feast on tasty *boquerones* spread with white anchovies, boiled egg, and remoulade; grilled octopus with potatoes, pea shoots, and spicy harissa vinaigrette; or crispy quail over posole with lime and chipotle. With only a few late night spots in Napa, Zuzu is ideal for a bite before or after a Napa Valley Opera House performance.

Sonoma County

Often eclipsed as a wine region by neighboring Napa Valley, this canton that borders meandering Marin County claims 76 miles of Pacific coastline, as well as over 250 wineries that take advantage of some of the best grape-growing conditions in California. Agoston Haraszthy established Northern California's first premium winery, **Buena Vista**, just outside the town of Sonoma in 1857. Today thirteen distinct wine appellations (AVAs) have been assigned in Sonoma County, where vintners produce a dizzying array of wines in an area slightly larger than the State

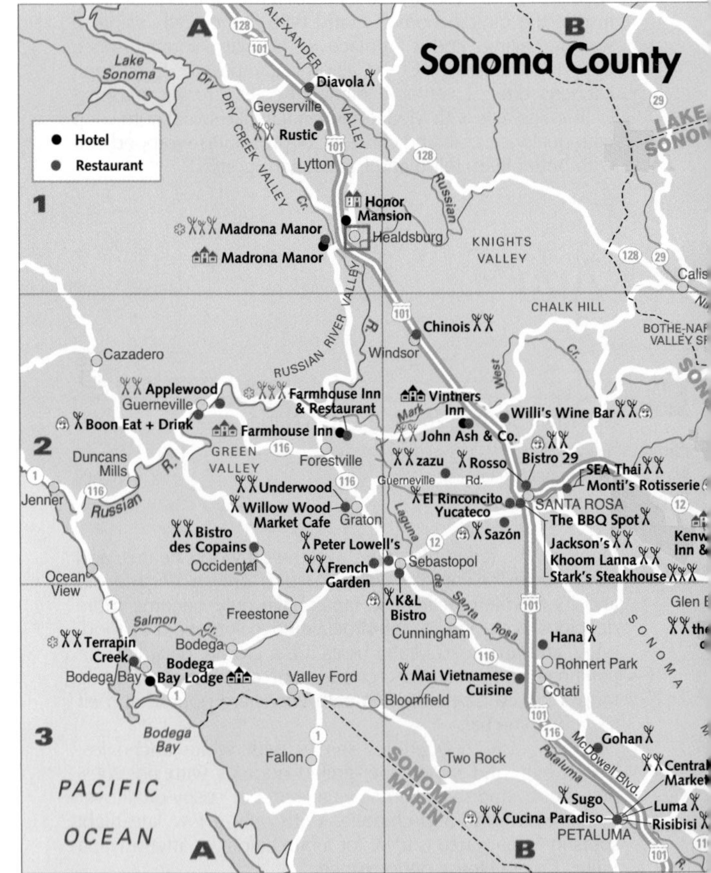

of Rhode Island itself. Along Highway 12 heading north, byroads lead to out-of-the-way wineries, each of which puts its own unique stamp on the business of winemaking. For instance, the Russian River Valley edges the river named for the early Russian trading outposts that were set up along the coast. This is one of the coolest growing regions in Sonoma, thanks to the river basin that offers a conduit for cool coastal climates. Elegant and well-liked pinot noir and chardonnay headline here, but Syrah is quickly catching up.

At the upper end of the Russian River, the Dry Creek Valley yields excellent sauvignon blanc as well as chardonnay and pinot noir. This region is also justly famous for its zinfandel, a grape that does especially well in the valley's rock-strewn soil. Winery visits in Dry Creek are a study in contrasts. Palatial modern wineries rise up along the same rural roads that have

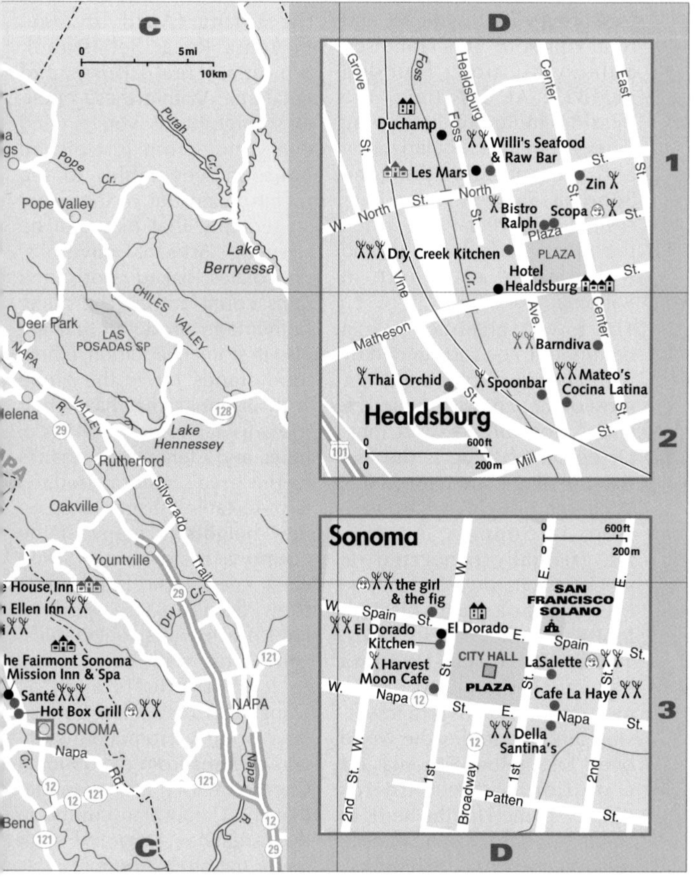

been home to independents for generations; and young grapevines trained into laser-straightened rows are broken up by the dark, gnarled fingers of old vines.

Sonoma County's inland most AVAs are Knights Valley and Alexander Valley. These two warm regions both highlight cabernet sauvignon. Nestled between the Mayacamas and Sonoma ranges, the 17-mile-long Sonoma Valley dominates the southern portion of the county. At its center is the town of Sonoma, site of California's northernmost and final mission: San Francisco Solano Mission, founded in 1823. At one time, the mission included a thriving vineyard before secularization and incorporation into the Sonoma State Historic Park system 102 years ago, when the vines were uprooted and transplanted elsewhere in Sonoma.

The town's eight-acre plaza continues to be surrounded by 19th century adobe buildings, most of them now occupied by shops, restaurants, and inns. Of epicurean note is the fact that building contractor Chuck Williams bought a hardware store in Sonoma in 1956. He gradually converted its stock from hardware to unique French cookware, kitchen tools, and other novelty foods. Today **Williams-Sonoma** has more than 200 stores nationwide, and is a must-stop among foodies the world over. Just below Sonoma lies a portion of the Carneros district, named for the herds of sheep (*los carneros* in Spanish) that once roamed its hillsides. Carneros is best known for its cool-climate grapes, notably pinot noir and chardonnay.

Pastoral Pleasures

Throughout this bucolic county–also referred to as SoCo by savvy locals–vineyards rub shoulders with orchards and farms that take advantage of the area's fertile soil to produce everything from apples and olives, to artisan-crafted cheeses. Sustainable and organic are key words here at local farmers' markets, which herald the spring (April or May) in Santa Rosa, Sebastopol, Sonoma, Healdsburg, and Petaluma. Within these open-air smorgasbords, you can find everything from just-picked heirloom vegetables to sea urchin taken out of the water so recently that may still be wiggling. Artisanal olive oils, chocolates, baked goods, and jams count among the many homemade products that are also in store. In addition, ethnic food stands cover the globe with offerings that have their roots as far away as Mexico, India, and Afghanistan. Thanks to the area's natural bounty, farm-to-table cuisine takes on new heights in many of the county's restaurants. Some chefs need go no farther than their own on-site gardens for fresh fruits, vegetables, and herbs. With easy access to local products such as Dungeness crab from Bodega Bay, poultry from Petaluma, and cheeses from the Sonoma Cheese Factory, it's no wonder that the Californian cuisine in this area has attracted such major national attention.

Applewood

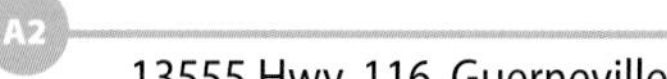

Californian

A2

13555 Hwy. 116, Guerneville

Phone: 707-869-9093 Dinner Wed – Sun
Web: www.applewoodinn.com
Prices: $$$

Tucked among the redwoods and rolling hills of wine country, Applewood offers much more than meets the eye—it is a serious spa, an inn, and clearly a destination dining spot. Surrounded by exceptional produce and primary ingredients, this Sonoma sparkler welcomes all into its serene dining room framed with floor-to-ceiling windows.

Having embraced a relaxed, product-driven cuisine, Applewood is conducive to enjoying a fuss-free yet well-made smoked Yukon Gold potato soup studded with crispy shallots; or cocoa-nib crusted rack of California lamb sauced with chimichurri and laid atop a pool of sweet potato purée and sherry-braised chorizo. Pair a quince frangipane tart with a selection from their ample coffee carte to understand what all the fuss is about.

Barndiva

Californian

D2

231 Center St. (bet. Matheson & Mills Sts.), Healdsburg

Phone: 707-431-0100 Lunch & dinner Wed – Sun
Web: www.barndiva.com
Prices: $$

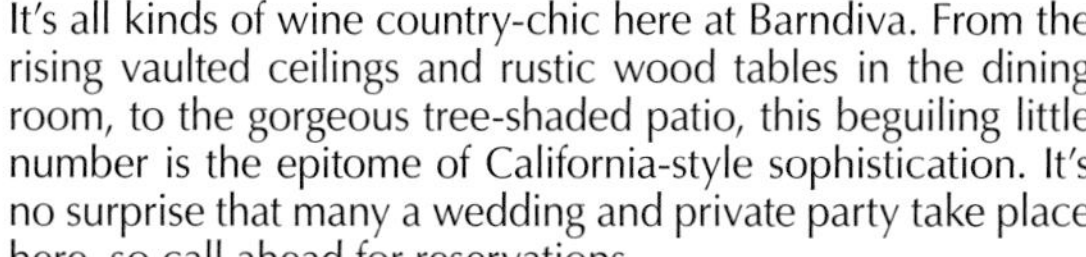

It's all kinds of wine country-chic here at Barndiva. From the rising vaulted ceilings and rustic wood tables in the dining room, to the gorgeous tree-shaded patio, this beguiling little number is the epitome of California-style sophistication. It's no surprise that many a wedding and private party take place here, so call ahead for reservations.

The exquisite menu has featured delights like creamy lobster risotto, and crispy pork belly with bean *cassoulet*. Dig into crispy young chicken, perfectly prepared, seasoned, and served over roasted artichoke hearts, root vegetables, and smoky pancetta, with a soft ricotta-egg yolk *raviolo* perched on top. The warm peach- and almond-frangipane tart with vanilla bean-thyme ice cream is a dream come true.

The BBQ Spot

Barbecue

B2

3448 Santa Rosa Ave. (bet. Robles Ave. & Todd Rd.), Santa Rosa

Phone: 707-585-2616 Lunch & dinner Tue – Sun
Web: www.thebbqspot.net
Prices: ⊜

This newcomer to Santa Rosa has a no-frills locale and is situated next to a tattoo parlor, but don't let the lack of ambience dissuade you, the little restaurant is turning out some seriously good barbecue. The menu has all the heavy hitters like succulent, falling-off-the-bone pork ribs that are smoky and caramelized with a sweet glaze, and tender pulled pork that is delicious on its own or drizzled with house-made spicy sauce. With sides like homemade baked beans and coleslaw to choose from, your barbecue sampler is complete. The restaurant is simple and causal with colorful linoleum floors, flat-screen TVs on the walls, and disposable utensils. Expect a low-key, local crowd, but as the word gets out, this place may get super busy.

Bistro des Copains

French

A2

3782 Bohemian Hwy. (at Occidental Rd.), Occidental

Phone: 707-874-2436 Dinner nightly
Web: www.bistrodescopains.com
Prices: $$

In the quaint town of Occidental, in a small cottage off of the main street, is Bistro des Copains. Take in the cheery yellow walls, wood burning oven, and red floral tablecloths. Vintage photos of the French countryside will have you instantly transported to Roquefort, where one of the owners spent part of his childhood at his grandparent's sheep farm.

Perfecting the setting is very traditional French bistro fare that might include onion soup to start; followed by *poisson du jour*, perhaps a simple and deliciously browned pan-roasted halibut, served over a pool of beurre blanc, and paired with a potato galette. One bite into raspberry shortcake filled with sweet whipped cream and plump berries, and you might even believe those memories are your own.

Bistro Ralph

D1

109 Plaza St. (bet. Center St. & Healdsburg Ave.), Healdsburg

Phone: 707-433-1380 — Lunch daily
Web: www.bistroralph.com — Dinner Mon – Sat
Prices: $$

Look for a pair of sidewalk tables to enter this local stomping ground overlooking the boutiques of Healdsburg's central plaza. Chef/owner Ralph Tingle's eponymous bistro has a whitewashed brick interior studded with metal accents, and a bar counter that bestows a view onto the open kitchen, where each season's bounty inspires the concise menu.

Order a carefully selected local wine or martini–always shaken, never stirred–then sit back to enjoy a delightfully chaste and contemporary spread. Lunch may bring fried Sichuan pepper calamari accompanied by a soy-ginger sauce; while ravenous appetites can opt for a hearty veal chop served with anchovy butter and sweet potato fries. Finish with a cheese board or one of a few homemade sweets.

Bistro 29

French

B2

620 5th St. (bet. D St. & Mendocino Ave.), Santa Rosa

Phone: 707-546-2929 — Dinner Tue – Sun
Web: www.bistro29.com
Prices: $$

This charming French bistro-meets-crêperie in downtown Santa Rosa specializes in the authentic dishes of Bretagne in the northwest of France. Bistro 29 has an authentic look to match the menu with deep red-painted walls, dark-framed mirrors, and crisp white linen. It is a popular spot with locals and families and the diminutive place is hopping at sundown.

Expect such traditional bistro items as a half head of butter lettuce dressed with a creamy *fromage blanc* dressing and then liberally sprinkled with chopped herbs. This is best trailed by a savory crêpe Lyonnaise filled with smoked lardons, caramelized onions, and melting cave-aged Gruyère. A runny egg tops this this authentic rendition and may leave you wondering how you got here without a passport.

Boon Eat + Drink

Californian

A2

16248 Main St. (bet. 4th & Mill Sts.), Guerneville

Phone: 707-869-0780 Lunch & dinner Thu – Tue
Web: www.eatatboon.com
Prices: $$

The cat's out of the bag. Boon Eat + Drink might be a bit off the radar (tucked in the picturesque town of Guerneville) but its seasonal Californian fare attracts connoisseurs from miles around. The modest storefront features a covered patio for outdoor dining and a quaint interior where aluminum chairs and simple wood tables allow the local, sustainable fare to shine.

When in season, Boon's flash-fried Brussels sprouts with olive oil and red chili flakes may be the best you've had. You may say the same of the grilled calamari set atop peppery arugula mingled with white beans; or Gleason Ranch-braised pork belly with black-eyed peas and sautéed garlicky greens. For dinner, try the grilled halibut with fennel braised gigante beans and basil pistou.

Cafe La Haye

Californian

D3

140 E. Napa St. (bet. 1st & 2nd Sts.), Sonoma

Phone: 707-935-5994 Dinner Tue – Sat
Web: www.cafelahaye.com
Prices: $$

Cafe La Haye is the curious yet wonderful collision of a bespectacled former college music teacher with seasonal ingredients and a charming house off Sonoma's town square. A local favorite since 1996, the bi-level dining room with a revolving art collection is constantly packed: make reservations or hold out hope for a seat at the tiny kitchen-facing counter.

The open kitchen provides an unobstructed view of the local produce that comprises the Californian cuisine. Be sure to ask for the daily risotto before embarking on such dishes as smoked trout with lemon-horseradish cream and shaved fennel; or roasted chicken frilled with grilled zucchini and oven-dried tomatoes. Seal your meal with a throwback and delicious butterscotch pudding.

Central Market

Mediterranean XX

B3

42 Petaluma Blvd. N. (at Western Ave.), Petaluma

Phone: 707-778-9900 — Dinner nightly
Web: www.centralmarketpetaluma.com
Prices: $$

This is a relaxed but packed spot in downtown Petaluma where huge painted canvases of cows adorn the walls. Chef Tony Najiola is the welcoming proprietor walking through the dining room chatting with guests, many of whom are regulars. He is clearly passionate about his menu which includes first-rate ingredients sourced from his own farm.

Foodies aim for seats facing the open kitchen where the chef can be seen creating Mediterranean-inspired dishes with care and precision. Starring local ingredients is a kale salad dressed in a light vinaigrette, tossed with shaved Parmesan, walnuts, and topped with a superbly fresh farm egg; or rainbow trout stuffed with wilted spinach, olives, and garlic, served with crispy paprika-seasoned potatoes.

Chinois

Asian XX

B2

186 Windsor River Rd. (at Bell Rd.), Windsor

Phone: 707-838-4667 — Lunch Mon – Fri
Web: www.chinoisbistro.com — Dinner Mon – Sat
Prices: $$

Chinois' owners have cornered the market on Asian cuisine in this neck of the woods (they also own Ume Japanese Bistro down the road), but in this case, monopolies aren't a bad thing. A delightful gem, delivering fresh flavors that are a welcome change from the sticky sweet sauces of other Asian spots, Chinois is Asian fusion without the confusion.

A little bit of this, a little bit of that, the menu proudly highlights curries from Thailand, dim sum from China, and noodle dishes from all over. It may seem like a tall order to blend so many different styles, but the kitchen executes this task flawlessly. Thanks to its wine country location, the Asian haven touts a respectable list of wines to accompany the beer selections.

Cucina Paradiso

Italian XX

B3

114 Petaluma Blvd. N. (bet. Washington St. & Western Ave.), Petaluma

Phone: 707-782-1130 Lunch & dinner Mon – Sat
Web: www.cucinaparadisopetaluma.com
Prices:

Nestled in downtown Petaluma, Cucina Paradiso kills with kindness. Chef/owner Dennis Hernandez and his wife, Malena, run their homey mainstay with a strong sense of family: the staff is a tight-knit group, regulars are greeted with kisses and hugs, while the rest of us are simply friends they haven't met yet.

Once a well-kept secret, Cucina Paradiso is flourishing in this spacious dining room bathed in sunny yellow with Gerbera daisies smiling from each table, all a far cry from its strip mall origins. The menu of homemade specialties is informed by the chef's Italian training, so as arias fill the air, find harmony in such dishes as rigatoni with spicy pork, red peppers, and creamy tomato sauce; or pillowy Gorgonzola gnocchi with chopped walnuts.

Della Santina's

Italian XX

D3

133 E. Napa St. (bet. 1st & 2nd Sts.), Sonoma

Phone: 707-935-0576 Lunch & dinner daily
Web: www.dellasantinas.com
Prices: $$

Just a few steps off the main square, through an iron gate, and down a brick pathway lies Della Santina's—a family-owned and operated Italian restaurant where guests are treated like part of the family. Coziness abounds from the garden patio with wisteria and olive trees, to the simple furnishings and family photographs.

The home-style Italian dishes are prepared with skill and may be exactly what your Italian grandmother would make. And you'd happily heed her urge to *mangia* with dishes such as the restaurants' signature *gnocchi della nonna* (super soft gnocchi in an herbaceous tomato sauce), and a hearty *panino* of garlicky pork sausage and roasted peppers, served with a side of rosemary potatoes. Have a glass of wine and enjoy the warmest of welcomes.

Diavola

Pizza

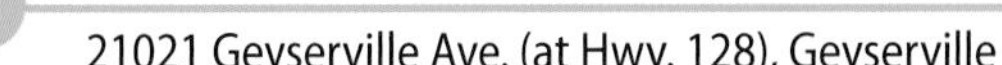

A1

21021 Geyserville Ave. (at Hwy. 128), Geyserville

Phone: 707-814-0111 Lunch & dinner daily
Web: www.diavolapizzeria.com
Prices: $$

Folks far and wide know to come to Geyserville for Dino Bugica's artisan-cured meats and pizzas. Once a brothel, the room's original wood floors, tin ceilings, and exposed brick exude history. And as for its decidedly tamer wares, find artisan hams, with whole legs hanging up front, as well as fresh sauces, sausages, and imported cheese available to take home.

A rosy pizza oven from Italy is hard at work at the end of the lengthy marble bar, where thin-crust pizzas are one-size-fits-all and decked with toppings ranging from the simple Margherita to smoked pork belly, meatballs, pine nuts, and raisins. Salads may include pomegranate, persimmon and *ricotta salata*. Roasted bone marrow, or crispy beef tongue are at the ready if pizza isn't your thing.

Dry Creek Kitchen

Californian

D1

317 Healdsburg Ave. (bet. Matheson & Plaza Sts.), Healdsburg

Phone: 707-431-0330 Lunch Fri – Sun
Web: www.charliepalmer.com Dinner nightly
Prices: $$$

Housed in Hotel Healdsburg, just off of the town's central square, Dry Creek Kitchen is the very picture of elegance. Its dining room is bedecked with sweeping flower arrangements, arching pillars, towering windows, and linen-topped tables; while round, banquet-style tables are perfect for families and larger parties.

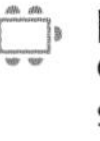

Tasty dishes like porcini *velouté* garnished with prosciutto chips and topped with cognac foam and a drizzle of scallion oil; or smoky-grilled lemon-marinated shrimp served on a salad of local greens tossed with brioche croutons and mandarin segments show off the kitchen's Californian aesthetic. Don't forget to gratify your sugar yen with a rich and dense Meyer lemon cheesecake finished with lemon curd and refreshing mint sorbet.

El Dorado Kitchen

Californian XX

D3

405 1st St. W. (at Spain St.), Sonoma

Phone: 707-996-3030 Lunch & dinner daily
Web: www.eldoradosonoma.com
Prices: $$

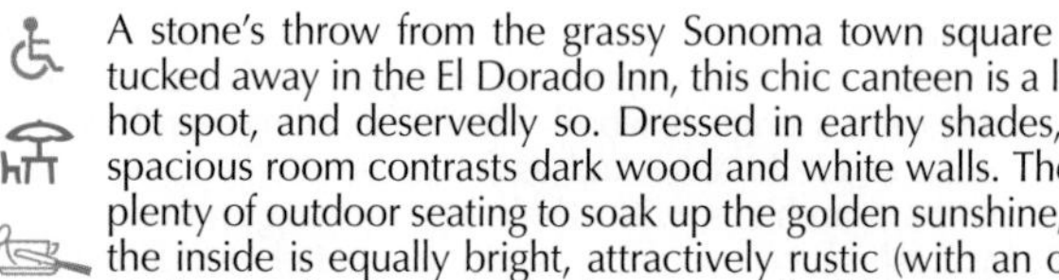

A stone's throw from the grassy Sonoma town square and tucked away in the El Dorado Inn, this chic canteen is a local hot spot, and deservedly so. Dressed in earthy shades, the spacious room contrasts dark wood and white walls. There's plenty of outdoor seating to soak up the golden sunshine, but the inside is equally bright, attractively rustic (with an open kitchen and salvaged wood communal table), and not the slightest bit cliché.

Utilizing the region's bounty, the kitchen turns out the likes of fried green tomatoes with pineapple salsa, or flaky Alaskan halibut with corn pudding, pea shoots, and shaved asparagus. The cheese plate sticks to West Coast producers, and desserts like warm rhubarb crisp make a strong case for seasonality.

El Rinconcito Yucateco

Mexican X

B2

3935 Sebastopol Rd. (bet. Campoy St. & Wright Rd.), Santa Rosa

Phone: 707-526-2720 Lunch & dinner daily
Web: N/A
Prices: ⊜

This small dining room specializes in dishes from the Yucatán region of Mexico. The spot may be fuss-free, causal, and basic, but the family who runs the place is super welcoming and convivial.

All meals start with homemade chips and spicy roasted chili salsa for dipping. *Auténtico* is to be found in the Yucatan specialty, *cochinita pibil panuchos*—black been purée sandwiched between two corn tortillas and topped with deliciously tender achiote-marinated roasted pork. Fresh tomato and pickled onions complete the flavorful creation. Fine fixings abound in the pineapple- and chili-marinated *al pastor panucho*; while the grilled chicken topped with cool, creamy avocado is simply *delicioso*! For those in a hurry, there is a weekend taco stand out front.

Farmhouse Inn & Restaurant ✿

Californian XXX

A2

7871 River Rd. (at Wohler Rd.), Forestville

Phone: 707-887-3300 Dinner Thu – Mon
Web: www.farmhouseinn.com
Prices: **$$$**

Farmhouse Inn & Restaurant

Miles away from anything other than vineyards and forest, this quaint two-story farmhouse restaurant lives amid eight small cottages. The dining room is painted yellow and olive, hung with intricate iron chandeliers, and decorated with a flowing mural border depicting country life. Casually dressed young couples and families relax and take in the ambience.

The menu of local and seasonal products changes frequently, yet the flavors in each dish always make sense without being overly complicated. Expect such first courses as house-made pillows of pasta holding enticingly salty Taleggio in an aromatic truffled beurre blanc with celery, green apple, and black truffle shavings. Next may come a simple but robust and beautifully roasted guinea hen with confit leg, squash bread pudding, and hearty beans; or slices of elk tenderloin fanned over squash spaetzle, set in an archipelago of pickled huckleberries, squash brunoise, and mâche. There's bound to be a rich Valhrona chocolate dessert for a sweet finish.

The aproned staff presents plates with synchronization, adding a traditional touch to the country feel. Intimate and comfortably warm, there is an aura of special occasion in the air.

French Garden

French XX

8050 Bodega Ave. (at Pleasant Hill Rd.), Sebastopol

Phone: 707-824-2030 Lunch & dinner Wed – Sun
Web: www.frenchgardenrestaurant.com
Prices: $$

At French Garden, the cuisine blows an air kiss to the classic Gallic bistro, but this actual garden is grounded in California. The Sebastopol favorite sources its leeks, cilantro, and piquillo peppers–to be sautéed with Manila clams for dinner–from its own bio-intensive farm. There you'll also find seasonal ingredients for such expertly adapted plates as traditional frisée salad, with bacon and a poached egg, and fluffy mushroom quiche.

As you would expect, French Garden boasts a pleasing terrace; on cooler nights, find a seat in the airy dining room or near the hearth in the lounge. Desserts are excellent here so don't miss out. With pistachio pastry crust, cranberry coulis, and toasted merinque, the lemon tart may be the most refined you've ever had.

Glen Ellen Inn

Californian XX

13670 Arnold Dr. (at Warm Springs Rd.), Glen Ellen

Phone: 707-996-6409 Lunch Thu – Tue
Web: www.glenelleninn.com Dinner nightly
Prices: $$

Charming and quaint, this restaurant serves well-prepared Californian fare from its home on the second level of the Glen Ellen Inn, lending the air of a favorite bed and breakfast. With carved wood chairs, glass-topped tables, and paper doilies, the setting is appropriately old-fashioned for a little *auberge*. On warm days, dine on a stone-tiled balcony overlooking the small garden. Servers are friendly and low-key at this homey spot.

Expect the likes of a velvety roasted parsnip and apple purée that is earthy, slightly sweet, and balanced by swirls of crème fraîche; or plump, steamed mussels plunged into a creamy, saffron-scented broth flavored with caramelized bits of pancetta and served with garlic crostini—perfect to sop up the broth.

Gohan

Japanese

1367 N. McDowell Blvd. (at Redwood Way), Petaluma

Phone: 707-789-9296 — Lunch Mon – Fri
Web: www.gohanrestaurant.com — Dinner nightly
Prices: $$

Sushi may be an unexpected choice of fuel while shopping at Pier 1 or Michael's, but Gohan is the pride and joy of its strip mall surrounds at Petaluma's Redwood Gateway Shopping Center. With crisp linen-topped tables, high ceilings, and an LCD fire in the high-tech hearth, this is an undeniably cool spot for lunch.

Serving classics like ribeye teriyaki and fresh hamachi sashimi, Gohan's menu has something for everyone. Fans of creative maki, though, have truly come to the right place. For a view of the chef in action, slip up to the sushi counter and watch as your fish is neatly sliced and expertly displayed. Don't miss the Cisco roll, stuffed with shrimp, avocado, and green bean tempura topped with crab salad and spicy orange *tobiko*.

Hana

Japanese

101 Golf Course Dr. (at Roberts Lake Rd.), Rohnert Park

Phone: 707-586-0270 — Lunch Mon – Sat
Web: www.hanajapanese.com — Dinner nightly
Prices: $$

For the full experience, park it at the sushi bar where the obliging chefs can steer you through the best offerings of the day. Rohnert Park denizens are wising up to this little gem of a spot, tucked in a hotel plaza next to the 101, and run by affable owner, Chef Ken Tominaga, who sees to his guests' every satisfaction.

Traditional, fresh sushi and Japanese small plates are the secret to Hana's success, though simply exquisite items like pan-seared pork loin with a ginger-soy jus, and pots of steaming udon also hit the spot. Chef's omakase is a fine way to go—six pieces of nigiri which could include toro, hamachi belly, kampachi, tai snapper, halibut with ponzu sauce, or sardine tangy from lemon juice and sprinkled with Hawaiian lava salt.

Harvest Moon Cafe

D3 — Californian X

487 1st St. W. (bet. Napa & Spain Sts.), Sonoma

Phone: 707-933-8160 — Lunch Sun
Web: www.harvestmooncafesonoma.com — Dinner Wed – Mon
Prices: $$

Harvest Moon Café is located on the main town square in Sonoma. Without an obvious façade, this place has become popular by word of mouth. They are known for their great weekend brunch where locals sip an oversized cappuccino and perhaps indulge in a savory dish of tender *gigante* beans served with chewy pieces of pancetta, sautéed garlicky Swiss chard and kale, and heartily topped off with two fried eggs.

Tourists join the mix at dinner. The café serves Californian fare made from local, seasonal ingredients, such as a crisp chicory salad tossed in tangy blue cheese dressing with caramelized grilled onions and smoky-salty bacon.

The charming café is adorned with wildflowers, an open kitchen and bar, as well as an outdoor patio for warm days.

Hot Box Grill

C3 — American XX

18350 Sonoma Hwy. (bet. Calle Del Monte & Hawthorne Ave.), Sonoma

Phone: 707-939-8383 — Lunch Thu – Sun
Web: www.hotboxgrill.com — Dinner Tue – Sun
Prices: $$

Hot Box Grill is Sonoma's definition of down-home family dining. Chef/owner Norm Owens can be spotted daily in the kitchen working side-by-side with his sous chef brother. Keeping it all in the family, Owens' wife, meanwhile, creates fantastic pastries and his sister-in-law is credited with creating the linoleum prints around the room.

Flower boxes line the front windows with views to the open kitchen, and the back wall doubles as a blackboard boasting the day's dressed-up comfort food specials. Each dish makes the most of local ingredients—think plump duck confit ravioli in spiced broth, or succulent fried Cornish game hen with shells and cheese. With sweet bites like the deliciously campy Valhrona S'mores tart, dessert should be mandatory.

Jackson's

Pizza

B2

135 4th St. (at Davis St.), Santa Rosa

Phone: 707-545-6900 — Lunch & dinner daily
Web: www.jacksonsbarandoven.com
Prices: $$

Chef/owner Josh Silver's Jackson's menu is created with families in mind. Still, the room is mighty sleek and curvy, dressed-up with high ceilings; while an espresso brown and deep crimson shade the walls. Contemporary wood tables and chairs look upon bright paintings, many of which were actually done by one of the chefs.

The open kitchen with its shiny fire engine red, wood-burning oven is for more than just pizza. An oven-roasted Cornish game hen shares the menu with a daily changing hot dog, and sandwiches too. Lamb meatballs, mac and cheese, oysters, and mussels all get the roaring fire treatment.

While the kids enjoy a giant carrot cake cupcake for dessert, moms and dads can choose from their list of Scotch, Ports, and stickies.

John Ash & Co.

Californian

B2

4330 Barnes Rd. (off River Rd.), Santa Rosa

Phone: 707-527-7687 — Lunch Wed – Fri
Web: www.vintnersinn.com — Dinner nightly
Prices: $$$

A trip to John Ash & Co. is the culinary equivalent of getting a massage. Set at the Vintner's Inn in Santa Rosa, the restaurant is surrounded by more than 90 acres of soothing vineyards and gardens and, miraculously, plentiful parking. A sun-soaked patio overlooks the terrain, but the romantic interior is equally plush with a toasty fireplace and terra-cotta hues.

White linens set the stage for organic Californian meals with a slight German inflection. Accompaniments of sauerkraut, cabbage, and spätzle hint at the chef's heritage, but the cuisine is generally worldly. A tasting menu might include salmon and cream cheese canapés with dill and briny capers; Canadian lobster tail with celery root purée; and a moist, herbaceous rack of lamb.

Khoom Lanna

B2 Thai

107 4th St. (bet. Davis & Wilson Sts.), Santa Rosa

Phone: 707-545-8424 Lunch & dinner daily
Web: www.khoomlannathai.com
Prices: $$

Although this Thai jewel might seem pricey to some, Khoom Lanna's generous use of fresh vegetables and unique ingredients in each of its dishes merits the expense. A brick façade (flanked by a wood awning adorned with windows and greenery) marks the entry into this charmign yet rustic Asian burrow.

Countering its vibe (mauve walls, linen-lined tables, lush flower arrangements, and Thai artifacts), servers are candid and casual. If *pad si ew* (noodles stir-fried with vegetables, tofu, eggs, and splashed with dark soy) or *plah gung* (succulent, smoky prawns tossed in tangy lime juice and dusted with toasted rice powder), aren't as fiery as you'd hoped, up the spice ante in a hearty dish of basil lamb glazed with garlic and red chilies.

K & L Bistro

B2 Californian

119 S. Main St. (bet. Burnett St. and Hwy. 12), Sebastopol

Phone: 707-823-6614 Lunch Mon – Sat
Web: www.klbistro.com Dinner nightly
Prices: $$

Husband-wife duo Karen and Lucas Martin steer the stoves at K & L, a quintessential bistro that takes great pride in its craft. The intimate neighborhood gem typically bursts with Sebastopol locals rubbing elbows at close-knit tables topped with butcher paper. Exposed brick walls and dark wood accents lend a homey polish, while the granite bar is a terrific spot to sit and swirl.

Rusticity reigns in the semi-open kitchen where a crackling mesquite grill turns out French bistro classics and Californian fare. Traditionalists might begin with warm duck confit, while others may prefer grilled Monterey Bay sardines or crispy pork belly with watermelon. A thick-cut pork Porterhouse, simply seasoned with salt and pepper, is a juicy cap to a chilly night.

LaSalette

D3

452-H 1st St. E. (bet. Napa & Spain Sts.), Sonoma

Phone: 707-938-1927 — Lunch & dinner daily
Web: www.lasalette-restaurant.com
Prices: $$

LaSalette is a passage to Portugal just off Sonoma's town square. While wooden Port wine crates and pumpkin-hued walls may aim to transport, you'll feel right at home thanks to Chef/owner Manuel Azevedo and his wife, Kimberly, who bring the flavors of his native Azores Islands to wine country. Peek into the open kitchen where a wood-burning oven roasts a variety of small plates for sharing. Try the linguiça with *queijo fresco*—a piece of pork-and-garlic sausage crowned with farmer's cheese and a Portuguese olive. A lunch special of *caldeirada* (fisherman's stew) unveils a fragrant lobster-saffron broth teeming with fresh seafood and fingerling potatoes; while *piri piri* fries are dusted with chile powder and served with a creamy garlic-herb aïoli.

Luma

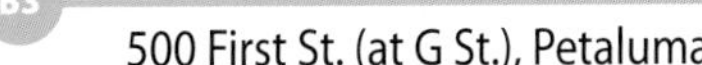

B3

500 First St. (at G St.), Petaluma

Phone: 707-658-1940 — Lunch Sun
Web: www.lumapetaluma.com — Dinner Tue – Sun
Prices: $$

The milk chocolate and caramel color palette isn't the only thing sweet about Luma, a Californian eatery that offers after-school specials and crayons for the kiddos on the industrial side of Petaluma. But Luma is also parent-approved with a small wine counter, sunny plant-lined patio, and plenty of savory fare to snack on before the key lime pie arrives.

Pizzas and pears hold court on a menu featuring the Pear & Blue, a thin-crust pie topped with the obvious. Other delights include wood oven-baked pears stuffed with blue cheese, walnuts, and cherries; and a Brie and blue *fonduta* with honey-pear syrup. Dinner may bring ancho-seared skirt steak over cannellini beans and *chimichurri*, or a roasted half-chicken served with mushroom bread pudding.

Madrona Manor 

Contemporary XXX

A1

1001 Westside Rd. (at West Dry Creek Rd.), Healdsburg

Phone: 707-433-4231 Dinner Wed – Sun
Web: www.madronamanor.com
Prices: $$$

Madrona Manor

This huge Victorian manor brings a quintessentially English feel to Dry Creek Valley. The wraparound porch offers views of the romantic gardens and fountain. Inside, antiques, floral-motif sconces, and heavy drapes tie together the garden theme. Crystal chandeliers softly light this special occasion spot frequented by couples and hotel guests. Elegance is clearly the operative word. All needs are met by the smartly dressed servers who clearly take pride in creating a relaxed atmosphere with just a hint of formality.

While the cuisine highlights classic technique with local Californian ingredients, some molecular moves do sneak in, especially in the slightly more ambitious tasting menus. Starters may include a lovely combination of large, fresh gnocchi served with nuggets of succulent lobster and finished with a light citrus jus. Successes have revealed tender venison served with crunchy purple beets and a red wine jus, or roasted duck breast with yellow wax beans, sliced apple, and a touch of earthiness in the sautéed matsutake mushrooms.

Be sure to eat your meat so you can have some pudding: as in a classic peanut butter-chocolate parfait in a jar with cookies and ice cream.

Mai Vietnamese Cuisine

Vietnamese

B3

8492 Gravenstein Hwy. (bet. Cotati Ave. & Hwy. 101), Cotati

Phone: 707-665-9628 Lunch & dinner Tue – Sun
Web: www.maivietnamesecuisine.com
Prices: ⊜

The cheery yellow walls, the delightful servers, the abundance of hospitality—this lovely Cotati spot is practically a mood enhancer. Tucked into the corner of a small shopping plaza next to Highway 101, the place is packed with loyal regulars craving fresh, tasty Vietnamese classics.

Dishes like lemongrass chicken and scallop curry share the menu with vermicelli and rice plates, as well as a list of refreshing Vietnamese shakes, including mango and durian (if you dare). *Pho* lovers can choose from several types, like *pho tai* with thinly sliced steak, vermicelli noodles, white onions, scallions, and cilantro swimming in a ginger-clove broth. Or go with a hearty barbecue plate of prawns, smoky-glazed pork, and egg roll served over rice noodles.

Mateo's Cocina Latina

Mexican

D2

214 Healdsburg Ave. (bet. Matheson & Mill Sts.), Healdsburg

Phone: 707-433-1520 Healdsburg
Web: www.mateoscocinalatina.com
Prices: **$$**

Skip the Mexican street-style food prominent in the Bay Area and head to this slam-dunk of a spot, where organic ingredients get whipped-up into a stunning array of succulent goodness. Credit is due to Chef/owner Mateo Granados for his serious cooking chops, Yucatán heritage, and devotion to healthy eating. Stone floors, mosaic-tiled tabletops, rustic wood tables, marigold walls, and sky lights create a gorgeous atmosphere, so snag a seat and get feasting.

Here you'll find tamales and tortillas made with olive oil instead of lard, and several scorching-hot varieties of homemade sauce—made from habaneros picked off the family's tree. These are also a delicious complement to smoky lamb carne asada; tender suckling pig *tamal*; or olive oil-guacamole *tacone*.

Monti's Rotisserie

American

B2

714 Village Court (bet. Farmer's Ln. & Hardmand Dr.), Santa Rosa

Phone: 707-568-4404 Lunch & dinner daily
Web: www.starkrestaurants.com
Prices: $$

Wrought-iron accents, colorful antique doors, and a quirky collection of decorative roosters give Monti's Rotisserie an unusual Mediterranean-cum-Southwest vibe where spit-roasted meats are the common denominator. Since opening in 2004, Monti's long wooden bar has beckoned shoppers to Santa Rosa's Montgomery Village for snacks like house-made charcuterie, Tunisian Dungeness crab "briks," and to-die-for homemade fries.

Of course, it's the smoky meats turned over smoldering coals that give the place its name. On Wednesdays, belly up for a spit-roasted leg of lamb; and Fridays bring the roast rack of natural-fed veal. On sunny Saturdays, take your protein to the trellised patio and dive into a crispy duck special coupled with a sweet and sour duck jus.

Peter Lowell's

Italian

B2

7385 Healdsburg Ave. (at Florence Ave.), Sebastopol

Phone: 707-829-1077 Lunch & dinner daily
Web: www.peterlowells.com
Prices: $$

You may refer to this Sebastopol eatery as a "sleeper": once just a little known spot to lunch, Peter Lowell's is enjoying a renaissance thanks to their chef who is championing the local, sustainable ethos and taking it to new heights with seasonal Cal-Italian cuisine made from organic ingredients sourced in Sonoma County.

Dine inside or out and be patient with the service—remember, good things come to those who wait. Meals might bring a bowl of beans and greens tossed in olive oil, lemon juice, salt, and pepper; cracker-thin pizza topped with squash blossoms and Calabrian chilies; and veal with saffron risotto. End on a sweet note with a light, moist, and spongy olive oil cake layered with ripe strawberries and mascarpone cream.

Risibisi

B3

154 Petaluma Blvd. N. (bet. Washington St. & Western Ave.), Petaluma

Phone: 707-766-7600 Lunch & dinner daily
Web: www.risibisirestaurant.com
Prices: $$

Named for a favorite risotto in the Friuli-Venezia Giulia region, Petaluma's Risibisi offers a true taste of the Italian city of Trieste. Owner Marco Palmieri hails from the Adriatic seaport and mingles a Californian sensibility with the traditional cuisine of his youth. He's had a Midas touch with restaurants further exemplified in this Sonoma charmer, which also embraces whimsy by dint of heavy ropes and brightly hued chairs suspended from the ceiling and brick walls adorned with art works.

The kitchen makes magic of such memorable fare as beef carpaccio garnished with arugula, capers, and shaved Parmigiano Reggiano; fluffy gnocchi with a choice of four sauces; and veal *involtini* rolled with prosciutto, spinach, and mozzarella in a cabernet-sage sauce.

Rosso

Pizza

B2

53 Montgomery Dr. (at 3rd St.), Santa Rosa

Phone: 707-544-3221 Lunch & dinner daily
Web: www.rossopizzeria.com
Prices: $$

For those who think that vino and *futbol* (read: soccer) don't pair well together, think again. At Rosso, Italian wines live in utter harmony with the flat screen TV. And while the sports channel may feel appropriate to the Creekside Center strip mall locale, the crisp pizza *Napoletana* is a divine departure abroad.

Owner John Franchetti did time at St. Helena's Tra Vigne before opening this pizzeria. Here, amidst an urbane vibe, you'll find crisp salads with smoked chicken and walnuts and, the highlight, chewy 12-inch pies with fresh ingredients that pay homage to the Slow Food Movement. Take a walk on the wild side and order the "goomba" pizza topped with spaghetti, meatballs, and saffron tomato sauce; or stay closer to home with a white pizza *funghi*.

Rustic

300 Via Archimedes (off Independence Ln.), Geyserville

Phone: 707-857-1485 Lunch & dinner daily
Web: www.franciscoppolawinery.com
Prices: $$

With every turn up the vineyard-lined hill that leads to the Francis Ford Coppola Winery, visitors begin to breathe deeply and relax a little more. At its peak, discover a Mediterranean château that feels like a swanky getaway, with a cabana-lined pool designed for daytime respite and a restaurant, Rustic, that's as luxe as it is homey—if you are Coppola himself, you are in fact right at home.

Themed around "Francis' Favorites," Rustic is a hodgepodge of wine ephemera, movie memorabilia, and foods from the director's past. From the *parilla* (an Argentine grill), look for sweet-and-savory ribs inspired by a Polynesian restaurant from the filmmaker's college days; as well as Mrs. Scorsese's lemon chicken with organic herbs and chocolate mousse "al Francis."

Santé

Californian

100 Boyes Blvd. (at Hwy. 12), Sonoma

Phone: 707-939-2415 Dinner nightly
Web: www.fairmont.com/sonoma
Prices: $$$

Santé is located in the Fairmont Sonoma Mission Inn & Spa, which is tucked off of Highway 12. This charming dining room has warm gold walls, woven rattan chairs, and views of the pool area. While corporate hotel guests make up much of the clientele, the service is friendly and the ambience relaxed.

The interesting menu unfolds such delightful presentations as a starter of "grown-up" macaroni and cheese studded with generous portions of Maine lobster and black truffles in a creamy fontina sauce. A trio of roasted rabbit rack, bacon-wrapped loin, and tender leg confit coupled with morels, favas, potatoes, and natural jus is fulfillment personified; while a towering Meyer lemon soufflé quivers delightfully at the end, eliciting many satisfied smiles.

Sazón

Peruvian

B2

1129 Sebastopol Rd. (bet. McMinn & Burbank Aves.), Santa Rosa

Phone: 707-523-4346 — Lunch & dinner daily
Web: www.sazonsr.com
Prices: ⚭

Take a chance on Santa Rosa's divey-looking Sazón, and the only broken heart will be the Peruvian *anticucho de corazón*, or traditional skewered beef heart from the busy open kitchen. It may be a tiny spot in an awkward locale, but know that all this leaves little room for disappointment. Elbow up to the high granite counter or slip into a small corner table; an outdoor counter is open to those in need of fresh air.

On warm days, a cold Inca Cola will help keep things cool. Know that you may need it: spicy *rocoto* and jalapeño peppers enliven the *causas limena*—balls of mashed potato infused with *aji amarillo* and topped with Dungeness crab. Also try creamy prawn chowder (*chupe de camarones*) and *pollo a la brasa*, rotisserie chicken with hand-cut fries.

Scopa

Italian

D1

109A Plaza St. (bet. Center St. & Healdsburg Ave.), Healdsburg

Phone: 707-433-5282 — Dinner nightly
Web: www.scopahealdsburg.com
Prices: **$$**

Like the lively Italian card game that gives Scopa its name, this Healdsburg hottie is one big, boisterous family meal brought to the table by Chef Ari Rosen and his wife (and resident oenophile), Dawnelise. The space is pint-sized, but the vibe is bustling, especially on Winemaker Wednesdays, when local vintners work the room and pour their wares at the six-seat marble bar.

Framed Scopa cards set the scene for dinners designed to share. Fill up on antipasti like spicy meatballs and crispy, piping-hot *arancini*. Try splitting a crusty artisanal pizza topped with wafer-thin prosciutto or the seasonal ravioli, but *nonna's* tomato-braised chicken is a dish that heartier appetites keep to themselves.

Check out baby sis Campo Fina just a few steps away.

SEA Thai

Thai

B2

2323 Sonoma Ave. (at Farmer's Ln.), Santa Rosa

Phone: 707-528-8333 — Lunch & dinner daily
Web: www.seathaibistrosr.com
Prices: $$

Parked on a cozy corner in the bustling Montgomery Village outdoor mall, Tony Ounpamornchai's authentic, upscale Thai-fusion bistro is more than a strip mall stop. Here, crimson walls crawl along a narrow dining space, and upscale Thai gets a Westernized spin in dishes like shrimp bruschetta, made with four squares of fresh, delicious bread topped with avocado, shrimp, cilantro, and spicy homemade Asian pesto. The lunch menu has plenty of goodies to choose from, though curry dishes are only served at dinner. For a fabulous finale, try the banana fritters with coconut ice cream—that should hush the aficionados complaining that prices here are higher than divier joints.

Folks in Petaluma enjoy the older sibling restaurant, SEA Modern Thai Cuisine.

Spoonbar

Mediterranean

D2

219 Healdsburg Ave. (bet. Matheson & Mill Sts.), Healdsburg

Phone: 707-433-7222 — Lunch Sat – Sun
Web: www.spoonbar.com — Dinner nightly
Prices: $$

Located just off the "green" h2hotel lobby, you'll know to anticipate eco-chic concrete floors, wood tables, brightly cushioned chairs, and glass doors that open onto the sidewalk on warm, sun-soaked days. The restaurant is super casual and relaxed, as befitting a favorite lunch/resting spot for all the Lycra-clad weekend cyclists.

The relatively healthy menu is a selection of Mediterranean dishes prepared with local Californian produce. Expect the likes of heart-warming fried polenta with creamy romesco and Comte cheese; delicate and moist fluke decked with an aromatic roasted lemon oil and hearty dandelion greens; *spaghettini* twirled with *bottarga*; or a deliciously tender pork shank paired with salty Padron peppers and Savoy cabbage.

Stark's Steakhouse

Steakhouse XXX

B2

521 Adam St. (at 7th St.), Santa Rosa

Phone: 707-546-5100
Web: www.starkrestaurants.com
Prices: **$$$**

Lunch Mon – Fri
Dinner nightly

Although it's the youngest of four siblings and related to the Willi's concepts and Monti's Rotisserie, Stark's has finally grown up and is hitting its stride as the sophisticated brother. On Santa Rosa's historic Railroad Square, this fine-looking retreat draws suitors with a baby grand piano, fireplaces, and a snug lounge offering a vast range of Bourbon and Scotch to go with an all day menu.

Unexpected starters like potato skin fondue or steak tartare with smoked chili aïoli are full of pizzazz. Iceberg and Caesar salads are classically represented; while grass-fed and dry-aged beef appeases those with meat in mind. Flesh rules here, but it shares space with seafood *a la plancha* like Arctic char massaged with Indian spices and cucumber-dill "raita."

Sugo

B3

5 Petaluma Blvd. S. (at B St.), Petaluma

Phone: 707-782-9298
Web: www.sugopetaluma.com
Prices: **$$**

Lunch & dinner daily

Housed behind a well-worn brick façade in Petaluma's Theater District, Sugo Trattoria offers a comely take on dinner and a movie, where classic films silently unfold on a white wall above the open kitchen. If this bit of art house entertainment isn't enough to take your mind off Sugo's strip mall locale, perhaps ambient music and candlelight are enough to transport you at last.

As the name suggests, Sugo's tiered dining room waves its flag for Italy with a hefty selection of bruschetta, including one topped with prosciutto, fig, and Brie; a daily ravioli; and *secondi* starring Californian produce—think pistachio-crusted salmon or artichoke chicken *piccata*. A panzanella salad makes a nice light lunch when paired with five-dollar wines by the glass.

Terrapin Creek ✿

A3 — Californian XX

1580 Eastshore Rd. (off Hwy. 1), Bodega Bay

Phone: 707-875-2700 — Lunch & dinner Thu – Sun
Web: www.terrapincreekcafe.com
Prices: **$$**

Terrapin Creek

Located in the picturesque town of Bodega Bay, Terrapin Creek is situated at the end of a tidy little sky-blue shopping complex. The dining room is divided in half, with an exhibition kitchen at front and a vibrantly colored larger area in back, flooded with sunlight. Wood chairs, a central fireplace, and small, paper-topped tables make the space seem no-frills and very charming. Everything here feels warm and welcoming from start to finish.

While lunch may be a simpler affair, dinner is a knock-out offering of absolutely delicious, ingredient-driven cuisine. Expect each skillfully prepared dish to favor skill over innovation, as in a crunchy salad of shaved radishes, cilantro, avocado, and cabbage in curry-lime vinaigrette, topped with three perfectly plump and freshly roasted sardines. The pan-roasted lingcod is golden brown and elegantly served with a tower of roasted sunchokes, baby bok choy, meaty mushrooms, a swirl of soy-enhanced dashi, and garnishes of finely sliced scallions and raw ginger.

At dessert, you just might find the silkiest and airiest cheesecake you've ever had, made here with lightly sweetened crème fraîche, a buttery graham cracker crust, and raspberry sauce.

Thai Orchid

Thai

1005 Vine St. (at Mill St.), Healdsburg

Phone: 707-433-0515
Web: N/A
Prices: ⊛

Lunch Mon – Sat
Dinner nightly

Rocking a no-frills vibe and nestled inside a bustling shopping center, this under-the-radar gem does Thai food right. Bold, delicious flavors may as well be the motto here at Thai Orchid, where local families can be found chowing on select favorites like spicy basil duck, pumpkin red curry, and *pad see ew.*

The simply appointed space shows off photos of the Thai royal family, artsy carved screens, and bamboo plants. Amid such ease, start on complex items like tangy *tom kha kai,* spicy coconut and lemongrass broth brimming with chicken, cilantro, and green chilies. The pork *pad ka prow*–a sumptuous platter of spicy garlic-basil pork with onions and red peppers–is a fine choice, as is the *kai-yang,* grilled smoky-sweet chicken with jasmine rice.

the fig café

Californian

13690 Arnold Dr. (at O Donnell Ln.), Glen Ellen

Phone: 707-938-2130
Web: www.thefigcafe.com
Prices: $$

Lunch Sat – Sun
Dinner nightly

The fig café is so much a fixture in Glen Ellen that she is practically a landmark. And with a deluge of natural light to illuminate vaulted ceilings and a friendly crowd, it's simple to see why the fig is a favorite among locals. The interior is casual and comfy and the Californian cuisine is consistent, approachable, and beautifully prepared.

Dinners frequently feature local ingredients and might include, you guessed it, a fig and chèvre salad with caramelized pancetta, pecans, and spicy arugula; crispy duck confit with glazed turnips over earthy French green lentils; butcher's steak with blue cheese butter; and fluffy lemon bread pudding with macerated berries and a bit of crème fraîche. In the mood for brunch? See you at the fig on weekends!

the girl & the fig

D3 — Californian XX

110 W. Spain St. (at 1st St.), Sonoma

Phone: 707-938-3634 — Lunch & dinner daily
Web: www.thegirlandthefig.com
Prices: $$

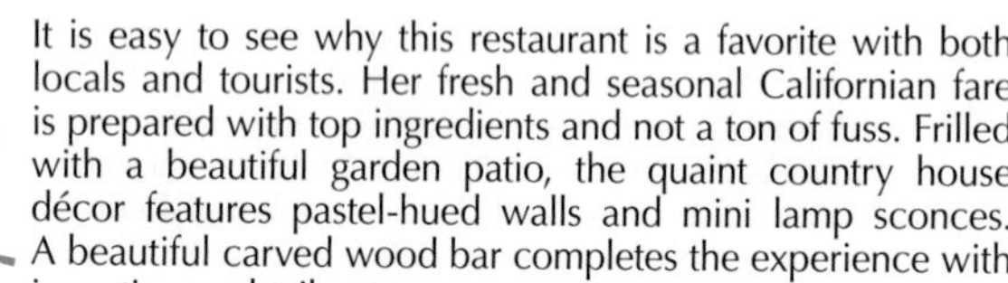

It is easy to see why this restaurant is a favorite with both locals and tourists. Her fresh and seasonal Californian fare is prepared with top ingredients and not a ton of fuss. Frilled with a beautiful garden patio, the quaint country house décor features pastel-hued walls and mini lamp sconces. A beautiful carved wood bar completes the experience with inventive cocktails.

A California-and-French influenced menu may divulge a delicate smoked trout salad—moist, flaky, and mingled with pea tendrils and baby red and golden beets; or pastis-scented steamed mussels with crispy frites. If you're looking for the fluffiest quiche Lorraine ever (studded with bacon and Gruyère and served with ultra-thin herbed matchstick fries), you've come to the right spot.

Underwood

A2 — International XX

9113 Graton Rd. (at Edison St.), Graton

Phone: 707-823-7023 — Lunch Tue – Sat
Web: www.underwoodgraton.com — Dinner Tue – Sun
Prices: $$

Graton may be little more than a cluster of restaurants and shops, but Underwood is where local winemakers gather to celebrate the harvest or make deals over good food and wine. The nickel bar has a saloon feel, especially when laden with classic cocktails and oysters. The red, riveted banquettes and heavy zinc-topped tables in the dining room conjure a French bistro, yet the cuisine is decidedly international.

The menu ranges from cheeses and salads to an eclectic selection of globetrotting small plates like hoisin-glazed baby back ribs, or Thai lettuce cups filled with pork seasoned with lemongrass and mint, alongside cucumbers, roasted peanuts, and rice noodles.

The Willow Wood Market Café across the street has the same owner and is a bit more rustic.

Willi's Seafood & Raw Bar

Seafood

D1

403 Healdsburg Ave. (at North St.), Healdsburg

Phone: 707-433-9191 — Lunch & dinner daily
Web: www.starkrestaurants.com
Prices: $$

Healdsburg locals have all new reason to clink glasses of Sonoma County wines: their beloved haunt, Willi's Seafood & Raw Bar, now has room enough for everyone. A couple of years since their expansion, Willi's rustic-chic interior continues to burst at the seams with regulars and tourists who come for seafood-focused small plates. Not to worry, the fab alfresco dining patio is still perfectly intact.

Ideal for sharing with a jovial bunch of friends, Willi's savory nibbles include fresh hamachi ceviche tossed with *pepitas* and *rocoto* chilies in zesty lime juice; salty, deep-fried Ipswich clams with shisito peppers and citrus aïoli; uni "Mac & cheese" with Sweet Bay scallops; and clam, mussel, or oyster "steamers" with green garlic butter and PBR.

Willi's Wine Bar

International

B2

4404 Old Redwood Hwy. (at Ursuline Rd.), Santa Rosa

Phone: 707-526-3096 — Lunch Tue – Sat, Dinner nightly
Web: www.starkrestaurants.com
Prices: $$

This roadhouse is easily missed when racing down the old tree-lined highway, if not for the packed parking lot. The name comes from a spot in Paris that pioneered serving American wines to the French 30 years ago. Nowadays, they serve over 40 wines by the glass and an eclectic menu of smaller plates. Inside, find a series of small, wood-accented rooms with a romantic and a ruby-red glow.

The multi-cultural menu is divided into Surf, Earth, and Turf—and if the Iberico pork loin is on offer, get it. In addition, try the skewed brick chicken with harissa, *tzatziki* sauce, and fried onion salad; Moroccan lamb chops; or goat-cheese fritters with smoked paprika and lavender honey.

Aspiring oenophiles should belly up to the bar for a real wine education.

Willow Wood Market Cafe

Californian

9020 Graton Rd. (at Edison St.), Graton

Phone: 707-823-0233 Lunch daily
Web: www.willowwoodgraton.com Dinner Mon – Sat
Prices: **$$**

Hospitality always pairs well with food—especially in California where that casual and cozy comfort is a distinct local pleasure. And stepping into the Willow Wood Market Cafe feels like returning to a welcoming home, or maybe a quirky sundries store stocked with good wine. Obscure specialty items for foodie friends and revolving local artworks hanging on the buttery yellow walls all combine to enhance this quaint eatery's charms.

Salads and sandwiches are tasty, but the menu revolves around many different homey renditions of piping hot polenta. The creamy cornmeal goodness has many guises, like garlicky rock shrimp with roasted peppers, or simply with goat cheese, sweet-roasted red onions, and pesto. Just about everything comes with garlic bread.

Yeti

Nepali

C3
14301 Arnold Dr., Ste. 19 (in Jack London Village), Glen Ellen

Phone: 707-996-9930 Lunch & dinner daily
Web: www.yetirestaurant.com
Prices: **$$**

Historic Jack London Village, with its gristmill from the mid-1800s, may seem like an unlikely spot for a Nepali restaurant. But, somehow the odd combination works. Pass a 25-foot water wheel to find the quaint Yeti. Large barn-windows open for fresh air and garden-views, while Himalayan and Indian influences are patent in the décor (artifacts and fabrics) as well as the cooking.

This is a peaceful spot to enjoy superlative Nepali dishes like momo, heart-warming Himalayan-style dumplings filled with ground meat and spices; perhaps followed by Himalayan pepper pot soup. Their version of chicken *tikka masala* (yogurt- and *garam masala*-marinated chicken in a creamy tomato sauce) is above par, especially when paired with a piping-hot garlic *naan*.

zazu

Californian

B2

3535 Guerneville Rd. (at Willowside Rd.), Santa Rosa

Phone: 707-523-4814 — Lunch Sun
Web: www.zazurestaurant.com — Dinner Wed – Mon
Prices: $$

You can't miss this red roadhouse on the fringes of Santa Rosa–and neither do the crowds–so expect it to be packed to the brim with boisterous groups on any given evening. The vibe is relaxed with mauve banquettes, shabby-chic décor, copper-topped tables, and friendly servers.

Embodying a sustainable and farm-to-table philosophy, the husband-wife team raises their own poultry and pigs; tend the restaurant's garden; and make their own wine. The menu features house-cured pork products such as plump and sticky-sweet dates wrapped in thick slices of artisanal bacon and grilled until crispy; and al dente pappardelle ribbons twirled with a robust Bolognese of crumbled pork sausage, wilted arugula, shaved Parmesan, crushed tomatoes, and fresh herbs.

Zin

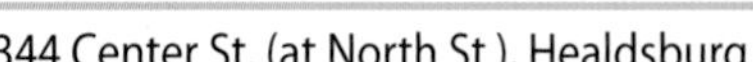

American

D1

344 Center St. (at North St.), Healdsburg

Phone: 707-473-0946 — Lunch Mon – Fri
Web: www.zinrestaurant.com — Dinner nightly
Prices: $$

A narrow window at the door lined with jars packed with preserved goodies is a portent to the homemade goodness inside. Casual, with polished concrete floors, high ceilings and walls hung with bright agrarian scenes overlook cork-lined tables below. The co-owners are sons of farmers, and that upbringing has not been forgotten in the cuisine.

The seasonal menu is laced with fresh spins on American classics, and their tempura-fried green beans with mango salsa are legendary in these parts. Southwestern zeal is evident in the crispy duck leg with pepper jelly or shrimp and grits with andouille sausage. Different blue-plate specials every night celebrate Americana.

There are always zinfandel tasting flights, with a half-dozen available by the glass.

Where to Stay

Stanyan Park

750 Stanyan St. (at Waller St.)

Phone: 415-751-1000
Web: www.stanyanpark.com
Prices: $$

30 Rooms

6 Suites

Stanyan Park

Stop and smell the proverbial roses at the Stanyan Park hotel. This delightfully chic turn-of-the century little hotel exudes the simple charms and quiet grace of a bygone era. Stanyan Park's roots are showing, and they're very proud of it (it's listed on the National Register of Historic Places).

Just across from Golden Gate Park and a mere stone's throw from the Natural History Museum, Hall of Flowers, and famed Japanese Tea Garden, its classic Victorian exterior has a doll house-like appeal. It may date back to the early 1900s, but the hotel's elegant and sensitive restoration ensures all modern comforts and conveniences. With just 36 rooms and suites, Stanyan Park feels a bit like a country inn or bed and breakfast (and, indeed, there is a complimentary continental breakfast). The accommodations are gracefully appointed with mahogany period furnishings and floral-patterned wallpaper; while the two-bedroom suites exceed expectations with complete kitchens, full baths, and dining rooms.

Rooms looking out over the park provide a tranquil setting, but all accommodations are blissfully quiet and intimate retreats perfect for turning off the outside world—if only for just a day or two.

Inn at the Opera

333 Fulton St. (at Franklin St.)

Phone: 415-863-8400 or 800-325-2708
Web: www.shellhospitality.com
Prices: $$

30 Rooms

18 Suites

Inn at the Opera

It has been performing nightly for more than half a century, but The Inn at the Opera continues to deliver a virtuoso performance. This European-style hotel was built to house visiting opera stars, but those who can't carry a tune will still feel right at home amidst the artists and art-loving patrons.

It enjoys a prime location just a few steps away from the Civic Center, War Memorial Opera House, and Davies Symphony Hall, making this a natural choice for visiting culture buffs. The rooms and suites are divided into whimsical categories ranging from Ballet and Concerto to Symphony and Opera. Even the smallest rooms feature kitchenettes, while the largest (none other than the Opera, of course!) sleeps four with two comfortable sitting rooms and two bathrooms. Antique-style furnishings set a traditional tone, while amenities, like iPod docking stations, are plentiful and certainly keep music junkies happy. The complimentary breakfast buffet is an added treat.

Business travelers and globe-trotters alike will appreciate such convenient features as fax, copy, and print services. Finally, an internet kiosk is also available for those techn junkies who just can't bear to stay "offline."

Phoenix

D1

601 Eddy St. (at Larkin St.)

Phone: 415-776-1380 or 800-248-9466
Web: www.thephoenixhotel.com
Prices: $$

41 Rooms

3 Suites

Joie de Vivre Hotels

Crash, but don't burn, at the super-hot Phoenix Hotel. This motor lodge with the mostest rests right on the edge of the trendy, and still seriously gritty, Tenderloin district.

Preppies need not apply at The Phoenix, which proudly flies its funk flag. Step right up to the front desk where a tattooed and multiply pierced artist, er, front desk attendant hands over the keys. Why bother with kitschy rock n' roll memorabilia when you've got the real thing—and it's jamming by the pool? From the Red Hot Chili Peppers and Pearl Jam to The Killers and The Shins, The Phoenix hosts, and even helps launch, the hottest bands. The lush courtyard is a hotbed of creativity that doubles as a stage for up-and-comers and superstars alike. Join the party, or just open the window to listen to the jam sessions that bring a whole new level to the phrase "in-room entertainment."

Expecting a moody, melancholic décor? Come on, where's that open mind? This young-at-*art* hotel turns that frown upside down with its upbeat 50s and vintage tropical flavor; the rooms are *Hawaii Five-ooh*.

Chill poolside or lounge in the swank bars of Chambers Eat + Drink, which hits all the right notes with its irreverent gourmet menu.

Bijou

111 Mason St. (at Eddy St.)

Phone: 415-771-1200 or 800-771-1022
Web: www.hotelbijou.com
Prices: $

65 Rooms

Bijou

It might be all about the green in the Financial District, but at Hotel Bijou, it's all about the silver. The silver screen, that is. This gem of a place, just four blocks from Union Square, is a true one-of-a-kind destination in downtown San Francisco.

Make your next Bay Area trip a visit of cinematic proportions at this stellar respite, where drama queens aren't just welcomed, they're celebrated. From its traditional movie house details to its classic Hollywood portraits, the hotel is a tribute to the film industry. Self-centered maybe, but what good star isn't? In this case, the star is San Francisco itself, which has romanced moviegoers in a number of films. Don't worry if you can't remember which ones, since the rooms are all named for a different one. Individually designed, the rooms display original movie stills and accents that play up to the namesake films.

Hotel Bijou has the standard offerings expected of a small hotel, but it's the mini theater that is the clear winner. Catch the free nightly double features here, where red velvet curtains and wooden chairs covered with plush purple seats and bronze art deco details capture the sophistication of old-school movie-going.

Clift

A2

495 Geary St. (at Taylor St.)

Phone: 415-775-4700 or 800-697-1791
Web: www.clifthotel.com
Prices: **$$$**

265 Rooms

107 Suites

Morgans Hotel Group

Don't take this hotel's location too literally—it might be steps from Union Square, but there's nothing *square* about the Clift. A purple walkway leads visitors into this fabulously fantastic world curated by Philippe Starck. Irreverent, unexpected, and surreal, its mind-bending and modern design is a little bit Alice in Wonderland and a whole lot of cool.

From a wildly out-of-proportion chair fit for a giant and a coffee table by Salvador Dali to Eames chairs, the haute hodgepodge weaves together an eclectic array of furnishings that pull double shifts as artwork. Lounge in the Living Room, sip and sup at the Velvet Room, but don't miss the Redwood Room. This city landmark, famed for its bar crafted from a single redwood tree, is soaked with a heart-stopping, handsome spirit.

The rich jewel tones and fiery red accent lighting lend a moody seduction to the lobby and public spaces, but the rooms and suites pull an about face with their fresh-as-a-spring-morning ambience. The look (crisp white linens and Starck's custom-designed blonde English sycamore furnishings) is light and airy, but a fanciful touch is ever-present (his wheelbarrow-style chair is a shout-out to Man Ray).

Diva

440 Geary St. (bet. Mason & Taylor Sts.)

Phone: 415-885-0200 or 800-553-1900
Web: www.hoteldiva.com
Prices: **$$**

116 Rooms

2 Suites

Rien van Rijthoven

This one's definitely not a wallflower and it's ahem, fitting, that the Diva is just two blocks from Neiman Marcus and Saks. This stylish boutique brims with personality and just a bit of wit. Take the façade: it may seem like a simple white brick exterior, but look again...it's all dolled up. The windows make peeping Toms out of passersby with cut-out shades of lace-corseted figures and sexy stockinged legs.

Speaking of legs, stroll those gorgeous gams across the hotel's sidewalk of fame, which showcases signatures of famous former guests. Even a demanding diva won't find fault (or call the fashion police) with this hotel's rooms and suites. It is pure 1940s old Hollywood glamour. Steel accents, lacquered furnishings, and a muted black, white, and gray palette create a Bogey-meets-Bacall setting. If your idea of a dapper Don is a teacup Pomeranian, don't frown (you'll get wrinkles) as the hotel is dog friendly.

Slip into something fabulous and slink downstairs for the evening sake hour. Because even divas need to make money, the hotel features a full-service business center where you can work in peace, while a just-off-the-lobby Starbucks proves this joint knows its crowd.

Galleria Park

191 Sutter St. (at Kearny St.)

Phone: 415-781-3060 or 800-792-9639
Web: www.jdvhotels.com
Prices: $$

169 Rooms

8 Suites

Cesar Rubio

Go ahead and answer. That's comfort calling, and it's waiting for you at the Galleria Park. Located in the heart of bustling downtown San Francisco, this adored hotel puts visitors in the center of it all. It is just a few blocks from Union Square's shopping and dining as well as the unique flavor of Chinatown, while the city's museums and cultural centers are all within easy reach.

Warm and hospitable service is a hallmark of this Financial District darling. From complimentary breakfast to evening wine hours, the hotel treats guests to a whole host of thoughtful extras. Eight floors are home to plush rooms and suites. Rich chocolate brown leather platform beds are set against mint-colored walls creating a casual elegance. The rooms have inspiring city or soothing courtyard views.

Work gatherings and other events are a cinch in the well-equipped function rooms, and a business center is on hand for 24-hour assistance. There's a gym of course, but for a little fresh air, lace up those sneakers and head outdoors to the park terrace. This lovely spot feels like a well-treasured secret, and with walking trails and park benches, it's a perfect way to fit in a little alfresco downtime.

The Inn at Union Square

440 Post St. (bet. Mason & Powell Sts.)

Phone: 415-397-3510 or 800-288-4346
Web: www.unionsquare.com
Prices: $$

29 Rooms

1 Suite

Greystone Hotels

Seeking that bed and breakfast charm without the commute to the country? The Inn at Union Square is the answer. This distinctive hotel offers the best of both worlds. It is just a hop, skip, and a jump away from Union Square, scenic Fisherman's Wharf, the cable cars of Powell Street, and several theaters, but the Inn's delightful atmosphere feels worlds away from the big city.

The Inn at Union Square radiates with a gentle pace and warm spirit that is just perfect for vacationers or city residents looking for an in-town getaway. However, it is also a natural choice for those in town to do business. Corporate travelers appreciate the business center, intimate meeting rooms, and walking distance to the city's Financial District.

The accommodations are done up with classic style boasting elegant mahogany period furnishings set against golden yellow walls and rich red fabrics. The Inn at Union Square is definitely a chocolate-on-your pillow kind of place, so expect plenty of smile-inducing touches throughout your visit. Complimentary breakfast and afternoon cocktails are included in the room rate. There is no in-house restaurant, but room service is available from nearby Morton's.

King George

A2

334 Mason St. (bet. Geary & O'Farrell Sts.)

Phone: 415-781-5050 or 800-288-6005
Web: www.kinggeorge.com
Prices: $

151 Rooms

2 Suites

Grevstone Hotels

Set just one block from the Geary and Curran Theaters in the heart of Union Square, the King George offers superior access to the city's world-class culture and entertainment. The professional and knowledgeable concierge handles everything from theater tickets and dinner reservations to tour arrangements in a snap. So what's the catch? Take it at face value; the King George is a royal flush. There is no need to pawn the crown jewels in order to live like a king at this spot.

The hotel's rooms have a wonderfully inviting ambience and are as comfortable as they are attractive. Classic, yet casual, the accommodations have European flair (tartan throws, floral patterns). Get caught with your hand in the candy jar—just one of the soft touches that make this hotel stand apart from the crowd. Dial in for room service and watch a movie on the flat-screen or take the elevator down to Winston's Lounge & Bar for a cocktail and some conversation.

The King George understands that no king or queen wants to be overthrown, so it makes minding the castle (or the office) a breeze with such features as lobby-located computer work stations and easy access to neighboring Bay Area corporations.

Monaco

A2

501 Geary St. (at Taylor St.)

Phone: 415-292-0100 or 866-622-5284
Web: www.monaco-sf.com
Prices: $$$

169 Rooms

32 Suites

Fred Licht/Kimpton Hotels

Boo hoo. The passport is expired and the private jet is grounded (or non-existent), but the glamour of the French Riviera and its principality of posh, Monaco, is calling. Don't leave the country, head downtown to Union Square and its glittering Hotel Monaco.

This hotel packs a serious punch when it comes to panache. The lobby is a glorious affair with soaring ceilings, sky-high floral displays, and a marble staircase that begs for a knockout to make a grand entrance. It's the stuff of legend, except that it's not. It's the Riviera redux, so fussy French it's not. Instead, this snazzy spot is fresh, flirty, and fantastic. The rooms and suites are at once playful and polished. Bold stripes in wild hues are eye-catching, while the furnishings keep it all grounded. Classic French details, like the fleur-de-lis and harlequin-style ticking, are reinterpreted with a modern spin. Surprises are abundant: spot that leopard-print bathrobe hanging next to the commode?

Bring a pet or borrow a fish for a little guppy love, bliss out at the luxurious spa, or dine in first-class style at Grand Café Brasserie & Bar. A turn-of-the-century ballroom, this stunning restaurant pours on the glitz.

Mystic

417 Stockton St. (bet. Bush & Sutter Sts.)

Phone: 415-400-0500 or 888-817-9050
Web: www.mystichotel.com
Prices: $$

72 Rooms

7 Suites

Charlie Palmer Group

Formerly the Crescent, the Mystic is benefitting from a makeover. Everything looks stylish as modern minimalism meets traditional. The lobby is bright and simply accoutred with white panel flooring, a small front desk area, and dark blue contemporary sofas attractively accented by bright red cushions. The hallways feature wood flooring laid with red carpeting—from there, a single small elevator transports guests to one of the 8 floors.

Rooms are fresh looking with updated amenities. The white-on-white palette is welcoming and a restful ambience can be found in beds laid with crisp white linens, a white lacquer headboard, and soothing pale grey carpet. Slender, polished cabinetry and a small desk in the window nook complete the furnishings. Vintage-looking mirror tiles, a clear acrylic desk chair, and a pop of color provided by a red glass ceiling pendant get an A for accents. Some rooms even have exposed brick walls, and bathrooms are fresh, too, featuring faux marble tiles.

The downtown location near Chinatown is central, and for those who aren't looking for frills, the hotel represents a good value. The hotel's restaurant and bar seem to be destinations in their own right.

Nikko

222 Mason St. (bet. Ellis & O'Farrell Sts.)

Phone: 415-394-1111 or 800-248-3308
Web: www.hotelnikkosf.com
Prices: $$

510 Rooms

22 Suites

Matthew Millman/Hotel Nikko

Travelers seeking a Far East flavor need not travel far or wide. It's right here in the middle of the city at the Nikko. Cultures collide with chic results at this East-meets-West Coast hotel.

With stories of shimmering glass that catch the sunlight, the amply sized Nikko cuts an impressive figure on the city skyline (not to mention its amazing views). Inside, it's clean and contemporary. The rooms and suites are a study in Zen and the art of Asian-style simplicity. Warm, polished woods and soothing colors lend a European grace to the accommodations, but the super-comfortable Subarashee Yume pillow-top mattresses, lavish Subarashee Ame showers, and slick in-mirror televisions are straight out of Japan. This Financial District gem doesn't stand on its good looks alone—it's the total package. Road warriors find their salvation, and surrender their stress, at the 10,000-square-foot fitness center, complete with a greenhouse-style swimming pool, health club, steam rooms, sauna, and shiatsu massages.

Classic Asian flavors are spotlighted at Anzu, but it's the Rrazz Room that brings a little razzle-dazzle and stars like Chita Rivera and Kenny G. to the otherwise serene Hotel Nikko.

Omni

500 California St. (at Montgomery St.)

Phone: 415-677-9494
Web: www.omnisanfrancisco.com
Prices: **$$$$**

347 Rooms

15 Suites

Omni

It's not just a coincidence that the Omni is right on the money. Originally built in 1926, the Italian Renaissance-style building once housed a bank. Today's guests count their lucky stars, not their dollars, but the place exudes old-money sophistication. Italian marble and Austrian crystal chandeliers lend a European elegance, but with a location right on the cable car line, the Omni is San Francisco through and through.

High ceilings, crown moldings, and traditional furnishings give the rooms and suites a classic appeal, while marble vanities surprise and delight in the guest bathrooms. Traveling with tots? Book the Kids Fantasy Suite, where yellow and blue (plus bunk beds, beanbags, and games) make other kids green with envy and parents giddy from a good night's sleep next door. The Omni offers many business services, while those on vacation are perfectly positioned for sightseeing, and can tag along on the hotel's complimentary guided walking tour.

With graceful Palladian windows and polished wood-paneled walls, Bob's Steak & Chop House has a private club ambience. Its mouthwatering Midwestern meats, succulent shrimp, and decadent desserts lure locals and visitors alike.

Rex

562 Sutter St. (bet. Mason & Powell Sts.)

Phone: 415-433-4434 or 800-433-4434
Web: www.thehotelrex.com
Prices: $$

94 Rooms

Rex

Small town charm with a big city address isn't just a pipe dream—at least at Hotel Rex. This Theater District hotel enjoys a prime location just one block from Union Square and the Powell Street Cable Car line. You can shop, tour, and even work until you drop and then head straight home to this delightfully inviting sanctum that pours on the charm.

If you've ever found yourself wishing you could have just one night with Gertrude Stein, Ernest Hemingway, or F. Scott Fitzgerald, the Rex is for you. This gracious style is inspired by the literary salons of the 1920s and 1930s. The intimate lobby is enhanced with framed sketches and oil paintings that look like they've been hanging for generations (they haven't been, but they're all done by local artists). The Library Bar takes the literary inspiration to heart—the menu is divvied up between short stories (appetizers), novels (entrées), and text books (sandwiches).

Downstairs has that classic globe-trotting look down pat (think wicker furnishings and lots of globes), but upstairs in the rooms and suites, the mood is airy and bright. Sunny yellow walls, striped carpets, and hand-painted lampshades *à la* Matisse...wait, is this Provence?

Serrano

405 Taylor St. (at O'Farrell St.)

Phone: 415-885-2500 or 866-289-6561
Web: www.serranohotel.com
Prices: $$

217 Rooms

19 Suites

David Phelps/Kimpton Hotels & Restaurants

Smack dab in the middle of the bustling Theater District, the Serrano knows how to put on a show. This baby is a star. Don't be fooled by the plain Jane, beige-brick exterior. It's just a front...one step past that front door and it's hello, high drama! Huge red marble columns and a hand-painted ceiling that's gunning for the Sistine Chapel...the lobby is mahvelous, darling. It looks serious, but this beloved boutique hotel isn't the least bit formal.

Golden yellow walls, red-and-white striped window dressings, and bed skirts show off a sunny sophistication with a subtle French accent in both the rooms and suites. Playful and upbeat without being a distraction, these rooms let you get your beauty sleep (on Frette linens, thank you very much). It's good to be bad here, where the Wicked Suite plays to its audience with a Land of Oz theme (and applause-worthy views of the surrounding theaters).

The Serrano definitely channels their good witch when it comes to services like morning coffee and tea, evening wine receptions, bikes for tooling around town, and gourmet grub at Jasper's Corner Tap. All this, and you can even tote Toto along for the ride at this pet-friendly hotel.

Sir Francis Drake

B2

450 Powell St. (at Sutter St.)

Phone: 415-392-7755 or 800-795-7129
Web: www.sirfrancisdrake.com
Prices: **$$$**

410 Rooms

6 Suites

David Phelps

You'll be quoting Oliver–"please Sir, I want some more"–but this San Francisco landmark is all prince and no pauper. It's certainly historic, dating to 1928, but resting on its laurels? No siree Bob. Instead, this palatial hotel takes the Old World and the New and sets them on a chic collision course. From the Beefeater-attired doorman who welcomes new arrivals to the lobby's gilded ceilings, antique crystal chandeliers, and seriously sweeping staircase, the Drake makes a lasting first impression.

Just when you thought you nailed their sensibility, something comes along to surprise you. Take one look at the sumptuous rooms and suites and the Old World is a distant memory. Shimmery silver, statement headboards...these accommodations are suffused with a sexy spirit that feels equal parts gorgeous guy and glamorous doll.

Generations have taken to this hotel for cocktails and conversation, and some things never change. Bar Drake totally nails that cool speakeasy style with its Rob Roys and Sazeracs from a master mixologist, but there's only one Harry Denton's Starlight Room. This tried-and-true nightclub with its 360-degree panoramic views showcases stars, both performing and twinkling.

Triton

342 Grant Ave. (at Bush St.)

Phone: 415-394-0500 or 800-800-1299
Web: www.hoteltriton.com
Prices: **$$**

140 Rooms

Markham Johnson

Take nine local artists and let them have at it in one building. No, it's not a new reality show; rather, the out-of-the-box thinking that has made the Hotel Triton a stand-out since the early 90s. Just across from the famous Chinatown Gate, the Triton is a wacky and wonderful kaleidoscope of color.

There isn't an inch of uncovered space on the lobby walls, where a trippy mural twists and turns with a groovy vibe. The mezzanine hosts solo shows and rotating thematic exhibitions. Got a Dead shirt? Pull it on and check right in to this hip (hippie?) spot. It's not just for 60s love children, though Jerry Garcia did envision one of the celebrity suites. Comedienne Kathy Griffin designed a celebrity suite that is far from laughable. Got a sweet tooth? The Haagen Dazs suite is complete with an ice cream cabinet that puts the mini-bar to shame. The individually designed rooms and suites appeal to all sorts of visitors with their uplifting colors and distinctive furnishings.

Just because it's artsy doesn't mean it's flaky, so expect lots and lots of creature comforts, like in-room spa services to soothe your senses, freshly baked cookies, and evening wine hours with tarot card readings.

Westin St. Francis

335 Powell St. (at Union Square)

Phone: 415-397-7000 or 866-500-0338
Web: www.westinstfrancis.com
Prices: $$$$

1137 Rooms

58 Suites

Elizabeth Fraiberg Photography

Don't settle for residing "near" Union Square when you can be right on it—the Westin St. Francis *is* Union Square. With its red awnings and stately architecture including marble columns, balconies, and intricate woodwork, this grande dame has been a hometown haunt for over a century. Those on a treasure hunt to spot San Francisco's legendary sights always include a visit to the St. Francis' Grandfather Clock. Suspended from the lobby ceiling, it's been a meeting place for residents and guests for generations.

With two towers boasting more than a thousand rooms between them, four popular restaurants, and comforts like an elaborate fitness center and spa, the Westin St. Francis is cherished among the corporate crowd. Everything about this hotel pays tribute to time-honored traditions. Revel in the classic crown moldings, crystal chandeliers, and tall ceilings of the rooms and suites located in the landmark building or take a Tower room or suite for some modern elegance and commanding city views.

Grab and go at Caruso's, enjoy all-day dining at the Oak Room, but let time really stand still for just a few moments at the lobby-located Clock Bar replete with classically-inspired cocktails.

Drisco

2901 Pacific Ave. (at Broderick St.)

Phone: 415-346-2880 or 800-634-7277
Web: www.hoteldrisco.com
Prices: **$$**

29 Rooms

19 Suites

Hotel Drisco is the preferred choice for travelers who want to leave the crowded spots behind and sample a taste of how the other half lives. This elegant hotel is ideally situated in the exclusive Pacific Heights neighborhood, where million-dollar view and mansions are just part of the allure. Welcome to the softer side of San Francisco. Skyscrapers dazzle on the horizon, but in Pacific Heights, it's all Victorian charms and boutique-lined streets.

Pillow menus, toiletries from a local perfume house, and Egyptian cotton triple sheeting are just a few of the niceties offered here. From morning chauffeur service to a bountiful breakfast that just so happens to be included in the rate, the little things add up to an exceptional experience. The rooms and suites, done up in a fresh and light palette, are comfortable and elegant.

Rev up with a workout, but be sure to spend a little quiet time in the Sitting Room, where coffee and tea are always brewing and scrumptious handmade biscotti make an appearance every afternoon. With excellent recommendations from the knowledgeable concierge and complimentary bikes for breezy tours, Hotel Drisco delivers Pacific Heights on a silver platter.

Kabuki

1625 Post St. (at Laguna St.)

Phone: 415-922-3200 or 800-533-4567
Web: www.hotelkabuki.com
Prices: **$$**

203 Rooms

15 Suites

Matthew Millman

Hotel Kabuki offers the ultimate chic cultural immersion. Set in the heart of the revitalized Japantown, this retreat is surrounded by authentic kimono shops, sushi bars, and bookstores that make this locale so unique.

Hotel Kabuki is the embodiment of sleek Japanese design. The uncluttered, clean look of the lobby instantly calms mind, body, and soul. Located just off the lobby, stroll through the serene Japanese-style gardens with a koi pond. The Zen spirit is alive all around, but it doesn't end there. The rooms and suites offer a *real* respite from the everyday. Shoji screens and vintage-style Asian art set a sense of peace, while beautifully patterned silks add a luxurious touch. Some rooms feature traditional Japanese-style soaking tubs, but for something truly out of the ordinary, book the traditional Japanese suite, complete with an in-room bamboo and sand garden.

Spa treatments are available in-room, but jump right in and get the full experience at the totally traditional Kabuki Springs & Spa. *Izakaya* are to Japan what the corner pub is to London, so stop by hotel Kabuki's O Izakaya Lounge for some sake and small plates that mix tradition with a little West Coast cool.

Laurel Inn

444 Presidio Ave. (at California St.)

Phone: 415-567-8467 or 800-552-8735
Web: www.thelaurelinn.com
Prices: $$

49 Rooms

Joie de Vivre Hotels

In ancient times, laurel wreaths were bestowed upon victors to symbolize achievement (kind of like that trophy for the 3rd grade spelling bee that's gathering dust in the basement). It's a tall order to take on a name like that, but this hotel does it with great aplomb.

Go ahead and blink because there's no chance you'll miss this place. It definitely strays from the Victorian-style pack in this Pacific Heights neighborhood just on the border of Laurel Heights. From its 50s-style neon sign to its funky, bright purple zig-zag awning, the Laurel Inn has a distinct retro vibe that offers something different. It has a shaken, not stirred, kind of sophistication with a touch of South Beach art deco mixed with a whole lot of swank. Upbeat without a trace of Pollyanna, the guest rooms sport a studio-like ambience with added space and extras like sofa beds and kitchenettes (in some rooms). Pull a plush purple chair up to the espresso-hued desk to write that presentation or chill out with Fido on the comfy couch. The Laurel makes being away from home oh-so-livable.

Pop down to the lobby for cookies and lemonade, but for something stronger, slink over to Swank Cocktail & Coffee Club.

Tomo

1800 Sutter St. (at Buchanan St.)

Phone: 415-921-4000 or 888-822-8666
Web: www.jdvhotels.com/tomo
Prices: $

124 Rooms

1 Suite

Cesar Rubio

If you know someone who suffers from Peter Pan syndrome, don't call a therapist; call and make reservations at this Marina marvel. Hello Tomo! This hotel in the heart of bustling Japantown doesn't want its hipster guests to ever grow up. Step off the hurried streets and into this pop art-influenced space that might have you feeling like you've stepping straight into a video game. Bright colors, wacky accents, and murals by Japanese anime artist Heisuke Kitazawa make this hotel truly one of a kind.

This property's rooms and suites take the average college dorm room and bump up the cool factor with bean bag chairs, simple IKEA-style blond wood furnishings, cheerful colors, and even plush monsters tucked into the beds. But, with Kitazawa's artistic creations in each dwelling, this is definitely not your teenager's dorm room. Get the whole gang together for a video game marathon in the over-the-top Players Suites. But, it's not all play and no work with high-tech amenities, ergonomically designed workspaces, and a well-equipped business center.

Despite its name, word has gotten out about Tomo's Mums Restaurant and Bar. This hot spot is all about shabu-shabu and an endless stream of sake.

The Ritz-Carlton, San Francisco

600 Stockton St. (bet. California & Pine Sts.)

Phone: 415-296-7465 or 800-241-3333
Web: www.ritzcarlton.com
Prices: **$$$$**

274 Rooms

62 Suites

The Ritz-Carlton, San Francisco

When it opened in 1909 as the western headquarters of the Metropolitan Life Insurance Company, this neoclassical landmark flanked by a row of stately Ionic columns was lauded as a "Temple of Commerce." A century later, as The Ritz-Carlton, the edifice crowning the eastern slope of Nob Hill can justly be called a temple of luxury and refinement.

A museum-quality collection of 18th- and 19th-century antiques and artwork decorates the public areas. While treasures such as Waterford crystal candelabras, 18th-century portraits, and Regency silver abound throughout the hotel. Restored with European charm, your home-away-from-home here comes with a featherbed and down comforter, a cozy robe and soft slippers, and a marble bath with a rain showerhead. On the Club Level, a dedicated concierge, continuous culinary offerings, and a private business lounge provide unparalleled pampering.

All the expected amenities apply. Take the time to work out in their fitness facility, then relax those tired muscles in the steam room before your soothing massage. Later in the day, the lobby lounge makes a gracious venue in which to linger over afternoon tea or a cocktail before retiring for the night.

The Fairmont

950 Mason St. (at California St.)

Phone: 415-772-5000 or 866-540-4491
Web: www.fairmont.com
Prices: $$

528 Rooms

63 Suites

Fairmont

Learn the true meaning of an oldie but goodie at the historic Fairmont. Reigning over the city from its prized location atop Nob Hill, The Fairmont has stood watch over San Francisco for more than a century. Nothing, not even the 1906 earthquake, could topple this grand lady and her indomitable spirit...just one of the reasons it is near and dear to the hearts of many.

This queen of the city retains a traditional charm. There's definitely not an ounce of boutique in this classic hotel, where more than 500 rooms, two restaurants, gardens with fountains, a wellness center, and more than 55,000-square-feetof ballrooms and function space are on display. It's impressive in that good, old-fashioned kind of way. The accommodations are luxuriously appointed with period furnishings and soft, pastel palettes. Many of them showcase stunning views, but those with balconies are extra special.

The Laurel Court & Bar is the perfect complement to the Fairmont tradition. Afternoon tea is a time-honored ritual at this white-glove establishment. Hold on to your hat at the Hurricane Bar, where thunder claps add a thrilling effect, or head to the South Pacific in the tropical-themed Tonga Room.

Nob Hill

835 Hyde St. (bet. Sutter & Bush Sts.)

Phone: 415-885-2987 or 877-662-4455
Web: www.nobhillhotel.com
Prices: $

52 Rooms

Nob Hill Hotel

The Nob Hill is old-world, period. Established in 1906 and fully restored in 1998, this hotel is all gleaming marble, alabaster chandeliers, ornate ceilings, and stained glass panels. Its period décor is matched only by its premier location in Nob Hill, one of San Francisco's most cherished and graceful neighborhoods.

Walking into one of the rooms or suites is truly like stepping back in time. These Victorian-styled accommodations are full of details, including antique furniture, hand-painted walls, windows framed with oversized silk drapes, and canopy beds dressed with velvet and satin bedding. Period art and antiques complete the tasteful look. The largest suites are a favorite with tourists for their added features like whirlpool tubs and garden-set patios.

Named for its lofty location, the hotel may look like an inn, but with lunch and dinner served at Colombini, it's clear that this spot is so much more than just a place to hang your hat. This Italian café and bistro plates up fresh seafood, steak, and pizza, along with signature risotto dishes in an intimate (read tiny: there are just ten tables so arrive early at breakfast if you want to sit) Tuscan-influenced setting.

Orchard Garden

466 Bush St. (at Grant Ave.)

Phone: 415-399-9807 or 888-717-2881
Web: www.theorchardgardenhotel.com
Prices: $$$

86 Rooms

Orchard Garden

Sorry, Kermit, but it is easy being green...if you're staying at the Orchard Garden Hotel. This eco-chic boutique hotel brings a much-needed dose of oxygen to the hustle and bustle of downtown. It is just blocks from Union Square's shops and restaurants, but this hotel's simple sophistication feels light years away from the city and its commercialism.

If green living has you conjuring up images of tree-huggers living in yurts, think again. Orchard Garden may have been designed to fit all the standards of a green building, but it's far more chic than commune. Light maple furnishings (certified by the Forest Stewardship, of course) and artwork from local artists create an instant sense of calm in the public spaces, while the cocoon-like rooms and suites are tranquility defined. Efficient water and temperature controls, organic bath products, and chemical-free linens are among the many eco-sensitive initiatives, but the only thing you'll notice is the comfort.

The area bursts with dining choices, but get back to (your) Roots, the hotel's award-winning organic restaurant. It might not be coming up roses, but Orchard Garden is definitely blooming. Just visit the rooftop garden for proof.

Argonaut

495 Jefferson St. (at Hyde St.)

Phone: 415-563-0800 or 866-415-0704
Web: www.argonauthotel.com
Prices: $$

239 Rooms

13 Suites

David Phelps

It may be named after those who came rushing in search of a fortune, but the Argonaut strikes gold of its own. Thanks to a special partnership with the San Francisco Maritime National History Park, this hotel has an unrivaled location nestled inside the historic Haslett Warehouse at The Cannery in Fisherman's Wharf. As if that's not enough to whet your appetite, the coveted hotel looks straight across to the sparkling San Francisco Bay and the Park's fleet of historic ships.

Large timbers, exposed brick, and even hefty warehouse steel doors are just some of the original details that can be enjoyed in the nautical and nice rooms and suites. The interiors could double for a Ralph Lauren ad–think anchor printed and striped royal blue, sunny yellow, and crisp white bedding and accents–but this salty dog is more sophisticated than kitschy. The Argonaut has all the amenities expected of a Kimpton member (evening wine hour and pet-friendly services), while the unique location accounts for a few bonuses (like the first-floor access to the Maritime Museum).

With its large bar, brick walls, and nautical memorabilia, The Blue Mermaid seduces diners with her many charms—and her chowder.

Bohème

444 Columbus Ave. (bet. Green & Vallejo Sts.)

Phone: 415-433-9111
Web: www.hotelboheme.com
Prices: $$

15 Rooms

Hotel Bohème

North Beach's strong Italian roots and beatnik past live together in perfect harmony at Hotel Bohéme. Pack a notebook (or a MacBook), since this one-of-a-kind hotel is the antidote to writer's block.

Hotel Bohéme is suffused with a palpable creative spirit that pays homage to North Beach's famous beats. From the black-and-white photographs and strong, inviting colors and palettes, to its literary and visual cues, the smoky haze of the 50s beat generation is evident throughout the hotel and it's enough to make an English literature graduate student weep with joy.

Settle in to one of the cozy, comfortable, and inviting rooms at the beautiful Bohéme, where it is easy to channel the spirit of Allen Ginsberg or Jack Kerouac. Cast-iron beds, mirrored armoires, and lavender or burnt-orange walls are a total throwback. Lampshades stitched together with 50s sheet music, torn Blue Note album covers, and paperback poetry book covers, blur the line between decoration and inspiration. Maybe that's why so many artists and writers continue to make this their home away from home.

The neighborhood's distinct European ambience, courtesy of the many Italian sidewalk cafés, isn't too bad either.

Four Seasons

B2

757 Market St. (bet. Third & Fourth Sts.)

Phone: 415-633-3000 or 800-819-5053
Web: www.fourseasons.com
Prices: **$$$$**

231 Rooms

46 Suites

Mary Nichols/Four Seasons San Francisco

Go on and say you're staying here because of the convenient location. It's true that the Four Seasons has a great site across from Yerba Buena Gardens and one block from the Moscone Center. It's just a little bit like saying you read Playboy for the articles. Nope, you're staying at the Four Seasons to be cosseted like a rock star. Nobody does modern luxury quite like this straight-away winner. Intuitive, yet never intrusive, the staff and service at the Four Seasons never miss a beat.

Like a moth to flame, the Four Seasons lures savvy visitors who eschew in-your-face conspicuous consumption. There are no marble columns or gilded staircases. It is sumptuous for the new millennium sophisticate, where the lobby is a wood-paneled jewel box-like space that glows with a soft light.

The accommodations are tastefully appointed with contemporary furnishings and gentle colors. Whether it's soundproof windows or extra-thick towels, every one of the amenities is thoughtfully considered. In-room spa services further enhance relaxation, though the spa's elegance is worth the elevator ride.

The signature Seasons restaurant always fits the bills with its steakhouse-style menu and casual elegance.

InterContinental

B3

888 Howard St. (at 5th St.)

Phone: 415-616-6500 or 888-811-4273
Web: www.intercontinentalsanfrancisco.com
Prices: $$$

536 Rooms

14 Suites

Rien van Rijthoven

For the city's latest and greatest, just look up to catch a glimpse of the glittering InterContinental. This glass tower shimmers in the sunlight as it rises 32 stories above SoMa. It doesn't get any more convenient than this hotel, which is adjacent to the Moscone Convention Center. The InterContinental sparkles and shines with all of the bells and whistles expected of a new millennium hotel. It's also the tallest LEED certified building in all of California, but who's counting?

The striking architecture is perfectly complemented by a cool and contemporary interior. The lobby's gleaming white marble floors are a soothing respite from the cacophony of the Convention Center, but the serenity doesn't end at the reception desk. Take in fantastic city views from the rooms and suites, where a modern elegance reigns. Every conceivable amenity is standard, and guests have access to a fully serviced business center, 24-hour fitness center with an indoor lap pool, and a luxurious spa with 10 treatment rooms and Vichy shower.

Who knew there were 120 different types of grappa? Bar 888 did, and this lobby-located cocktail lounge serves them, along with other drinks, in its stylish setting.

The Mosser

B2

54 4th St. (bet. Market & Mission Sts.)

Phone: 415-986-4400 or 800-227-3804
Web: www.themosser.com
Prices: $

166 Rooms

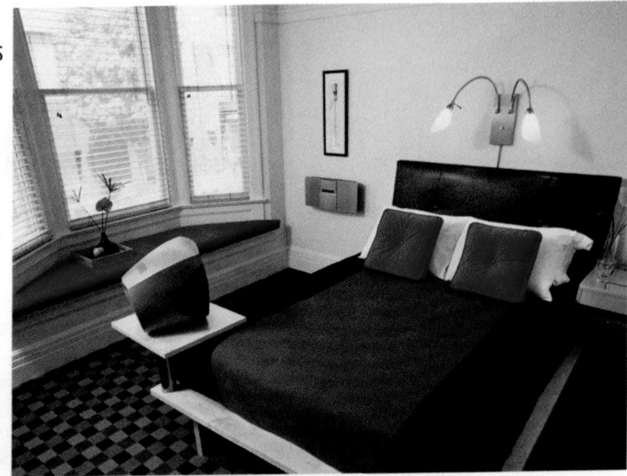

The Mosser

Looking for proximity to the Moscone Convention Center but want something with a less corporate feel? The Mosser is your spot. This delightful hotel shares a highly individual and warm, hospitable spirit with all its guests; one also feels like it has a past because it does. It is snuggled inside a historic building that dates to 1913. You can't fake good bones like this, where crown moldings, high ceilings, and unique architectural touches lend an aristocratic air.

While the lobby shows off a historic flavor with a slight sense of whimsy, the rooms and suites are definitely modern. Geometric-patterned carpets, blond wood platform beds, and punchy accents, like the lipstick red window seats, are very au courant. There isn't a stuffed suit in sight at this refuge, though doing business is a snap with custom-designed writing desks and executive swivel chairs. Lunch and dinner are served at The Mosser's restaurant, Annabelle's Bistro and Bar. This glorious space, where bistro meets the Belle Epoque, recently underwent a glorious restoration.

Still not swayed by this hotel's unique beat? Groove on over to the hotel's state-of-the-art music and media studio to lay down some tracks.

Palace

2 New Montgomery St. (at Market St.)

Phone: 415-512-1111 or 888-625-5144
Web: www.sfpalace.com
Prices: $$$$

519 Rooms

34 Suites

Palace Hotel, San Francisco

Mirror, mirror on the wall. Who's the grandest of them all? Why, the Palace, of course. This grande dame proudly shows off her old-world refinement.

Lauded as an icon and modeled after legendary hotels in Paris and London, this sanctuary has been a little slice of Europe in the heart of the city for over 100 years. It doesn't follow trends; it honors traditions. Afternoon tea at the Garden Court is as wonderfully regal as it gets. Set underneath the greenhouse-like roof with crystal chandeliers, Oriental rugs, and lush plantings, the Garden Court is fit for a queen. Even the less formal spots on the property are extraordinary. The Pied Piper Bar & Grill, famed for its Maxfield Parrish mural, is considered one of the world's best bars. Its clubby appeal extends to the menu (club sandwiches, oysters Rockefeller), which smacks of American traditions.

The guest accommodations, appointed with mahogany furnishings and period accents, echo the Palace's grand conventions. Old-world style doesn't translate to old-fashioned amenities, where a comprehensive fitness center includes a heated indoor swimming pool and 53,000 square feet of function space to host the city's top weddings and balls.

Palomar

12 4th St. (at Market St.)

Phone: 415-348-1111 or 866-373-4941
Web: www.hotelpalomar-sf.com
Prices: $$$

179 Rooms

16 Suites

David Phelps/Kimpton Hotels

Want the shopping and dining of Union Square, proximity to the businesses of the Financial District, *and* a front-row seat to the action of the thriving SoMa district? Look no further than the Palomar. Resting at the crossroads of these three distinctive neighborhoods, this boutique hotel serves up San Francisco in style.

Hotel Palomar is a hip spot that looks good and feels even better. Dark furnishings, bright red accents, as well as contemporary artwork and objects set the rooms and suites apart, but the creature comforts really seal the deal. Everything and anything is here for the asking. Feeling a little lonely? Call down and have the front desk deliver one of their pet goldfish for the duration of your stay. Hotel Palomar even pampers guests with paws; the concierge is on hand to help with suggestions for enjoying a dog's eye view of San Francisco. Eco-sensitive practices and an evening wine hour are among the pleasant little (human-focused) touches at this hotel.

From complimentary bikes and a morning running club to the onsite fitness center, keeping fit was never so easy. Overdid it on the treadmill? Work out the kinks with a luxuriously relaxing in-room massage.

St. Regis

C2

125 3rd St. (at Mission St.)

Phone: 415-284-4000 or 877-787-3447
Web: www.stregis.com
Prices: $$$$

214 Rooms

46 Suites

Joe Fletcher

St. Regis wasn't the patron saint of high style, but the namesake hotel certainly makes a compelling argument. This temple of sophistication is a perfect example of why SoMa is so hot. Blending the historic Williams building with a 40-story modern tower and a museum (the Museum of African Diaspora), The St. Regis takes the hodgepodge and makes it haute.

This is not your grandmother's St. Regis. Far from traditional, the striking interiors are as sleek as an Armani suit. The spare drama will have you asking...is this the lobby or a modern installation? It's understandable, after all, with the adjacent African museum and the Museum of Modern Art across the street. Contemporary verve and sophisticated serenity come together in the divine rooms and suites. Mozambique wood doors, Bella Crema marble, Pratesi bedding, and St. Regis signature butler service—it's luxury at its finest.

The Remède Spa stretches out in style with 9,000 square feet (including an indoor infinity pool) dedicated to refined renewal and soothing sessions. Breakfast and lunch with a local bent are served in the light-filled, sage green-and-white Vitrine, but nothing beats a table in the sun on the Yerba Buena Terrace.

Vitale

D1

8 Mission St. (bet. Steuart St. & The Embarcadero)

Phone: 415-278-3700 or 888-890-8688
Web: www.hotelvitale.com
Prices: $$$

180 Rooms

20 Suites

Hotel Vitale

It's right on the waterfront set along the revitalized Embarcadero. It's urbane and chic with a definitive tranquility. So what's the catch? Nothing, unless it's the fresh fish at the Ferry Building's renowned gourmet marketplace located right across the street. Hotel Vitale takes the feel of a destination spa and brings it to the heart of the bustling city. This hotel seems to have a lock on stylish serenity. The lobby is a warm and inviting space defined by white brick columns and bamboo walls. It's like Asian Zen mixed with a bit of rustic lodge.

The rooms and suites are the very definition of urban retreats. The interiors look like how a wonderful deep breath feels—relaxing, rejuvenating, and peaceful. Winsome blue-and-white, floral-patterned bedding lends a bit of the country to these city oases. With rainforest showerheads and supremely comfortable soaking tubs, guests may never want to leave.

Hotel Vitale's crowning achievement is certainly its penthouse-located spa, complete with outdoor soaking tubs and a soothing bamboo garden. Was it the Thai Herbal Infusion body treatment or the inspiring Bay Bridge views that left you feeling revitalized? Nobody is keeping track.

W - San Francisco

181 3rd St. (at Howard St.)

Phone: 415-777-5300
Web: www.whotels.com
Prices: **$$$**

395 Rooms

9 Suites

W San Francisco

The 'W' doesn't really stand for wonderful, witty, or wow, but all perfectly sum up the style of this corporate-loving hotel. Set in the heart of downtown SoMa, the W is right across the street from the Moscone Convention Center and sits adjacent to the renowned San Francisco Museum of Modern Art. Mixing business with pleasure was never so easy, or frankly, so attractive.

Cool and contemporary design? W-San Francisco wrote the book on it—it has always been synonymous with suits, tourists, and local revelers, and this bustling city property lives up to all of the hype. Curvy furnishings and bright colors lend a sexy and upbeat ambience to every one of the sleek rooms and suites.

The 5,000-square-foot Bliss Spa in the W puts the fabulous in fitness. Nothing captures this hotel's lively spirit quite likes its perennially hip bars and restaurant. Equal parts lounge and art gallery, the Living Room is cherished for its libations and tunes, while the sexy cool blue lighting at Upstairs Bar & Lounge is just right for flirting with new friends. The eye-popping, black-and-white beauty and sustainable cuisine give Trace Restaurant more than just a trace of modern sophistication.

Claremont

41 Tunnel Rd., Berkeley

Phone: 510-843-3000 or 800-551-7266
Web: www.claremontresort.com
Prices: **$$$**

263 Rooms

16 Suites

The Claremont Hotel Club & Spa

It is impossible to avoid falling in love with the Claremont. This Bay Area darling is filled with legend and romance. It all began with a Kansas farmer who struck it rich and built his dream "castle." Later sold, largely destroyed by fire and even apparently won in a game of checkers, the Claremont has a storied past indeed.

Today's Claremont improves on a legend. Boasting the largest convention facilities in all of the Bay Area, this resort–just down the road from UC-Berkeley–is a popular spot for corporate events. Rolling lawns and a relaxed pace make this cherished refuge equally well-suited to those seeking a quick getaway from the city. The rooms and suites are appointed with a classic elegance and fitted with thoughtful amenities, but it is the views of the San Francisco bay and city skyline that are truly unforgettable. Join the Club at the Claremont. This comprehensive facility has it all—tennis courts, two lap pools and a kids pool, spa, and a 20,000-square-foot fitness facility with more than 60 group classes.

Hungry from those seemingly limitless activities? Three restaurants, ranging from poolside and a casual brasserie to the more formal dining room, are on the mark.

Lafayette Park

B1

3287 Mt. Diablo Blvd. (bet. Carol Ln. & Pleasant Hill Rd.), Lafayette

Phone: 925-283-3700 or 877-283-8787
Web: www.lafayetteparkhotel.com
Prices: $$

138 Rooms

Lafayette Park

Take the distinguished spirit of a French château and combine it with West Coast laid-back luxe and you have the lovely Lafayette Park Hotel & Spa. This East Bay pearl is definitely not suffering from a Napoleonic complex. It is consistently ranked as one of the region's favorite and finest spots for spa days and weekend getaways.

It's just 30 minutes to San Francisco from this resort that rests in the rolling hills of Lafayette, but it's a peaceful world unto its own, complete with colorful courtyards filled with trickling fountains. The sunny yellow estate borrows the best details from French Norman architecture and re-imagines them with a modern accent. Interiors are romantic and inviting, offering an updated take on tradition. Bold, yet calming, the rooms and suites use royal blue, red, and gold for a typical French feel, while plush canopied beds and walnut furnishings further add to the refinement.

The Duck Club and Bistro at the Park present an enticing array of mouthwatering selections. The pièce de résistance at the Lafayette Park is its lovely garden terrace and pool. The poolside country garden-inspired spa brings a whole new meaning to stopping and smelling the roses.

Casa Madrona

801 Bridgeway, Sausalito

Phone: 415-332-0502 or 800-288-0502
Web: www.casamadrona.com
Prices: $$$

63 Rooms

Spa

Casa Madrona Hotel & Spa

Just across the iconic Golden Gate Bridge and a ferry ride from San Francisco, Sausalito wins the prize for charming the pants off its visitors. This picturesque waterfront community woos travelers with a charming downtown brimming with tempting shops and restaurants, while just above, petite cottages and million-dollar mansions are stacked into the cliffs.

In the heart of it all, Casa Madrona has been sharing the joys of Sausalito with travelers since 1885. It's listed on the National Register of Historic Places, but this small hotel feels astoundingly fresh and brand new. Set on a hillside overlooking Richardson Bay in the middle of downtown, Casa Madrona is breezy sophistication at its best. And then there are those views. Gaze out over the sailboats of beautiful Sausalito and the hills of Belvedere that linger beyond, and it is no wonder why guests feel like they have this special place entirely to themselves. Sit back and relax in the privacy of a guest room or hillside cottage, where a contemporary bungalow sensibility soothes body and mind.

The Spa at Casa Madrona is a vision of beauty with a crisp navy and white palette and a wide array of rejuvenating therapies.

Cavallo Point

A3

601 Murray Circle (at Fort Baker), Sausalito

Phone: 415-339-4700 or 888-651-2003
Web: www.cavallopoint.com
Prices: $$$$

142 Rooms

Kodiak Greenwood

Resting within the Golden Gate National Park, the exceptional Cavallo Point has arguably the best vantage point for taking in the beauty of the San Francisco Bay. It is red, white, and green all over here—where the majestic Golden Gate Bridge looms large in the background, charming white cottages are sprinkled along the emerald-green lawns, and an eco-minded contemporary lodge is terraced into the hillside. Cavallo Point may have a rich history as the former U.S. Army Post Fort Baker, but the only strict orders given these days are to relax and unwind.

Decisions, decisions. Is it going to be the historic cottages or the modern lodge? The former officers' residences sway guests with out-and-out charm, original architectural details, country décor, and even rocking chairs on the porches; while the hillside eco-rooms impress with bamboo furnishings, radiant heated floors, gas fireplaces, and panoramic views.

Total renewal is the point, whether you're enjoying a nature hike through the grounds or blissing out at the excellent Healing Arts Center & Spa. Learn something new with a resort cooking class or just leave it to the experts and savor refined cuisine at the restaurant and bar.

The Inn Above Tide

30 El Portal (at Bridgeway), Sausalito

Phone: 415-332-9535 or 800-893-8433
Web: www.innabovetide.com
Prices: **$$$**

29
Rooms

Jay Graham

Don't have a sailboat for enjoying Sausalito's coastal charm? No problem. A room at The Inn Above Tide will do just fantastically fine. As its name suggests, this inn is located directly above the water—you can't possibly get any closer without getting wet. Slightly tucked away from it all, yet convenient to the many delights of town, The Inn truly shares the best of Sausalito with guests. In its enviable location, the sound you'll hear is the gentle lapping of the waves lulling you to sleep.

Step inside one of the rooms and feel the tension just float away. If you can tear your eyes away from the view, you'll find sophisticated, coastal-cool accommodations fitted with luxurious and romantic amenities. The all-encompassing views from every room are equal parts decoration and entertainment, and most rooms feature private decks for further enjoyment. In-room massages and select spa services are the ultimate indulgence.

Greet the morning with The Inn Above Tide's lovely breakfast spread before setting out on one of the available bikes for a spin around town. Then head back before sunset to enjoy a glass of wine and nibble of cheese. Romance washes over you at The Inn Above Tide.

Nick's Cove

A1

23240 Hwy. 1 (near Miller Park), Marshall

Phone: 415-663-1033
Web: www.nickscove.com
Prices: **$$$$**

9 Rooms

3 Suites

©2012 frankenyimages.com

Pulling into Nick's Cove off Highway 1 feels like a trip back in time—probably because it is. This pristine and pastoral cottage community overlooking Tomales Bay has been here since the 1930s. Nick's shares an authentic spirit of the California coast. Its cottages, mostly on land, but with five on pilings over the beach, have a rough-hewn simplicity. They are the real deal, built by hand by immigrants who wanted to get away to the coast.

Simple A-line frames were nailed together piece by piece and that legacy has been maintained, albeit with a few, ahem, modern, amenities. Luxurious linens, wood-burning stoves, bathrooms with heated ceramic tile floors, some with deep-soaking bathtubs......Nick definitely never had it this good. There are 12 distinctive cottages, each with its own charm. From the old-school paneling in Al's fisherman's-style cottage, to the dinghy-shaped bathtub in the waterfront Nicolina and scenic vistas at Bandit's Bungalow, there is a surprise in store for everyone within each unique hideaway.

Nick's isn't just about the cottages though. After hours, stroll to the lighted bar (shack) at the end of the pier, and enjoy an expertly mixed cocktail by candelight.

The Ritz-Carlton, Half Moon Bay

1 Miramontes Point Rd. (at Hwy. 1), Half Moon Bay

Phone: 650-712-7000 or 800-241-3333
Web: www.ritzcarlton.com/hmb
Prices: **$$$$**

239 Rooms

22 Suites

Mark Norberg

Drive along the serpentine roads of Highway One and you'll come face to face with Half Moon Bay. This town's stunning natural beauty and carefree attitude captures the very essence of the Northern California coastline. And it's just 23 miles southwest of San Francisco, making it a perfect choice for city dwellers looking to dip their toes in the water.

There's no better place to enjoy Half Moon Bay than the breathtaking views at the Ritz-Carlton. Set high above the crashing surf on craggy cliffs carpeted in emerald-green grass, the baronial-style palace brings a bit of Scotland to this side of California. Rolling out the red carpet, this resort is a veritable playground for adults and children alike. World-class golf on two championship courses is a property highlight, but there's so much more. Tennis and swimming (indoor) and a 16,000-square-foot spa, oh my! Rooms, suites, and guest houses are sophisticated havens fitted with luxurious amenities. Suites that look over the crashing waves of the Pacific, and rooms with terraces and fire pits are worth the splurge.

It's burgers and beers with a view at the Conservatory Lounge, while ENO is a wine, cheese, and chocolate heaven.

Rosewood Sand Hill

2825 Sand Hill Rd. (at I-280), Menlo Park

Phone: 650-561-1500 or 888-767-3966
Web: www.rosewoodsandhill.com
Prices: **$$$$**

91 Rooms

32 Suites

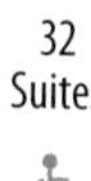

Rosewood Hotels & Resorts

Yahoo! Finally someone figured out that business and pleasure can indeed live happily ever after. The Rosewood Sand Hill puts a little bit of sizzle and style in Silicon Valley—this resort is tucked in the hills near Menlo Park. The architecture recalls the tradition of Craftsman design and adds a modern spin. Designed to seamlessly blend with the rugged natural landscape, the Rosewood Sand Hill isn't splashy, but it is seriously sophisticated.

Rooms and suites are done up with soothing earth tones and a chic, contemporary sensibility. Original art, marble baths, and of course, state-of-the-art technology ramp up the luxury factor. All have private balconies or terraces with enchanting views of the gorgeous courtyard gardens, an inviting swimming pool, or the Santa Cruz Mountains.

Business is a breeze here and the professional, friendly, and anticipatory service staff are standout as well. But it's really downtime that the Rosewood does best. Chill out in the sleek and sanctuary-like Sense Spa, which definitely lives up to its name for engaging all the senses. Of course, it's perfectly fine to simply hang out by the heated pool, perhaps with a cocktail in hand, and daydream.

Stanford Park

C4

100 El Camino Real (at Sand Hill Rd.), Menlo Park

Phone: 650-322-1234 or 866-241-2431
Web: www.stanfordparkhotel.com
Prices: $$$

134 Rooms

29 Suites

Stanford Park Hotel

The Stanford Park Hotel is proof positive that not everything in San Francisco's Silicon Valley has to be cutting edge to be cool. The location simply can't be beat. Adjacent to Stanford University, the namesake hotel provides unparalleled access to this world-renowned university and surrounding Palo Alto. Steal away to this four-story English colonial-style hotel, where secluded and lush garden courtyards, a private library, and a museum-worthy collection of art all lend a European sophistication. The warm glow from the lobby's red brick fireplace sets the tone for this gracious hotel where guests are treated to small hotel charm and large hotel amenities.

The oversized rooms and suites are the embodiment of romance. Features like four-poster, canopied beds, fresh flowers, and traditional, period furnishings feel grand, yet inviting. The beautifully landscaped courtyard garden is home to a sparkling heated swimming pool that is perfect for a watery workout, while the fitness center is equipped with all of the latest machines.

In-room dining, a Starbucks Barista at the Park, and the classic American-style Menlo Grill Bistro & Bar round out the Stanford Park hotel's offerings.

Cypress

10050 S. De Anza Blvd. (at Stevens Creek Blvd), Cupertino

Phone: 408-253-8900 or 800-499-1408
Web: www.thecypresshotel.com
Prices: $$

224 Rooms

Cypress

When the businesses of Silicon Valley call, stay at the luxurious Cypress hotel. This beloved respite puts you in the heart of it all. Located just minutes away from San Jose and such esteemed companies as Apple and Hewlett-Packard, the Cypress enjoys a peaceful setting at the foot of the Santa Cruz Mountains in the heart of Cupertino.

It's all within reach, but the hotel's lush grounds and stylish Italian villa atmosphere might just convince you to skip that morning meeting. Rich colors and resplendent details show off a jaunty old-meets-new sensibility in the lobby and public spaces. Polka-dot walls, geometric-patterned carpets, padded velvet headboards, and playful accents (leopard-print accent pillows) create a dazzling look in the rooms and suites. In keeping with its locale, the in-room technology is state-of-the-art. Kimpton's signature services, which range from spa treatments and wine receptions to pet-friendly and children's programs, round out the comforts.

Take a seat by the firepit and enjoy a cocktail before dinner at the adjacent Park Place Restaurant. Fresh from a renovation, the restaurant draws crowds who relish their fresh and inventive New American cuisine.

De Anza

E3

233 W. Santa Clara St. (bet. Almaden Blvd. & Notre Dame Ave.), San Jose

Phone: 408-286-1000 or 800-843-3700
Web: www.hoteldeanza.com
Prices: $$

95 Rooms

6 Suites

Alex Johnson

Hotel De Anza is a sophisticated surprise in the heart of San Jose. Set within walking distance of the HP Pavilion and the Convention Center, it is a natural choice for Silicon Valley business travelers, but this hotel also speaks to visitors who need a casually elegant escape.

With its retro neon rooftop sign and its classic art deco exterior, De Anza looks like it could fit right in along Collins Avenue in South Beach. But, don't judge a book by its cover. Inside, the hotel feels more modern Mediterranean than 50s vintage. The lobby's large columns, tall ceilings, and soft colors are the first sign that guests will be treated with care and warmth. The accommodations are defined by the same casual elegance that pervades the interiors. All rooms are spacious and comfortable, but for a blowout experience, book the Penthouse Suite, with two balconies, fireplace, and in-room steam room and Jacuzzi.

From the small plates at Hedley Club Lounge to inspired Italian cooking at La Pastaia, the De Anza answers the call when hunger strikes. Got the midnight munchies? Wander down in that fluffy robe and raid their pantry for a cookie or sandwich. Seriously, it's encouraged (and complimentary).

Valencia

355 Santana Row (bet. Olin Ave. & Tatum Ln.), San Jose

Phone: 408-551-0010 or 866-842-0100
Web: www.hotelvalencia-santanarow.com
Prices: $$$

196 Rooms

16 Suites

Hotel Valencia

San Jose's Santana Row is like a little slice of leisure in the heart of Silicon Valley. While convenient to business centers and offices, this lively locale's vibrant mix of shops, restaurants, and entertainment takes visitors away from to-do lists and spreadsheets.

There's no better way to experience the flavor of Santana Row than by staying at the hotel Valencia. Walk past the buzzing restaurants and look for the graceful arch, capped off with an ironwork sign, that beckons guests past the pastel-hued façade. The hotel envelops you in its chic sophistication. Mediterranean influences abound, but Valencia mixes it up with worldly and modern accents (the larger-than-life Buddha at the end of the red-lit hallway, for one).

The rooms and suites are at once spirited and soothing. Dark and handsome with padded leather headboards and faux fur throws, they ites are at once spirited and sexy, yet serene and soothing.

The Valencia's dining and entertainment rivals the best of Santana Row. The rooftop wine terrace, Cielo, serves up views with its varietals, while the Vbar Lounge is hip and high-tech. With such edgy and flavorful dishes, orange you glad you made reservations at Citrus?

Auberge du Soleil

180 Rutherford Hill Rd. (off the Silverado Trail), Rutherford

Phone: 707-963-1211 or 800-348-5406
Web: www.aubergedusoleil.com
Prices: $$$$

31 Rooms

21 Suites

Spa

Trinette Reed

Yes dearest, it's true. The sun will come out tomorrow, and you can bet your bottom dollar that it will be shining on the gorgeous Auberge du Soleil. Like the fine wines from the Napa Valley, this French country inn only gets better with age. It all began with a (relatively) simple idea: to recreate the pastoral pleasures of a Provençal-style restaurant in the heart of wine country. Soon, the gourmet country cooking drew epicureans from all over, and those weary wine drinkers needed a cozy place to land. Voila! The Inn, and the Auberge du Soleil's legacy of luxury, was born.

The Auberge's rooms and suites are a delightful blend of French country and California contemporary design. These accommodations are perfectly suited to romance, with wide-planked oak floors, sunny orange-tinted bedding, fireplaces, and private terraces overlooking the enchanting gardens, valley, or hillside. From the nature-inspired spa with views extending to the vineyards and olive grove, to a serene swimming pool set within the lush landscape, the natural beauty of this stunning milieu can be enjoyed in a variety of settings.

Watch the sun set by the fire or outdoors on the wraparound deck at the Bistro & Bar.

AVIA Napa

1450 1st St. (at School St.), Napa

Phone: 707-224-3900
Web: www.aviahotels.com
Prices: $$

83 Rooms

58 Suites

Alex Hayden

Don't waste another minute debating the designated driver, since the AVIA Napa lets all guests live it up. This boutique hotel's location in the revitalized West End area of downtown, places it within walking distance from the upscale shops, gourmet restaurants, and 15 different tasting rooms showcasing the region's finest wines.

AVIA's sparkling personality is evident at first glance—just look at that lobby. It has a reworked French-meets-funk feel with sexy red velvet couches, a swirly-patterned carpet, and vintage mirrors. Yes, that ivory doe statue certainly adds a playful touch. Stumble home to serious refinement in the rooms and suites. The gorgeous beds pull double shifts as function and fashion with crisp white linens, soothing moss green accents, and drop-dead gorgeous chocolate brown leather headboards. Comfort is king here, where gleaming all-white marble bathrooms boast rainfall showerheads.

Put down that Merlot and sip something new with those delish truffle-oiled portobello fries at the Riddling Rack Wine Bar or indulge in the chic comfort food at AVIA Kitchen's breakfast and dinner. Order "to the terrace" and snack in style by the fire pit or in a cozy corner.

Bardessono

6526 Yount St. (at Finnell Rd.), Yountville

Phone: 707-204-6000 or 877-932-5333
Web: www.bardessono.com
Prices: **$$$$**

62 Suites

Sammy Dyess Todd

You could say that green is considered the gold standard here, but you'd be wrong—it's platinum. This embodiment of eco elegance is one of just three U.S. hotels to reach LEED platinum certification. And green is just oh-so-good at this modern complex nestled on the historic Bardessono family farmstead in the center of Yountville. From grapes to galleries, this sanctuary presses together the total Napa Valley experience.

Innovation and sensitivity collide with impressive results. Whether it's locally sourced stone and salvaged woods or cutting-edge, energy reduction technology, the hotel lives and breathes its environmental values. From the artisan-crafted coffee to the carbon fiber bicycles, the dogma is in the details. But don't worry; they won't make you compost your own garbage. It is as marvelous as it is mindful. The sustainable sophistication in the rooms and suites is proof that luxury is not a four-letter word. Sleek and serene, even the most style-minded sybarite can't find a bone to pick.

All this plus, indulgent, soul-nourishing, and nature-based spa treatments, hand-crafted bath products, and a shimmering rooftop pool. Clean living never looked, or felt, so good.

The Carneros Inn

4048 Sonoma Hwy., Napa

Phone: 707-299-4900 or 888-400-9000
Web: www.thecarnerosinn.com
Prices: $$$$

76 Rooms

10 Suites

Mark Hundley

It's called wine country for a reason. Ditch downtown and head for the hills to The Carneros Inn. This resort has 27 acres of apple orchards and rows and rows of twisted vines all to itself. Well, sort of. They're willing to share with lucky guests. The Carnernos Inn may have a bucolic appeal, but there's definitely nothing hee-haw about this stylish getaway. Traditional country architecture (think barns and silos) is given an industrial chic overhaul here, which brings a whole new meaning to the phrase "fresh farmed."

Supremely private, the resort boasts individual cottages, suites, and homes. Fireplaces, bathrooms with both indoor and outdoor showers, French doors that open out to private terraces, and a country-chic décor define the welcoming environment.

Whether it's quality time or alone time, The Carneros Inn fits the bill. Gaze at the grazing cows and horses from the adults-only, infinity-edge pool or splash around at the family pool. There's a fitness barn for working up a sweat, an award-winning spa for mind-body therapy, and a whole lot of comfort food (citified chicken and waffles) with some haute cuisine thrown in for good measure (it's still Napa) at five dining spots.

Hotel Yountville

6462 Washington St. (at California Dr.), Yountville

Phone: 707-967-7900 or 888-944-2885
Web: www.hotelyountville.com
Prices: $$$$

71 Rooms

9 Suites

Hotel Yountville

Hotel Yountville may be one of the newest resorts to hit the wine country, but its stone buildings with covered porches reek of a time-honored elegance. Set on five acres in the heart of renowned Yountville, this hotel puts it all in glorious perspective (for an especially magical point of view, book a nearby hot air balloon ride).

The resort's beautifully manicured gardens, rolling hills, and cypress-lined swimming pool share the distinctive charm of a European village. It certainly feels far from the madding crowd, but this resort is within walking distance of Yountville's legendary restaurants and boutique-style shops. Revel in the luxuries of Italian linens, deep-soaking bathtubs, and rain and steam showers in the well-appointed rooms and suites. From wood-beamed ceilings and four-poster beds to stone fireplaces and enchanting views of Hopper Creek, these accommodations ooze refined romance.

Spa AcQua delivers a serene one-two punch (so to speak). Regular treatment rooms have private gardens, while the couples' suites have double-sized tubs and fireplaces. There's no need to hike too far for fine food: just hop over to Hopper Creek Kitchen for luscious, locally focused dishes.

Lavender

2020 Webber Ave. (bet. Yount & Jefferson Sts.), Yountville

Phone: 707-944-1388 or 800-522-4140
Web: www.lavendernapa.com
Prices: $$

8 Rooms

Lavender

This Yountville inn so perfectly captures the essence of Provence that it sends Francophiles into fits of delight. Just go ahead and try to find a place that exudes more charm than this French country inn. Good luck with that. The inn is comprised of four buildings, but nothing captures the heart like the gray-shingled heritage home. Heard of shocking pink? This hotel has cornered the market on shocking lavender, which lines the windows of the historic gray-shingled home for a whimsical touch.

The guest rooms are straight out of the sunny French countryside. Warm yellow walls, pots filled with sprigs of lavender, wicker chairs, and beds swathed in classic Provençal prints all add up to an adorable and cheery ambience. From gas fireplaces and private patios (some boasting Jacuzzis) to in-room spa services, Lavender pours on the relaxation.

Lavender also pulls out all the stops in true bed and breakfast style. The breakfast buffet is as beautiful as it is bountiful and the afternoon cocktails and hors d'oeuvres reception is a delicious delight. Is that the smell of freshly baked cookies? It sure is. And with Le Belge chocolates left at turndown, Lavender wishes sweet dreams indeed.

Maison Fleurie

6529 Yount St. (at Washington St.), Yountville

Phone: 707-944-2056 or 800-788-0369
Web: www.maisonfleurienapa.com
Prices: $$$

13 Rooms

Four Sisters Inns

You don't need to speak a word of French to see how Maison Fleurie gets its name. This delightful French country inn's brick-and-stone façade is covered in lush vines (hence the name "flowering house"). Comprised of three buildings on a beautifully planted half acre property, it is easy to get swept away by the charms of Maison Fleurie, but with a location that puts it just around the corner from the renowned French Laundry, it's as convenient as it is charming.

Guest accommodations are tucked inside the main house, carriage house, and bakery building. Gingham printed pillows, floral patterned bed coverings, and rustic oak furnishings define the darling French country décor. Is that a teddy bear on your pillow? It sure is, and there's a Le Belge chocolate, too. Larger rooms have fireplaces and decks overlooking the landscaped pool, while the "petite" rooms are indeed as diminutive as they sound.

Maison Fleurie is a bed and breakfast, so mornings are appropriately delicious with freshly baked breads and muffins, quiches, and casseroles. The delicious personal touches continue throughout the day with warm and fresh cookies in the afternoons and evening wine and hors d'oeuvres.

Meadowood

900 Meadowood Ln. (off the Silverado Trail), St. Helena

Phone: 707-963-3646 or 800-458-8080
Web: www.meadowood.com
Prices: **$$$$**

41 Rooms

44 Suites

Meadowood Napa Valley

Calling it a resort simply doesn't do it justice. Meadowood is so much bigger than that. Gracious world unto itself? Now that's more like it.

It's not surprising that Meadowood was once a private country club. Nestled on 250 private acres, this place exudes white-glove, blue-blood elegance. Its grand clubhouse-style building and cozy cottages have an upper-crust, almost New England guise, but step inside and there's no mistaking Meadowood's airy, country-cosmopolitan flair for anything but West Coast. Chirping birds and sun-dappled, lush grounds invite quiet reflection and relaxation, but Meadowood is a true paradise, not to mention playground, for active travelers. Tennis, swimming, biking, hiking, and even croquet are among the activities, while the nine-hole golf course is a rare treat in the Napa Valley. The top-notch spa blankets guests in serene style and features a comprehensive nature-based menu.

Anyone can taste wine, but with Meadowood's program, guests drink in the traditions and legacies behind Napa's famed vineyards. Poolside, terrace, grill, or dining room... take your pick (or picnic) from a variety of lovely settings featuring Meadowood's award-winning cuisine.

Milliken Creek Inn & Spa

1815 Silverado Trail, Napa

Phone: 707-255-1197 or 800-835-6112
Web: www.millikencreekinn.com
Prices: **$$$**

11 Rooms

1 Suite

Milliken Creek Inn & Spa

You've definitely seen them before. They're the CDs with covers of rushing rivers washing over shiny stones that promise to put a little Zen in that daily commute. Don't settle for a soundtrack of serenity when you can have the real thing. Milliken Creek Inn & Spa is that place. Set on three acres of lush grounds fronting the Napa River, this resort is the antidote for civilization. And that gentle trickling water sound? It's not a recording.

There are just a dozen rooms at this wonderful place. From rattan ceiling fans and plantation chairs to private decks overlooking the river, these accommodations promise guests the world. Antique-style maps and black-and-white photographs lend an expat flavor, while muted colors (khaki and cream), French bath products and marble baths soothe and seduce.

Guests are treated with kid gloves (and to breakfast and afternoon cocktails) by a superior staff that is unobtrusive, yet available at a moment's notice. Laze in luxury and enjoy the respite from society at their soul-stirring spa. Resting riverside, this fantastic facility shares its surroundings with exceptional therapies like grapeseed body polishes and soothing stone treatments.

Napa River Inn

500 Main St. (at 5th St.), Napa

Phone: 877-251-8500
Web: www.napariverinn.com
Prices: $$$

68 Rooms

Napa River Inn

Change your tune and try something different on that next wine country sojourn. The Napa River Inn rocks with an urban beat. Set within a two-acre riverfront complex bursting with bars and restaurants, there's simply nothing else like it around.

Everything old is definitely new again at the Napa River Inn. The historic mill, built in 1884, is a Registered National Landmark, but there are no cobwebs or fuddy-duddys milling about this place. Restored maybe, but revitalized for sure. The Inn is the crown jewel of this downtown Napa landmark. Step inside a guestroom and it's easy to see why: fireplaces, balconies, and river views are among the usual offerings. From claw-foot tubs to exposed brick walls, historic rooms sport a number of charming details. Just when you thought it couldn't get any better, there's a knock at the door...it's breakfast in bed, courtesy of Sweetie Pies Bakery.

Napa River Inn's unique setting means that guests have a bevy of dining and entertainment opportunities at their fingertips. From day spas to a roster of restaurants running the gamut from Pan-Asian to French country to jamming jazz clubs and live entertainment on the plaza, it's all here for the taking.

Rancho Caymus Inn

1140 Rutherford Rd. (off Hwy. 29), Rutherford

Phone: 707-963-1777 or 800-845-1777
Web: www.ranchocaymus.com
Prices: $$

25 Rooms

1 Suite

Rancho Caymus Inn

This warm and inviting all-suite inn is smack dab in the middle of Napa in downtown Rutherford. All it takes is five minutes and you'll have your pick of dozens of celebrated wineries, but chances are you'll want to stretch out and stay awhile right here. Gracious hospitality isn't just a buzzword at this hotel, where it's been two decades and four generations of one family that have worked hard to make Rancho Caymus one of the wine country's finest lodgings.

From a wrought-iron gate and secluded courtyard with trickling fountain to a classic red-tiled roof draped with vines and luscious blooms, Rancho Caymus shares a classic Spanish Colonial allure that is echoed throughout its public and private spaces. All suites, furnished with hand-carved black walnut beds, handmade wrought-iron light fixtures, and 100-year-old oak-beamed ceilings, speak to the heritage of hacienda-style architecture and design. Stoke the fires of romance with a wood-burning fireplace or step out to the private balcony for a breath of fresh air and a better view.

Rancho Caymus isn't just near the wineries; it has its own. Stop by Flora Springs for a taste before sitting down to a meal at the inn's own restaurant.

Solage

755 Silverado Trail (at Rosedale Rd.), Calistoga

Phone: 707-226-0800 or 866-942-7442
Web: www.solagecalistoga.com
Prices: $$$$

83 Rooms

6 Suites

Solage Calistoga

Solage brings in the funk (but not the noise) to Napa Valley. Set in the mountains just steps from Calistoga, Solage isn't your average room with a view. This resort jazzes up the already scenic setting with an impressive collection of art that is sprinkled throughout the interiors and grounds. Contemporary sculptures, tranquil landscape paintings, and sculptural twig pieces convey an industrial-salvaged sophistication. The young staff is well-intended but may lack polish.

The architectural style reflects the farming heritage of the region, just only with a more fabulous feel. And the studio-style lodgings? Well, they've got that whole light-filled and airy thing down pat. The polished concrete floors and pebble stone-floored showers are a tad cold, but the very essence of eco-chic.

Room service, known here as in-studio dining, is totally orgasmic, organic cuisine. Tell your foodie friends that you ordered a mudslide in the middle of wine country and you'll elicit a wince. You don't have to tell them it's a signature mineral-rich mud treatment at the spa. It's more than ok to "drink" the water here, where Calistoga's legendary hot springs have cured ails for centuries.

Villagio Inn & Spa

6481 Washington St., Yountville

Phone: 707-944-8877 or 800-351-1133
Web: www.villagio.com
Prices: $$$

86 Rooms

26 Suites

David Shipman

Home to just as many Michelin stars as it has in the night sky, plus Hollywood divas seeking refuge from the paparazzi, along with an Oscar-winning director and his pet project vineyard, Napa Valley covers everything from star gazing to star grazing. But where are the normal (read: Bentley-free) people? They are all at Villagio Inn & Spa. This lovely resort takes the best of Italy and transplants it to the middle of Yountville on the 23-acre Vintage estate. Color-soaked, villa-style buildings are set within lush Mediterranean-style gardens at this totally Tuscan spot that promises elegance and comfort at a pretty price.

Set along cobblestoned pathways that snake through the fountain-filled gardens, the sunny rooms are a welcome sight for weary travelers with lemon walls, warm wood furnishings, deep-soaking bathtubs, and fireplaces.

If you weren't already wearing flip-flops, Spa Villagio would knock your socks right off. This 16,000-square-foot spa truly offers a slice of paradise. Cascading waterfalls, quiet reflecting pools, indoor and outdoor fireplaces, and a treatment menu that literally covers everything from head to toe. If you can't achieve inner peace here, just give up.

Vintage Inn

C2

6541 Washington St., Yountville

Phone: 707-944-1112 or 800-724-8354
Web: www.vintageinn.com
Prices: $$$

72 Rooms

8 Suites

The Vintage Estate

Set within the 23-acre Vintage estate, the Vintage Inn is the sister property to the Villagio Inn & Spa. In a yin to its yang, the Vintage is a French château to Villagio's Tuscan villa. The guest rooms are pure French country charm. Wood-beamed ceilings, French antique furnishings and accents, and vases bursting with sunflowers are torn straight from the pages of a Provence design book. Enjoy the comforts of added touches like wood-burning fireplaces, private patios or balconies, and oversized Jacuzzi bathtubs.

The Vintage Inn treats its guests like old friends. Celebrate the beginning of a new day at the champagne breakfast buffet or sample delicate tea sandwiches and scrumptious scones at the afternoon tea—both gifted to guests by the hotel.

Soak up the sun by the pool or chill out in the shade in one of the cabanas before or after a game of tennis, Pilates class, or a work-out at the fitness center. Skip over to the sister Spa Villagio for an out-of-this-world (or body) experience. From wining and dining to biking and ballooning, Napa Valley's treasures await just outside the door. Then again, Vintage Inn's many charms make a pretty convincing argument to just stay put.

Bodega Bay Lodge

103 Hwy. 1 (near Doran Beach Rd.), Bodega Bay

Phone: 707-875-3525 or 888-875-2250
Web: www.bodegabaylodge.com
Prices: **$$$**

84 Rooms

Woodside Hotels

Ruggedly handsome and windswept...it's not a Hollywood hunk, it's the Sonoma coast. This exquisitely beautiful stretch of moody coastline has a lock on serenity, yet it is just an hour north of the Golden Gate Bridge. It is a veritable paradise for naturalists and outdoor enthusiasts with a limitless variety of fresh air fun, but with Sonoma wine country's wineries nearby, epicureans can get in on all of the joy, too.

Set on a gently sloping hillside overlooking bird-filled marshes, flower-covered dunes, and Doran Beach, the Bodega Bay Lodge enjoys one of the region's best locations. The A-frame, stone-covered lodge and cabins define rustic refinement both indoors and out. Come inside and warm up by the fire before retreating to the cozy comforts of the exceedingly spacious guestrooms and suites. From the soft, calming palette to the unobstructed bay and ocean views, the look is coastal sophistication. And the feel? It's plush without pretension.

Soak away your stress in the heated outdoor pool or relax with a coastal-themed treatment at the spa. The Duck Club Restaurant spotlights the region's award-winning wines, artisan cheeses, and farm-fresh produce with postcard-perfect views.

Duchamp

421 Foss St. (at North St.), Healdsburg

Phone: 707-431-1300 or 800-431-9341
Web: www.duchamphotel.com
Prices: $$$

6 Rooms

Duchamp Hotel

Duchamp is the reigning champ when it comes to style in Sonoma. This tiny resort's artistic flair would make its namesake proud. If you've ever wanted to go into hiding without forsaking any of life's luxuries, Duchamp is for you. Set in the Russian River Valley in the little town of Healdsburg, Duchamp is the ultimate hideaway. Private and sequestered just doesn't describe it. It's more like an estate belonging to an über-rich benefactor of the arts.

Stay in one of just six cottages shaded by 50-year-old olive trees. A sexy and spare design defines the interiors, where concrete floors have fluffy faux fur rugs and bare walls are left unadorned. The bathrooms are the picture of industrial chic with stainless-steel vanities and sinks. But really, were you expecting anything less from a hotel whose namesake made quite a name for himself with a urinal? The look may be minimalist, but the amenities are far from it. Fireplaces, high-definition flat-screens, oversized spa showers...it's all too much.

The sleek swimming pool sits in the middle of it all tempting visitors to take the plunge. Dive into Napa wine tasting with an exclusive private tasting and tour of the Duchamp Estate Winery.

El Dorado

405 1st St. W. (at W. Spain St.), Sonoma

Phone: 707-996-3220 or 800-289-3031
Web: www.eldoradosonoma.com
Prices: **$$**

27 Rooms

Peter Medilek

You might not be panning for it, but you'll discover gold at the El Dorado. Set right in the heart of historic Sonoma Plaza, this 27-room boutique hotel truly shines. Browse the stalls at the weekly farmers market, peruse the many charming shops, or tuck into a meal at one of many fine dining venues all just steps away. Oh, and then there is a little something called the Dry Creek Valley here too. Life is good, indeed, at El Dorado hotel.

This place is the embodiment of effortless-chic—there's not a trace of country; instead El Dorado captures that airy, urban sanctuary style. The accommodations blend a fresh, garden-inspired design (think green walls, nature-themed art) with modern elements (four-poster, frame-only beds). French doors lead to private balconies with views of the Spanish Plaza and garden courtyard. The eco-sensitive practices (filtered water in the fridge, bath amenities) feel as thoughtful to guests as they are to Mother Nature.

The ground floor lounges and outdoor heated pool and terrace have seemingly cornered the market on that chilled-out vibe. For more of that luxuriously laid-back spirit, hit up the Corner Café for an array of local wines and beers.

The Fairmont Sonoma Mission Inn & Spa

100 Boyes Blvd. (bet. Arnold Dr. & Hwy. 12), Sonoma

Phone: 707-938-9000 or 800-441-1414
Web: www.fairmont.com
Prices: $$$

166 Rooms

60 Suites

The Fairmont Sonoma Mission Inn

The Fairmont Sonoma Mission Inn & Spa isn't following trends. This granddaddy of old-school Sonoma is a legend. It occupies a land rich with healing mineral springs that have lured tourists for centuries. Opened in the 1920s to welcome travelers in search of a little R&R, this Spanish Colonial-style hotel is a full-service resort that is as suited to corporate events as it is to couples and families. French country charms are evident in the accommodations. Some rooms are in the fully restored historic building, while the suites are housed in the new wings.

Stay at the Sonoma Mission Inn to enjoy some of the most comprehensive amenities available in the wine country. There is a championship golf course, an alluring swimming pool set within lush gardens, and a world-class spa where the focus is on those famed healing waters, of course!

The resort is also home to a panoply of restaurants as wide ranging as the activities. Dine at the Golf Club Grill or poolside, hit up two bars complete with thrilling cocktails, or sink your teeth into old-fashioned American comfort food at the Big 3, where patrons have been feasting for more than fifty years. Who said there was a world outside?

Farmhouse Inn

7871 River Rd. (at Wohler Rd.), Forestville

Phone: 707-887-3300 or 800-464-6642
Web: www.farmhouseinn.com
Prices: $$$$

6 Rooms

12 Suites

Farmhouse Inn

If an authentic experience is on your itinerary, the Farmhouse Inn should be your first and only stop. This delightful country inn sums up the best of Sonoma with its award-winning restaurant, country comfort, and warm spirit in the heart of the Russian River Valley. It's all in the family at the Farmhouse Inn, which is owned by a brother-and-sister duo. They're not pretending to be innkeepers with the mostest, but Joe and Catherine Bartolomei do put on a terrific show. Fifth-generation farmers, vineyard owners, and natives, they are the real deal.

Whether you're snuggled in to a Main House room, cozied up in a cottage, or stretched out in a Barn Suite, these accommodations have oodles of charm. Service is definitely their pleasure, with everything from handmade bath soaps to freshly baked cookies at turndown. You won't need a rooster to wake you once you've had a taste of the farm-fresh breakfast served each morning. Eggs straight from the Bartolomei's own farm and pastries fresh from the oven-yum!

With therapies incorporating their heirloom cider apples, spring forest honey, and fresh herbs, the spa takes the farm-to-table concept from the dining room to the treatment room.

Gaige House Inn

C3

13540 Arnold Dr. (at Railroad St.), Glen Ellen

Phone: 707-935-0237 or 800-935-0237
Web: www.gaige.com
Prices: **$$$**

12 Rooms

11 Suites

Joie de Vivre Hotels

Go East, young man, at the Gaige House. It's all about the Zen at this stylish Asian-inspired hotel. Located in the Sonoma Valley in Glen Ellen, Gaige House Inn is a perfect home base for exploring the area's wineries and plentiful outdoor activities; but its rave-worthy design and first-rate amenities make it a destination unto itself.

The Gaige House Inn enjoys a picturesque setting nestled on three acres of plush gardens and tree-lined paths along the Calabazas Creek. This spot alone could calm the nerves of a raving lunatic, but coupled with the soothing, Asian-style accommodations? Sorry, stress, but it's just not a fair fight.

Retreat to one of the rooms in the main house, where the Queen Anne style of the original home blends with quiet Asian influences. Go whole hog with one of the stand-alone studio suites. Boasting private entrances, decks, fireplaces, and whirlpool tubs or two-person showers, these accommodations are just waiting to romance couples. Everything from Buddhas to gilded Thai-style headboards spotlights the Eastern influence.

In-room spa treatments are available, but with the creekside spa's delightful setting (complete with a Zen garden), why stay home?

Honor Mansion

A1

14891 Grove St. (bet. Dry Creek Rd. & Grant St.), Healdsburg

Phone: 707-433-4277 or 800-554-4667
Web: www.honormansion.com
Prices: **$$$**

13 Rooms

Scout's honor—this one is a keeper. Honor Mansion's privileged guests have four acres all to themselves. Set on a luscious landscape, Honor Mansion is a truly relaxing getaway that feels worlds away, yet its location just a short walk from downtown Healdsburg means never having to say no to shopping.

There are just 13 unique accommodations at Honor Mansion. Hand-carved furniture, fireplaces, private patios, and winsome Victorian décor lend a distinguished air to the mansion rooms, while the cottages share a breezy elegance. The four Vineyard suites are the largest quarters, and while each has a distinct flavor, all cram in lots of creature comforts.

From eggs Benedict and Grand Marnier French toast to the gorgeous buffet, breakfast is an art at Honor Mansion. While many of the rooms spotlight views of the lovely koi pond, Honor Mansion isn't all about lazing about in luxury (though that's perfectly fine, too). This inn functions more like a full-service resort, with everything from competition croquet courts and a PGA putting green, to tennis and basketball courts, and a lap pool with two poolside pavilions. Who has time for wine tasting with all that Honor Mansion has to offer?

Hotel Healdsburg

25 Matheson St. (at Healdsburg Ave.), Healdsburg

Phone: 707-431-2800 or 800-889-7188
Web: www.hotelhealdsburg.com
Prices: $$$$

51 Rooms

4 Suites

Hotel Healdsburg

Urbanistas who can't stomach leaving behind the comforts of the city should let their manicured fingers do the talking and book themselves right into Hotel Healdsburg. Set in the heart of historic downtown, this hotel is a little bit (wine) country with a little bit rock and roll.

Just steps from Healdsburg Plaza's hip dining and shopping, Hotel Healdsburg ensures that hipsters are never far from their favorite pastimes of shopping and dining. Trends are trendy for a reason so go ahead and yield to the super-cool Hotel Healdsburg. These are a few of this hotel's favorite things: pecan wood floors covered with Tibetan rugs; poured concrete bathroom counters; and Italian glass Bisazza tile showers. It's like an around-the-world party of chic design, and the glamorous guests are wrapped around its fingers. Feeling soured by the standard offerings at other spas? Hotel Healdsburg's Meyer Lemon Sage body polishes, massages, and herbal wraps will have you puckering up for a kiss. But really, tip with bills, not *besos*.

Live jazz, weekend yoga, and wine tastings are all part of this retreat. The pool is a totally cool hangout, or snag a seat and snack at the Grand Fireplace Lounge.

Kenwood Inn & Spa

B2

10400 Sonoma Hwy. (bet. Kunde Dr. & Kunde Winery Rd.), Kenwood

Phone: 707-833-1293 or 800-353-6966
Web: www.kenwoodinn.com
Prices: $$$$

27 Rooms

2 Suites

J. Nichole Smith

If you're looking for a place where you can meander along pathways that lead to luxuriant courtyards set with fountains and serene ponds, then Kenwood Inn & Spa is your Eden. This adults-only inn promises an intimate and romantic hideaway, and boy, does it deliver. Each of the rooms and suites has its own private entrance. Inside, the accommodations are the very picture of European-inspired rustic refinement. Rich and regal reds and golds lend a traditional, sumptuous feel, while the striped- and floral-patterned fabrics are straight from the country. Featherbeds dressed in Italian linens and fireplaces are just two ways that Kenwood doesn't miss a chance to enchant its guests.

Days begin with a complimentary breakfast that encourages lingering. Spend an afternoon by one of two shimmering saline pools or succumb to a regionally-inspired treatment at the spa.

The dreamy Mediterranean influences continue to the restaurant, where wrought-iron chairs and textured, sunny yellow walls speak of Italy. The menu highlights local produce with a modern Mediterranean bent. Enjoy the warmth of the fire in winter or head outdoors to the terrace to feel the warmth of the sun on your face.

Madrona Manor

A1

1001 Westside Rd. (at West Dry Creek Rd.), Healdsburg

Phone: 707-433-4231 or 800-258-4003
Web: www.madronamanor.com
Prices: $$$

17 Rooms

5 Suites

Madrona Manor

Now this is the place to play out that lord or lady of the manor complex. It is just so easy to get swept up in the romance of Madrona Manor, which looks like it arrived straight from the pages of a Brontë novel. There is simply nothing else like it in Sonoma County. This Victorian-era mansion enjoys an unparalleled beauty. Nestled on eight lovingly tended gardens dotted with flowers, fruit, and vegetables, Madrona Manor is tucked in the hills above Sonoma's Dry Creek Valley in Healdsburg. This place just begs for brides and grooms, but you don't have to exchange vows to fall in love with this one-of-a-kind hotel.

Turn back the clock at Madrona Manor, where the rooms and suites reflect the elegance of a kinder and gentler time. From original antiques and champagne slipper bathtubs to roaring fireplaces, these accommodations keep grand traditions alive. Larger lodgings may be discovered in the Garden Cottage or in the recently converted 1920s-era schoolhouse.

Wend your way through the orchards and gardens, stretch out in the sun by the lovely pool, sip sunset cocktails on the classic veranda, or cozy up by the fire at Madrona Manor, which minds its manners in grand style.

Vintners Inn

4350 Barnes Rd. (at River Rd.), Santa Rosa

Phone: 707-575-7350 or 800-421-2584
Web: www.vintnersinn.com
Prices: $$$

44 Rooms

Vintner's Inn

Seeking Italian good looks and charm? The Vintners Inn has a lock on it. This exclusive inn rests on 92 acres of rolling vineyards in Sonoma's Santa Rosa. It's certainly appropriately named, since it's owned by Healdsburg's renowned Ferrari-Carano winery, but the Vintners Inn stands on its own two perfectly groomed feet.

With sprawling hills that seem to stretch into infinity, it's easy to get wrapped up in it all at Vintners Inn, but trips to area vineyards are a snap from this convenient and central location. Three two-story buildings house the accommodations that await the arrival of wine country visitors. Set around a lovely, flower-filled courtyard complete with a trickling fountain, the rooms and suites exude elegance and intimacy. Carved stone fireplaces, canopy beds, and classic floral prints lend a traditional air to these restful private spaces. The Spa's complete treatment menu offers a wide variety of massages and facials. For an extra touch of romance, book a couples' treatment.

The Front Room Bar & Lounge's stone-cut fireplace and handcrafted fir and blue mosaic tile-topped bar set a casually sophisticated scenery that's just right for thirst quenchers and appetizers.

Peter L. Wrenn / MICHELIN

Indexes

Where to **Eat**

Where to **Stay**

Alphabetical List of Restaurants

Q

R

S

Y

Z

Restaurants by Cuisine

Afghan

American

Asian

Austrian

Barbecue

Basque

Brazilian

Burmese

Californian

Cambodian

Chinese

Contemporary

Cuban

Eastern European

Ethiopian

Filipino

French

Japanese

Cuisines by Neighborhood

San Francisco

Castro

Civic Center

Nob Hill

North Beach

Richmond & Sunset

SoMa

WINE COUNTRY

Napa Valley

American

Barbecue

Californian

Contemporary

French

Gastropub

International

Italian

Japanese

Latin American

Mediterranean

Mexican

Pizza

Seafood

Spanish

Steakhouse

Thai

Vietnamese

Sonoma County

American

Asian

Barbecue

Californian

Contemporary

French

International

Peter L. Wrenn / MICHELIN

Starred Restaurants

Within the selection we offer you, some restaurants deserve to be highlighted for their particularly good cuisine. When giving one, two, or three Michelin stars, there are a number of elements that we consider including the quality of the ingredients, the technical skill and flair that goes into their preparation, the blend and clarity of flavours, and the balance of the menu. Just as important is the ability to produce excellent cooking time and again. We make as many visits as we need, so that our readers may be assured of quality and consistency.

A two or three-star restaurant has to offer something very special in its cuisine; a real element of creativity, originality, or "personality" that sets it apart from the rest. Three stars – our highest award – are given to the choicest restaurants, where the whole dining experience is superb.

Cuisine in any style, modern or traditional, may be eligible for a star. Due to the fact we apply the same independent standards everywhere, the awards have become benchmarks of reliability and excellence in over 20 countries in Europe and Asia, particularly in France, where we have awarded stars for 100 years, and where the phrase "Now that's real three-star quality!" has entered into the language.

The awarding of a star is based solely on the quality of the cuisine.

Exceptional cuisine, worth a special journey

One always eats here extremely well, sometimes superbly. Distinctive dishes are precisely executed, using superlative ingredients.

Excellent cuisine, worth a detour

Skillfully and carefully crafted dishes of outstanding quality.

A very good restaurant in its category

A place offering cuisine prepared to a consistently high standard.

Bib Gourmand

This symbol indicates our inspectors' favorites for good value. For $40 or less, you can enjoy two courses and a glass of wine or a dessert (not including tax or gratuity).

Under $25

Brunch

Late Dining

Alphabetical List of Hotels

Notes

Michelin

Notes

Michelin

The Michelin Adventure

It all started with rubber balls! This was the product made by a small company based in Clermont-Ferrand that André and Edouard Michelin inherited, back in 1880. The brothers quickly saw the potential for a new means of transport and their first success was the invention of detachable pneumatic tires for bicycles. However, the automobile was to provide the greatest scope for their creative talents. Throughout the 20th century, Michelin never ceased developing and creating ever more reliable and high-performance tires, not only for vehicles ranging from trucks to F1 but also for underground transit systems and airplanes.

From early on, Michelin provided its customers with tools and services to facilitate mobility and make travelling a more pleasurable and more frequent experience. As early as 1900, the Michelin Guide supplied motorists with a host of useful information related to vehicle maintenance, accommodation and restaurants, and was to become a benchmark for good food. At the same time, the Travel Information Bureau offered travellers personalised tips and itineraries.

The publication of the first collection of roadmaps, in 1910, was an instant hit! In 1926, the first regional guide to France was published, devoted to the principal sites of Brittany, and before long each region of France had its own Green Guide. The collection was later extended to more far-flung destinations, including New York in 1968 and Taiwan in 2011.

In the 21st century, with the growth of digital technology, the challenge for Michelin maps and guides is to continue to develop alongside the company's tire activities. Now, as before,Michelin is committed to improving the mobility of travellers.

MICHELIN TODAY

WORLD NUMBER ONE TIRE MANUFACTURER

- 69 production sites in 18 countries
- 115,000 employees from all cultures and on every continent
- 6,000 people employed in research and development

Moving for a world

Moving forward means developing tires with better road grip and shorter braking distances, whatever the state of the road.

CORRECT TIRE PRESSURE

RIGHT PRESSURE

- Safety
- Longevity
- Optimum fuel consumption

-0,5 bar

- Durability reduced by 20% (- 8,000 km)

- Risk of blowouts
- Increased fuel consumption
- Longer braking distances on wet surfaces

forward together
where mobility is safer

It also involves helping motorists take care of their safety and their tires. To do so, Michelin organises "Fill Up With Air" campaigns all over the world to remind us that correct tire pressure is vital.

WEAR

DETECTING TIRE WEAR

MICHELIN tires are equipped with tread wear indicators, which are small blocks of rubber molded into the base of the main grooves at a height of 1.6 mm. When tread depth is the same level as indicators, the tires are worn and need replacing.

Tires are the only point of contact between vehicle and the road, a worn tire can be dangerous on wet surfaces.

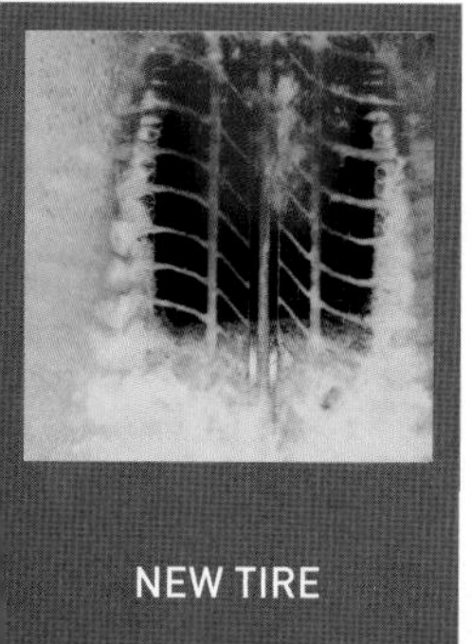

NEW TIRE

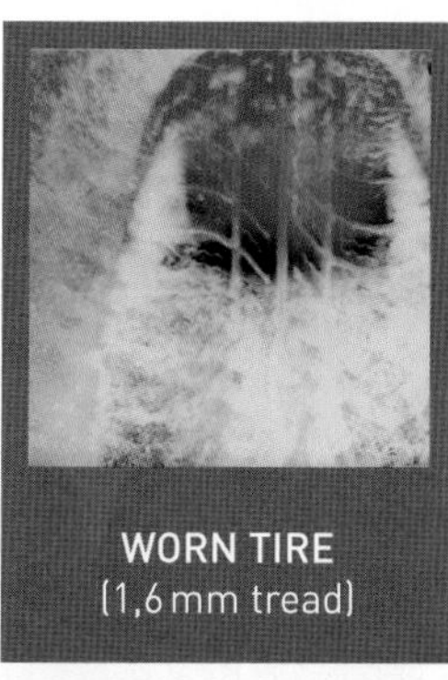

WORN TIRE
(1,6 mm tread)

The photo shows the actual contact zone on wet surfaces.

Moving forward
means sustainable mobility

INNOVATION AND THE ENVIRONMENT

By 2050, Michelin aims to cut the quantity of raw materials used in its tire manufacturing process by half and to have developed renewable energy in its facilities. The design of MICHELIN tires has already saved billions of liters of fuel and, by extension, billions of tons of CO2.

Similarly, Michelin prints its maps and guides on paper produced from sustainably managed forests and is diversifying its publishing media by offering digital solutions to make travelling easier, more fuel efficient and more enjoyable!

The group's whole-hearted commitment to eco-design on a daily basis is demonstrated by ISO 14001 certification.

Like you, Michelin is committed to preserving our planet.

Chat with Bibendum

Go to
www.michelin.com/corporate/fr
Find out more about Michelin's history and the latest news.

QUIZ

Michelin develops tires for all types of vehicles. See if you can match the right tire with the right vehicle…

A 1

B 2

C 3

D 4

E 5

F 6

G 7

Solution : A-6 / B-4 / C-2 / D-1 / E-3 / F-7 / G-5

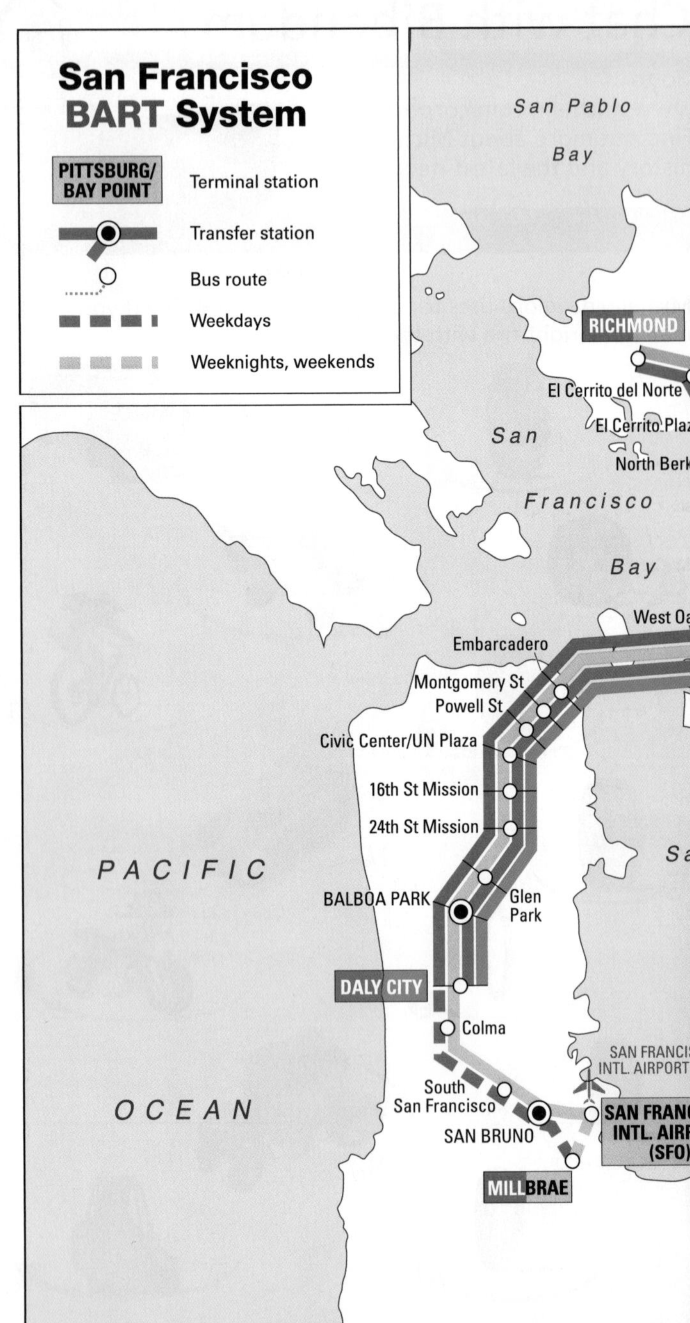
San Francisco
BART System
PITTSBURG/
BAY POINT
Terminal station
Transfer station
Bus route
Weekdays
Weeknights, weekends
San Pablo
Bay
RICHMOND
El Cerrito del Norte
El Cerrito Plaz
North Berk
San
Francisco
Bay
West Oa
Embarcadero
Montgomery St
Powell St
Civic Center/UN Plaza
16th St Mission
24th St Mission
PACIFIC
BALBOA PARK
Glen
Park
DALY CITY
Colma
SAN FRANCIS
INTL. AIRPORT
South
San Francisco
SAN BRUNO
SAN FRANC
INTL. AIRF
(SFO)
MILLBRAE
OCEAN
Sa

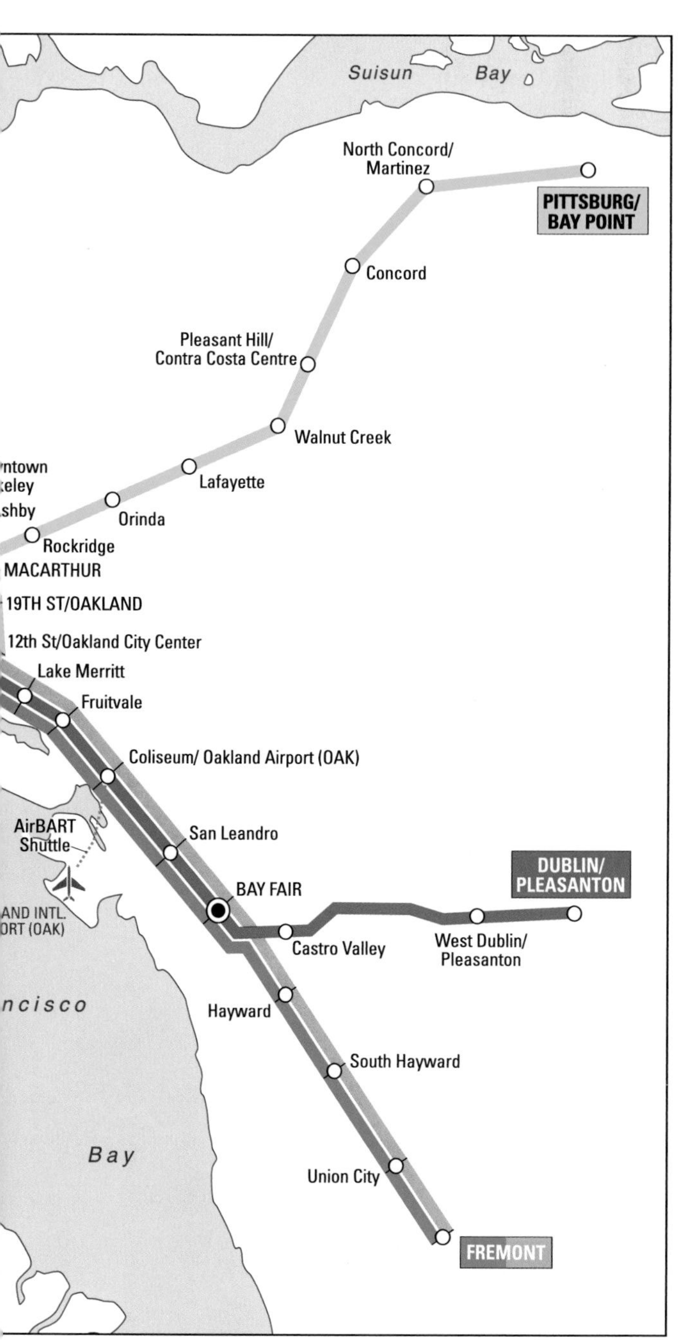
Suisun Bay
North Concord/ Martinez
PITTSBURG/ BAY POINT
Concord
Pleasant Hill/ Contra Costa Centre
Walnut Creek
Lafayette
Orinda
Rockridge
MACARTHUR
19TH ST/OAKLAND
12th St/Oakland City Center
Lake Merritt
Fruitvale
Coliseum/ Oakland Airport (OAK)
AirBART Shuttle
San Leandro
BAY FAIR
DUBLIN/ PLEASANTON
Castro Valley
West Dublin/ Pleasanton
Hayward
South Hayward
Bay
Union City
FREMONT

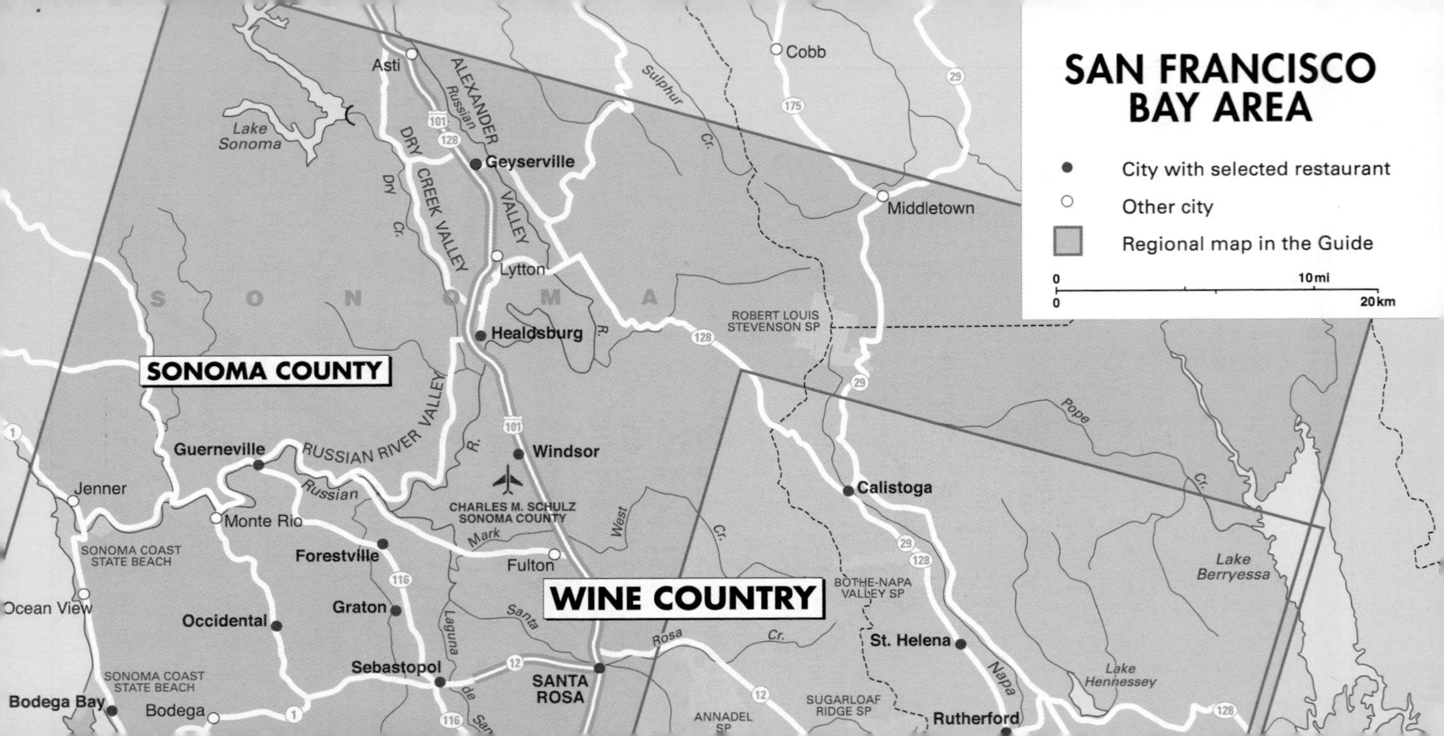

SAN FRANCISCO BAY AREA
City with selected restaurant
Other city
Regional map in the Guide
0
10mi
0
20km
SONOMA COUNTY
WINE COUNTRY
Asti
Lake Sonoma
ALEXANDER VALLEY
Russian
DRY CREEK VALLEY
Dry Cr.
Geyserville
Lytton
Healdsburg
R.
S O N O M A
Cobb
Sulphur Cr.
Middletown
ROBERT LOUIS STEVENSON SP
Pope
Cr.
Lake Berryessa
Lake Hennessey
Calistoga
BOTHE-NAPA VALLEY SP
St. Helena
Napa
Rutherford
SUGARLOAF RIDGE SP
ANNADEL SP
Rosa
Cr.
Santa
SANTA ROSA
West
Cr.
Windsor
CHARLES M. SCHULZ SONOMA COUNTY
Mark
Fulton
RUSSIAN RIVER VALLEY
Russian
Guerneville
Jenner
Monte Rio
Forestville
Graton
Occidental
Sebastopol
Laguna de San
SONOMA COAST STATE BEACH
Ocean View
SONOMA COAST STATE BEACH
Bodega Bay
Bodega
1
12
29
101
116
128
175